PATRICK BISHOP has emerged as the outstanding historian of the wartime RAF with such classics as *Fighter Boys*, *Bomber Boys* and *Target Tirpitz*. He was a foreign correspondent for twenty years covering many conflicts, including Afghanistan, the subject of his widely acclaimed *3 Para*.

Praise for *Air Force Blue*:

'After Bishop's pilot's eye views of the war in *Fighter Boys* and *Bomber Boys*, *Air Force Blue* counts as a publishing event. It won't disappoint readers who already know they like Bishop's way of writing history from the point of view of those who lived it … [he] examines with admirable and perhaps surprising detachment the timely hypothesis that there was something rather special about the RAF in the Second World War'
                                          GILES WHITTELL, *The Times*

'What Mr Bishop does so well is to show how the RAF came to be such a distinctive and effective force technically, strategically, tactically, geographically, politically and socially … a masterful work of technical, political and social history'
                                          JONATHAN GLANCEY, *Country Life*

'Many excellent and vivid stories … a blending of social and operational history that works splendidly … Bishop is excellent on the social mix of the RAF … A virtue of this book is that Bishop writes with shrewd confidence about nuances: he knows his subject inside out, and avoids the romanticism that mars many such histories … this is a terrifically readable, authoritative book that told me many fascinating things I did not know'
                                          MAX HASTINGS, *Sunday Times*

'As a former war correspondent with more than thirty years' experience, Bishop brings journalistic strengths to his second career as a popular historian: an easily readable and exciting writing style, a knowledge of what fighting means to those at the sharp end, a nose for the nub of the story, and an admirable compassion for the victims of war on all sides … a book that at once educates, explains and excites'   *BBC History Magazine*, Book of the Month

Also by Patrick Bishop

PATRICK BISHOP

AIR FORCE BLUE

THE RAF IN WORLD WAR TWO

WILLIAM COLLINS

William Collins
An imprint of HarperCollins*Publishers*
1 London Bridge Street
London SE1 9GF

WilliamCollinsBooks.com

First published in Great Britain by William Collins in 2017
This William Collins paperback edition published in 2018

1

Copyright © Patrick Bishop 2017

Patrick Bishop asserts the moral right to
be identified as the author of this work

A catalogue record for this book is
available from the British Library

ISBN 978-0-00-743315-5

Maps by John Gilkes

Printed and bound in Great Britain by
CPI Group (UK) Ltd, Croydon CR0 4YY

MIX
Paper from
responsible sources
FSC
www.fsc.org
FSC™ C007454

TO HEN

ANGEL GIRL IN CHIEF

Contents

Maps

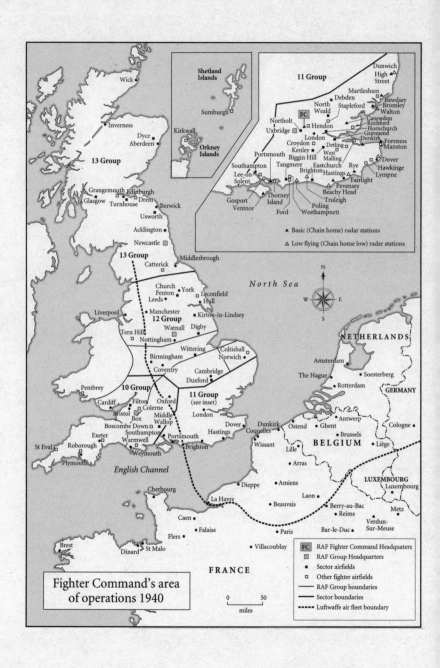

Fighter Command's area of operations 1940

Wick

Shetland Islands
Sumburgh

Kirkwall
Orkney Islands

Inverness

Dyce
Aberdeen

13 Group

Grangemouth Edinburgh
Glasgow Drem
Turnhouse Berwick

Usworth
Acklington
Newcastle

13 Group

Middlesbrough

Catterick

Church Fenton York
Leeds Leconfield
Hull

Liverpool Manchester Kirton-in-Lindsey
12 Group

Tern Hill Watnall Digby
Nottingham

Wittering Coltishall
Birmingham Norwich

Coventry Cambridge

Duxford

Pembrey **10 Group** Oxford **11 Group**
Cardiff Filton Middle (see inset)
Bristol Colerne Wallop London
Box Dover
Boscombe Down Hastings
Exeter Southampton Portsmouth
St Eval Warmwell Brighton
Roborough Weymouth

Plymouth

English Channel

Cherbourg

Caen
Falaise
Flers

Brest
Dinard St Malo

FRANCE

Villacoublay

North Sea

N
W E
S

NETHERLANDS

Amsterdam
The Hague Soesterberg
Rotterdam

GERMANY

Antwerp
Dunkirk Ghent Cologne
Coquelles Ostend Brussels Liège
Wissant BELGIUM

Lille
Arras LUXEMBOURG
Dieppe Amiens Luxembourg
Laon
Beauvais Berry-au-Bac Metz
Reims
Paris Bar-le-Duc Verdun-Sur-Meuse
La Havre

Inset: 11 Group

Dunwich
High Street
Martlesham
Debden Bawdsey
North Stapleford Bromley
Weald Walton
Northolt Canewdon
FC Hendon Hornchurch Rochford
Uxbridge London Detling Gravesend
Croydon Dunkirk Foreness
Kenley West Manston
Portsmouth Biggin Hill Malling
Southampton Tangmere Eastchurch Dover
Lee-on- Brighton Rye Hawkinge
Solent Hastings Lympne
Pevensey Fairlight
Gosport Thorney Beachy Head
Ventnor Island Truleigh
Ford Poling
Westhampnett

▲ Basic (Chain home) radar stations
△ Low flying (Chain home low) radar stations

FC RAF Fighter Command Headquaters
▪ RAF Group Headquaters
■ Sector airfields
□ Other fighter airfields
— RAF Group boundaries
— Sector boundaries
···· Luftwaffe air fleet boundary

0   50
miles

Main Bomber Command
stations in the UK

0   10   20   30   40   50

miles

*North
Sea*

○ Group HQ
• Airfield

• Croft

Leeming •

Skipton-on- • Thirsk • Wombleton
Swale • Topcliffe
Dishforth • • Dalton
• Tholthorpe
Linton-on-Ouse • • East Moor   Carnaby •
Allerton ○   Full Sutton •   Driffield •
Marston Moor • ○ *YORK*   Lissett •
Rufforth • • Pocklington
Elvington •   Leconfield •
Riccall • • Melbourne
Burn • • Holme-on-Spalding-Moor
Breighton •
Snaith •   North Killingholme •
Sandtoft •   Elsham Wolds •
Lindholme • *SCUNTHORPE* • Kirmington
Doncaster • • Finningley   • Grimsby
Bircotes ○   • Blyton   • Binbrook
Bawtry •   Sturgate • Hemswell • • Kelstern
Worksop • Faldingworth • • Wickenby • Strubby
Gamston • Ingham •   • Ludford Magna
Scampton • • Dunholme Lodge
LINCOLN   • Fiskerton
Ossington • • Wigsley Skellingthorpe • • Bardney   • Spilsby
Swinderby ○   • East Kirkby
Winthorpe • • Woodhall Spa
Waddington • Balderton •   • Coningsby
Syerston • • Fulbeck   Metheringham •
Newton •
Langar • • Bottesford
Church Broughton •   ○ Grantham
○ Eggington
Tatenhill • • Castle Donington • Saltby
Wymeswold •
Lichfield •   • Cottesmore
• Woolfox Lodge
North Luffenham •

• North Creake
Sculthorpe • • Little Snoring
Foulsham •   • Oulton
Great Massingham •   • Swannington
West Raynham •   — • Attlebridge
Swanton Morley • Bylaugh Horsham St Faith •
Downham Market • • Marham   Hall
• Watton
Methwold • • Bodney
Feltwell • • East Wretham

Nuneaton •
Bruntingthorpe • Market
Bramcote • Harborough   Polebrook •
Bitteswell •   • Upwood   Mepal • • Witchford • Lakenheath
Husbands Bosworth • Desborough • Warboys •   Mildenhall •
Harrington • Alconbury •   Waterbeach •   • Honington
Honiley • Molesworth • Huntington ○ Wyton •   • Tuddenham
Wellesbourne   Graveley •   ○ Exning
Mountford Little Staughton • Oakington • • Newmarket
• Gaydon   Bourn •   *CAMBRIDGE*   • Chedburgh
Stratford • Chipping Warden • Tempsford • • Stradishall   • Wattisham
Edgehill •   Gransden Lodge •
Hinton-in-the-Hedges • • Silverstone Bassingbourn • Wratting Common • Woodbridge •
Croughton • Turweston • Cranfield • Steeple Morden • • Ridgewell
Barford St John •   • Little Horwood
Finmere • ○ Winslow
Enstone • • Bicester • Wing
Upper Heyford • • Westcott • Cheddington
Weston-on-the-Green • • Oakley

Mount Farm •
Benson •
High Wycombe
Hampstead • HQ Bomber Command
Norris

LONDON

N
W E
S

Main targets in Europe

0   100   200   300

miles

Range circles are measured from Lincoln

⊙   ○   Bomb targets

Stockholm

E D E N

Baltic Sea

Copenhagen

Sassnitz
Peenemünde
Warnemünde   Swinemünde
⊙ Stettin

EAST
PRUSSIA

Danzig ⊙

S O V I E T
U N I O N

• Minsk

E R M A N Y

Berlin ⊙
otsdam ⊙

• Warsaw

Magdeburg
○ Dessau
Leipzig
○ ○
Leuna
Chemnitz

Dresden
⊙

P O L A N D

Prague •

Pilsen
•

C Z E C H O S L O V A K I A

• Krakow

Nuremberg
○
Schwandorf
⊙ Regensburg

• Linz

Vienna •

• Bratislava

R U M A N I A

⊙ Munich
Berchtesgaden

A U S T R I A

H U N G A R Y

• Budapest

Bucharest •

Trieste
•

Belgrade •

B U L G A R I A

I T A L Y

Adriatic Sea

Y U G O S L A V I A

• Sophia

The Mediterranean, Levant
and Southern Europe

N
W · E
S

0   100   200   300
miles

Black Sea

Athens

CRETE

CYPRUS

SYRIA

Sea

LEBANON
Beirut ·   · Damascus

Gambut ·   · Bardia
Tobruk

PALESTINE

El Adem ·
Sidi Rezegh ·
Sollum
Halfaya
Mersa Matruh

C Y R E N A I C A

Aboukir
Alexandria ·
Fuka ·
El Alamein ·

Jerusalem ·

Sidi Haneish
Sidi Barrani
Ma'aten Bagush

Abu Sueir ·
Port Tewfik ·

TRANS-
JORDAN

Cairo ·

EGYPT

to RAF Shaibah
(Basra)
→

*Red
Sea*

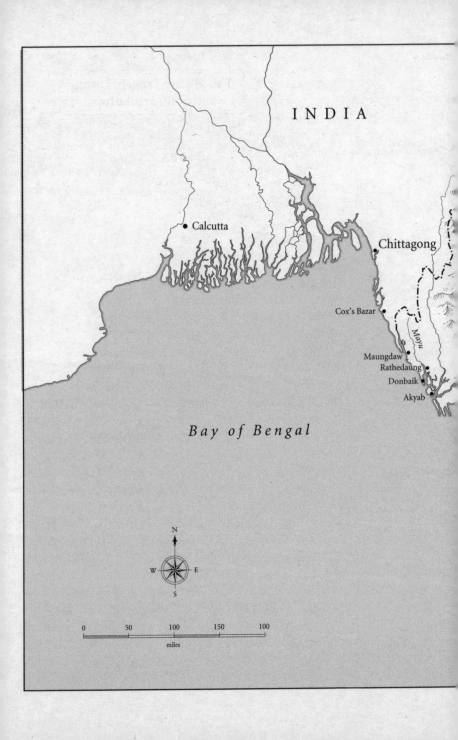

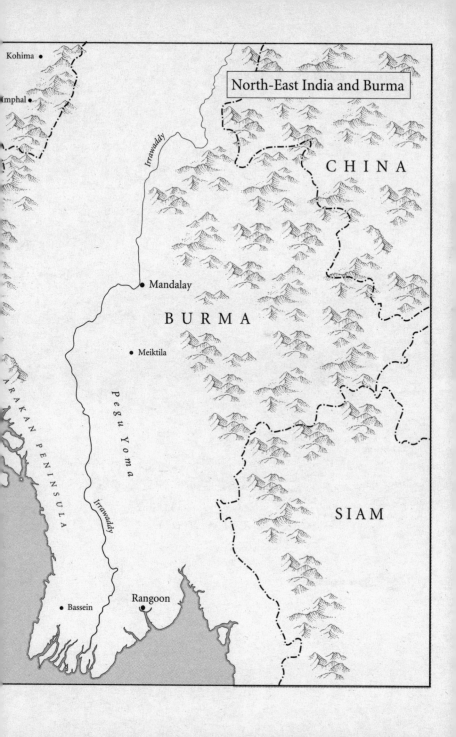

North-East India and Burma

Kohima

Imphal

CHINA

Irrawaddy

Mandalay

BURMA

Meiktila

ARAKAN PENINSULA

Pegu Yoma

Irrawaddy

SIAM

Bassein

Rangoon

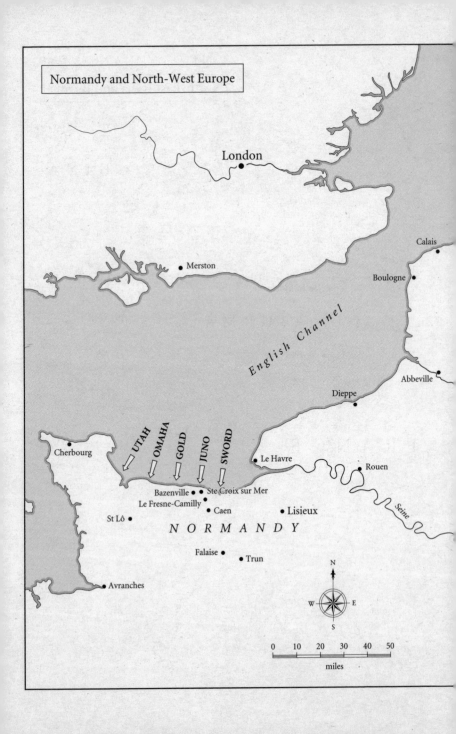

Normandy and North-West Europe

London

Calais

Boulogne

Merston

Abbeville

English Channel

Dieppe

Cherbourg

Le Havre

Rouen

UTAH OMAHA GOLD JUNO SWORD

Bazenville ● ● Ste Croix sur Mer

Le Fresne-Camilly ●

● Caen

St Lô ●

Lisieux ●

Seine

N O R M A N D Y

Falaise ●

● Trun

Avranches ●

N
W ⊛ E
S

0 10 20 30 40 50

miles

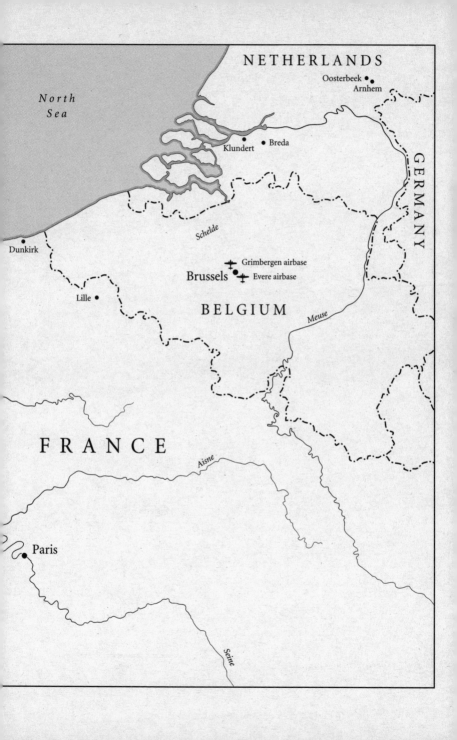

Prologue

Firstway

In the spring of 1944 the chief information officer with the Royal Air Force permanent delegation in Washington, DC, reported back to London on how the service was regarded on the other side of the Atlantic. 'We cannot hope to *enhance* the prestige of the RAF,' he wrote. 'Throughout the world it is a household word, and in the United States its reputation is so high that in some quarters it is almost regarded as something apart from, and superior to, Britain.'[1]

The Americans were not easily impressed. Since joining the war they had become the dominant partners in the alliance and the attitude of US commanders towards the British Army and Navy could be tinged with a condescension that was sometimes amused and often exasperated.

The information officer's report, smug though it sounded, was essentially accurate. The RAF *was* seen differently. Unlike the other services, it attracted quasi-automatic admiration and respect. American airmen regarded their British comrades as something like equals; energetic, efficient and providing an operational contribution that added real weight to the Allied war effort.

In March 1944 when the report was written, Britain and the US had settled on the command structure for the forthcoming great invasion of northern Europe, and Dwight D. Eisenhower was chosen as Supreme Allied Commander. Eisenhower knew who he wanted as his second-in-command: Arthur Tedder of the RAF, who he had got to know intimately during the Mediterranean and Italian campaigns. 'Ike' had been Tedder's best man when he married for the second time. Tedder was Eisenhower's 'warm personal friend'[2] and the man he most admired and trusted among the British high command.

The US military's assessment of the quality and worth of their allies was based initially on observation, then on direct experience. For the first ten months of the war the Army's record was one of debacle and defeat in Norway and France ending in the ignominy of Dunkirk. In North Africa, it floundered against a weaker enemy, and a golden chance for a quick ending was squandered when Churchill decided to switch forces to Greece in a hopeless attempt to stem the Nazi invasion. The eventual victory at El Alamein was the result of a marked numerical superiority in men, guns, tanks and aircraft. It was the first and last time that a British and Commonwealth force would beat the Germans on their own. Thereafter almost all of the Army's effort in the West would be in conjunction with, and ultimately subordinate to, the Americans.

At sea, the war disobligingly failed to develop along the lines that the Admiralty had planned for. There would be no major fleet show-down between the Royal Navy and the Kriegsmarine and the huge and expensive battleships the admirals set such store by absorbed commensurate resources and manpower, which had to be diverted from more productive activities in order to protect them. The Navy did, of course, secure at great cost and effort the sea lanes that kept Britain in the war, but the Battle of the Atlantic was a struggle for survival rather than an advance towards victory. Fighting it took all their time and British warships did not contribute anything to the US Navy's campaign in the Pacific until January 1945.

The information officer's belief that the Air Force was perceived as something 'apart from' and 'superior to' Britain was telling. The Americans did not do sentimentality. The notion that cultural and historical connections meant that Britain was owed deference had long ago vanished. Some in the British military and political estab-lishment did not seem to have noticed that things had changed. Transatlantic visitors were used to being talked down to by their hosts, who drew on centuries of imperial wisdom to instruct and correct. Americans believed they had little to learn from a nation that was fast losing its world-power status and in the space of a generation had twice been forced to turn to them for salvation.

Their dealings with the RAF brought a pleasant surprise. In the early autumn of 1940, when America was still more than a year away from entering the war but already supplying Britain with materiel, a delegation toured Egypt. Colonel Harvey S. Burwell of the US Army Air Forces (USAAF) was greatly impressed by the spirit of the pilots and ground crews, praising their 'superb morale, extraordinary patience and wonderful courage'.[3] He met Tedder, then head of the RAF's Middle East Command, and some of his senior officers and was relieved to find that 'the [British] supercilious superiority so objectionable to Americans is rarely exhibited'. The impression persisted so that the information officer was able to state in his 1944 report from Washington that 'many people who dislike the British would not say a word against the RAF'.[4]

This image of unstuffiness was reinforced by a well-orchestrated stateside propaganda effort, promoting the RAF's achievements and personalities. Guy Gibson, hero of the May 1943 Dams Raid, was pressed into service as an ambassador. In September that year he swept across North America charming interviewers, reporters and radio audiences and receiving the sort of reception normally accorded to movie stars. Humility was not a quality readily associated with Gibson at home. Abroad, however, he was seen as a 'thoroughly nice, modest young man with a good sense of humour'.[5]

Above all, he was unmistakeably a great warrior. The Dams Raid was an epic feat of arms. It immediately attracted the attention of the Hollywood director Howard Hawks, who invited Gibson to stay with him in Los Angeles. Hawks commissioned a script from Flight Lieutenant Roald Dahl, a former fighter pilot then serving as a press attaché in Washington (though this version foundered on the objections of Barnes Wallis, the scientific brains behind the operation).

The Air Force projected confidence, aggression and efficiency. Whatever the Americans thought about Britain's contribution on land and sea, no one could deny that in the air it more than pulled its weight. The first American bombs fell on Europe in August 1942. In the twenty-nine months that followed, the USAAF never matched the tonnages showered down by the RAF. It was only in January 1945 that they began to pull ahead. The final balance showed that, in the bombing war in Europe, Bomber Command dropped 873,348 tons of ordnance and the United States Eighth Air Force 621,438.[6] In this field of the great Allied endeavour in the West, the British were seen to deliver more and suffer more than the US in both men and machines.[7]

At the business of strategic bombing, British aircraft were the best in the world. The Avro Lancaster and Handley Page Halifax were the same size as their American counterparts, the Boeing B-17 Flying Fortress and Consolidated B-24 Liberator. However, they carried much heavier bomb loads; 10,000lb against the Fortress's 5,000lb.[8]

So when Americans looked at the RAF they saw an organization that did not conform to their notions of Britishness but something more akin to themselves, matching them for ambition, efficiency and swagger. Military forces mirror the values of the society they spring from. The image of Britain that the RAF presented in the glass was not the same as that reflected by the Army and the Navy. The old services represented the past. The airmen were the incarnation of how new Britons viewed themselves: modern, competent, democratic and reluctant to give to those above them the automatic deference that had hitherto been expected.

This picture of the RAF was widely accepted both inside and outside its ranks. As a result of the great attention paid to it by the press, the radio and the newsreels, the Air Force came to be seen as a repository of a new set of national values. It was a development that suited the government's information strategy and it was soon endorsed as a recurrent trope of British propaganda. The approach carried hidden risks. In it was contained an implicit promise that the ethos the RAF enshrined would be given political expression and influence the future shape and direction of the country once the war was won.

As the conflict approached, the people of Britain absorbed the idea that the Air Force would play the dominant role in the coming struggle, as the guarantors of their survival and the agents of eventual victory. On 1 October 1938, the first issue of the weekly news magazine *Picture Post* appeared. It was lively, outspoken, thoroughly modern in outlook and almost immediately won a big circulation and considerable political influence. The second issue carried a long article entitled simply 'The RAF', part of a series intended to shed light on 'our great national institutions'.[9] It was written by Nigel Tangye, a young journalist-about-town who was also a pilot and officer in the RAF reserve. Tangye had good connections with the Air Ministry and it would have been surprising if he had not checked with them before making the momentous claim that 'the RAF holds today a position of importance higher than the Army or Royal Navy'. The duties of the Air Force of protecting the national territory, preserving vital sea trade routes, defending the empire and lending aid to allies amounted to 'everything which for hundreds of years has been the function of the Royal Navy'.

Publicity frequently stressed its 'democratic' nature, compared to the other services. 'Officers and men in the Royal Air Force share a common spirit which is unknown either in the Army or the Navy,' wrote Tangye. 'So much of the Navy's time is spent in scrubbing decks, so much of the Army's in massed drilling. But the Air Force Machines have to fly every day, and the crews of each are bent on keeping them in tip-top condition.'

It was never presented as a classless organization. That would have been too much to claim in a society which, though lines were blurring, was still strictly defined by birth, money, education, accent and manners. It did, however, seem something like a meritocracy in which the near-revolutionary notion that competence was more important than background had taken hold.

The Air Force needed a large cadre of expert tradesmen to keep it flying. They came, largely, from the lower-middle and upper-working classes, and the educational gap between other ranks and officers was consequently narrower than in the Army and Navy. The need for aircrew opened the door to the officers' mess to young men who would never have passed muster in the 1920s and 1930s.

The literary types sent in the early years of the war by the Air Ministry on fact-finding tours of bases to gather propaganda material were struck by the varied origins of the officers they encountered. The Oxford don Lord David Cecil noted after a visit to a bomber station in 1941 how 'compared with the Army or Navy the men of the RAF seem very diverse … very varied … drawing its members from every sort of rank and profession'.[10]

Sitting down to dinner in the mess he found on one side of him 'a boy fresh from a public school; on the other side a bank clerk; opposite, a New Zealander, next to him a garage worker, next to him a law student'.

The service was too young, he concluded, to have 'evolved a traditional type' to which all must conform: 'Their upper lips are not too stiff. On the whole their manners tend to be expansive. There is often a touch of jaunty flamboyance in the way they walk and speak and wear their uniforms, with an elegant identification bracelet glinting on the wrist.'

Air Force style was in bright contrast to the dowdiness of the other services. As a boy watching the build-up to D-Day around his home in the West Country the military historian John Keegan was disappointed that the British soldiers he saw 'wore khaki from top to toe … so ill-cut, shapeless and hairy that I could find almost nothing in its wearers to admire'.[11] When the Americans arrived he and his school friends were amazed at 'how different they looked from our own jumble-sale champions, beautifully clothed in smooth khaki …' They were even more impressed by the 'number, size and elegance of the vehicles in which they paraded about the countryside in stately convoy', so unlike the 'sad collection of underpowered makeshifts, whose dun paint flaked from their tin pot bodywork' that the Army had to make do with.

No one had to feel sorry for the RAF. The aircrew could equal their Yank counterparts in swank and dash and even the earthbound 'erk' had the edge over his 'brown job' and matelot comrades. Their uniform may have been of serge but they wore a collar and tie to go to work and their hair, curling from under their distinctive two-button side caps at a length that would have given a sergeant-major apoplexy, was as like as not gleaming with Brylcreem.

It was no longer the case that all the nice girls loved a sailor. In October 1939 'Just An Airman' wrote to *Picture Post* complaining that after joining the Air Force his girlfriend had dumped him and since then he had found that 'no decent girl seems to look at an airman'. He went on: 'I am five feet 10 inches tall, good at sports and reasonably good looking. Once I had girlfriends. Now the only place I seem welcome is at the public house.'[12]

His self-pitying and possibly self-serving missive produced an avalanche of positive responses, a selection of which was printed over a double-page spread. 'I, as a young lady of nineteen, was very surprised to read your correspondent's letter,' wrote Joyce Dickinson of London Road, Rainham, Gillingham, Kent.[13] 'Many young ladies, including myself, admire members of the Royal Air Force and feel especially proud when we read of their daring and brave exploits on the Western Front and over Germany. He may rest assured that although one girl has turned him down, many of us would like the opportunity to make his acquaintance.'

From Wallasey in Cheshire 'An Admirer' declared: 'I think many readers will agree with me when I say that the RAF is the finest of the three services. I am not saying anything against the Navy or the Army ... but I prefer the Air Force.'

It was little wonder that when conscription began more men exercised their right of choice in favour of the Air Force over the other services. The RAF seemed immune to the criticism that the Army in particular sometimes attracted. The war in the air got off to just as bad a start as it did on land and sea. Bomber Command's early record was one of continuous failure and heavy, pointless losses, and the pattern was maintained by all branches of the service in the campaigns in Norway and France. Government propaganda and a co-operative media skated over this truth.

Then, in the summer of 1940, in full view of the population, Fighter Command won the Battle of Britain, supercharging national morale and gilding the Air Force with an aura of success that never tarnished. 'The RAF are the darlings of the nation!' wrote John Thornley, a twenty-nine-year-old salesman from Preston, Lancashire, in his diary in July 1940.[14] 'What magnificent chaps the RAF pilots must be,' he declared a month later as the Battle approached its climax.

By the end of the summer its reputation seemed unassailable. Britain's city-dwellers proved remarkably willing to overlook Fighter Command's inability to protect them from the nightly Blitzes that devastated their homes in the winter of 1940–41, preferring to blame politicians for the lack of counter-measures. Major flaws in the Air Staff's thinking and preparations such as its blind faith in strategic bombing and the initial failures to co-operate effectively with the Army and Navy were never really exposed to public view. The RAF's numerous critics in the upper echelons of the other services complained that it appeared subject to different rules from the ones they had to obey. Often it seemed a law unto itself, holding, in the opinion of the soldier-historian Bernard Fergusson, 'an unwritten charter direct from the war Cabinet' that allowed it to direct bombing policy and decide on what types of aircraft were needed without having to consult with soldier and sailor colleagues.[15]

In two previous books, *Fighter Boys* (2003) and *Bomber Boys* (2008) I told the story of the RAF in the Battle of Britain and the Strategic Offensive against Germany, conveying events, emotions and attitudes as much as possible from the perspectives of the participants. In this final work in the trilogy, I hope to extend the field of vision to the whole of the Second World War. A comprehensive history is impossible in one volume. There was too much being done by too many people. Instead I have tried to examine essential aspects of the RAF wartime experience, both for those flying and those on the ground in selected battles and theatres, in the process, I hope, colouring in the RAF's distinct identity. So this is not a chronicle of the war in the air. It is about the spirit of the Air Force, its heart and soul.

Again, I have tried to see things through the eyes of the players, relying wherever possible on contemporary documents, diaries and letters and, where they are not available, memoirs and reminiscences. I was lucky enough to meet and interview many veterans during my earlier research and could draw on their memories of other parts of their service not covered in previous books. There is, I was pleased to discover, still much rich material lying undiscovered in the archives which provides new evidence and insights.

This book is about many things but a recurrent theme is the special relationship that the Air Force enjoyed with the nation at this uniquely testing time in its history. For much of the war the RAF was Britain and Britain was the RAF. The conflict arrived in the middle of a time of great transformation, when British characteristics and attitudes were undergoing profound changes.

Among the girls who responded to 'Just An Airman' was Joyce Robinson of Firstway, Raynes Park, London SW20. She, too, was an Air Force fan, admiring 'the spirit of adventure which prompts a man to join'.[16] The street is half a mile from where I grew up. It was built in the 1920s by an energetic master builder called George Blay who turned much of what was then countryside into suburbia. It is a tree-lined cul-de-sac of nice, three-bedroomed terraced houses, with bay windows, timberwork on the façades and ample back gardens. They cost £675 (with 85 per cent mortgages available) and were a few minutes' walk from Raynes Park station on the Southern Electric railway which ran straight in to Waterloo. Thousands of streets like Firstway were springing up around Britain's cities at the same time.

The families who lived in them were members of the most over-looked and underappreciated stratum of the social layer cake – the lower-middle class. The cautious patriarchs of these 'quadrants', 'crescents', 'drives' and 'walks' left each morning for their jobs as clerks, draughtsmen, shopkeepers and minor civil servants while Mum stayed home to clean and cook. Their children raised their eyes to broader horizons. I have not managed to discover anything about Joyce Robinson but I have imagined her: playing tennis at the club round the corner in Taunton Avenue, watching Clark Gable in *Gone With the Wind* at the Raynes Park Rialto, taking the District Line to Hammersmith to dance at the Palais, perhaps driving with a boyfriend to a roadhouse on the Kingston by-pass.

It was this emerging Britain which provided the wartime Air Force with much of its man- and womanpower as well as enriching its identity and ethos. There were fewer men and women in Air Force blue than there were in Navy blue or khaki. The Second World War was nonetheless in many ways an RAF show. From the beginning to the end it was the spearhead of almost every action and effort. Not only did it lead the way to victory, it shaped the contours of peace.

1

The Big One

The faint feeling of dread that was always there in the bad old days was absent this morning. Dawn was still several hours away and inside the chilly briefing room eighteen crews from 9 Squadron were gathered to hear their orders. They smoked and chatted, waiting for the CO to arrive to reveal the location of the target. Occasionally there was a burst of laughter. Today the hilarity sounded unforced and not just a cover for jangling nerves. The date was 25 April 1945 and Germany was in its death throes. One precious thought united the 126 men present: in twelve hours' time their war might be over and they would never have to do this again.

If so, it seemed likely they were going out with a bang. The previous evening the CO had toured the messes advising drinkers to take it easy as 'something special' was in the offing.[1] The word from Flights was that the fuel order was for 2,154 gallons per aircraft.[2] That meant an extra-long trip. And what was the BBC doing here? Next to the platform at the front of the room a reporter and technician were fiddling with microphone and disc recorder.

The large map of Europe on the wall behind the platform offered a clue. It was the first thing the crews looked at when they trooped in. The red tape that traced their route to the target 'started at Bardney, our base, ran down to the South Coast and across the Channel,' remembered Flight Sergeant Fred Whitfield, who, though 'tour expired' after completing thirty trips as a rear gunner, had volunteered to carry on.[3] 'At that point it diverted across France on a dog leg and ended up in Southern Germany.' Whitfield's first thought was that it 'looked like a daylight raid on Munich'.

The orderly officer called the crews to attention and with a scraping of chairs they got to their feet as Wing Commander Bazin walked down the aisle followed by his specialist officers, stepped onto the dais and began the briefing.

Jim Bazin, DFC and bar, seemed indestructible. Born in Imperial India, raised in a comfortable middle-class family in the North East of Britain, he served as a part-timer in an RAF auxiliary squadron for four years before the war and fought from the first day to what was now surely almost the last. By any reckoning of the odds he should have been dead several times over. Whatever terrors he had experienced had left no outward mark on him. When he spoke, it was in a cultured, amused accent, more like a university professor than a warrior.

'Well, Gentlemen,' he announced. 'This is the big one.'[4] He explained that at this late stage in the war they were being given a chance to land a blow on the man who had started it all. They were off to bomb Hitler's mountain retreat at Berchtesgaden. 'Your particular aiming point for this attack is the house where this gentleman is supposed to live,' he told them. 'Whether he's there is another matter.' He paused for a second before going on. 'But no doubt there will be plenty of people there to benefit from it.'[5] The room rocked with laughter.

They settled down as the met, navigation and intelligence officers delivered the weather forecast and took them through the technicalities of route, plan of attack and expected opposition. When they finally filed out into the Lincolnshire night, heavy with the muddy smell of the surrounding fields, everyone was talking excitedly. They had all heard of Berchtesgaden, of course. To the older ones who remembered it from pre-war newsreels, it brought back memories of Chamberlain and Munich and national humiliation. For the younger airmen it was a name from the news bulletins, one of the three main military headquarters from which Hitler directed his forces. None of those who planned Bomber Command operations had seen fit to attack it before. Now, for reasons that no one explained in the briefing, the time had finally come.

The sky was clear and the moon, one day away from fullness, silvered the ridges of the potato fields surrounding the base. The aerodrome stood just north of the village of Bardney on the plain which stretches north from the Lincolnshire fenlands to the rising hills of the Wolds. It was one of more than a hundred bomber stations built during the early years of the war, a standard pattern of three concrete runways and three hangars, interspersed with utilitarian huts and sheds where the airmen, ground crews and WAAFs ate, washed and slept.[6]

There were two hours to take-off and much to be done beforehand. Operations boiled down to a succession of routines which had to be followed to the letter if you wanted to succeed and survive. But first they would eat, a meal that had long ago become a cliché: bacon and eggs and wodges of bread and margarine, washed down with American canned orange juice and mahogany-coloured tea.

They cleared their plates and headed for the crew room to climb into multi-layered flying gear and pick up their parachutes. For those who needed it there was a detour to the latrines to empty their bowels before they all climbed into canvas-covered four-ton lorries that trundled them out to dispersal where the bombers loomed, casting long moon shadows on the tarmac. The ground crew had been there for hours, refuelling, bombing up, checking the control surfaces and undercarriage, fussing over the machine as if it was their own lives that were at stake.

Those flying were swaddled like Michelin men but it still felt cold. The metal tube of the fuselage carried its own special chill. They climbed the five rungs of the ladder, through the hatch behind the gun turret amidships, and struggled to their posts. Pilot, flight engineer, navigator, bomb aimer and wireless operator wriggled forward to the nose, clambering over the thick spar that pinned together the bomber's 102-foot wingspan. The gunners settled into their solitary nests behind them.

Each man began to run through the litany of checks and drills, second nature now from years of training and practice. For the gunners it took a few minutes. For the pilot and flight engineer it was more like half an hour. Then the pilot shouted down to the ground crew that he was 'ready for starting'. A mechanic jumped forward to work the Ki-Gas pump and prime the carburettor of the first engine. Someone swung a white torch to indicate which engine to fire up first. From his seat, squeezed in next to the pilot, the flight engineer flipped on booster coil and main ignition switches and opened the master fuel cock. The pilot thumbed the starter button and with an explosive thud and a volley of flame and smoke, one by one the Merlin engines burst into life, filling the rural silence with a deep-throated roar. In the farms and villages around the bomber bases the noise was now as familiar as birdsong.

More minutes passed before the dials showed every engine had reached the right temperature and pressure. It was a laborious business but there was no rushing it. The machine was what got you there and got you home. This day of all days, with the finishing line in sight, was no time to get careless.

A-Able was the first away. It was 5 a.m. and still pitch-black but the clear sky promised a fine day. The Lancaster moved off jerkily, stopping and starting as the pilot tested the flaps and brakes. It rolled onto the runway, waiting for the signal on the Aldis lamp mounted on the control van to flash from red to green. Lining the tarmac were the usual party of WAAFs and ground staff gathered to wave and smile and pray for a safe return. This morning there were others present. Standing among them were the BBC reporter and soundman who had been at the briefing. That evening the journalist's report, delivered in a bright, modern voice, very different from the plummy tones of the pre-war Corporation, would go out on the evening news:

'Hallo BBC. This is Brian Bliss with Bomber Command. It's Zero Hour, the attack is on and the first Lancaster's swinging into position at the head of the runway right opposite me now … here she comes … remember this is the squadron which sank the *Tirpitz* and now they're off to Berchtesgaden with twelve thousand pounders. *Twelve thousand pounders!* And they're taking the attack literally to Hitler's doorstep!'[7] Millions of listeners heard the engine note rising sharply as the revs climbed, then fading as Bliss, almost shouting now, announced that 'A-Able is off … a marvellous sight as she races by!'

In Q-Queenie, rear gunner Fred Whitfield sat in his turret and waited with the rest of the crew for their turn. After thirty operations together they knew each other as well as they did their own families.

They were ordinary men from all over Britain. The pilot, Ron Adams, came from Wembley, London, Larry Brown the flight engineer was from Leeds, bomb aimer Phil Jackson from Nottingham, navigator Jim Lynam from Scunthorpe, wireless operator Jack Faucheux from Romford and the mid-upper gunner Frank Stebbings from Tunbridge Wells. Fred Whitfield was a Geordie, born in South Shields.

Starting operations in the aftermath of D-Day, they had bombed V weapons sites, marshalling yards, bridges and U-boat pens, before resuming the assault on German cities. They had been shot up by a night fighter and only made it home thanks to the skill and determination of 'Lucky' Adams who, though only twenty-one, was in Whitfield's eyes 'the best pilot in the RAF'. The gunners gave as good as they got. Whitfield and Stebbings had several kills to their credit, and the crew's 'press-on' spirit had earned them four Distinguished Flying Medals and one Distinguished Service Cross between them. It had needed courage, skill and the closest teamwork to come through these trials and their faith in each other was strong. The raid they were about to embark on seemed less hazardous than most. But everyone knew of a crew that had bought it on their last mission. While he waited Whitfield 'closed my eyes for a couple of minutes and had a few words with my God'.[8]

Then Q-Queenie was shuddering with the pent-up kinetic energy of four Merlin engines as Ron Adams jammed on the brakes and opened the throttle to maximum revs. He eased off and the Lancaster bounded forward. At about 50 knots (57mph) Whitfield 'felt the turret lift as the tail wheel left the ground. "90 knots, 100 knots, 120 knots," said the engineer, reading the speed. The skipper eased back on the control column. Queenie was airborne. We climbed, slowly gaining height'.

Once all aircraft were at 10,000 feet they formed a loose gaggle, and set course for Cap Gris Nez near their rendezvous with the squadron with whom they would be spearheading the raid. 617 Squadron were friends and rivals and their base was only a few miles from Bardney at Woodhall Spa. The two operated together often, specializing in missions requiring great skill and accuracy, and as Brian Bliss reminded his listeners six months before had finished off Hitler's last remaining battleship with a volley of 'earth-quake' bombs as she lay crippled in Tromsø fjord. The exploit had added extra lustre to the reputation of 617, already famous as the Dam Busters. However, as their sister squadron liked to point out, they were relative sprogs in the bombing game, having been created only two years earlier, whereas 9 Squadron dated back to 1914 and had been in continuous action from the very start of the war.

The sister squadrons made up just a small part of a huge force bearing down on Berchtesgaden. The pre-dawn sky of eastern England was thick with aircraft heading in the same direction. Three hundred and fifty-nine bombers were being thrown into the attack. Guiding them were sixteen Mosquitoes from Path Finder Force, equipped with special navigation aids to fix the target, tucked, safely until now, in the folds of the Bavarian Alps. Only five years before, an armada of this size was a distant fantasy. Yet this was not even the biggest raid of the day. An even larger formation was heading off to the North Sea island of Wangerooge, to smash up shore batteries that menaced Allied shipping delivering supplies to the port of Bremen for the armies encircling Berlin.

The RAF of April 1945 bore little resemblance to the organization Jim Bazin had joined eleven years before. In that time it had expanded enormously, evolving from a tight, professional elite drawn mainly from the top layers of society into a vast structure, more than a million strong. It had long ceased to be an overwhelmingly British enterprise. Scattered among the squadrons today were Poles, Australians, New Zealanders, Rhodesians, Americans, Canadians, Frenchmen and Dutchmen, Norwegians and Danes, only some of the sixty nationalities which had found a home in the Air Force.

The spirit of amateurism that still flickered in the pre-war service had long ago been snuffed out by the demands of war and replaced by a ruthless professionalism. Five years and eight months before, 9 Squadron had taken part in the first proper British air raid of the war. On 4 September 1939, together with 149 Squadron, they flew in appalling weather across the North Sea to attack German warships lying near Brunsbüttel. They had only dead reckoning to get them there and their twin-engine Wellingtons were loaded with primitive bombs. Against great odds, most of the raiders managed to find the target area but it was covered with cloud and fiercely defended by flak and fighters. Only one crew claimed to have hit anything. Two 9 Squadron aircraft were brought down and all ten on board killed. There would be hundreds of other futile sorties before the RAF began to function efficiently as a war machine. Now the process was complete. The days of wasted effort and useless sacrifice were long gone and the British and American air forces enjoyed almost total mastery of the skies of Europe.

The shoals of Lancasters cruised on, dark and ominous in the moonlight, pausing to circle at their rendezvous point above the towns of Arras, Valenciennes and Laon near the Franco-Belgian border. Then, with 9 Squadron and 617 Squadron in the lead, they set off south and east towards the Alps and Berchtesgaden.

The crews had been given their specific targets at early morning briefings at nineteen bases spread over the bomber counties of Yorkshire, Lincolnshire, Nottinghamshire and Norfolk. The lead squadrons had the most difficult task. Their objectives were, as Bazin warned his men, 'very, very small indeed'[9] and hidden in the pine-covered clefts of a tall mountain range. The first was the Eagle's Nest, a spectacular pavilion, built for Hitler as a retreat and diplomatic reception centre on top of a rocky spur called the Kehlstein, 6,000 feet above sea level. The second was Hitler's house, the Berghof, which sat, five miles down the mountain, on the shoulder of the humped ridge known as the Obersalzberg. The surrounding area was enclosed by fences and guard posts. Inside the security zone some of the leading figures of Hitler's court – Hermann Goering, Martin Bormann and Albert Speer – had built villas and the rock beneath it was honeycombed with bomb shelters and storerooms. The complex also housed a communications centre from where Hitler could keep in touch with his commanders.

The chances of a direct hit on either target were slight. With the armament 9 and 617 Squadrons were carrying, however, perfect accuracy was not essential. At the start of the war the biggest weapon in the RAF's armoury was the 500lb General Purpose bomb. It contained more metal than explosive and many of those produced were duds. Today the thirty-two aircraft of the lead squadrons were carrying 12,000lb 'Tallboys', aerodynamically optimized dart-like missiles devised by the engineering genius Barnes Wallis that plunged deep into the ground before exploding, creating an earth-quake effect that devastated everything around.

Behind them came a stream of bombers from the Main Force, the workaday squadrons which had spent the last three years smashing Germany's cities, causing and suffering appalling casualties. They would attack in two waves. Their main objective was the most prominent feature on the Obersalzberg, the barracks which housed the SS troops who guarded Hitler and his entourage.

Was he there or wasn't he? It seemed unlikely, but it was left to squadron commanders to raise or lower the expectations of their men as they saw fit. Bazin had chosen to play down the possibility. Others decided it would be enjoyable to hint that Hitler might well be at home. Either way, this was an operation most were proud to be part of, something to tell the grandchildren they were beginning to allow themselves to believe they might one day have.

The Dam Busters were led by Squadron Leader John Brookes, who was also in overall charge of the operation. The honour should have gone to their CO, Wing Commander Johnny Fauquier but he had been told by his superiors that he had exceeded his permitted number of operations and would not be on the trip. The blunt-spoken Canadian did not bother to hide his annoyance when he spoke to Brookes at the briefing. 'I'd like to have this target in my log book,' he told him. 'In fact I would like to have this target tattooed on my arse, but you have got to lead it.'[10]

The route took the bombers southwards towards Paris. There they turned again, south and east cruising at a steady 145 knots and ninety minutes later saw the snow glowing pink as the sun broke over the ramparts of the Swiss Alps.

At points along the way they were joined by more than two hundred Mustangs from RAF Fighter Command and the US Eighth Air Force. For most of the war the bombers had gone forth alone with only their on-board guns to protect them from flak and fighters. Now long-range escorts shepherded Allied bombers to and from their raids. Today there scarcely seemed a need for them.

H-Hour had been set for 9 a.m. As the bombers droned closer, the people of Berchtesgaden blithely went about their morning routines. Hitler's presence had seemed like a blessing at first, bringing attention and excitement to the valley. The modest villa he had first rented in 1928 had been transformed over the years into something more suited to a man of destiny. The result was what one architectural historian described as 'a combination of *faux* rusticity and imposing grandeur akin to a Thurn und Taxis princess decked out in a haute-couture dirndl'.[11]

At the heart of the house was the Great Hall. It was the size of a hangar, furnished with elephantine armchairs and hung with tapestries and paintings by Italian masters. Set into the northern wall was a picture window, thirty yards square, which, thanks to an ingenious mechanism, wound down into a recess in the floor. It was, enthused Diana Mosley, wife of the Blackshirts' leader Oswald Mosley, 'the largest piece of glass ever made ... through it one sees this huge chain of mountains and it looks more like an enormous cinema screen than like reality ...'[12]

As well as being the closest thing that Hitler had to a home, the Berghof made useful propaganda. It was a backdrop against which he could demonstrate his more human side. He was pictured in

Uncle Adolf

trilby, loden jacket and flannels, feeding deer and smiling at flaxen-haired little girls. It was a place for relaxation where he breathed the mountain air and stood at the enormous window looking out at the Untersberg, where legend had it that the twelfth-century Holy Roman Emperor Frederick Barbarossa lay sleeping, awaiting the hour when he would rise again and build a German empire that would last for a thousand years.

It was also a place of business, an ideal setting in which to impress or intimidate the politicians who trooped there in the countdown to the war. Stamped in the memories of the older airmen were images of an infamous visit that had taken place six and a half years earlier. On the morning of 15 September 1938 the Prime Minister Neville Chamberlain arrived at Berchtesgaden to try and avert another European conflagration. Hitler was demanding that Czechoslovakia allow the ethnic Germans of the Sudetenland to unite with the fatherland or face invasion. By the end of the meeting, Chamberlain was persuaded it was worth sacrificing Czechoslovakia for the sake of a shameful peace. Twelve months later the Second World War began.

Allied bombers had since wrecked every major German city killing hundreds of thousands. Berchtesgaden had been left alone and was barely touched by the war. The local economy boomed, supplying the Nazi colony which expanded as the elite moved their families and wealth out of bomb-blasted Berlin. Hitler was a frequent visitor. Between 1939 and 1944 he spent more time at the Berghof than he did in the capital, but nine months ago he had left and not been seen again.

That Wednesday morning there was one very senior Nazi in residence, however. Hermann Goering had turned up at his villa to join his family a few days before. He left Berlin on 20 April, Hitler's birthday, and had tried to persuade the Führer to go with him to Berchtesgaden. The overture had been rejected contemptuously. As he drove out of the city and Allied air raids began, Goering and his entourage ducked into a public shelter. 'May I introduce myself,' he declared as the bombs rained down. 'My name is Meyer.' It was a bitter joke. Years before he had promised that if British bombers ever struck Germany 'you may call me Meyer' – a very common

German, and also Jewish, name. Astonishingly, the huddled crowd burst into laughter.[13]

His flight brought him no nearer to safety. On arrival at the villa, Goering had made an ill-judged attempt to take over leadership of the Reich, in accordance with an agreement struck with Hitler in June 1941 that he should assume the powers of the Führer should he be captured or incapacitated. The move was interpreted as an act of treachery, and that morning two senior SS officers had showed up, pistols in hand, to arrest him.

The drama was interrupted when, up and down the valley, the air raid sirens sounded. Despite interference from the mountains on the Pathfinders' 'Gee' electronic navigation systems, the lead aircraft arrived almost exactly on time, just before 9 a.m. Squadron Leader Brookes of 617 squadron was to bomb first. His target was the Eagle's Nest. It was extremely hard to spot from the bombing height of 15–16,000 feet. Neither Brookes nor his bomb aimer were able to identify anything that was worth wasting a Tallboy on. Three of the following aircraft did drop their bombs, but none scored a direct hit.

Then it was 9 Squadron's turn. As they approached the Berghof, the flak batteries set into the valley sides were banging away, pumping up streams of accurate flak at the bombers coming in at between 14,000 and 15,000 feet. Flight Lieutenant G. J. Campbell broadcast later on the BBC that he saw a ridge flash below him as his pilot Flying Officer J. Buckley brought him 'almost dead ahead of the house. I had a perfect run up and released my twelve-thousand pound bomb with the house dead in the sight.'[14]

Campbell's Tallboy was fuzed at twenty-five seconds.[15] From a Lancaster following close behind, rear gunner Flight Sergeant E. J. Cutting watched 'a twelve thousand pounder land about a hundred yards from Hitler's house'.[16] There was 'a terrific flash and though we were flying pretty high we could hear the explosion above the roar of our engines and the whole plane seemed to rock,' he told radio listeners. Then 'great piles of earth came shooting up, high into the sky. I thought to myself well, even if that's a bit short, it must have damaged the place. But just at that moment there was another flash, followed by a huge explosion. One of the other aircraft had planted its twelve thousand pounder bang on the target.'

By now the Main Force squadrons had arrived and the sky over the valley was dangerously crowded with huge aeroplanes. Cutting's pilot reported at the post-operation debrief that 'interference from other aircraft was so great' that he was unable to identify the target on the run-in and was ordered by the master bomber controlling the operation from another Lancaster not to bother making a second effort. Another pilot, Squadron Leader James Melrose, stated that 'just as the bomb aimer was preparing to drop the bomb, the aircraft was narrowly missed by a bomb from [an] aircraft above, and the target was accordingly overshot and it was impossible to bomb'.[17] Fred Whitfield's main concern was the anti-aircraft fire. The gunners had found their range and 'the sky was black with flak'.[18] The bomb aimer, Phil Jackson, seemed unaware of the shells rocking their kite as he talked Ron Adams in. Then Q-Queenie 'appeared to leap a thousand feet in grateful thanks for being relieved of five tons of metal'. Relief was brief. A few seconds later he heard a 'huge bang ... we went into a steep dive. The port engine was on fire.' Then came 'another almighty bang' apparently caused by one of the giant bombs hitting the top of the mountain. This blast hurled Q-Queenie upwards, blowing out the flames licking around the engine in the process. Swinging his turret to port Whitfield looked back up the inside of the aircraft for damage and saw jagged holes in the fuselage but the Lancaster flew on unperturbed. As they turned away he had a grandstand view of the Main Force attack.

Their target was the SS barracks, about a hundred yards from the Berghof. From the bellies of the aircraft, 4,000lb, 1,000lb and 500lb bombs tumbled out. Some fell on a hotel next door to the Berghof used for housing visitors, others on the villa of Martin Bormann who had managed to secure a prime spot for his house right next to his master. Emmy Goering was in her bedroom when she heard the first explosion. Her first thought was for her daughter and she 'ran to Edda's room but the governess had already taken her to the shelter', in the cellar of the house.[19] Next, she sought her husband and found him shaving, apparently unconcerned. He told her to go to the shelter but said he would not be joining her. When she insisted on staying with him, he relented. Had he not, his story might have ended there. One bomb landed in the swimming pool a few yards from the window of his study. The blast brought down the roof of the villa and collapsed the main staircase.

The bombs fell on innocent and guilty alike. When the sirens sounded school children were ordered to return home. Ten-year-old Irmgard Hunt was hurrying back with her sister Ingrid and friends when they 'began to hear the droning of bombers overhead'.[20] They were given a lift by a passing SS driver who let them out near their house. As the car drove off the first explosions erupted. The noise of the bombs was 'hellish'. It was followed by 'an enormous storm-like wind that would have blown me off my feet had I not gripped the rough bark of the nearest spruce and pressed myself against it ... We waited for a pause after each explosion to race to the next tree before the blast of air hit us.'

They reached home and crouched with their mother in the basement flinching from the 'horrendous noise that engulfed us, even in the cellar'. Next day Irmgard and Ingrid walked back to school. 'As the Obersalzberg came into view we saw the devastation. The plateau had become a chaotic brown-and-black mess of tree stumps that looked like charred matchsticks, dark craters and smoking ruins. "It's all gone", I said to myself.'

Half of the SS barracks was demolished. The villas of the elite were wrecked. Emmy Goering had left her jewellery in the house and was relieved when a servant found it among the wreckage. The Berghof had been gutted and the great picture window that had delighted pre-war guests was no more than a hole in the wall. The bombs had killed thirty-one in their usual indiscriminate fashion, with local civilians and foreign slave workers as well as SS troops among the casualties.

The raiders had suffered, too. Two Lancasters were brought down by flak. One crash-landed without casualties. Another, F-Freddie from 619 Squadron, provided a last story of heroism from the RAF's war. With the machine fatally damaged, the Canadian pilot Wilf DeMarco ordered the crew to jump while he held the aircraft steady. Three got out alive. The other three went down with their skipper.

The bombers landed at their home bases between noon and two o'clock. Because of the battering it had received, Q-Queenie was excused joining the queue of aircraft circling the base and given permission to land at once. Ron Adams made a smooth touchdown and taxied to dispersal where they were met by the ground crew eager to hear their adventures and dispensing cigarettes. After eight hours without a smoke, Fred Whitfield remembered, the first puff 'was pure nectar'.[21] When, in bomber bases up and down the east of England, the crews sat down to be debriefed by station intelligence officers, the same observation was repeated over and over. During the entire eight-hour trip they had not seen a single German aeroplane.

The exploit covered the front pages of the following day's newspapers. 'Hitler's Chalet Wrecked' was the headline in *The Times*. The *Daily Express* lead announced: 'Hitler Bombed Out – 5-tonners right on der Fuhrer's house', adding that 'Berchtesgaden was the target that every bomber pilot had longed to attack for nearly six years'.

Nobody asked why it had never been hit before now. Nor was the military usefulness of the exercise questioned. The truth was that the Berghof had been mentioned frequently when target lists were being drawn up but had always been rejected. Allied intelligence knew about the deep bomb shelters dug to protect the leadership and reckoned the negative publicity of a failed attempt to finish Hitler was not worth the effort. Later the calculation changed. The fear now was that the bombers might succeed, and the defence of Germany would pass to the hands of someone more competent and rational.

On 25 April 1945, with Hitler's empire reduced to a few square miles in the heart of a burning city, there was less reason than ever to attack Berchtesgaden with such extravagant force. None was offered. The raid on Hitler's mountain retreat was an overwhelmingly British operation, in conception and execution, with American aircraft playing only a secondary role. Its purpose was thus symbolic and the message was from Britain to the world. Hitler had started the war, and it was the British alone who had stood out against him. It had taken a great coalition to defeat him but without that initial defiance there might have been no victory. Smashing Berchtesgaden was a reminder of that truth. It was fitting that it was the Royal Air Force that delivered the blow.

2

A Cottage or a Castle?

One afternoon in the middle of the war Group Captain Arnold Wall sat down to tea and biscuits with Lord Trenchard, who was revered as the 'Father of the Royal Air Force'. Wall taught at the RAF Staff College and was preparing a lecture on the early history of the service. Among the questions he had for the great man were two that were 'pretty trivial', but which he 'felt personal curiosity about'.[1] The first was how it was that the RAF got its famous blue uniform.

There were 'two legends about this, both picturesque' in circulation, and he hoped Trenchard might be able to settle the matter once and for all. One claimed that in 1917 the textile mills of Bradford had received an order to weave a million yards or so of light blue cloth for the Tsar of Russia's cavalry. After the October Revolution, this was left on their hands. Thus, when the RAF officially came into being on 1 April 1918, there was a vast stock of surplus material going cheap that suited their requirements.

In the other version, the staff officer charged with choosing the colour was the beau of a musical comedy star named Lily Elsie, famous for starring in the London version of *The Merry Widow*. When samples were brought to him for a decision he decided to consult his girlfriend. '*This* is it,' she is alleged to have replied, picking out the shade that the RAF has worn ever since, 'because it matches the colour of my eyes.' Trenchard was 'most apologetic' but could throw no light on the matter.

On the second subject – the origin of the RAF ensign – he was more helpful, saying 'Yes, yes. I can tell you something about that.' Trenchard recalled his staff coming to him with a sketch of the design. It featured the RAF red, white and blue roundel, originally devised to deter trigger-happy Tommies from blasting at friendly aircraft from their trenches, set on a sky-blue background. They warned him, however, that the Royal College of Heralds had ruled the roundels unacceptable as they were 'not heraldry'. Trenchard resolved to take the matter up with the King. On his next meeting with him he brought the design along and explained the difficulty. 'Well, Trenchard,' said George V, 'if it wasn't heraldry before, it will be from now on.' And he signed the drawing there and then.

Gilded Lily

The ensign anecdote sounds plausible enough. Trenchard was not the man to make up a tale about his sovereign. The truth of the origin of Air Force Blue remains obscure, though gossip certainly favoured the second version. John Slessor, who went on to be one of the outstanding figures of the wartime RAF, recalled being summoned one evening in October 1918 with other senior officers to a meeting in Salisbury to discuss sending reinforcements to France where the Germans were in full retreat. Before the main business began there was some light relief. Mark Kerr, a former senior naval officer who had switched to the Air Force, was to model the first uniform. As Kerr stepped forward into the light of a reading lamp in the new rig, the audience reacted with mirth and incredulity. '[It] was terrible,' Slessor recalled, 'a nasty pale blue with a lot of gold all over it, which brought irresistibly to mind the gentleman who stands outside the cinema.'[2] He reported that 'rumour had it that it was a joint design by Mark Kerr and Miss Lily Elsie, though I'm sure that this was a libel on a beautiful and talented lady who has far too good taste ever to have been party to such an atrocity. Fortunately, it was short lived …'

These foundation stories say much about how the RAF saw itself – and how it wanted others to see it – in the first years of its existence. Unpicking the Russian story – the yarn about the yarn – reveals some enduring components of the RAF image. One is an aura of romance. The Air Force was being linked to what was traditionally the most dashing arm of the military. The message was that aviators were the aerial equivalent of the cavalry, bold, colourful and brimming with elan, éclat and all the other French words that go with sabre-wielding men on horseback. But there is also a suggestion that they were the target of some resentment from their dowdier colleagues. The implication was that the authorities had decided that, rather than weave a new cloth for the new service, they would have to make do with a quartermaster's windfall.

The second version reinforces the element of romance and introduces a raffish note. Lily Elsie was a big star of the day whose picture was plastered over mass-circulation illustrated papers. She was also married (as was Mark Kerr). Perhaps significantly, her playboy husband's fortune came from a family business that made textile machines. Here the RAF is presented as the sort of outfit that has in its upper ranks officers who hang out with beautiful celebrities. The tale gives the impression of modernity and a devil-may-care attitude to traditional proprieties.

Without stretching things too far, the ensign anecdote also carries a subtext. In this submerged narrative, the infant service, whose values are illustrated in an attractive and innovative design, runs up against the dreary forces of tradition in the form of the heralds. But where there's a will there's a way and help is at hand from an unusual quarter. Young and brash the newcomers may be, but the King recognizes them for the loyal liegemen that they are. At a stroke the hindrance is removed. There will be plenty more obstacles across their path in the journey ahead, the tale implies, but they will be approached and dealt with in the same undaunted manner.

The RAF's image developed naturally from the activities of the Royal Flying Corps in the First World War. The first task it was given was one that traditionally had been done by the cavalry – scouting the movements of the enemy. Once the front lines had solidified and trench warfare began, airmen mapped the battlefield, spotted for the artillery and clashed with enemy aviators trying to do the same thing.

At this stage they were a mere adjunct of the ground forces and did what the Army asked them to. But the nature of their activities meant they received a disproportionate amount of attention.

Aerial combat over the trenches seemed a clean, chivalrous business compared to the industrial carnage below. The isolated nature of much air fighting drew attention to individual warriors and the 'ace' was born. Both sides' propaganda boosted their own airmen heroes. In Britain William Leefe-Robinson, Mick Mannock, Albert Ball and James McCudden, all VC winners, were household names. The last three died flying. Aerial combat was clearly a very dangerous business but outwardly at least the airmen displayed a cheerful fatalism: 'Here's a toast to the dead already' ran a favourite song in the RFC's well-lubricated messes, 'three cheers for the next man to go.'

The airmen very quickly formed an identity that set them apart from soldiers and sailors. It was an attractive one, a blend of gallantry, individualism and insouciance in the face of death. The small-scale, tactical work they did was unsuited to the sort of regimented discipline that shaped the Army and Navy. They were old-fashioned warriors in modern fighting machines. These perceptions would persist long after this early 'heroic' age of air fighting was over.

Between 1917 and 1939 the Air Force would move from the periphery to the centre of British military thinking, planning and expenditure. The development was the result of two growth spurts, both of them brought about by fear of German air power. The Royal Air Force itself was conceived in the panicky atmosphere generated by continuing German air raids on Britain. Attacks by Zeppelins killed 500 civilians by the end of 1916 and diverted 17,000 servicemen from other duties. In the summer of 1917 long-range Gotha bombers struck London, killing and wounding nearly six hundred people in the initial raid. The fear felt on the streets spread upwards. 'One would have thought the world was coming to an end,' sniffed the Chief of the Imperial General Staff Sir William Robertson after attending an emergency cabinet meeting in July. 'I could not get a word in edgeways.'[3]

Something had to be done. The War Cabinet appointed the South African soldier-statesman Jan Smuts to investigate. His first, short recommendations arrived quickly and focused solely on improving the air defences of the London area.

His follow-up report, delivered only a month later, went much further. From the flimsy evidence of the air raids, Smuts drew a vision of the future. He was now convinced that there was 'absolutely no limit' to the use to which aeroplanes could be put. 'The day may not be far off,' he predicted, 'when aerial operations with their devastation of enemy lands and destruction of industrial and populous centres on a vast scale may become the principal operations of war, to which the older forms of military and naval operations may become secondary and subordinate.'[4]

This was quite a claim to advance on the basis of a few air raids. By making it, Smuts set a pattern for extravagant extrapolations, unsupported by serious data, of what air power might do that persisted through the years ahead and which profoundly shaped the development and condition of the Royal Air Force as it prepared for the next big war.

His prophecy was followed by an equally momentous proposal. He recommended that henceforth the RFC and its maritime equivalent, the Royal Naval Air Service, should no longer be tied strictly to the tactical needs of the Army and Navy and the two should be amalgamated in a single Air Force under the political control of a new Air Ministry. The Smuts plan was adopted and implemented with a speed that was remarkable even in wartime. The Royal Air Force came into being on 1 April 1918, the first – and for some years the only – independent air service in the world.

The original set-up was makeshift. The Air Ministry was initially sited in the Cecil Hotel, a second-class establishment in the Strand, before moving to a Portland stone block at No. 1 Kingsway, named Adastral House after the wonderful motto the RAF had inherited from the RFC – *Per Ardua ad Astra*. But the first great leap had been made and the airmen had their chance at reaching for the stars.

In less than four years the status of airmen had soared. Initially the lackeys of the traditional services they were now their nominal equals. The grant of independence had come out of nowhere. No one serving in the air had asked for it. Indeed, there were some in the RFC, including initially Trenchard himself, who were sceptical of the value of a third service, though it did not take him long to change his mind.

The airmen had been handed independence on a plate. They soon learned they would have to fight to keep it. The Army and Navy saw the measure as a temporary aberration. Once the flap was over and the war won, they set about trying to kill off the upstart and claw back control of their air assets.

The fight for survival that ensued had a profound effect on the fundamental character and outlook of the RAF. From birth it was forced to develop theories and practices that justified its existence and techniques for fending off a predatory Army and Navy, both operating from positions of massive institutional strength.

The Navy was particularly persistent. The Admiralty had a solid claim that as the Fleet was central to Britain's defences, anything connected to it should come under its control. The creation of the

Fleet Air Arm in 1924 still left naval aviation in the hands of the RAF and it was not until May 1939 that the Admiralty won it back. The Army felt that it had not been properly compensated for the loss of the RFC and senior officers complained constantly that the RAF showed no interest in providing for its legitimate needs. The belief that the Air Force was primarily out for itself ran deep in the traditional services. It was true that the RAF fought its corner hard in the early years of its existence, but self-interest was essential for self-preservation.

Mutual suspicion and misunderstanding, breaking occasionally into open bureaucratic warfare, placed a heavy strain on relations between the services that would last into the early years of the next war, hampering Britain's ability to fight it.

The RAF had to tread carefully in the post-war atmosphere of military cost-cutting that slashed budgets to the bone, a general loathing of war and a deep reluctance to contemplate the dreadful thought that Britain might one day have to fight another one. The newcomers were last in the queue for resources. Even getting kitted out in the new blue uniforms was a struggle. The Royal Army Clothing Department which dealt initially with supply, appeared unwilling to accept the change. 'Without presuming to criticize the decision of the Air Council, I venture to submit to you the following considerations,' wrote its director, General Sir Benjamin Johnson, in July 1918.[5] He went on to urge them to make sure they were happy with their choice as 'nothing could be worse for the prestige of the Air Service than the adoption of a colour which it might be found faded, went shabby or showed dirt and dust marks easily'. Eight years after the birth, the Treasury were still complaining that they had not been consulted about the clothing costs (which admittedly came to about £1.5 million).[6]

In the face of this resentment and a government which begrudged every shilling of military expenditure, the RAF needed outstanding leadership to keep it on its feet. It was provided by Hugh Trenchard who, as Chief of the Air Staff, was the professional head of the RAF for eleven of the first twelve years of its life. 'Boom' Trenchard dominates the story of the early days, simultaneously forbidding and benign, the patriarchal figure of the foundation myth. He claimed to dislike being referred to as the 'Father of the RAF' but had no difficulty accepting all the other accolades that would be heaped upon him over the years. Trenchard was a failure until he was forty. He was born in 1873, the son of a soldier turned failed West Country solicitor and a mother whose father had been a naval officer. He was supposed to join the Navy but flunked the entrance exam to Dartmouth then twice failed to pass muster for the Army academy at Woolwich. He finally scraped into the Royal Scots Fusiliers and spent the next nineteen years in India and Africa.

His career was going nowhere when in 1912, inspired by a letter from a brother officer describing ecstatically his experiences with the newly formed Royal Flying Corps at their aviation school on Salisbury Plain, he decided to try it for himself. He was immediately entranced – not with flying for he was too big and clumsy to be a good pilot – but with the opportunities it offered, for the military and for himself. Qualities the Army overlooked were appreciated in the RFC and promotions came rapidly. Three years later he was officer commanding in France.

Trenchard inspired something close to adulation among the generation of officers who led the RAF into the war and his thinking pervaded their outlook. Even after he was long gone from office, his protégé Arthur Tedder, who, as deputy to the Supreme Allied Commander in Europe, Dwight D. Eisenhower, was one of the busiest men in the world, still found time during the 1944 invasion to write to the old man asking for his advice.

He was seen to possess a quality that was not obvious in any other military figure of the time. 'There are some rare people in whose presence one instinctively and immediately feels: here is a really great man,' declared 'Jack' Slessor who first met him when a young RFC officer in France.[7] 'I felt it [then] ... and I have felt the same about him ever since. It is difficult to define that quality of real greatness. Self-confidence without a trace of arrogance, a contemptuous yet not intolerant disregard for anything mean or petty; the capacity to shuffle aside non-essentials and put an unerring finger on the real core of a problem or the true quality of a man, a sort of instinct for the really important point; a selfless devotion to the cause of what he believed to be true or right.'

Those who served with him felt they had been gilded by the association. 'I'm one of the Boom boys,' boasted Air Marshal Sir Hugh Walmsley in later life. 'He put the fear of God into me but by God I loved him.'[8] He even managed to be a hero to his valet. The humorous, intelligent Maurice Baring, who as his adjutant saw him at very close quarters in the First World War, thought him 'one of the few big men of the world'.[9]

Trenchard had many failings. He could be bombastic, dogmatic and often got things badly wrong. He shamelessly interfered in Air Force matters long after leaving office, with the result that 'all his successors up to the end of the war had to cope with his promptings and criticisms'.[10] And despite his military disdain for civilian manoeuvrings, he could intrigue as enthusiastically as any grubby politician if he thought the cause was worth it.

In many ways, though, his reputation is deserved. He was a formidable operator in the corridors of Whitehall, forceful with officials but knowing when to bend, and showed a subtle understanding of political realities, tending to tell his masters what they wanted to hear. His methods intensified friction with the other services, but they worked. The historian Malcolm Smith, who took a sceptical view of the great man, nonetheless concluded that 'Trenchard's extraordinary personality was, without doubt, one of the greatest assets of the RAF in its fight for survival ... when it was likely to have been wound up, if the other services had had their way'.[11]

His claims to greatness went further than that. He devised the institutions and established the traditions that enabled the Air Force to merge quickly into Britain's institutional landscape. He oversaw the development of the strategic theory that – rightly or wrongly – placed offensive air power at the centre of Britain's defence arrangements. Above all, he gave the RAF its identity, its self-belief and its credo, which was implanted in the DNA of the service in the years after the Great War by a cohort of disciples, suffusing the RAF 'with a vigour and aggression, a mixture of dogmatism and iconoclasm, characteristic of the Father of the Royal Air Force' himself.[12]

Trenchard initially stuck loyally to the Army chiefs' view that aeroplanes should be strictly subordinated to their own terrestrial needs. He began to change his mind after being given command of the 'Independent Force', which emerged from the deliberations of the Smuts inquiry. Its purpose was to give the Germans a taste of their own medicine by launching air raids into enemy territory to attack war industries. The campaign achieved little apart from killing German civilians but the notion of using aircraft to pursue strategic rather than simply tactical war aims was planted. Trenchard would end up the most energetic and effective preacher of the primacy of air power in future conflicts and the need to place an offensive air policy at the centre of all planning, organization and procurement.

Trenchard was a notoriously bad speaker but he had a physique and presence that more than made up for his inarticulacy. No one who met him forgot the experience. Many did meet him, for he clung to his baby long after his guardianship was ended, and he pops up often in memoirs and diaries, carrying out inspections and delivering pep talks, indulged by his old protégés who were reluctant to suggest his visitations might be inconvenient.

Arnold Wall, the officer who quizzed Trenchard about the origins of Air Force Blue, remembered a freezing day in December 1926 when he came to the RAF College at Cranwell to inspect the passing-out parade. Even at this early stage Trenchard's stature was immense. Wall, a young New Zealander in his first term as a cadet, noted every detail as he passed by. His first impression 'was of bigness. He was a tall man, heavily built, bearishly, this accentuated by his great-coat, his head seeming on the small side for a man of his size. Heavy eyebrows, shaggy; eyes deep set and rather close set, very keen in expression but friendly; greying moustache worn rather more heavily than was fashionable. His whole bearing was kindly and interested; an amiable Great Bear.'[13]

The parade trooped into the gymnasium for prize giving and speeches. All the cadets knew that Trenchard's nickname was 'Boom' on account of his penetrating voice. They 'were curious to discover whether he would speak to us in the voice of a howitzer, but in this he was a disappointment. He was gruff, certainly, and loud and clear but not a boomer ...'

Early in 1929 Wall went to RAF Uxbridge to hear Trenchard, who was stepping down as Chief of the Air Staff (CAS), deliver a farewell speech. 'I don't remember much of what he said, but one of the metaphors sticks in the mind,' he wrote. 'He stressed that all he and his contemporaries had been able to do since the RAF was formed was to lay "foundations (long pause), foundations for the future (pause). For you fellows to build on (pause). Could be a cottage, could be a castle. I don't know (pause). Nobody knows. Whichever it is, hope you'll find that the foundations are sound, strong ..."'

Laying a 'sound framework on which to build the service' had been one of Trenchard's main aims when he resumed the post of CAS in the spring of 1919 (a brief earlier stint had ended in his resignation after repeated clashes with the Air Minister, Lord Rothermere). The other was to find a role for the RAF that would justify its existence. Unlike his predecessor and rival Frederick Sykes, he understood the need for modesty and frugality. He came up with a proposal for how an Air Force, now pared down to a tenth of the size it had attained by the end of the war, could be employed in a way that projected military power effectively and cheaply.

The concept was called 'force substitution'. It meant simply that instead of relying on expensive ground forces to keep down rebellious natives in hot and dusty corners of the empire, the RAF could do the job by deploying a few aeroplanes. Inevitably, the idea raised Army hackles. The new boys were seeking to take over work that had previously been done by soldiers. Winston Churchill, who was both War and Air Minister, backed the idea, however, and henceforth the RAF would be engaged heavily in imperial policing.

The first success came early in 1920 when they crushed an uprising by the Dervish leader Mohammed Abdullah Hassan in Somaliland. The 'Mad Mullah' was defeated in a few weeks at a cost of £77,000 – 'the cheapest war in history' it was said.[14]

In one year, 1929, the RAF was in action in Iraq, Aden, Sudan, and the North-West Frontier. Its achievements were vaunted by the Air Minister Samuel Hoare in the House of Commons. In Iraq, it was 'the encroachment of certain tribes many miles over the Iraq frontier and the butchery of large numbers of men, women and children' that triggered operations. In Aden, it was 'the kidnapping of two sheikhs friendly to Britain'. In Sudan, it was 'the murder of a British Commissioner, a Greek trader and several natives'. The results were very satisfactory. 'The operations were carried out successfully with scarcely any casualties amongst either the Air Force or the native population,' Hoare reported. As a result of all this activity the RAF lost only one man. As for cost, the Aden mission came to £8,000, where 'under the older conditions of warfare the expenditure would have run into perhaps £6 millions'.[15]

These operations were of little use in preparing aircrews for modern warfare. Few of the tribesmen they subdued had ever seen an aeroplane, let alone had the means to shoot one down. Nor did they provide much practice in Army–Air Force co-operation. They did, however, have the beneficial effect from the airmen's point of view of keeping the RAF firmly in the public eye and in the minds of politicians.

At home Trenchard was anxious to establish and build up an institutional framework that would consolidate the Royal Air Force's independence forever. He set out to form a new generation of officers and airmen by training them from the outset in Air Force thought and method.[16] Cranwell – the first air academy in history – opened in February 1920. Alongside it was established the School of Technical Training to provide a pool of skilled ground crews.

The first Cranwell cadets were housed in a hutted camp formerly occupied by the RNAS planted on the windswept plain of south Lincolnshire. In time it would grow into a grand establishment that could hold its own with Sandhurst or Dartmouth. In October 1934, the Prince of Wales opened the new College Hall. The architect Sir James Wood had chosen the Royal Hospital in Chelsea, home to Army pensioners since 1692, for inspiration. The structure was a gigantic metaphor for Trenchard's approach. The brick and stone elevations and large dome looked as if they had been there for centuries. In fact, the classical exterior was all façade and the building was held up by thoroughly modern steel beams.

Cranwell graduates were, as the founder intended, a small and exclusive clique, 'the very heart and centre from which the RAF derives her vitality', as an inter-war Air Secretary Lord Londonderry described it.[17] This was the nucleus around which the service would grow. Trenchard made the ability to fly an aeroplane well a basic condition of entry to the RAF's future elite. As well as being a flying school, the college taught aviation technology and aeronautics alongside a basic academic curriculum. The course lasted two years and at the end the graduates passed out as 'General Duties Officers' ready to take their place wherever the service required them and in time to rise to the summit of the RAF.

There were two entries a year, and in the period between the wars the total number of annual entrants never exceeded seventy-one.[18] Entrance was by competitive examination, the same one sat by candidates for Dartmouth and Sandhurst, followed by interview. The college preferred candidates who came towards the top of the list (Sandhurst was prepared to consider anyone in the first hundred).[19] Before the college opened an Air Ministry Committee under Lord Hugh Cecil was set up to consider what sort of boy they were looking for. It concluded that RAF officers required a higher technical ability than was needed in the Army. As to character, they were seeking those with 'the quality of a gentleman'.[20] By this they did not mean 'a particular degree of wealth or a particular social position but a certain character'. This sounded egalitarian, a statement that the RAF was a modern service in tune with the democratic mood of the age. The problem was, as the Cecil report admitted, how to find candidates with the required education and qualities 'without excluding from the service men of small and humble means'.

Cranwell cost money – a hundred pounds a term, which was the same as the fees to a good public school. Parents also had to find another hundred pounds for uniform and books. This was far beyond the means of most British households. Six full scholarships worth £105 were awarded each year. But even if a grammar school boy's parents could scrape the funds together he was still at a disadvantage. Many public schools had separate, specialized curricula for boys trying for Sandhurst and Dartmouth and it was easy for them to extend the service to Cranwell aspirants.

In practice then, the selection process and entry requirements meant Cranwell was dominated by the sons of the affluent middle and upper classes and the products of the public school system. Of the 929 schoolboy entrants who passed through between 1920 and 1939, all but ninety-three went to fee-paying schools.[21] The public schools represented at Cranwell ranged from Eton, which sent twenty cadets, to small, long-vanished colleges for the sons of the shabby genteel, which sent one or two. The biggest block came from the Victorian foundations which sprang up in the nineteenth century to raise the soldiers, sailors and administrators needed to run Britain and its empire. Wellington, built as a national monument to the Iron Duke, provided the most with fifty. Other schools with strong military traditions were well represented. Cheltenham sent twenty-eight, Tonbridge and Imperial Service College twenty-two, and Marlborough and Haileybury twenty. Of military-minded schools, only Harrow, with five entrants, was under-represented.

The Cranwell course was rigorous and for much of the period the conditions were spartan. The cadets were marooned in the back of beyond. Sleaford, the nearest town, offered few temptations; one reason Trenchard had chosen the site was its distance from the fleshpots of London. After the rigours of boarding school, most of the entrants found it easy to cope. Peter Townsend, son of a colonial civil servant, arrived at Cranwell in 1933 from Haileybury where life at the outset at least was 'hard and sometimes cruel [and] there was no one to help us but ourselves ... Survive your first two years at Haileybury and you could survive anything.'[22] At Cranwell he 'submitted, gladly for the most part, to the intensive and variegated process which was to mould me as a pilot, an officer and a gentleman'.

Brian Kingcome, another son of the empire, started in 1936 after leaving Bedford School, which had developed strong links with Cranwell. 'The college schedule was very civilised,' he remembered.[23] 'Each day, including Saturday, began with an early morning parade, and there was a church parade on Sunday. Parades were followed by classes, including an hour or so a day of flying instruction. Wednesday and Saturday afternoons were set aside for sport. We dined formally in mess each night from Monday to Friday. From Monday to Thursday we wore mess kit consisting of leg-hugging mess overalls strapped under half-Wellingtons, with black tie, blue waistcoat, stiff shirt and butterfly collar.' Dining in mess at weekends was optional when the dress code was slightly more relaxed – a suit on Saturdays and tweed jacket and flannels on Sunday.

Smartness was something of a fetish for the authorities. Tim Vigors, from a family of Anglo-Irish landowners, set off in January 1939 for his first term at Cranwell with hair cropped considerably shorter than he had worn it at his old school, Eton. On the train he bumped into an acquaintance, also Cranwell-bound, who advised him it was still too long, so he stopped off at a barber shop for another trim. On his first morning he lined up on the parade ground in regulation suit and bowler hat for inspection by a large and fierce warrant officer, who, after prowling up and down the line, stopped menacingly in front of him. He then 'bellowed at the top of his voice, for the whole of Cranwell to hear, "What do you think you are sir? A bloody woman! Go and have yer hair cut!" Vigors hurried off for his third visit to the barber in two days.[24]

The reverence for spit and polish, for parades and bull, was at odds with the reputation of the wartime RFC. On the 'dromes of the Western Front dress codes and discipline were relaxed and drilling and parading were not highly regarded. The emphasis on appearance was another instance of the determination of Trenchard and his followers to show that the RAF could match the other services in every department, down to the precision of their marching and the shine on their boots. The attitude rubbed off on some of the cadets, who, when the next war came, would frown on what they saw as the casual attitude of the greatly expanded service.

Soaked in the public school ethos, Cranwell offered a huge variety of sports and activities. There was rugby, football and cricket, of course, but also athletics, squash, tennis, badminton, fencing, hockey, swimming, boxing, basketball, rowing and water polo. The surrounding countryside offered shooting, fishing and above all riding to hounds. Lincolnshire was prime fox-hunting country and the Quorn and the Belvoir would sometimes meet at the college. Riding was voluntary but encouraged. The belief that a good horseman made a good pilot, dating from the first days of aviation, was still strong, 'the thinking being that the sensitive hands which could coax the best from a horse would be those most suited to the delicate controls of a flying machine'.[25] The same applied to yachtsmen, and a declared enthusiasm for sailing always went down well at interviews. The course included history, English, foreign languages, though as the college authorities admitted, in 1935 the officer responsible for organizing the academic programme faced a 'difficult and sometimes ungrateful task'.[26]

The cadets were attracted principally by the thrill of flying. There was certainly plenty of theory on offer from the course lectures on engineering and aerodynamics. The practice, though, was something else. Townsend reckoned that in his two years at Cranwell he clocked up only 157 hours of flying time, the same as a Luftwaffe trainee amassed in nine months.[27] One reason for not letting cadets get airborne too often was that flying, particularly for novices, was still a very dangerous business. They started off on the Avro Tutor, a small open-cockpit biplane with a 240hp engine which, according to Kingcome, was 'completely vice-free' and 'stood up to the cruellest abuse with a happy smile'.[28] Then in their second year they moved on to 'service type' aircraft. The Bristol Bulldog, which arrived in November 1933, was fine when flying straight and level, but, as Peter Townsend discovered, in a spin 'she was a bitch'.[29]

Putting an aeroplane into a deliberate spin then getting out of it was a regular exercise. One day Townsend was aloft with his instructor Flying Officer A. F. McKenna, a 'burly, smiling man with a rolling gait like a sailor'. They climbed to above 8,000 feet, which given the aircraft's proclivities was set as the minimum height at which the manoeuvre should be attempted, then McKenna in the rear cockpit told his pupil through the Gosport speaking tube to 'spin her to the left off a steep turn'. Townsend pushed the stick forward and the Bulldog spiralled briskly downwards. After three turns McKenna told him to 'bring her out'. Townsend followed the prescribed counter-intuitive drill of shoving the stick forward again and applying opposite rudder but nothing happened. He wrote:

> We were sinking rapidly and I was conscious of an eerie hush, of the clatter of the engine's poppet valves and the reek of burning castor oil … of the propeller, in a slow tick-over, brushing the air, of the air rushing past my ears and through the bracing wires, making them whine, while the aircraft pitched and tossed in a sickening, circular movement, totally, hopelessly, out of control. 'I've got her!' yelled McKenna, now far from

cheerful. Banging open the throttle lever, pumping the stick, kicking the rudder, he tried to rock the Bulldog back into flying position. In vain. 'Get ready to jump,' shouted McKenna and I moved my hand to the quick release of my ... harness, praying to God that I should not have to pull it. With throttle, stick and rudder McKenna kept fighting the Bulldog. We were down to 2,000 feet when at last he brought her back to an even keel with just enough height left to dive and pick up flying speed. His voice, now very quiet, came through the speaking tube: 'That was a near one. Now climb her up again and we'll do another.'

Others were not so lucky. During Townsend's time at Cranwell a mid-air collision killed two instructors and two cadets. Their dismembered bodies had to be collected from trees and fields for burial. The perils of flying training did not end there. Of the young men who passed through Cranwell between the wars, sixty-two were killed in flying accidents, many more than died in RAF operations in the same period.[30]

The Apprentice Schools were set up with the same devotion to excellence. Obviously, the RAF depended on a high level of mechanical expertise to function. Trenchard decided that the best way to create a dedicated workforce of career technicians was 'to enlist the bulk of our skilled ranks as boys and train them ourselves'.[31] The Apprentice Training Schemes started in April 1920. The Army and Navy tended to draw their recruits from the ranks of the young, poor and unskilled. The RAF, declared a 1934 article, was 'different from any other Service. The aircraftmen are the elite of their class. All, by comparison with former days, are educated. A great many of them are well-educated ... in no other Service is there closer association between all ranks.'[32]

Applicants had to have the School Certificate, an exam normally sat at the age of sixteen with papers in five subjects including English, mathematics, a foreign language and a science. Most British children left school at the first legal opportunity aged fourteen to find jobs and contribute to the family budget.

Candidates were nominated by local education authorities and sat a competitive exam which included papers in maths, experimental science and English. The intake was much bigger than Cranwell – upwards of three hundred a year. The great disparity in numbers reflected a basic fact about the nature of air forces. To function, the RAF needed a longer logistical and support tail than the Army or even the Navy and ground personnel greatly outnumbered fliers. By 1945, in an Air Force numbering more than a million, only 17.7 per cent flew aircraft. The function of the other 82.3 per cent was to project them into battle.[33] Even so, the Apprentice Schools could not fill all technical manpower needs and qualified tradesmen had to be recruited directly from civilian life to make up the shortfall.[34]

Successful applicants for apprenticeships were expected to serve at least ten years with two on the reserve. Clothing, food and lodging was free and boys under eighteen got one shilling, then one and sixpence a day, the older ones three shillings. Those destined for the larger trades – the fitters who serviced the engines and the riggers who looked after the airframes – were trained at Halton, a former Rothschild mansion in Buckinghamshire which had been bought by the War Office at a knock-down price. Those specializing in wireless technology were housed in a school on the Cranwell complex.

Trenchard's enthusiasm for the apprentice scheme was as great as his devotion to Cranwell. Those who passed through it would be known as 'Trenchard's Brats'. In some ways the Apprentice School mirrored the college. The boys lived a regimented life in which competition in everything was encouraged and smartness was enforced. Hubert Rawlinson, who arrived at Halton as a sixteen-year-old from Bolton in late August 1939, found himself plunged into an austere world where almost every minute was accounted for and rules governed virtually all human activity. After a bone-shaking ride from Wendover station in three-ton lorries with solid rubber tyres the new boys were set down at Bulback Barracks.

'We came to a halt by a huge parade ground and climbed down from the vehicles,' he wrote.[35] 'A roll call was made and we were then taken to three gigantic barrack blocks, each having six large rooms with rows of beds either side. Each bed had a wooden locker alongside, a wooden box which could be padlocked underneath the bed, and a steel locker fastened to the wall above. Underneath the wall locker were three clothes pegs fastened to a frame. The beds were made in two halves, the front sliding into the rear; no springs but thin metal slats ... upon the beds stood three square biscuit mattresses, five brown blankets, two calico sheets and a head bolster. Twenty of us were placed in each room ...' After this sobering beginning they were taken across to the dining hall for their first taste of service cuisine: rissole and chips followed by suet pudding and custard.

After three weeks of square bashing and PT they were assessed to determine which trade they would be trained in for the next three years. The order in which they were interviewed was set by their place in the entry exam results. The strong message the boys received was that they had entered a meritocracy and that success would be determined by talent and hard work. Rawlinson was selected as a metal rigger, the trade responsible for maintaining and repairing airframes. The archaic sounding term was justified in an era when many of the aircraft the RAF flew were still partly constructed of wood, canvas and wire and the pear-drop smell of the acetone used to 'dope' the canvas stretched over biplane wings permeated workshops and hangars.

The boys marched everywhere, back and forth every morning and evening to the workshops, twice a week to half a day of academic lessons in the school building, always to the tune of a band made up of older apprentices equipped with bagpipes, trumpets, fifes and drums. On Sundays, church parade was compulsory.

At weekends, after Saturday morning fatigues, the boys were allowed off the camp to visit Aylesbury, Tring and Wendover. They were on public display, representatives of the Royal Air Force, and correctness in behaviour and dress was essential. For these outings they had to wear 'best blues': breeches, puttees, boots and tunics with 'dog-neck' collars, set off with a swagger stick tucked under the arm. Only those over eighteen were allowed to smoke and then not in barracks.

After three years and several progress tests apprentices sat their passing-out examinations; one week for academic subjects and a second for their trade. Failures were re-mustered as aircraft hands, the dogsbodies of the RAF. The rest were then sent off to start their careers on a starting pay of twenty-six shillings and sixpence a week – good money for an eighteen-year-old in the 1930s.

Halton created something that had never been seen in the British armed forces: a body of educated NCOs and skilled technicians, confident in their abilities and well aware of their vital function in the organization. It showed in their attitude. T. E. Lawrence, writing to Air Vice Marshal Oliver Swann, noted that RAF officers 'were treated by the men off parade as rather humorous things to have to pay respect to'.[36] They tended to regard officers as ordinary humans, rather than, as Army and Navy other ranks were expected to, as more exalted and evolved members of the species. This relationship between commissioned and non-commissioned wearers of Air Force Blue was to be a defining characteristic of the new service, one that harmonized with the spirit of the times and the mood of the skilled lower classes on whom it would have to rely.

The gap between the two was slowly closing. Unlike the other services the RAF offered real opportunities for social mobility. When drawing up his strategy for the training of pilots who would be mostly officers, and ground crew who would be NCOs and other ranks, Trenchard had left a window open. It was decided that the best three apprentices from each entry would be awarded cadetships at Cranwell at the end of their time at Halton. The scheme also included Wireless School apprentices. Together they would send 124 boys to the college in the years between the wars, more than 10 per cent of the total intake.[37]

For Halton boys who had spent two years living twenty to a hut, Cranwell, where each cadet got a room of his own and had the services of a batman, must have seemed like luxury. The Brats, though, were unlikely to have been overawed by their surroundings or their classmates. They were already well versed in service ways and armoured with the confidence that came from hard-earned success. Two Halton boys won the Sword of Honour in the inter-war period, Patrick Coote in 1930 and John Badger in 1933. Both were killed in the war before they could achieve their full potential but, on the whole, apprentices who made it to Cranwell were destined for the top. The first Halton entrant, Walter Dawson, ended up an air chief marshal. Among the rest who passed through in the years between the wars were an air marshal, eleven air vice marshals, twenty air commodores and thirty group captains. Of the relatively small number who failed to make it beyond the rank of Flight Lieutenant, all but a handful attended at the end of the period and lost their lives in the war while still junior officers.[38]

The elite cadres that emerged from the college and training schools were far too small to satisfy even the limited manpower demands of the RAF in its shrunken post-war existence. Aviation was a young man's game and the active life of a pilot was relatively short. If everyone who flew an aeroplane had a permanent commission, the service would soon fill up with underemployed and expensive officers whose flying days were over.

Several solutions emerged. One scheme was to create a new class of airman pilots, drawn from the ranks. The preference was for men with 'a high standard of education and efficiency', showing the qualities of 'pluck, reliability, alertness, steadiness, keenness and energy'. Rather than lose their technical skills they would not receive commissions but were classed as sergeant pilots. They were expected to serve for five years then go back to their old trades.[39] In 1939, about a quarter of the pilots in RAF squadrons were NCOs, giving a core of toughness and skill to every unit. They had won their wings the hard way and would be regarded with slightly nervous respect by the younger newcomers who flooded in later.

Most of the flying personnel needs were supplied by the invention of the Short Service Commission (SSC). In 1924 the Air Ministry advertised for 400 young officers for flying duties. They were to be British-born and of pure European descent who would serve up to six years and then move onto the Reserve of Air Force Officers (RAFO). According to the official RAF account in the interwar years these men 'formed the bulk of officers ... the Air Force was essentially a short service force and its flyers were birds of passage'.[40]

In 1925 Trenchard backed a scheme suggested by some RFC veterans who studied engineering at Cambridge after the war to start a university air squadron. The idea spread to Oxford, then London, then elsewhere. He also got government backing for an Auxiliary Air Force of weekend fliers, the RAF's equivalent of the Army's territorial units. The pilots were amateurs who flew in their own time in aeroplanes supplied and maintained by the RAF and the squadrons would have a marked local character. The Auxiliary Air Force provided a home for men from affluent homes to meet up in a patriotic cause and enjoy each other's company. The atmosphere was clubby and exclusive and in some units the whiff of snobbery was strong.

These structures were bold and imaginative departures from contemporary military norms. The RAF's top officers, and those rising behind them, hardly seemed like radicals. They almost all came from conventional military backgrounds and on paper differed little from their Army and Navy counterparts. Trenchard was succeeded as CAS in 1930 by John Salmond, the son of a major general who, after Wellington and Sandhurst, had fought in the Boer War before taking up flying and transferring to the RFC. On 1 April 1933 he handed over to his brother Geoffrey who lasted only twenty-seven days in the job before dying. His replacement was Edward Ellington, a former gunner.

The rising generation of RAF officers, the men who would lead the RAF into the war, also came from the same strata of society in which the generals and admirals were traditionally nurtured. They were, on the whole, courteous (though there were some notable exceptions) and valued 'form'. They liked to hunt and shoot, fish and sail and their politics were conservative. Like their Army and Navy contemporaries who made it to the top, they could be vain, overbearing and unscrupulous in the pursuit of advancement and glory.

They differed from their peers in sharing a heightened sense of the possibilities of the new. It was this spirit that had led them into the air in the first place. All had been attracted by the excitement of aviation. They were risk-takers, hazarding not just their lives at a time when flying was a very dangerous game, but also their careers, for opting for the RFC was a gamble for anyone planning a long-term military future. And they were by and large an intelligent bunch: sharp, inquiring and well-educated, at a time when brain power was not regarded as a cardinal military virtue. Arthur Tedder read history at Cambridge and had just started in the Colonial Service when the Great War broke out. Trafford Leigh-Mallory was a Cambridge contemporary, planning a career as a barrister. Sholto Douglas, a professor's son, studied Classics at Oxford. Cleverness was prized and the cleverest, it was generally agreed, was Charles Portal, Winchester and Christ Church, Oxford, and 'the accepted star of the Air Force' as Churchill called him when appointing him Chief of the Air Staff in October 1940 at the young age of forty-seven (his Army and Navy opposite numbers were fifty-eight and sixty-four respectively).[41]

Not least, they looked different from their Army counterparts. The most senior, the best-known soldiers – Alan Brooke, Bernard Montgomery, Harold Alexander – sported Edwardian-era moustaches proclaiming their membership of a military caste. Portal and Tedder were clean-shaven. Tedder, with his fresh face and jutting pipe, cut a very unmartial figure, more like a liberal university professor than a man of action. Portal's hooked nose and hooded eyes did not look British at all, and he reminded Peter Townsend of 'an Arab sheikh'.[42]

Despite his relative youth, Portal would show himself the most detached and composed of the wartime chiefs of staff. He was as cool and hard as marble. High intelligence did not equate with an excess of human sympathy. This thoroughly modern warrior was as ruthless as any traditional commander and did not flinch from accepting or inflicting casualties. A spirit of restless aggression would pervade the direction of the wartime RAF, stimulated by a cadre of senior officers, most of whom had passed through Trenchard's kindergarten. The approach guaranteed a high casualty rate among those who flew. The question was whether the expenditure was matched by the results.

3

Smoke and Mirrors

In March 1934, Stanley Baldwin, the dominant figure in the National Government, announced in Parliament that henceforth it was official policy that 'in air strength and air power this country shall no longer be in a position inferior to any country within striking distance of its shores'.[1] That meant Germany. The great transformation in the RAF's fortunes had begun. It was now launched on a race to keep up with the Luftwaffe as German air power evolved from nothing to threaten domination of the skies over Europe.

Baldwin's words marked an end to wishful thinking. The physical and economic catastrophe of the last war had made a new one unbearable to contemplate, for government and people alike. Since 1919 defence spending had been governed by the 'Ten Year Rule' founded on the supposition that the country would not be engaged in a major conflict in the decade to come. Hard-headed Tories like Baldwin had become enthusiasts for Utopian formulas for world peace, embodied in the international disarmament talks which opened, attended by every major world power, in Geneva in February 1932.

The Ten Year Rule was scrapped in 1932 after service chiefs warned that the armed forces would soon be incapable of defending the empire. The Geneva talks effectively collapsed when Hitler pulled Germany out of both the conference and the League of Nations in October 1933.

With the Baldwin speech disarmament was all but buried. So too were the niggardly defence budgets that had starved the services of funds during the 1920s. When the purse strings were loosened it was the Air Force that benefited most. Once the poor relation of the forces, the Air Force was suddenly the Treasury's favourite son. In 1930 it received by far the smallest share of the military budget: £16.75 million compared with £55.75 million for the Navy and £40.15 million for the Army.[2] By 1939 it was getting the largest: £105.70 million against the Navy's £97.96 million and the Army's £88.29 million.

The money was emphatic proof that the Air Force was now at the heart of Britain's defence strategy. In the thirty years since the advent of heavier-than-air flight, air power had assumed the same vital significance as sea power in ensuring the defence of the nation.

Between 1934 and 1939 the government authorized a series of schemes to expand the RAF at a rate that would maintain numerical parity with the Luftwaffe in the hope that this would deter aggression. When it became clear that this was unrealistic the emphasis switched from quantity to quality. The aim became to shape a force that would be able to withstand an initial onslaught from the air, and in time strike back. Existing programmes were scrapped and new ones devised in a desperate effort to keep up with an ever-changing reality. Such was the pace of events that only one of the eight expansion plans – Scheme F – was completed.

The favoured status of the Air Force was the result of several intertwined developments. There was a general conviction, shared by amateur and expert alike, that air power would determine the outcome of future conflicts. It followed that a powerful Air Force was the best means of deterring potential enemies. It also offered the hope that, if war did come, it could be fought without the need to send British troops to the Continent, an awful prospect for a society in which the memory of the trenches was still raw. All these notions were promoted with arriviste confidence by air power lobbyists inside and outside the RAF.

Trenchard and the Air Staff did not support the more extreme doctrines circulating in international military and political circles, which held that aeroplanes could win wars on their own. They answered the question: 'what is the RAF really for?' with a theory of air power that has been described as 'strategic interception'.[3] This held that, until now, in wars between nations, one side had tried to beat the other by defeating its land and sea forces in battle. The coming of air power changed all that. Aeroplanes could reach out to undermine the enemy's capacity and will to fight. They would do so by smashing up war factories, power supplies and transport systems. As the targets were in populated areas, the onslaught would have a devastating effect on civilian morale. Trenchard was fond of quoting a maxim that had no basis in observable fact that 'the moral effect [of bombing] is to the material in the ratio of ten to one'.[4]

Sooner rather than later the pressure would become unbearable. Civilians would clamour for protection and soldiers would be withdrawn from the front to try and defend them. Public support to continue fighting would evaporate and the enemy's leaders would be forced to sue for peace. The prospect of mass civilian deaths and spectacular violence raised obvious ethical questions. They were to some extent answered by the claim that air power would put an end to the long agony of defensive terrestrial warfare as seen in the trenches of the Western Front. New wars would be short and sharp but less bloody in the long run than the old ones.

All this had profound implications for the futures of the Army and Navy. Trenchard was careful not to claim that the new reality would make the old services redundant. The Navy would have an important role undermining the enemy's war economy by exercising its traditional function of imposing a maritime blockade and securing Britain's supply lines. The Army would still have to defeat the enemy forces in the field – though these would be much weakened as a result of air action. If the Air Force claims were accepted, though, it would mean that in a time of crisis it would have a privileged call on resources and a dominant voice in war councils. It was a recipe for bad blood.

The supposedly scientific prognostications of the air professionals chimed with the instincts of the civilian amateurs. Politicians needed little persuasion about the menace posed by aerial warfare. Stanley Baldwin's doom-laden speech in the House of Commons on 10 November 1932 revealed how deeply the message had penetrated. Baldwin had twice been Prime Minister and was now the leader of the Conservative Party which dominated the National Government led by Ramsay MacDonald. He had been foremost in pressing for an international convention to outlaw, or at least limit, the use of aircraft as weapons of war. Now, with the Geneva conference in its death throes, he had nothing to offer but despairing prophecies.

The speech is remembered for his warning that 'the bomber will always get through', a phrase that struck home immediately. It was only one of a number of utterances that must have curdled the blood of everyone reading the next morning's papers.[5] He had now abandoned the hope that agreements to curb air power could ever work. The stark conclusion was that 'the only defence is in offence, which means that you have got to kill more women and children more quickly than the enemy if you want to save yourselves'.

One of the many striking things about the speech is the sense of dread that it sets out to create even though there was at that stage no European war in prospect. Hitler and the Nazis were new on the scene and were still presumed to be subject to the normal laws of diplomacy and power politics.

As the decade progressed the spectre raised by Baldwin would haunt the political landscape. The future arrived more rapidly than he imagined and the distant nightmare began to feel like imminent reality. Mass media stoked anxieties. The Alexander Korda film *Things to Come*, based on H. G. Wells's novel, was released in 1936. It painted a picture of a London-like metropolis being bombed back into the Dark Ages by an unstoppable wave of enemy bombers. The movie was a critical and commercial success, the sixteenth most popular at the box office that year.

It was to the RAF that everyone looked for protection from these horrors and it was happy to offer reassurance. Adastral House had a plan for dealing with the mounting threat from Germany. Almost every senior officer who mattered was an adept of the cult of the bomber. For John Slessor the paramountcy of bombing was 'an article of faith'.[6] Slessor was thoughtful and articulate, a Trenchard protégé who had ghosted his writings and speeches and from 1937 was *de facto* head of the plans department that translated doctrine into practice. He and his colleagues envisaged a scenario in which deterrence broke down and the Luftwaffe launched a huge air assault on Britain to land a 'knock-out blow' and deliver a swift victory.

The RAF needed fighter aircraft that would 'provide a reasonable chance of parrying a knock-out blow'. But the real protection would be provided by a 'striking force' of bombers mounting a massive counter-offensive. Slessor admitted later that 'our belief in the bomber was intuitive' and that until war broke out 'we really did not know anything about air war on a major scale'.[7] The excuse was that there was a lack of hard evidence to work on. The RAF had little recent practical experience – bombing villages in Waziristan taught no lessons. There seems to have been no systematic military analysis of air operations in the wars in China, Abyssinia and Spain.[8]

'Jack' Slessor

The absence of data did nothing to undermine the Air Staff's confidence in the doctrine. It rested unsteadily on several untested propositions. One was that airspace was so vast that British bombers would be able to proceed directly to the task of destroying the enemy's war industry relatively unhindered. But what was true for British bombers would presumably be true of German ones. Surely, at some point, a battle would have to be fought to gain air supremacy in order to avoid an endless attritional cycle of attack and counter-attack?

Another was that bombing would have a devastating effect on enemy morale. Again if that was so – and some critics argued from the evidence of the Spanish Civil War, where the bombing of Barcelona by the Nationalists in March 1938 had galvanized Republican resistance, that if anything the opposite was the case – then British morale would be similarly affected. To the first the airmen had no answer. The second could only be dealt with by the assertion that innate racial superiority meant that, whereas Britons could 'take it', Germans couldn't.

Despite these obvious flaws the views of the Air Staff were generally accepted in Downing Street, Whitehall and Westminster. They harmonized with the mood of the times and the priorities of politicians. Everyone was desperate to avoid a war, especially one that meant sending troops to fight again on the Continent. Building up the Army and Navy could only provoke the Germans. Building up the Air Force might deter them. Expansion was seen as a defensive measure, popular with government and public alike. The decision to go ahead with it was essentially a *political* not a strategic choice. Once taken, the Air Force hogged both the public limelight and the Treasury's still limited largesse.

The Army and Navy boiled with exasperation at the favour bestowed on the new boys. It bubbles in the diaries of Henry Pownall, a sharp-eyed Army officer who watched the process from his seat on the secretariat of the Committee for Imperial Defence which brought together the professional service heads, cabinet ministers and senior officials. 'The public cry is all for the Air Force [first], Navy a distinct second, and the Army a very bad third,' he complained after a major report into how to repair the country's run-down defences that paved the way for rearmament was unveiled in February 1934.[9] 'The RAF have got too much,' he snapped a few months later as the details of how the budget would be carved emerged.[10] The Army's appeals for funds to build up a field force to send to France in time of war received a stony reception. 'Everyone will shout loud enough for the Army to practise as an Army when war comes but in peace it is the Cinderella of the Services,' wailed Pownall in 1938.[11]

It was not just about money. There was resentment at the tremendous strategic airs the Air Force had given itself. 'A constant bone of contention in our discussions was the role to be played by the Air Force,' wrote Major General Sir John Kennedy, the Army's Deputy Director of Plans on the eve of the war. 'Both the General Staff and the Naval Staff opposed the fanatical efforts of the Air Staff to press upon us their theory that the war would be decided by the action of air forces almost unaided by the other two services.'[12]

They were also aggrieved by the RAF's extreme reluctance to divert resources to meet their particular needs. The Army and Navy 'fought hard and unsuccessfully for the provision of adequate specialized air forces, properly trained and equipped for the support of naval and military operations'. The airmen's attitude was combative and defensive. Kennedy claimed that a senior officer at the Air Ministry had told him that the Air Staff regarded such co-operation as a 'prostitution of the Air Force'.

The fight for a share of air assets would go on far into the war. In the high-level meetings where defence priorities were decided the admirals and generals could only grind their teeth while the RAF got their way. 'The politicians were much attracted by the Air Force doctrine,' recalled Kennedy. 'The soldiers and sailors could never persuade the cabinet or the defence committee to settle the dispute in a way we thought right, either before or during the war.'[13]

For all their perceived cockiness, the newcomers showed respect towards political authority and voiced their arguments softly. Edward Ellington, CAS for the crucial 1933–7 period, was regarded by his own senior officers as being too deferential in the company of politicians. His successor, Cyril Newall, was more forceful but got on well with Lord Swinton and Sir Kingsley Wood, the air ministers who presided over the expansion period.

The Air Marshals' approach contrasted favourably with the high-handed ways of the soldiers and sailors. The Army brass barely bothered to disguise their contempt for Leslie Hore-Belisha, Secretary of State for War from 1937 to 1940. 'An obscure, shallow-brained, charlatan political Jewboy' was Pownall's verdict.[14] Their treatment of him is revealed in an episode recounted by Kennedy when he was taken on a tour of the front in northern France by Lord Gort, commander of the British Expeditionary Force, in November 1939.

> It was a cold, wet windy morning. We motored through the rain to the western side of the British salient ... on our way we crossed Vimy Ridge. Gort got us out of our cars ... he made Hore-Belisha climb a very muddy bank and kept him shivering in the howling gale while he explained the battle fought there in the 1914–18 war. In spite of his discomfort Hore-Belisha kept up a good appearance of polite interest. By this time his patent leather boots must have been giving him hell.[15]

There were further stops at other windswept battlefields. They paused at a château to meet the French commander and were taken to an attic window for yet another *tour d'horizon*. Gort deliberately 'opened a window and let in a piercing draught on Hore-Belisha; when we went out again into the rain he shouted jovially, "Isn't it a grand day!"'[16]

This schoolboyish bullying was all the more extraordinary given that Gort owed his appointment to Hore-Belisha's patronage. Nor would the War Minister be thanked for the great efforts he made in cabinet to obtain funds and equipment for the army Gort now commanded. Edmund Ironside, who Hore-Belisha appointed as Chief of the General Staff, was equally obnoxious towards his patron. Ironside, an outstanding linguist, gleefully recounted to Kennedy over lunch one day in his club how he had instructed his political master not to try and address French commanders in their own tongue: 'I told him that his French was Le Touquet French – good enough for talking to Mademoiselle X on the *plage* but no good for military conversations.'[17]

The hostile and surely anti-Semitic attitudes of Gort and Ironside were in sharp contrast to the warm relations between the RAF and Sir Philip Sassoon, Under Secretary of State for Air between 1931 and 1937. Sir Philip was rich, Jewish and unmistakeably gay.[18] He was famously generous and hospitable and every summer hosted the annual camp of the Auxiliaries of 601 (County of London) Squadron, of which he was honorary CO, at Port Lympne, his sumptuous country house on the Kent coast. In between flying, the young airmen lounged around the twin swimming pools in the grounds and there was a party every night. Sassoon's death aged only fifty in June 1939 caused the Air Force real sorrow. At a meeting of the Air Council ten days afterwards much of the discussion was taken up with whether or not to cancel the RAF garden party held each year at Trent Park, another Sassoon mansion in Hertfordshire, as 'the absence of Sir Philip would revive memories and cast a gloom over the proceedings'.[19]

Expansion piled enormous bulk on the organizational skeleton devised by Trenchard. In April 1934, on the eve of the great transformation, the RAF had 814 aeroplanes at home and abroad. When the war broke out it had 3,860.[20] The Air Force's new physique might look impressive but was there real muscle underneath? The speed of events in Europe had the Air Ministry perpetually scrambling to keep up. The Nazis' obfuscations about the extent of their own expansion programme meant there were no solid metrics on which to base the pursuit of parity. The result was that much of the budget was squandered on unsatisfactory aircraft which were ordered mainly to create the illusion of strength – an attempt at 'scaring Hitler by "window dressing"', as senior officers privately admitted to each other.[21]

The political imperative for numerical parity with the Luftwaffe had taken little account of the quality of the aircraft. In a time of fast-changing technology the policy was shockingly wasteful. The Air Ministry ordered new types in the knowledge that they would be out of date before they reached the squadrons. The Fairey Battle light bomber was known to be a dud from the outset, underpowered and short-ranged, yet more than 2,000 were bought before a halt was called, leaving their crews tethered to a lethally useless machine when the fighting began.

The RAF could argue that it was not their fault. Building a modern air force was hampered by the underdeveloped state of the domestic air industry and the government's laissez-faire economic policy. In Germany, the Nazis ensured that aircraft manufacturing was at the service of the state and the national airline Lufthansa was to a large extent the Luftwaffe in sheep's clothing. A senior Rolls-Royce executive, Willoughby Lappin, visited the Heinkel works on the Baltic coast in April 1936 and on his return reported his findings to British intelligence. Workers started their shifts at 6.15 a.m. and finished at 5.15 p.m., with two fifteen-minute meal breaks. 'The most significant thing,' he noted, 'is probably the fact that everyone young and old is disciplined and is thinking nationally, whether from fear or choice does not matter ... the Government are solely responsible for the policy and working of all the aircraft factories and the directors thereof have no control except to provide the Air Ministry with what they require.'[22]

In Britain the state gave limited support to a range of smallish 'family firm' constructors, who had to pay the costs of developing new designs themselves and competed for orders when the Air Ministry issued specifications for a new type. Until late in the day, British governments avoided intervening, refusing to allow the international situation to interfere with the principle of 'non-inter-ference with the flow of normal trade'.[23]

The result was a piecemeal approach to design producing a pleth-ora of types. Multiplicity meant a lack of mass-production capacity and, though this was remedied when the government paid big motor manufacturers like Austin and Rootes to build 'shadow facto-ries' for airframes and engines, there was a reluctance to mobilize industry on a war footing until it became absolutely necessary. Ultimately the failures and shortcomings were a consequence of Britain's political system – what happened when a free-market democracy tried to prepare for total war.

Each side used smoke and mirrors to try and persuade the other that there was no point in trying to outdo them in the air. They engaged in a pantomime of good fellowship which looks surreal at this distance in time. The fraternizing began at the instigation of the

RAF when in the spring of 1936 the Air Minister Lord Swinton invited General Erhard Milch to Britain.

General Milch was the man who could claim most of the credit for building up the Luftwaffe in the space of a few years from a puny collection of ill-assorted aircraft into the most feared air force in Europe. The Germans reciprocated and a party of senior RAF officers toured Luftwaffe facilities and aircraft factories the following January.

On 17 October 1937, Milch was back again, together with his chief of staff, Lieutenant General Hans-Jürgen Stumpff and Major General Ernst Udet, an internationally famous air ace and head of the Luftwaffe's technical division. Arriving at Croydon Airport Milch declared he had come to 'destroy mischievous rumours and create an atmosphere of comradeship and friendliness'.[24]

The programme that followed gave the impression that Britain was welcoming a trusted ally rather than a potential enemy. The day after arriving, Milch was taken to Buckingham Palace for an audience with King George VI. The itinerary covered almost every aspect of RAF operations, including visits to Cranwell and Halton and tours of the new shadow factories. Everything was done to make the Germans feel at home. At a cocktail party at the Carlton Hotel in the West End of London attended by everyone who was anyone in the British aviation world, the RAF band struck up the 'Badenweiler Marsch', which was always played at Hitler's public appearances, as well as 'Old Comrades' and 'Our Flag Flutters Before Us', a marching song of the Hitler Youth.[25]

On 19 October the Germans were given the run of the bomber station at Mildenhall in Suffolk. It was occupied by 99 and 149 Squadrons, both equipped with Handley Page Heyford biplane heavy bombers which lined up in facing ranks on the grass runway for the visitors to inspect. According to *The Times*, the German officers, who were dressed in Luftwaffe uniform, 'sat in the cockpits, waggled the controls, trained movable guns in their turrets, had bomb trapdoors opened for their inspections [and] asked questions which were readily answered ...'[26] They were then treated to a mass flypast by an assortment of the bombers then in service: Vickers Wellesleys, Fairey Battles, Handley Page Harrows and Bristol

Blenheims. Lunch was served in the officers' mess. The table was decked out in the red, black and white Nazi colours.

The eagerness to please created moments of black farce. On 23 October Air Vice Marshal Victor Goddard, the RAF's deputy director of intelligence, took the Germans to Hornchurch in Essex which was home to two fighter squadrons. They were equipped with Gladiator biplanes which were swift and elegant but antediluvian compared to the sleek Messerschmitts now arriving at Luftwaffe fighter units. They did have one piece of equipment that was bang up to date – the latest optical reflector sights. Pilots had been told by the station commander Group Captain 'Bunty' Frew that 'if the Germans ask about the sight, keep mum'. So when General Milch peered into the cockpit of one of the Gladiators and inquired how the sight worked, the pilot, Bob Stanford Tuck of 65 Squadron, replied smartly: 'I'm sorry, General, it's so new, I've not yet found out.'[27] Tuck was 'quite appalled' when 'suddenly AVM Goddard interrupted and proceeded to give him the full details'. According to one version of the story, when Goddard had finished Tuck suggested: 'Sir, perhaps General Milch might like to take one home with him as a souvenir?'

The visit was presented by government and press as a hopeful sign that Hitler could be curbed. *Flight* magazine, the aviation bible, claimed that 'when the British mission visited German air force centres in January last, the members all felt that they knew, understood and respected their German hosts. It is permissible to hope and indeed to believe that the German party under the leadership of General Milch returned to Germany with the same feeling.'[28]

Others doubted that the Germans were fooled for a minute. Winston Churchill, the arch opponent of the government's policy of non-provocation, did not believe that the performance would have the slightest deterrent effect. It was, he wrote to the powerful Cabinet Secretary Maurice Hankey, 'a desperate effort ... to present a sham'. The truth was that at the Mildenhall display Bomber Command had struggled to 'put little more than a hundred bombers in the air – the great majority of which (as the Germans will readily see) can barely reach the coast of Germany with a bomb load'.[29]

Churchill's assessment of the RAF's power to intimidate was accurate enough. The Heyfords the Germans inspected had double-decker wings and fixed undercarriages and belonged to a bygone age. The machines in the flypast looked modern but were underwhelming in almost every department. The Battle was powered by a Rolls-Royce Merlin engine but carried only two single machine guns to defend itself and had a range of a sparse thousand miles. The Harrow, classified as a 'heavy', could manage a 1,250-mile round trip but was pathetically slow. The Wellesley 'medium' was capable of long distances but was also sluggish. The Blenheim, another medium, was the fastest of the lot, but was able to penetrate only to the fringes of German territory. These were the aircraft with which the RAF's bomber squadrons were currently equipped.

Better performing aircraft were emerging from the pipeline – the Whitleys, Wellingtons and Hampdens with which the RAF would fight in the first years of the war. But long-range aeroplanes capable of carrying a substantial bomb load were still in development. It would be twenty months before the Stirling, the first of the four-engine 'heavies', made its maiden flight. The Halifax did not start flying operationally until March 1941, the Lancaster a year later. In the meantime, the RAF would have to make do with machines which were plainly inadequate for the very ambitious role that had been claimed for them.

The Milch visit was merely a reminder of what the Air Staff already knew: that the service was utterly unprepared for war. Bomber Command – which had been created in a major structural reorganization of the Air Force in 1936 – had nothing in its armoury that was likely to cause Hitler to hesitate. Fighter Command, set up at the same time, was in better shape. It would be some time, though, before it had the machines and the system of detection, command and control needed to deploy them efficiently enough to withstand a mass attack. As things stood in the autumn of 1937, the Air Force was incapable of either deterring, defending or retaliating.

Slessor and the planning staff had already laid out the situation in stark terms in a paper to Newall a few days after he took over as Chief of the Air Staff on 1 September 1937. It stated that they would be 'failing in their duty were they not to express the considered opinion that the Metropolitan [i.e. home-based] Air Force in general and the Bomber Command in particular, are at present almost totally unfitted for war; that unless the production of new and up-to-date aircraft can be expedited, they will not be fit for war for at least two and a half years; and that even at the end of that time, there is not the slightest chance of their reaching equality with Germany in first line strength if the present German programmes are fulfilled'.[30]

The warning produced yet another scheme – J – but unlike its predecessors this was more than a mere exercise in upping the numbers. Quantity gave way to quality. The plan was based on what the Air Staff considered to be its minimum strategic requirements rather than on hoped-for deterrent effect, or some ill-defined numerical 'parity'. The goal was to have 3,031 front-line aircraft at home and abroad available by April 1941, that is 800 more than in Scheme F – the last one to get government approval.

As always, most of the new aircraft would be bombers, which would outnumber fighters by a factor of two to one. Nothing that had happened since the start of expansion had shaken the Air Staff's belief in the proposition that a big bomber force was the foundation for all air strategy. When submitting the new scheme for government approval, the Air Minister Lord Swinton made it clear 'there is no question of altering the ratio of fighter and bomber squadrons in the sense of reducing bomber squadrons to make fighter squadrons'.[31]

Faith in the offensive had blinded the Air Force professionals to the meaning of technological, military and political developments, the significance of which was dawning on amateur, civilian minds. Britain's defensive situation was improving fast. The domestic aircraft industry was at last producing fast, modern, low-wing monoplane fighters that could at least hold their own against the Luftwaffe. At the time Scheme J was proposed, 600 Hurricanes were on order from Hawker and the first small batch would start to arrive on squadrons at the beginning of 1938.[32] An order had been made for 310 Spitfires from Supermarine, though delays and complications meant production was stalled. Radar infrastructure was expanding rapidly. The first five stations in the Chain Home radar network covering the approaches to London became operational in 1938.

The Air Staff could take the credit for having identified and backed two world-beating fighters and for moving fast to exploit Radio Direction Finding. What they failed to grasp fully was the damage these developments had done to the premises on which their theory of air power rested. The combination of radar, the sophisticated command and control system that it made possible and fast, well-armed fighters seemed to provide a plausible shield against an attempted 'knock-out blow'.

The implications were spelled out by one senior officer who saw clearly the new reality. Hugh Dowding was appointed commander-in-chief of Fighter Command when it was created in July 1936, having been passed over for CAS in favour of Newall despite being his senior. He was regarded by his peers as humourless, earnest and aloof and well suited to his nickname, 'Stuffy'. Before his appointment he had been in charge of research and development at the Air Ministry and it was largely on his initiative that the Hurricane and Spitfire were ordered. He had no scientific training but was open to new ideas and soon grasped the significance of RDF. It was he who devised the finely tuned system of collating raw radar reports and sightings from ground observers, filtering them through control centres and translating the refined information into orders to the fighter squadrons.

Dowding's views ran head-on into the prevailing orthodoxy. He rejected the notion that counter-attack by bomber was the best form of defence in favour of a simpler idea. 'The best defence of this country is Fear of the Fighter,' he wrote. 'If we are strong in fighters we should probably never be attacked in force. If we are moderately strong we shall probably be attacked and the attacks will gradually be brought to a standstill ... if we are weak in fighter strength, the attacks will not be brought to a standstill and the productive capacity of the country will be virtually destroyed.'[33] The overwhelming duty of the Air Force, he argued, was to secure the safety of the home base. Dowding's views were heresy to the bomber cult. It took courage to maintain his beliefs in contradiction to the overwhelming official wisdom but he did so tenaciously, in the words of the official historians choosing 'neither to understand other arguments, nor to compromise, nor even to accept with good grace the decisions that went against him'.[34]

On his own, Dowding was unable to deflect the Air Staff from the fixed notion that inspired all their strategic thinking. It needed an outsider to do that. The first major challenge to the primacy of the bomber arrived from an unexpected quarter. Sir Thomas Inskip came from a line of stolid West Country solicitors and parsons and was known, if at all, for his parliamentary objections to a new version of the Book of Common Prayer. The announcement early in 1936 that he was to be moved from his post as Attorney General to the newly created position of Minister for the Co-ordination of Defence was greeted with derision and incomprehension. The role had been created by the Prime Minister, Stanley Baldwin, in an attempt to harmonize the rearmament effort. It was a vitally important job and big names were bandied about to fill it, among them Winston Churchill's. Baldwin eventually decided Inskip was a safer bet, a decision that was approved by the Chancellor of the Exchequer Neville Chamberlain who noted in his diary that while he would 'excite no enthusiasm' he would 'involve us in no fresh perplexities'.[35] Inskip would confound the low expectations set for him.

When Scheme J arrived on his desk he coolly reassessed the *a priori* assumption contained within it that it was essential for Britain to possess a bomber strike force to match that of the Luftwaffe. To the quiet, God-fearing lawyer, it seemed that for the time being at least the emphasis should be on defence rather than offence and priority given to fighters. Admittedly, if war came that would mean that Britain would suffer more damage than it could inflict, but 'the result would not at once be critical'.[36] He believed that Germany did not have the resources to sustain a prolonged war and would therefore have to 'knock us out in a comparatively short time'. The best course was to concentrate on warding off the initial assaults while preserving military and economic strength for a long-drawn-out fight which Britain would win through its superior staying power. He was prepared to propose an increase of only £100 million on top of the existing allocation for the previous expansion scheme. If the money was to be used effectively, the Air Ministry should spend it on relatively cheap fighters rather than expensive bombers.

The airmen fought back vigorously against this impertinent rejection of the professional wisdom that suffused their thoughts and actions. Swinton reiterated the mantra that 'counter attack still remains the chief deterrent and defence' and warned that 'we must not exaggerate the possibilities' arising from radar and other developments. He also mounted a political defence, suggesting strongly that the change of direction would play badly with the public, making it seem as if the government was abandoning its public promises to keep up with the Germans in the air.

He had misread the changing mood. It was the here and now that mattered currently, not theories for the future. When the whole question of defence expenditure was considered in cabinet on 22 December 1937, it was Inskip's view that 'parity with Germany was more important in fighter aircraft resisting aggression, than in the offensive role of bombers' that prevailed.[37]

The Air Ministry was now compelled to work with him to draw up a new scheme – K – which reflected the reversal in policy. The bomber force was reduced from ninety squadrons to seventy-seven and allowance was made for only nine weeks of reserves, at the end of which, Newall observed bitterly, 'the war would have been lost'. The numbers of the front-line fighter force remained the same at thirty-eight squadrons and 532 aircraft but there would be more than half as many again in reserve.

The Inskip intervention was taken badly by the Air Staff who resented an amateur trespassing on their territory and, as they saw it, endangering Britain's security purely for the sake of financial expediency. The assault on the thinking that had sustained the Air Force for much of its short life was most resented by the chief evangelist. The fact that he was nine years retired did not stop Trenchard from publicly and privately denouncing the shift to fighters. 'The old man was obstinately unrelenting – not only at this time but even after the war broke out – about adherence in any circumstances to the bomber policy,' John Slessor remembered.[38] It would turn out that, in the short term at least, Inskip was right and the Air Staff were wrong. This realization did little to shake the faith of the bomber cult, an attitude that would have profound consequences when the time came for Britain to fight on land and sea.

4

Brylcreem Boys

The great lexicographer of slang Eric Partridge recorded that in 1937 soldiers and sailors began to refer to their Air Force colleagues as the 'Glamour Boys'.[1] The term was not necessarily admiring or affectionate. A little later on the RAF attracted another nickname. They were the 'Brylcreem Boys', a reference to their habit of slicking their hair with a best-selling pomade. The manufacturers, County Chemicals of Birmingham, were delighted with the association. In 1939, launching the 'handy active service tube' they chose to dress the model in Air Force forage cap and tunic and during the war a glossy-haired airman appeared regularly in their advertisements. It was only many years later that the man in the ads, one Tony Gibson, was revealed as a conscientious objector who did several stints in jail for his beliefs.[2]

Hair cream and the Air Force seemed to go together. The product had a practical use. Richard Passmore, a wireless operator/air gunner on Blenheims in the early part of the war, recalled how his 'side cap hung above my ear at angle which mocked gravity and was a mute testimony to the adhesiveness of Brylcreem'.[3] However, the main point of it was that it allowed you to look like an up-to-the-minute civilian male while wearing military uniform.

Like many of the trends adopted by the youth of Britain in the 1930s, the trend for sculpted men's hairdos was imported from America via Hollywood movies. The notion of glamour was a contemporary one. If any branch of the armed services had claim to it, it was the Air Force.

The RAF's modern image gave it a marked advantage over the other services in the competition for human resources. Expansion required men as well as machines, to fly them and to service them. In 1933 the RAF needed only one recruiting depot to fill its manpower needs, and took on less than a thousand extra men in addition to the regular Halton and Cranwell intakes. By the spring of 1938 there were eleven depots and thirty-one sub-depots which over the next eighteen months scooped up 43,795 recruits. With the introduction of conscription and the outbreak of war the numbers exploded. Between September 1939 and January 1942, 789,773 joined the ranks. By the time recruiting was halted in 1944, nearly 1.2 million men and women were wearing Air Force Blue.[4]

Trenchard had identified the need for manpower structures that were light and simple yet strong enough to support a rapid increase in numbers when needed. Initially, the system worked very well. In peacetime, in addition to the small core of regulars, the RAF could rely on a steady throughput of short service commission officers to supply most of its aircrew requirements. After doing their time they then passed into the Reserve of Air Force Officers (RAFO). The front-line squadrons were backed up by the amateurs of the Auxiliary Air Force and University Air Squadrons.

By early 1936, with the likelihood of war growing by the month, it was clear that these sources would soon dry up once the fighting began and a much bigger reservoir of aircrew would be needed. The

experience of the last war had taught that 'casualties in air warfare are high and the replacement of wastage is an even greater problem for a personnel than an equipment department'.[5] The need to make good the 'wastage' – the term must have struck some as inhumane even then – prompted the creation of a pool of airmen who had received at least a basic level of flying training. They would learn theory at evening classes in city schoolrooms and practise at civilian air schools at the weekend, in readiness to fill the gaps torn in the front line when hostilities commenced.

The RAF Volunteer Reserve (RAFVR) hastened the transformation of the Air Force from a tiny elite dominated by the comfortably off and privately educated into a mass organization drawn from every level of Britain's sharply stratified society.

From the outset it was presented as a democratic endeavour. 'The social and political setting of the time had considerable influence on [the] proposed scheme and there was strong popular feeling against any "caste" or "old school tie" attitude', the RAF internal narrative recorded.[6] It was 'visualized as a collection of young men drawn from the middle class in its widest sense and with no suggestion in its organization of a pre-determined social hierarchy'. In time it would be hailed as a great RAF innovation but the credit for the initial concept belongs as much to the imagination of an Air Ministry bureaucrat as it does to the progressive instincts of the Air Staff.

W. L. Scott was working for Air Commodore Arthur Tedder in the Air Ministry's training department when he was set the problem of finding pilot material from new sources. He had won a DSC with the Navy during the previous war and went on to be knighted for his labours in the Civil Service. Despite his conventional background, he seems to have had a sympathetic understanding of the contemporary mood. He realized that to get the numbers it needed the Air Force would have to reach beyond the social groups it felt comfortable with and embrace the young men growing up on the suburban streets of modern Britain.

Britain in the 1930s was changing shape. Towns that had not altered for centuries were being transformed by giant cinemas and blocks of flats. The surrounding fields filled up with new housing, arranged in 'crescents', 'avenues' and 'drives' lined with mock-Tudor houses. The people who lived in them often also owned them. They worked in modern jobs in offices and factories and when they wanted fun looked to America to entertain them. They watched American films at the Odeon and danced to American music at the local Palais, which they drove to in small cars mass-produced by Morris and Austin. They had little reason to regret the passing of old Britain. They were interested in the future, and determined to have a place in it, and not on terms of deference or inferiority.

It was to this generation that the RAF now turned, but with some caution.[7] Scott's initial memo warned that the sort of men they were looking for were unlikely to take kindly to strict military discipline. Instead, 'the desire to fly, patriotism, and retaining fees large enough to count in a young man's weekly budget will be the means of attracting our reservists'. In addition, he proposed, it was important that the whole experience was fun. 'Socially the reserves must be a great success,' he wrote. 'The young men must enjoy their evening meetings and their weekends.'[8]

This concept was a major departure from conventional military structures and a lot for the Air Staff to swallow. Its members had spent their lives inside an institutional cocoon where they kept company with each other and followed traditional leisure pursuits: riding, shooting, fishing and sailing by day, dining and playing bridge together by night. They knew those below them on the social scale only as servants or other ranks. They were unfamiliar with the new world emerging beyond the gates of the base and were not sure how much they liked it. To them the growth of mass consumerism was an affront in a time of crisis. 'If even a fraction of the energy, material and organizing capacity now being diverted to such non-essential channels as the production of unnecessary motor-cars, luxury cinemas and blocks of flats were directed ... to the production of modern aircraft, we could overcome our present dangerous difficulties ...' complained an Air Staff paper in November 1937.[9]

Nonetheless, after a few initial queries, the Director of Training Arthur Tedder backed the scheme. Tedder came from a conventional establishment background. He was the son of a senior civil servant, went to Whitgift School, then Magdalene College, Cambridge, where he studied history. He entered the Colonial Service but volunteered for the Army when war broke out. An accident resulted in a serious knee injury which seemed likely to keep him out of the fighting. Desperate to escape the tedium and ignominy of a cushy rear echelon job, Tedder harassed the authorities until he was finally accepted for pilot training with the RFC. In the summer of 1916, while the Somme offensive was raging, he was a flight commander with 25 Squadron which was carrying out constant bombing raids and reconnaissance missions and suffering heavy losses. On 17 July they were inspected by the RFC commander Hugh Trenchard, whose policy of all-out aggression was driving the high casualty rate. In a letter to his wife Rosalinde, Tedder reported that he 'had to go round with him while he looked at our machines. He asked a lot of questions, but made absolutely no comments, except "Yes."'[10] Trenchard had seen something he liked in the twenty-six-year-old officer. He would 'foster many careers during the next 30 years' among the men who served under him on the Western Front, wrote his biographer, Vincent Orange, but 'none more so than Tedder's'.[11]

With Tedder's support the basic format was adopted. Putting the scheme to the Treasury, the Air Council proposed 'to open the new force to the whole middle class in the widest sense of that term, namely the complete range of the output of the public and secondary schools'.[12] Until now, anyone seeking entry to the RAF would have been initially graded as to whether or not they were officer material primarily on the grounds of their social class. In the new circumstances this was considered 'inappropriate'. Instead entry was to be 'on a common footing, airman pilot or observer and promotions to commissioned rank will be made at a later stage in accordance with the abilities actually displayed'.

It amounted to a near-revolutionary challenge to the assumptions that governed the closed world of the British military. In the previous war, death and injury had cleared a path for lower-class men to receive the King's commission. In peacetime the old barriers were quickly re-erected. In principle at least, the RAFVR established a new universal criterion for officer selection: it meant that candidates would be chosen, not on the grounds of which school they went to and which accent they spoke with, but on the basis of whether they were any good or not.

Expansion also created a need for more short service officers. To attract the numbers needed, advertising campaigns were mounted and standards relaxed. The results were unwelcome to some career officers who preferred the old exclusivity.

The gentleman fliers of the Auxiliary Air Force had been similarly dismayed by the creation of the RAFVR which opened the club doors of weekend service aviation to Tom, Dick and Harry. All AAF Squadrons were exclusive to a certain extent, some ludicrously so. Outfits such as 601 (County of London) were founded in 1926 by Lord Edward Grosvenor who recruited the first members from the White's club bar. Originally the Auxiliaries were all bomber squadrons and in the words of the RAF narrative 'truth to tell, not very highly rated as such'.[13] However 'they had no inferiority complex: very much the opposite in fact. Indeed, some of the squadrons were inclined to look down on the regulars, as the cavalry in the army used to look down on the infantry.'

When planning for the RAFVR began it seemed that the AAF provided a natural nucleus around which to build an organization to train the newcomers. It resisted all pressure to do so, being 'reluctant to sacrifice its exclusive character to serve wider interests' as its 'standard of expenditure and social rigidity were incompatible with a democratic reserve'.[14] Frederick Bowhill, the Air Council member responsible for personnel, thought the Auxiliaries might be open to recruiting a reserve of accountant and stores officers 'who might have been thought socially acceptable'. Instead opposition 'was so violent that the suggestion was hastily dropped'.[15]

Some AAF members and some regular officers saw themselves as the paradigm of the upper-class warrior, bold and courageous but taciturn and emotionally restrained. These types populate the quasi-autobiographical stories of John Llewellyn Rhys, son of a Welsh rector who, after public school, in the early 1930s gave up a place at Oxford to join the RAF. He combined a love of flying with literary ambitions and began publishing short stories in 1936. In one, 'Too Young to Live', the narrator is in hospital recovering from an unspecified injury. In the neighbouring bed is a young pilot, dying slowly from the effects of a crash after only his second solo flight.

That afternoon he began to talk to me again, telling me about his people, who were in India, and how they hated him flying and how his mother had prophesied that his career as a pilot would end in disaster … it seemed they had a place in England, a house in Suffolk in the lovely wooded country on the Norfolk border. There was a lot of game there and he wanted me to promise to come up for some shooting … 'The riding's grand too; you could have Magpie, and there's bags of hunting and we'd go into market on Wednesday and drink with the farmers …'[16]

England Is My Village, which appeared in 1940, describes the atmosphere in the officers' mess as the Wing Commander briefs his men on the eve of a big operation.

Robert heard his instructions and memorized them with an ease born of practice, but the words seemed meaningless, rattling like hail on the roof of his mind.

'Any questions?'

But they were all old hands and no naïve youngsters among them wanted to make themselves heard.

'Well … good luck! I know you'll put up a good show,' his voice was suddenly shy, 'I wish they'd let me come with you.'

They went back to the ante-room, went on talking, reading … Robert sat down by a friend. They had been together for years but were in different squadrons.

'If anything,' Robert's voice was quiet as he flipped the pages of a magazine, 'if anything were to happen to … slip up … tomorrow, would you attend to the odd detail?'

'Of course, old boy.' The other puffed his pipe alight, swung the match until it was extinguished.

'Tomorrow?'

'Yes.'

'Tough show?'

'Tough enough.'[17]

Robert does not return from the op. Rhys, a flight lieutenant in a bomber squadron, was killed on active service in August 1940.

This portrayal of an Air Force staffed by strong, silent men from good county families was more an expression of how some airmen liked to see themselves rather than a reflection of reality. The illusion was unsustainable. The social distinctions that marked the pre-war RAF soon became blurred when the fighting began. As the first clashes thinned their ranks and veterans were posted away, the AAF squadrons could no longer maintain their exclusivity and had to accept whoever they were sent as replacements. By the end of the Battle of Britain only five pilots remained from 601's pre-war strength. The sixty-one men who washed through the squadron in the months of the Battle made up what was by then a typical Fighter Command motley of RAFVR sergeants, former SSC pilots and Czech and Polish airmen rejoining the fight.[18]

Even so, some important aspects of the pre-war style survived to become embedded in the Air Force ethos and form a salient part of its image. British airmen, whatever their origins, disliked show-offs and insouciance and understatement were the form. Air Ministry officials who during the war organized morale-boosting visits by veterans to aviation factories had to urge them to speak vividly about their experiences. An official account noted that 'the reluctance of the aircrew personnel to "shoot a line" as they called it, had to be overcome'.[19] Above all, pre-war professionals, auxiliary amateurs and the citizen fliers of the wartime service were united in an all-but-unquestioned willingness to face any odds and accept any risk.

Scott and Tedder identified the desire to fly as the most powerful inducement in attracting aircrew candidates. Nowadays it is quite hard to appreciate the fascination with aviation that gripped young men – and women – growing up in the 1920s and 1930s. The jeremiads preached by politicians about the huge potential for evil created by the invention of the aeroplane had little effect on the young. In their minds, it was the magic of flying that prevailed.

In the 1920s and 1930s aviators, male and female, enjoyed the celebrity and sometimes the rewards of film idols. The British couple Amy Johnson and Jim Mollison were world-famous. Amy was small, dark and gamine and looked as good in the severe fashions of the day as she did in leather helmet and sheepskin flying jacket – a paradigm of modern womanhood. She was born in Hull in 1903, where her father was a prosperous businessman, and studied economics at Sheffield University only to end up as a secretary in a solicitor's office in London.

She found her métier when she joined the London Aeroplane Club, gaining a ground engineer's as well as a pilot's licence. Backed by her father and wealthy air enthusiasts she made a record-breaking solo flight to Australia in 1930 inspiring a popular hit, 'Amy, Wonderful Amy'. In 1932 she met and immediately married Mollison, a Glasgow-born flier and former RAF short service commission officer and instructor at the Central Flying School. They competed as a team in air races and were fêted as 'the Flying Sweethearts'. The marriage crumbled after four years, due it was said to Mollison's drinking and inability to cope with his wife's fame. When the war came she joined the RAF as an Air Transport Auxiliary pilot delivering service aircraft around the country and died in mysterious circumstances after baling out from an Airspeed Oxford over the Thames Estuary in January 1941.

Aviation attracted the wealthy, fashionable and aristocratic but it was also promoted as a marvel of the new democratic age that should be open to everyone. No one pushed this message harder than Alan Cobham. Even in an industry not lacking energetic egotists, Cobham stood out. He flew with the RFC in the First World War, then joined de Havilland as a test pilot before making a series of flights to Australia and around Africa for which he was knighted by King George V. He played himself – the starring role – in a 1927 silent movie, *The War Commander*. In 1929 he set out on an air tour of Britain to encourage a trade-boosting programme of municipal airport building under the slogan 'Make the Skyways Britain's Highways'. His great achievement, though, was to get a generation of British boys and girls airborne. Cobham believed that 'air-mindedness' was best started early. The airliner he flew around the country was called 'Youth of Britain' and on the first tour of Britain the Castrol oil magnate Lord Wakefield paid anonymously for 10,000 children to get a first taste of 'going up' in it.

His proselytizing drive, as well as a keen business instinct, led him to dream up an event which he hoped would 'embed itself in the public consciousness as deeply as Pancake Tuesday or Fireworks Night', by persuading hundreds of towns around the country to host their own National Aviation Day.[20] Cobham provided the spectacle with a team of 'aces', dashingly kitted out in white flying overalls manning up to fourteen aircraft. They laid on exhilarating displays, putting the aircraft through rolls, inverted loops, and 'falling leaf' manoeuvres as well as clambering out of the cockpits for displays of wing-walking. In 1933 they visited 306 venues in the British Isles and 800,000 people paid to see them. Ticket prices were low – 1s. 3d. for an adult and 6d. for a child – but, to Cobham's exasperation, many others watched for free from what he called the 'Aberdeen Grandstand' – neighbouring high ground.[21]

Part of the huge appeal of Cobham's Flying Circus was the chance for punters to get airborne and about one in four of those who attended did so. This could be done sedately, in a multi-seat airliner or, more thrillingly, in the rear cockpit of one of the smaller planes. The tickets were priced for a wide range of pockets: a pound for a white-knuckle full aerobatic flight (about £60 today), 10s. for a seat in the opening Grand Formation Flight or 4s. for a four-minute flip.

For thousands of the young men who flew with the Royal Air Force in the Second World War, this was their initiation to the air and for many it was as powerful and unforgettable as a first sexual encounter. Charles Fenwick, son of a captain in the Royal Engineers, was in his early teens when Cobham's circus came to Rough Common just outside Canterbury. His aunt Edie took him to watch the show. Fenwick had never seen an aeroplane before. What followed was a *coup de foudre*. 'Soon after we arrived the first plane taxied out and flew off into the lovely clear morning sky,' he recalled, 'and sitting behind the pilot was a young boy.'[22]

Fenwick was 'green with envy'. Then Edie offered to treat him to a 'flip' and a few minutes later he was climbing into the rear cockpit of an elderly Avro 504. He had barely time to strap himself in 'before we were rumbling across the field. After a final frenzied race across the meadow the rumbling suddenly stopped and my heart followed suit as I left the earth for the first time.' Many years after the event he wrote: 'the thrill as we climbed up and away from the solid old Earth will never fade. I was dumbfounded ... we sailed over Hall Place and peered down into the rookery as the inmates squawked their way to safety ... there was our home, the Claverings, looking for all the world like a doll's house. On, on we flew. This was utterly stupendous ...' When he left school Fenwick went to the aircraft manufacturer Short Brothers as an apprentice, joined the Volunteer Reserve six months before the outbreak of war and flew Hurricanes in the Battle of Britain.

Boys who were not lucky enough to take a joy ride could fantasize about flying, their imaginations stimulated by a vast range of juvenile literature featuring aeroplanes and aviators. Lively mass circulation comics like *Modern Boy* were full of now-forgotten flying adventurers such as Jaggers of the RAF and Scotty of the Secret Squadron. The greatest of them all was James Bigglesworth. Biggles was the creation of W. E. Johns who had a brief but dramatic career as a bomber pilot with the RFC on the Western Front. Shot down in the last weeks of the war, he was captured but managed, briefly, to escape. He stayed on in the post-war RAF as a recruitment officer. On leaving he turned to editing, writing and illustrating on aviation themes. In 1928 he became editor of *Popular Flying* where Biggles appeared in the first of many short stories. In September 1932 a collection appeared called *The Camels Are Coming*. It was the start of a literary phenomenon. Johns was prolific and Biggles books flowed from his pen sometimes at the rate of four a year.

The characters were reasonably close to life and the detail and plots rang true. The young readers were not spared the realities of air fighting including the prospect of a ghastly death burning alive in a slow descent. But against this was set the camaraderie and gaiety of squadron life and the compelling figure of Biggles himself. Cool, technically competent and skilful yet understated, full of pluck and vitality, he was a hero made for his time.

Before long he would have a female counterpart. In 1941 Johns followed up with the first in the 'Worrals' series featuring the adventures of Joan Worralson of the Women's Auxiliary Air Force and her sidekick Betty 'Frecks' Lovell. Johns revealed that the character was based on two women fliers of his acquaintance, Amy Johnson and Pauline Gower. As well as setting up her own joy-riding and air taxi service in Kent, Gower wrote stories with air themes for the *Girl's Own Paper*. She would go on to head the Air Transport Auxiliary during the war.

The Air Ministry exploited the glamour of aviation to burnish the RAF's reputation and appeal. The annual Hendon Air Display and the Empire Air Days put on at RAF stations around the country from 1934 to 1939 emphasized the excitement of flying rather than the realities of aerial warfare with spectacular demonstrations of stunt and formation flying. Sometimes they included mock imperial policing operations in which aircraft dropped flour bombs on villages inhabited by rebellious 'Whatnot' tribesmen or on fake wooden battleships. The main purpose, though, was to impress and entertain.

In official publications the RAF naturally emphasized its defensive and deterrent role. The bomber force was designed for a *counter-offensive* not to launch aggressive war. This was a British version of air power framed by national characteristics of restraint and reserve, with rearmament presented, reasonably enough, as a reluctant necessity. A pre-war recruiting poster showed a young family picnicking on the cliffs on a sun-drenched summer day. Father and son are looking upwards at a flight of twin-engine bombers heading out to sea while mother and daughter prepare tea. The copy reads 'Air Defence is Home Defence'.[23]

When it came to attracting the specialist ground tradesmen needed to service the expanded squadrons, the RAF used a different approach, which ignored the prospect of war and made no appeal to duty and patriotism. The competition for skilled men was fierce, and there were plenty of well-paid jobs available in war industry factories. Advertising campaigns played up the prospect of travel and adventure and the attractions of outdoor life over a dreary works in the Midlands. A poster that appeared in 1939 showed a smart, confident figure in side cap and overalls, probing efficiently at an aero engine above the exhortation: 'Come on, skilled fitters! Your experience will earn you the finest job ever: and with it – security, good prospects and a grand outdoor life'.[24]

The inducements on offer were strong even in supposedly prosperous parts of the country. Len Hayden was brought up in Henham-on-the-Hill in Essex, one of nine children who lived in a three-bedroom house without running water. He left school at fourteen and did a series of menial jobs in local haulage and engineering companies which offered little pay and no security but where he picked up a knowledge of mechanics. One winter morning early in 1939 he arrived at work after pushing his bike for eight miles through thick snow only to be sent home for turning up late.[25]

It was then that he made up his mind to respond to a newspaper advert seeking air mechanics for the RAF. He decided against telling his parents. His father Billy had been a reasonably prosperous coal merchant and dairy farmer before the previous war. He volunteered for the Army in 1916 and served in the trenches where he was poisoned by mustard gas. His health, and his prosperity, never returned. 'Time after time he would return home [from hospital treatment] and try and rebuild his business, each time only to succumb to bouts of pneumonia and pleurisy caused by his wartime service,' Hayden remembered.[26] He scraped a living as a middleman buying cattle for local farmers and a 19s. 6d. weekly pension, squeezed out of the War Office after the intervention of the local MP. His son reflected that it was 'no wonder tears trickled down his cheeks' when he called home late in 1940 to say goodbye before following his squadron to North Africa. 'He must have been thinking how a grateful nation would treat us when we returned from "our" war.'

The recruiting campaigns were almost too successful. In March 1939 Charles Portal, then in charge of personnel at the Air Ministry, reported that there was a shortfall of fitters, wireless and electrical mechanics, instrument makers and armourers. However, he concluded, 'basically the problem is not volunteers but the facilities in which to train them'.[27] The inability of the training machine at every level to keep pace with the increase in men and machines would contribute much to the RAF's multiple failures in the opening stages of the war.

Like their Army and Navy counterparts the men who ran the RAF regarded their service as a manifestation of British identity and a repository of British virtues. They were wary of outside attempts to portray it, no matter how great the resulting publicity might be. In July 1937 the weekly meeting of the Air Council which brought together the Air Minister Lord Swinton, his deputy and the top staff officers discussed a Hollywood proposal to make a movie with an RAF theme. British settings were popular with American audiences and Metro-Goldwyn-Mayer had recently set up a subsidiary, MGM-British, to develop co-productions.

One of the first projects was *Shadow of the Wing*. It had a screenplay by a Briton, Sidney Gilliat, but box office considerations demanded an American lead and Clark Gable, already a star, had been picked by Louis B. Mayer himself to play the hero. The minutes of the meeting record have Swinton stating that he was 'strongly in favour of films as valuable recruiting agents' – both the Navy (*Brown on Resolution*) and the Army (*OHMS*) had already co-operated with film makers in an effort to boost their appeal. However, he was 'in some doubt in this case as to whether we could or should acquiesce in an arrangement whereby the leading role – that of a Royal Air Force pilot – was to be taken by an American actor, Mr Clark Gable, who might prove to be possessed of a strong American accent'.[28]

He was followed by the CAS, Air Marshal Edward Ellington, who in a characteristic contribution affirmed that 'he too was opposed to such an arrangement but added that he did not know whether the actor in question had such an accent'. The senior civil servant at the Air Ministry, Sir Donald Banks, raised the possibility that MGM might be prepared to accept a British actor, though he warned that if they insisted on this point 'he feared that the company would abandon the project'. This prompted a discussion as to possible British stars. Leslie Banks (no relation to Sir Donald), a well-known character actor of domestic stage and screen but with no pretensions to stardom, was 'generally felt to be the most suitable'. The item concluded with Swinton proposing that he sit down that evening with his deputy to study a Clark Gable film and decide whether or not his accent was acceptable.

In the event neither was able to make the screening. However, at the next meeting Ellington reported that he had since seen Gable play the English seaman Fletcher Christian in *Mutiny on the Bounty* and found him 'not offensive in any way'. The consensus remained that a Brit would be better. Seven months later there was still no progress. Sir Donald ventured that 'he rather suspected that our modest display of enthusiasm for Mr Clark Gable who had been Mr Mayer's selection might to some extent account for the film proposal to have hung fire ...' (Clark Gable went on to fly several combat missions as an air gunner with the USAAF.)

Shadow of the Wing never made it to the screen but there were plenty of other air movies to keep audiences happy. Doom-mongering efforts like *Things to Come* were outnumbered by productions that showed military aviation in a heroic light. *The Dawn Patrol* was so popular it was made twice in the space of eight years. The second version starring Errol Flynn, Basil Rathbone and David Niven was a box office hit when it came out in 1938. It was an unsparing account of the life of Royal Flying Corps pilots operating on the Western Front in the summer of 1915 when German Fokker *eindecker* fighters were winning the battle for air superiority over the trenches. The men of 59 Squadron are a hard-drinking, fatalistic bunch. Among them are two friends, Dick Courtney and Douglas Scott, played by Flynn and Niven. They are at odds with their leader Major Brand (Rathbone) who has lost sixteen of his pilots in the previous fortnight, most of them greenhorns fresh from flying training school. The mental strain on a commander forced to send novices to almost certain death is convincingly depicted. But it also reinforces the propaganda message broadcast by both sides during the real war, which presented air fighting as a clean, almost chivalrous business in contrast to the industrial carnage going on in the mud below. Courtney is killed after shooting down the German ace von Richter. The film ends with an image of inescapable duty as Scott orders the remnants of the squadron off on another dawn patrol.

To many British boys who watched it, the film acted not as a dire warning about the perils of life in the Air Force but as a call to their spirit of courage, sacrifice and adventure. 'It may sound a bit odd and unlikely but this film really did have a tremendous influence on me,' remembered Charles Patterson.[29] 'It struck me that though casualties were very heavy it was much the most wonderful and exciting way to go to war ... some strange, but as it turned out accurate, instinct told me that if I was going to fight, this was about the only way that there was any chance of my doing it successfully.' As a Mosquito pilot with Path Finder Force, Patterson would take part in some of the most audacious daylight raids of the war, dropping his bombs and then filming the results of the operation for later analysis.

The multitudes who read aviation magazines and followed the air races and the fortunes of celebrity aviators had little chance of becoming pilots themselves. Flying instruction at most clubs and commercial schools during the 1930s cost two pounds an hour when a young man starting out in a clerical or factory job would be pleased to get two pounds a week. A course aimed at securing a basic 'A' licence cost anything from £15 to £35.

The RAFVR offered a passport to the enchanted domain. It was open to any male between the ages of eighteen and twenty-five with a reasonable level of secondary education. Those accepted would receive flying training gratis as well as an annual grant of £25. The educational requirements were a barrier to a large proportion of British males, most of whom left school at fourteen. Many who came forward were from the ranks of the comfortably off. But there were also large numbers of bank clerks, shop assistants, and minor civil servants eager to seize what seemed a God-given chance to break out of their dull existences and realize their fantasies.

Despite the obvious attractions of the offer, the Air Staff felt the mood of the country was tricky. They detected a hostility to 'militarism' and were alarmed by the prevalence of pacifist sentiments. At an Air Council meeting in May 1936 Frederick Bowhill complained that 'at present the Press give great prominence to pacifist manifestoes, particularly those from seats of learning, but make no attempt to inculcate a feeling among the youth of the country that service in its defence was a fine thing'. He proposed that 'we ought ... to aim at bringing about a change of heart in the Press'.[30]

Sensibly, the tone remained sotto voce, with publicity stressing adventure rather than patriotism, a wise approach given the mood of the times. In 1936 the Peace Pledge Union, inspired by a canon of St Paul's Cathedral, was in its heyday, attracting hundreds of thousands of supporters across the political spectrum, united in their renunciation of war and determination to work to remove its causes.

As the threat from Germany mounted attitudes hardened and the service chiefs' concerns about the willingness of the younger generation to fight would prove unfounded. When looking back, few would cite the worsening international situation or a sense of duty as a compelling motive for volunteering. 'I was walking down the Strand and there was an RAF recruiting office with a poster in the window and it said "London businessmen join the RAF and fly aeroplanes at the weekend"', said Maurice Leng who was just starting out in the advertising business. 'There were no patriotic reasons. I was interested in motor-racing but it was an expensive sport and I couldn't possibly afford the cost of a decent car ... here was this wonderful opportunity for flying these super aeroplanes provided by the government and that is exactly what I did.'[31] Brian Considine was a trainee at Unilever when he joined in January 1939. 'I was nineteen and I don't think I was bothered by [the political situation],' he recalled.[32] 'It was a way to learn to fly which was an expensive thing to do. In fact instead of paying out of one's own pocket one was actually going to be paid to do it.'

Some who went on to have gallant wartime careers enjoyed emphasizing the unheroic motives that had impelled them into the Air Force in the first place. Christopher Foxley-Norris, who flew Hurricanes in the Battle of Britain, liked to claim that his main reason for joining the Oxford University Air Squadron was the £25 signing-on fee. It enabled him to buy a car which his older brother had told him was essential if he was to have any chance of attracting a girlfriend.[33] But he also admitted that though life in the squadron was 'enormous fun, at the same time most of us realized there was going to be a bust up ... but at least some of us were doing something about it while the rest were just sitting around'.[34]

Tony Smyth, a graduate chemist working at the paint manufacturer Manders, did not 'join the RAFVR ... from patriotism, but only to increase my pay and show me the world'.[35] Like Foxley-Norris he soon learned that the fun came at a price. When in the spring of 1937 he began his basic training as part of the first intake of volunteers at Prestwick elementary flying school near Glasgow, the CO in his welcoming address left them in no doubt as to what it was they were being trained for. 'He told us ... that the remilitarization of the Rhineland by Hitler had showed the world that German expansion as proposed in "Mein Kampf" was serious. An enlargement of the RAF was essential ... to produce a reserve of civilian aircrew.' As time passed the truth that they were learning to fight as well as fly became increasingly apparent.

If war was coming, the Air Force seemed a good place in which to spend it. Almost everyone eligible to fight had someone close to them who had been killed or maimed in the previous war and most of the casualties had been suffered in the trenches of the Western Front. Reluctance to repeat the previous generation's experience was a powerful factor in choosing to serve in the relatively clean-seeming element of the air.

Tony Iveson's police inspector father had been 'shot on the first day of the Somme and very badly wounded. He had a huge scar on his chest ... All my generation knew how horrible it had been.'[36] Growing up in York he heard his elders talk in ever more pessimistic terms about the crisis in Europe. 'I knew that there was going to be a war and I knew who it was going to be with so I came through my teens with that in my mind.' Early on he resolved that when it came 'I just wanted to fly'. Iveson joined the RAFVR and flew in the Battle of Britain before eventually joining 617 Squadron – the Dam Busters.

There was also the question of comfort. The RAF seemed to offer a cushier existence than you could expect in the Army or Navy. Sir Edwin Lutyens had been among those consulted on the design of the stations that sprang up in the 1930s. They were built to high specifications and airmen, or at least officers, were thought to live well. Charles Patterson was self-aware enough to know he could 'never have stood up to the rigours of fighting on land and in the dust and heat and dirt'. When later at a recruiting interview he was asked why he wanted to be a pilot he boldly replied, 'because the only way that I could consider it possible to fight was if one was provided with central heating and constant hot water'.[37] The group captain heading the panel 'gave me a broad smile and nodded approval and said: "Accepted. Recommended".'

The first RAFVR entrants began training in April 1937. Tedder saved money by using the network of flying clubs across the country to supply the infrastructure, with the instruction being supervised by the RAF's Central Flying School.[38] The reservists did basic training at an initial six- or eight-week course, at the end of which they were expected to go solo, then returned to their regular jobs and kept up training at weekends at local airfields operating under contract with the Air Ministry. The volunteers had only a semi-detached relationship with the RAF. They did not wear uniform and were part of a mass reserve rather than organized into squadrons like the Auxiliaries.

They started flying on Tiger Moths and similar easy-to-master aircraft and gradually progressed on to new types like the Avro Cadet before finally getting to grips with aircraft then in service in the squadrons. They also attended night classes in local towns to study basic aeronautics and navigation.

For those who had never flown the initial trip could come as an unpleasant surprise. Bob Doe, who, despite having left school at fourteen with no qualifications was accepted into the RAFVR, got his first taste of flying in June 1938. He worked as an office boy at the *News of the World* and took the train from Fleet Street to Hanworth aerodrome in south-west London for his first 'air experience'. The machine was a Blackburn B2 in which pilot and pupil sat side by side. His instructor, a former stunt pilot with the Cobham circus, was, like him, a big man and they had to 'sit a bit sideways' to make room for each other. 'I remember thinking how thin the sides of the airframe were and that it would not take much to fall out,' Doe remembered.[39] 'I was afraid of falling through it. When he banked the thing to turn round, looking down at the houses about four hundred feet below, it was a weird feeling. Quite frankly I was petrified ...'

When they first got their hands on the controls novices learned that simple aircraft were delicate creatures and the sensations of handling were both disturbing and thrilling. Edward Hearn, a trainee estate manager from Folkestone, 'was surprised to find the joystick extremely sensitive and even slight pressure had an effect on the machine'.[40] He felt he was 'handling something so delicate that even a slight touch would send us tumbling earthwards'. Repetition brought familiarity and then confidence until the day came to go solo, a great, never-to-be-forgotten moment in every pilot's life.

Hearn was a slow learner. The average time taken by pupils to go solo was ten hours. In his case, it was fourteen. Decades later he could still 'distinctly remember this first venture alone in the air ... strapped in, propeller swung, goggles down, I opened up the throttle and it was the feeling of power as speed was gathered over the grass that gave me assurance and stability'. Hearn made three careful left-hand circuits without mishap. This was the easy part. Getting down was the problem. The training school canteens buzzed with stories of pupils who had come in to land fourteen or fifteen times before summoning the courage to put the aircraft down. Some finally had the decision made for them when they ran out of fuel. A rough landing did not qualify for 'that would mean a bounce and if the bounce was a real banger that would have meant opening up the throttle and going around again'. Hearn eventually brought the machine in smoothly, cutting the engine a few feet from the ground and drifting in to roll smoothly over to his relieved instructor.

The plan was to recruit 800 potential pilots a year but it soon became clear that the quota would easily be filled. The supply of pilot recruits, particularly in the London area, much exceeded the demand.[41] The problem was that everyone wanted to be a pilot. Few were interested in the less glamorous roles of observer – the contemporary term for navigators – and wireless operator/air gunner. The difficulty was solved when surplus pilots were diverted to fill the gaps in aircrew needs. By the time the war began there were 6,646 pilots in the ranks of the RAFVR; 1,623 had been trained as observers and 1,948 as wireless operators/air gunners.

The function of the RAFVR as a reserve did not last long. When the war started it became an administrative designation and the principal route for aircrew entry into the RAF. All those who applied for aircrew duties on their own initiative or chose the RAF when registering as required by the National Service (Armed Forces) Act which came into force in September 1939 joined its ranks. They were identified by a brass and cloth 'VR' worn on tunic lapels and shoulders. In 1943 the badges were phased out as they were considered divisive, though the surviving Auxiliaries were allowed to keep their distinguishing 'A'.

The airmen who went into battle with the Luftwaffe were a compound of professionals and amateurs and represented a broad social and geographical swathe of Britain. The fusion was remarkably successful. In the judgement of the internal narrative, borne out by and large by the testimony of the participants, 'so complete was the amalgamation that the distinctions of peacetime between the component parts ceased to be discernible and the memory of them failed to have any significance'.[42]

Those leading the force in the rush to war had managed to create a solid identity for a hugely expanded organization that would only get bigger with time. It was shared not only by the fliers but by the much larger number of men and women who kept them in the air.

5

'There's Something
in the Air'

When the war broke out there was no repetition among the civilian population of Britain of the 'tragic enthusiasm' of August 1914. Most of those of fighting age fell in reluctantly, but quietly, with the demands that a succession of government decrees made of them, starting with the April 1939 Military Training Act. They accepted the need to serve, not because they wanted to, but because Hitler had given them no choice.

Full-scale conscription began on the first day of hostilities with the passing of the first National Service (Armed Services) Act and all males (with significant exemptions) between the ages of eighteen and forty-one were liable to call-up. The upper age limit for men was later increased to fifty-one, and from December 1941 single women and childless widows between the ages of twenty and thirty were required to report for war service.

On call-up, men had first to register, usually at their local Labour Exchange. There, they were asked to make a profoundly important choice. Which branch of the armed services would they prefer to spend their war in? Thus was created a popularity contest between the Army, Navy and Air Force. Initially, the RAF won it hands down. Of the 230,000 men aged twenty to twenty-two registering for the first conscription proclamation of 21 October 1939, nearly 30 per cent said they wanted to join the Air Force. The Navy was second with 17 per cent.[1] The rest appear to have taken the fatalistic decision to go where they were sent. In February 1941, when the conscription net was thrown wider to scoop up nineteen-year-olds, nearly 50 per cent opted for the RAF against 18 per cent for the Navy.[2]

Many decided not to wait to be summoned but reported to one of the Combined Recruiting Centres dotted around the country to volunteer for the Air Force. Indeed, enlistments by those outside the conscript age range outnumbered pressed men until well into 1940.

RAF recruiting staff could therefore afford to be choosy as they surveyed each new crop of sprogs. In the first five years of the war, of those who volunteered before waiting to be called up about one in six were rejected. Among those who waited to be summoned before plumping for the Air Force, the washout rate was brutal. Less than half of those interviewed by recruiting officers made the grade (463,773 out of 1,054,348), and many of them were shunted off to the Army.[3]

In the first sixteen months of the war, 203,239 volunteers were accepted into the RAF, together with another 140,462 who opted for the Air Force on being called up.[4] Having succeeded in joining their preferred service, each man had another crucial – and potentially fatal – choice to make. At an early stage they were asked whether they wanted to serve in the air or on the ground. Of the 343,701 who entered in that initial period only about one in ten – 35,267 – were assigned to aircrew duties.[5] Among younger men, a figure of 13 per cent of aircrew optants was normal until recruiting tailed off in 1944.[6]

Why was it that so many ended up earthbound? It was not a simple question of choice. One reason was that far more technical tradesmen were needed than aviators, and anyone with a relevant skill would be steered towards a ground job. Another major factor was the high standard of physical fitness and intelligence set for those who volunteered for flying duties. Flying required a higher degree of academic ability than most military activity and, initially, priority was given to those with more than the legal minimal level of secondary education.

In 1939 four out of five children left school at fourteen when free education more or less ceased.[7] The result was that the great majority of the first-wave applicants were automatically excluded from a flying career. Gloucestershire boy F. S. Reed had enjoyed a ten-shilling joy ride at the RAF aerodrome at South Cerney and was 'hooked on flying'. When the war came he decided to join the Air Force but 'having no academic qualifications I didn't have a hope of being accepted for pilot training'. Instead he 'applied to join the RAF ... as a flight mechanic. If I couldn't fly them then at least I could work on them.'[8] Fate determined that he would spend most of the war servicing aircraft in a flying training school in South Africa.

A job on the ground had many attractions. Working as a skilled tradesman brought greater standing and a higher level of satisfaction than an Army or Navy other rank could expect. This status was reflected in the uniform for, unlike his counterparts, from 1938 onwards the 'erk' wore a collar and tie (it was six years before the Army caught up). Initially at least, there seemed a diminished likelihood of being sent overseas. It was also evident that ground crew duties carried less risk than serving in the air, or indeed anywhere. The importance this factor played in the decision-making process is hard to calculate. Wing Commander Jimmy Lawson of the Air Ministry Personnel Department recorded in a memorandum that 'it is believed that a number of young men enlisted voluntarily or opted for the RAF on ground duties with the knowledge that such employment was the least dangerous in any of the services'.[9]

How Lawson, who elsewhere in the document shows himself to be sensible and humane, arrived at this conclusion was not made clear. It cannot have been his intention to portray aircraftmen as shirkers. Those who served on the ground anyway displayed their own brand of fortitude, enduring long hours in all weathers and often miserable conditions, and could show the same selfless disregard for their own lives when duty called, as an entry in the diary of 217 Squadron recording an air raid on their base at St Eval in Cornwall in May 1941 shows: 'A/Cs Collier and Ball put up a very good show by towing a bowser which was on fire away so that it could burn out in safety. One of them actually had to climb under the bowser to attach a cable to it. Their prompt and courageous action undoubtedly saved another aircraft from destruction.'[10]

There was a steady flow of non-flying personnel who, despite intimate knowledge of the dangers involved, gave up a safe billet to volunteer for operations. It was not as straightforward a process as the authorities made it appear and answering the call did not guarantee acceptance, even at times when the need appeared to be urgent. 'Chaps, driven by boredom, volunteer continually for Air Gunnery, but they aren't accepted,' wrote John Sommerfield to a colleague in November 1940. He was a former public schoolboy and a Communist who had fought with the International Brigades in Spain before joining up as a lowly aircraftman. 'In the meantime the RAF goes on inserting 11 inch double column ads [in newspapers and magazines] for men to be aircrew.'[11]

An initial insistence on education to School Certificate standard was eventually dropped on the grounds that it 'debarred many excellent candidates otherwise suitable'.[12] Nonetheless it is clear that many who wanted to fly could not because they had not been given the basic education that would prepare them for the rigorous classroom training that all aircrew roles required. Geoffrey Goodman was bright and ambitious but his war-invalid father had been unable to find steady work and he had left school early. He was seventeen when the war broke out, working as cub reporter for a small magazine in Camden Town, north London. His Jewish background and left-wing sympathies reinforced his determination to fight Fascism and he felt flying with the RAF – 'the most dramatic of the three services' – was the best way to do it.[13] When, having added a year to his age, he turned up at a recruiting office near Euston station, he found it was not as easy as that. 'I wanted to go straight into aircrew [but] I didn't have the required qualifications,' he said. 'I remember arguing with the recruiting sergeant who told me that once [I] was in I may be able to remuster.' At the reception centre at Cardington he was advised to volunteer to train as a radio mechanic as an entrée to aircrew. While training at Cranwell a flight lieutenant told him he would be better off specializing in photography – a tip he followed and which led to him eventually being commissioned as a reconnaissance pilot. Goodman found that 'about a third of the groundcrew lads wanted to get into aircrew – it didn't matter what it was. If it wasn't as a pilot then as a navigator or air gunner.' The stumbling block was education – or lack of it. They 'wished to do so but they were very much aware that they didn't have the ... qualifications to tackle the aircrew course'.

In the first five years of the war RAF numbers increased sixfold – from 175,692 in September 1939 to 1,185,833 in July 1944.[14] This stupendous growth spurt required production-line methods to manage and for many recruits the plunge into uniform was disorienting, often shocking. They were passing from the realm of the comfortable and familiar into a baffling new domain that seemed unconnected with the civilian universe, filled with noise, discomfort and a total absence of privacy. The first stop for all, whether you were destined to be a pilot, a fitter or a 'general duties' dogsbody was one of the reception centres like Uxbridge, on the fringes of west London, Cardington in Bedfordshire, or Padgate, Lancashire, where you swapped your civvies for a uniform and acquired a service number that would henceforth be welded to your name.

Padgate was a vast, ugly, hutted camp near Warrington. No one who passed through its gates retained any happy memory of the place. 'My main impression of Padgate is parading and waiting in biting cold and rain,' John Thornley, a twenty-nine-year-old printer's rep from Preston, confided to his diary after arriving there in December 1940. 'The camp is built on marshy ground and is open to all winds.'[15] Even young men who knew poverty and overcrowding felt the rawness of the place, and cringed at the constant state of exposure in which it seemed they would henceforth live. The nakedness was literal. Almost the first order an RAF entrant received was to drop his trousers and pants, prior to an inaugural 'FFI' (Freedom from Infection) inspection, one of many he would undergo in his career.

Nineteen-year-old Norman Lee, who had left his reserved occupation job with an engineering firm in Yorkshire to emulate his twin brother and volunteer for aircrew, arrived in Padgate in November 1941. For his first FFI he and his comrades 'were lined up in a hangar facing the open side with only a sheet of hessian as a very inadequate screen between us and a crowd of WAAFs who giggled and made faces through the window of a low building opposite.'[16] Then 'to complete our embarrassment, as soon as the inspection was over we were marched straight into that self-same building' where the female spectators served them plates of gristly brawn.

For gently brought-up young men like Sam Pritchard, the son of a Wesleyan minister who turned up in the spring of 1940 on his way to becoming a navigator, Padgate brought his first, rather dismaying, close encounter with the British proletariat. The thirty men in his barrack room 'contained what I suppose must have been a cross-section of British society; a few types with a reasonable education and the remainder representing rapidly dwindling standards [down to] a group of foul-mouthed objectionable young men'.[17] His first night was 'miserable and unforgettable ... lying in a bed with no sheets on; a mattress and a pillow filled with straw, looking round for a sympathetic or understanding face ...'

By this rough immersion, the RAF might have unintentionally been doing the new boys a favour. It was sink or swim. To survive you had to cling to the nearest kindred spirit, and the experience encouraged instant and often lasting friendships. There was sanctuary, too, in the humour that pervaded everything: strong, black and subversive. Surreal wit combated their surreal new circumstances. As everyone constantly told everyone else, 'if you can't take a joke, you shouldn't have joined'.[18]

Sam Pritchard and his comrades soon discovered ways to circumvent the obscenity-flecked rule of the NCOs who drilled them. A 'favourite stratagem was to start giggling or laughing on parade whilst punctiliously and smartly obeying all the orders barked at us. This would first puzzle the corporal and then drive him to foul-mouthed hysteria ... eventually when [he] finally accepted the impracticality of charging all of us under King's Regulations, he would lower his voice to offer an extra pass out of camp if we "stopped our bleeding laughing"'.

Any manoeuvre that thwarted authority or made it look ridiculous delighted men who were, on the whole, determined to hang on to their status as civilians in uniform. During his initial training my father Ernest Bishop was in a group being taught self-defence by an overbearing PT corporal instructor. One by one, the teacher invited each man to 'take a swing', then promptly knocked him flat when he obeyed. Come my father's turn, he warned the corporal that he had 'done a bit with the gloves', as indeed he had, fighting as 'Tiger' Bishop at the Blackfriars Ring in London. 'They all say that,' sneered the corporal, and waved him on. Moments later the instructor was stretched out cold on the gym floor and Ernie did not have to buy beer for a fortnight.

Places like Padgate were purgatorial rather than hellish and the suffering was temporary. Sam Pritchard's grim memories were soon blotted out in the summer of 1940 by the far more agreeable experience of No. 2 Initial Training Wing, based in Cambridge University. Pay parades took place on the lawn in front of King's College Chapel and in the evenings he and his fellow trainee pilots and navigators toured the pubs. They were a superior crowd to the reception centre clientele. The majority were grammar school boys like himself but there was also 'a goodly proportion from Public schools, and some even who had completed a university course', as well as Australians, New Zealanders and Canadians.[19] For the first time he 'met other young men in their early twenties who were smarter, richer, better-looking, better-educated and more amusing than I considered myself to be'.

In the RAF you tended not to linger anywhere for too long. Specialized requirements and constant technological advances meant long training periods at a variety of establishments. It took Ted Mace, who signed on as an aircraft electrician, a full year of more or less continuous instruction at various technical schools before he was posted to a squadron.[20]

Aircrew training was more intensive. Pilots went through nine phases of instruction before they flew their first operation, and when bottlenecks in the system developed early in the war, periods of 'deferred service' at home extended the process. Even training for a relatively uncomplicated trade such as air gunner was a protracted business. Norman Lee volunteered in November 1940 but did not take to the air with 428 Squadron until the summer of 1943.[21]

The RAF's geographical reach spread enormously in the course of the war. The empire had greatly helped its training needs by agreeing to flying training schools in the wide skies of Canada, Australia, Rhodesia, South Africa and elsewhere. With expansion, new bases sprang up all over each new theatre of war and old ones were enlarged. Air Force life could thus be amazingly peripatetic, with constant moves from training course to training course, from station to station, from one end of the country to the other and to every corner of the globe. An airman might find himself shivering in Iceland, hard up against the Arctic Circle, cursing the flies in the

Nile Delta, or sweating in the sultry humidity of Takoradi on the Gold Coast (Ghana) of Africa.

However grim your current circumstances there was always the prospect of change. 'It is like living in a cross between a public school and a concentration camp,' wrote John Sommerfield, in 1941 shortly after arriving at Silloth, a remote station in Cumberland.[22] 'The town of Silloth is hideous, small and unpleasant ... Cumberland has the highest average rainfall in Great Britain ...' Before long, though, he was writing notes on the nature of the Western Desert ('the sinister shadows of stones at sunrise, the purplish sunset shadows that dramatize sand ripples into mountain ranges ...') that he would put to good use when he resumed his career as a novelist and short story writer after the war.[23]

Wherever they went, the airmen carried with them a comforting, familiar ethos to sustain them. In its short life, the RAF had developed its own way of speech, some of it the legacy of its Army and Navy origins, much of it new. Like Sommerfield, Roderic Papineau was a writer who served in the ranks. Both acted as field reporters for Tom Harrisson, one of the founders of Mass Observation, set up in 1937 to study the lives of ordinary people and which continued its work into wartime. In May 1941, while with 256 Squadron in Blackpool, he compiled an 'Airman's Vocabulary' recording the usages he heard around him in workshop, NAAFI and pub.[24]

He and his comrades were 'erks', a term that applied to all other-ranks ground staff. Its origin would never be satisfactorily explained. Even Eric Partridge failed to nail it and his theory, proposed in his 1945 *Dictionary of RAF Slang*, that it was a corrupted abbreviation of 'air mechanic', does not convince.[25] 'Type' was a handy alternative to 'bloke'. Aeroplanes were 'kites' or 'crates'. The rumours that hung like ground mist over base and depot (as they did over all military establishments) could be graded for reliability as 'the real griff' – almost certainly true, through 'pukka gen' – quite possible – to 'duff' or 'shithouse gen' – almost certainly bollocks. An expression that seems unique to the RAF was 'by the centre!', usually with an expletive inserted, to indicate 'amazed and outraged disgust or surprise'. It does not appear to have lingered long in use after the war though Sam Pritchard chose it as the title for his memoir.

Some phrases had a different meaning for ground staff than for fliers. According to Papineau, when an erk was 'shooting a line' he was 'pretending to unwarranted expert knowledge'. When a pilot did the same he was making some exaggerated boast, usually in the bar, and his utterance might well be recorded in the squadron 'line book'. The 9 Squadron book reports Pilot Officer Arnold announcing loftily one night: 'No I'm not keeping a diary, but I have the press cuttings of my flights ...'[26] A 'shaky do' on the ground was a 'disappointing or unsatisfactory affair'. In the air, it meant a terrifying near-death experience, and was all the more eloquent for its understatement. A word that meant the same to all was 'wizard' – 'superb', according to Papineau.

Life in the RAF may not have been uniformly 'wizard' and, as in all branches of the military, the hours passed against a background buzz of moaning about the incompetence, laziness and stupidity of those in authority. Yet the overwhelming impression received from contemporaneous diaries and letters and subsequent fictional and factual accounts of the experience was that it was, by and large, positive, even enjoyable at times, and that if there had to be a war and you had to be in it, then the Royal Air Force was the place to be. The strong desire not to end up in the Army – still regarded as a stronghold of bovine generals and ovine troops – is often cited as a motivation, particularly in ground staff memoirs (which are far less numerous than those left behind by aircrew). But there was more to it than that. The RAF seemed modern, dashing and somehow less formal. Like the Navy, it also seemed to actually be doing something. According to Papineau, the Air Force nickname for sailors was affectionate and respectful – 'tars' or 'matelots'. The Army, however, were 'brown jobs' or 'the unemployed'. They themselves were 'The Firm', a term that indicates pride, purpose and efficiency.

Naturally this ebullience could easily be interpreted as cockiness and there were some, not just among their military peers, who found the high spirits of the junior service irritating. The avalanche of admiring mail published in the innovatory illustrated news magazine *Picture Post* in the early months of the war, following a letter from an anonymous erk complaining that 'no decent girl seems to look at an airman', contained a few caveats. 'I must say it's not true that no decent and respectable girls look at airmen,' wrote A. M. 'I know several … (I for one). But some of them are so sure of themselves, always talking about drink etc.'[27] 'I have come to the conclusion that foul manners are the badge of the Air Force,' wrote a middle-aged woman who had served with the Army in France in the First World War, after being subjected to rough or ribald comments from RAF men in Kensington Gardens on two occasions. The bulk of the postbag, though, was gushingly, blushingly positive. 'I was very surprised at your letter as I always imagined airmen were considered heroes' ran one from a nurse. 'I envied my girlfriend whose heart is in the sky and who is now knitting air-force blue socks! The fact that it's such a stiff test to get in always made me imagine that airmen are he-men!'

The RAF's appeal was felt everywhere. The Duke of Edinburgh confided in a BBC interview on his seventieth birthday that he would have volunteered for aircrew had he not been pressured by his uncle Louis Mountbatten to join the Navy.[28] It seemed to attract a disproportionate number of celebrities of one sort or another. Aircrew trainee Edwin Thomas was delighted to tell his mother that among his intake group at the Torquay reception centre was the England fast bowler Ken Farnes who was so tall that 'he has got to wait three months for a uniform because the RAF can't find one to fit him'.[29] Farnes was later killed when his aeroplane crashed on a night-flying exercise. His England colleague Bill Edrich flew with Bomber Command, won a DFC and finished the war as a squadron leader. Another famous cricketer Cyril Washbrook served as a PT instructor.

Tommy Farr, the Tonypandy ex-miner who had fought Joe Louis for the world heavyweight boxing title in 1937, volunteered the day after war broke out and 'wanted to be an air gunner or an observer'. During a routine medical while training he was found to have a defective ear and eye, probably the result of punishment in the ring, and given a medical discharge. 'I feel very miserable about it all,' he said when the news became known. 'I was very happy with food and conditions in the RAF and believe me I am terribly sorry to leave the force.'[30]

Actors flocked to the RAF. Richard Attenborough, Richard Burton, Denholm Elliott, Rex Harrison, Christopher Lee and Donald Pleasence all served. So too did the playwright Terence Rattigan whose *Flare Path* was an early example of the dramatic potency of the RAF experience. Not all showbiz aspirants were welcomed. David Niven made his way back from Hollywood in the autumn of 1939 but withdrew after a bruising first interview. On arrival at the Air Ministry he was besieged by secretaries asking for his autograph which got him off to a bad start with the group captain assessing him.

'The man restored order and eyed me with distaste,' Niven remembered.[31] 'He knew who I was. Unless he was blind he couldn't have avoided it. Nevertheless, he went through the motions of asking my name and occupation and what I wanted to do. When I told him, he pursed his lips, sucked in some breath with a whistling sound and shook his head.' He then asked him whether he knew Wilfred Lawson, a highly regarded theatre and screen player who had flown as a pilot in the last months of the First World War and had rejoined the colours. Niven replied that he was a 'wonderful actor'.

'He's also a heavy drinker,' said the officer. 'We took him on and we've had trouble with him ever since.' By now Niven was losing patience and told him: 'I've come seven thousand miles at my own expense and I'd like to join the RAF.'

'So I've read,' the officer replied. 'But we don't encourage actors to join *this* service.' At this point Niven stormed out, and ended up in the Rifle Brigade after a chance encounter in the Café de Paris nightclub.

Musicians were also drawn to the Air Force. The number of well-known artistes volunteering or choosing to join encouraged the authorities in 1940 to form the Royal Air Force Dance Orchestra. Among the fifteen members were several who had played in the Bert Ambrose Orchestra, the hottest act of the day, including saxophonist Harry Lewis who was married to the band's vocalist Vera Lynn. They became famous as The Squadronaires, by far the best known of the service dance bands, and played all over the country as well as being broadcast on the BBC and cutting records for Decca. They generated a lush, big-band sound, and their great hit 'There's Something in the Air' would ever after evoke for hundreds of thousands of servicemen and women memories of crowded dance halls, the smell of cigarette smoke, perfume and spilled beer and the last bus back to camp.

For aircrew, the progress to a squadron was long and jerky and there were many obstacles to overcome before you finally got into action. Edwin Thomas was eighteen and a half when the war started. Like many, probably most, who aspired to fight in the air, he wanted to be a pilot. He was summoned to the combined recruiting centre in Romford on 29 October 1940 for assessment for the RAFVR, by now the conduit for most wartime entrants. Edwin had the benefit of a secondary education at Canterbury Road Senior School and Snaresbrook College in east London but his reports marked him down as a plodder. 'He is a thoroughly honest and trustworthy lad,' declared his head teacher, T. H. Moore. 'He has shown earnestness and painstaking ability in his work. In manner he is quiet, serious

Band of brothers: The Squadronaires

and gentlemanly.'[32] Thomas's weekly letters home to the family's semi-detached mock-Tudor home in the east London suburb of Wanstead describing his life as a trainee provide a detailed account of the rigours and disappointments of the process, as well as a touching picture of youth, innocence and devotion to duty. The meeting with the selection board went well. A week later he was installed at the Babbacombe Hotel near Torquay, about to begin a fortnight's drilling with forty-nine other novices before being sent off to a two-month course at an Initial Training Wing (ITW).

They were starting on the lowest rung of the ladder, classified as Aircraftmen 2nd Class (Group V) and receiving 2s. a day pay. From the beginning cash, or the lack of it, looms large in the correspondence. 'It is amazing how much money is spent on necessities such as copying ink [and] the VR badges that aren't on the uniform and cost 6d a pair,' he wrote on 13 November. There were no complaints about the food, though. 'For breakfast yesterday we had porridge, fried egg and mashed potatoes, bread and butter, marmalade and a terrific mug or two of tea,' he reported. 'For dinner: a lovely stew with potatoes and veg: for sweet an apple conglomeration with custard and an apple: for tea plenty of liver and gravy, bread and butter, jam and a piece of fruit cake. Cake every day. Supper: jug of milk, liver between two crusts and a slice of cake.' In the evenings there were trips into town 'to play billiards snooker or table tennis and end up with a glass of Devonshire cider ... we are too broke to get tipsy.'

By mid-December he was at the Initial Training Wing at Pembroke College, Cambridge, one of five colleges requisitioned by the Air Ministry to house about a thousand trainees. The course was a mixture of gruelling classroom work – navigation, signalling by Morse and Aldis lamp, armaments, maths, law and administration, hygiene, ship and aircraft recognition – combined with large doses of PE. Like all the armed forces the RAF was keen on the noble art, believing it cultivated a fighting spirit. 'I put my name down for boxing,' he wrote, 'and in the afternoon had three rounds with a fellow of my own weight.' His partner 'had never boxed before and his defence was an opponent's dream'. Later the PE instructor, a corporal called Harry Mizler and a celebrated East End Jewish bantamweight who represented Britain in the 1932 Olympic Games in Los Angeles, 'bounced medicine balls on our stomachs to strengthen the muscles'. They then set off on a two-mile run.

Soon after arriving at the ITW Thomas suffered the first of a series of disappointments. He learned he had done badly in a grading test and his chances of selection for pilot training had taken a blow. To keep his hopes alive he would have to get more than 60 per cent in the maths exam. If he failed, he would have to re-muster as a wireless operator/air gunner. With characteristic stoicism he knuckled down to 'special maths swotting with friends after hours'. Like many others, he was learning that 'if you want to be a pilot you have to work like blazes'. However, he told his mother 'if I get through the maths test it will all have been worthwhile'. It was not to be. It is not difficult to imagine his mother Helen's feelings as her first-born child reported sheepishly in his next letter that he had some 'rather disappointing news to tell you. I did not pass the maths exam.' After learning of his failure he had been interviewed by a squadron leader who told him that he would be given another chance. It meant, however, that he would be assigned to another group of trainees: 'I shall not leave Cambridge but I shall lose all my friends.'

A few months later he was writing with the 'sad, sad news' that he had failed his navigation exam. His bid to become a pilot was over and he was offered the choice of being discharged from the service, re-mustering as a wireless operator/gunner or being assigned to a ground job. 'Naturally I said I would go for WOP/AG,' he told his mother. 'If I had my discharge I should only go into the army eventually – and I do want to make a go of it in the RAF.' His pride had been hurt. A postscript to the letter adds, 'Tell anyone who enquires that as I failed the exam for pilot I have *volunteered* for WOP/AG.'

Edwin spent the next two years moving around the country from training unit to training unit, until at last, at the end of March 1943, he was posted to 78 Squadron at Linton-on-Ouse near York. On 2/3 April he took part in his first operation, bombing the port area of Saint-Nazaire. The relief of getting the first trip out of the way and 'without a scratch on K for Kathleen [their Halifax]' shone out of the letter home. 'The whole business was little different from an ordinary cross-country flight,' he wrote. 'But what gave us all a thrill was when we crossed the French coast and knew we were well on our way to the target.' He finished by reporting that 'we have been searching for ideas for a name for our kite. Most names fellows have chosen for their kites are indelicate. Much to my crew's pleasure I hit upon the idea of "Happy Go Lucky." The decision was unanimous.'

Bad weather meant that it was two weeks until the next mission. On the night of 16/17 April 78 Squadron took part in a mass attack on the centre of Mannheim, a regular 'area' target at this stage of the war. Eighteen aircraft were lost. Edwin's was among them and all the crew were killed. A friend of the family called Lydia wrote a few days later offering what little comfort there was. 'It is some consolation to know that Edwin was so very keen on the Air Force and would not have wished to be in any other Service,' she wrote. She added: 'The RAF are marvellous boys and to hear them going over night after night does make one's heart ache.'

In the search for words to soften the blow of death it was often asserted that the victim had died doing what they wanted. In the case of Edwin Thomas it was obviously the truth. His letters brim with the pride of belonging and pleasure in the company of his fellow airmen. He never seems to have been lonely and made friends early who meant a lot to him. 'I am with a grand set of fellows,' he wrote after arriving in Blackpool for his wireless operators' course. On his twentieth birthday 'the whole gang went on a binge ... Stanley, Stinker, Baxter (wee Scotsman, ex-Corporal Gordon Highlanders) and Ronnie Wells plus two girls who are holidaymaking and staying in Stanley's billet. I'm afraid we all had too much to drink.'

The arrivals and departures of wartime life meant friendships were often fleeting but no less real for that. Edwin's friend Malcolm, who he met at the Cambridge ITW course and was selected for pilot training, wrote to him in Blackpool months after they separated to say, 'I miss you like anything, you know, Edwin and I don't think I'll find a friend to replace you in this service.' He signed off: 'My best wishes to any of the lads up there and the same a hundred times over to yourself. See you soon, maybe over Berlin ...'

Compulsory female war service only come into effect in early 1942. Until then, the Women's Auxiliary Air Force, which was created on 28 June 1939, was staffed by volunteers. Between September 1939 and December 1940 14,546 came forward. The following year the numbers jumped to 81,928. The increase was largely due to the introduction of a second National Service Act in the autumn that made it clear that conscription for women between the ages of twenty and thirty was in the offing. The result, the Air Ministry narrative noted, was that 'recruiting offices were inundated with applications ... just before Christmas in one week alone over 7,000 completed application forms were received'.[33] After January 1941 the WAAF started receiving conscripts. Over the course of the war, however, volunteers greatly outnumbered National Service recruits by 180,704 to 33,932.

For women, the attraction of the Air Force over the other services was not as obvious as it was for men. They would have little contact with aeroplanes, as at first they were not considered for ground trades and there was no question of them serving as aircrew. Later some women were used as delivery pilots in the Air Transport Auxiliary but these had already obtained pilot's licences for themselves and it was only in 1944 that seventeen WAAFs were trained to do the job.[34] At the outset, the Air Ministry's attitude was more restrictive than had been the case at the end of the First World War. The majority of the 32,000 women in the Women's Royal Air Force – the forerunner of the WAAF – had done traditional jobs as typists, clerks, cooks and cleaners, but some broke into fields that were hitherto the preserve of men, working as fitters and riggers.

According to the RAF's own account the early WAAF recruits were 'in the main patriotic women who were inspired by the spirit of adventure'. Sylvia Drake-Brockman was a well-educated forty-year-old spinster from a military family who was employed as private secretary to the Chairman of the Stock Exchange in the City of London when the war broke out. It was an 'easy job' and she had 'elegant hours and no Saturday work'.[35] As time passed she became 'increasingly restless and anxious to do something for the war effort'.

In July 1940, at the start of the Battle of Britain, she applied to join the WAAF. Turning up at the RAF's recruiting headquarters at

Victory House in Kingsway for processing she found the place awash with like-minded women. 'What a crowd was waiting with me,' she wrote. 'All sorts of conditions of girls and of all ages ...' The applicants had a first encounter with 'one RAF and four WAAF doctors to examine different parts of our anatomy'. There was a long wait for the result. Then a 'card was handed to me marked FIT. Great relief and joy.'

A fortnight later she arrived at the West Drayton reception centre to the west of London where recruits were rolling in at a rate of a hundred a day. She was feeling 'rather tired and depressed' when she got there, not helped by 'some small boys outside the camp calling out "turn back before it's too late!"'. The message was repeated that evening when the newcomers were 'addressed by a Flight Officer who spoke to us all sufficiently sternly about not joining if we were, any of us, under age, so that one little girl bobbed up and admitted the offence and was told she would be returned to her home the next day'. They were also given a final chance to 'get out of the WAAF if we felt we could not take the final plunge ... twenty-four hours to think things over before taking an irrevocable step'. This practice would continue until 1941, whereafter there was no allowance made for second thoughts.

Sylvia spent a restless first night in a quarter 'like a council house' with some other new girls. Almost every WAAF memoir makes unaffectionate mention of the 'biscuits' they had to sleep on, three thin three-foot by three-foot squares of straw-filled canvas, laid down on a slatted bedframe. Bedclothes consisted of two unbleached sheets and three hairy blankets in Air Force Blue and there was a straw-filled bolster for a pillow. The next day was taken up with 'waiting for enrolment, getting enrolled (which meant turning into a cipher – 896991), waiting to get kitted, getting kitted – waiting for meals, waiting again and more waiting'.

Sylvia's secretarial background meant she was selected as a 'clerk, general duties'. Her job meant that, somewhat to her regret, she was excused much of the initial drilling. Instead she attended endless lectures. 'It seemed to my somewhat confused mind that the system was; when in doubt, send the recruits to a lecture. In this way I heard lectures on service etiquette, office routine and

correspondence, hygiene, sanitation, VD and again hygiene, sanitation and service etiquette.'

During the two-week initial training she was called to an interview by the female camp commandant and asked if she would like
to put her name forward for a commission as an administrative
officer. Sylvia was pleased to accept the offer as 'much as I was
enjoying my experience in the ranks I knew that I would get very
tired of the continual herding and lack of privacy before long'. There
was also 'a better reason – I felt confident that I would do more
good as an officer as I was and always [had] been very interested in
my fellow human beings'.

Sylvia's name was duly submitted to the Air Ministry. Later she
discovered that she had been recommended on the grounds of her
'education, personality and service connections'.

When a woman officer arrived to interview her 'the first question
I was asked was "why I had joined the WAAF when I had so many
relations in the Army". I replied that I liked the sound of the WAAF
and thought it was a good idea to break fresh ground.' She did not
confide 'another childish reason which influenced me: that I liked
the uniform better than the khaki of the ATS!' The drily humorous
and humane memoir that Sylvia Drake-Brockman left behind on
her death in 1978 makes it clear that the next five and a half years
were among the happiest in her life. She thrived on the responsibility denied to her in civilian life, was appreciated by her superiors
and held several important command and staff jobs. She also found
fulfilment in the camaraderie of service life and in acting as a stern
but affectionate big sister to her charges.

Sylvia was born at the tail end of the Victorian era and came from
the sort of family whose members made a profession of serving
Britain and its empire and had been well rewarded for doing so. To
a younger generation of women growing up in an era of expanding
independence and diminishing deference, the pull of duty was felt
in different ways. Marjorie Chaffe was twenty when the war began
and working in a book-binding plant in Southwark. She did not
volunteer for war service but when the Blitz began in September
1940 worked as a part-time firewatcher and member of Air Raid
Precautions. For reasons she could not understand she was classed

as doing essential war work in a 'reserved' occupation. Even if she had not been, as she explained in a frank memoir published twenty-five years after the end of the war, there were 'lots of reasons' why girls like her held back from rushing to the recruiting centres.[36] There was the 'obvious one of discipline and regimentation. Once you'd signed on the dotted line your life was no longer your own. What's more you didn't even know how long you would have to serve because you signed up for the duration of hostilities.'

But there were 'lots of other reasons too, petty no doubt, but all having to be taken into consideration when deciding just how far our patriotism was going to stretch'. One was uniform. 'Stockings must have lost more recruits than any other item,' she wrote. 'All the girls loathed them. They were thick, a ghastly blue and made the slimmest legs look twice their size.'

WAAF headgear did not suit the styles of the time. 'Rita Hayworth and Dorothy Lamour wore their hair cascading onto their shoulders … so civilian girls did the same. But on joining up, you either had to have your hair cut, or else dress it in such a way that it not only fitted under your cap but was also well above your collar.'

A bigger deterrent was family pressure. Almost all war work, be it in the services or employment in a war industry factory, meant moving away from home. Parents who had lost one or more sons to the forces were reluctant to see a daughter fly the nest to some possibly distant and inaccessible location.[37]

Boyfriends also presented a major difficulty. They 'didn't like their girls in uniform. They didn't mind who else's girl joined up, as long as theirs didn't.' Marjorie considered this 'natural enough … if he was a civilian himself he didn't want to walk down the road with the equivalent of an able seaman or an aircraftman who saluted every officer that came into sight, and if he was in the Forces he didn't want his girl running the gauntlet of hundreds of his own kind in camps all over the country.'

When conscription for young, single women came into force in January 1942, the matter was settled. When Marjorie was eventually summoned to do her National Service like everyone she could choose between the nursing services, the Land Army, the fire services, work in a war factory, or joining the WRNS, ATS or WAAF. She 'didn't like blood' and 'by no stretch of the imagination could conjure up a picture of myself mucking out a pigsty at five o clock in the morning'. She had had enough of factories and felt she had done her time firewatching, 'so it had to be the Forces'. Having lived through the Blitz she wanted to do something that had a direct impact on the enemy. 'The most aggressive jobs that a girl could do in the Army or Air Force was either to work on a gun site or the balloon barrage. So as I was feeling pretty aggressive after two years of air raids ... and preferring blue to khaki, I decided to go on the barrage.' Teaming up with two other Londoners, Rene and Dolly, who would be her best friends for the rest of her service, they set off to the reception centre at Gloucester, 'pleased at having gained the service we wanted' but with 'a few qualms about what sort of reception we would get as conscripts among a lot of volunteers'.

Marjorie's natural bolshiness made her impatient of the 'rules and regulations ... flung at us from all sides' which Sylvia accepted as the inescapable idiocies of service life. They were different ages, came from different backgrounds and had different expectations of what life could and should bring. Yet their years in the WAAF seem to have been among the most fulfilling in their lives, never to be regretted or forgotten.

6

'Tragic, Criminally Tragic'

Looking back at the first moments of the war, John Slessor recalled his feelings when, a few minutes after Neville Chamberlain's Sunday morning broadcast, the sirens sounded in London. He was in the Central War Room in Whitehall, talking to Lord Chatfield, until recently commander of the Navy, now Minister for Co-ordination of Defence. 'It was an odd sensation,' he wrote in a memoir published in 1956, 'standing there wondering whether this was in fact the "knock-out blow" to which we had given so much thought in the past two years.'[1]

The air raid warning was a false alarm, triggered by the appearance of a small aeroplane carrying Captain François de Brantes, the French assistant military attaché, on his way back from a visit to Paris. It would be another year before London suffered a serious attack from the air.

As the RAF's Director of Plans, Slessor had been deeply involved in the preparations for war. Now it was here he felt strangely relieved. As the all-clear sounded he was cheered by the thought that 'at least that awful period of indecision and uncertainty was over'.

Mobilization of the Air Force was already in full swing. Telegrams flew around the country ordering squadron members to break off their leave and return to bases now humming with activity. Guy Gibson rushed back from an idyllic Indian summer vacation swimming and sailing with his girlfriend on the Pembrokeshire coast to his bomber station at Scampton in Lincolnshire to see 'tractors driving around the perimeter roads in the sweltering heat, some with long bomb trailers bouncing behind; others pulling our Hampdens along cinder tracks far into the country to dispersal points fairly safe from enemy bombs. All around the airfield, sand-banked gun emplacements were being put up by aerodrome defence squads, but there were not many guns.'[2]

There was a lull on Sunday morning, when airmen stopped what they were doing to gather round wireless sets and hear Neville Chamberlain's announcement. Many accounts mention the 'heavy', 'solemn', 'defeated' tones of his voice. But there was also a message of defiance and hope, which inspired some of those listening, in which the character of the war was clearly defined. 'It is the evil things that we shall be fighting against,' the Prime Minister declared. 'Brute force, bad faith, injustice, oppression and persecution – and against them I am certain that the right will prevail.'

His words were followed by a burst of action. The staff of the RAF Flying Training School at Gravesend had orders to evacuate as soon as the declaration came, so as to clear the airspace around London for the coming battle. The chief instructor, Peter Johnson, had been given a sealed envelope giving the destination to which the school's aircraft were to be flown.

They took off immediately after the broadcast. Their wartime base would be Castle Bromwich near Birmingham and to reach it they were given a route that diverted them around London. 'It was a beautiful day with unlimited visibility,' he remembered. 'I had reached about two thousand feet when looking around to see all my flock were following, I was riveted, and I admit appalled, by an extraordinary sight. Over the southern suburbs, and behind them all over London, the balloon barrage was rising. The ungainly shapes, dozens of them, all fully inflated, were slowly rising to their operational height. Seen from the air it was a truly awesome spectacle, not least because of its implications. The only conclusion I could draw was that, even before the British declaration of war, a German air fleet had taken off almost certainly to raid London.'[3] When they landed to refuel at Hullavington in Wiltshire he was told that the balloons had been launched in response to the false alarm.

The fighter pilots of 43 Squadron, based at Tangmere at the foot of the West Sussex Downs, were waiting beside their Hurricanes at five minutes' readiness to take off when they were told the Prime

Minister was about to speak. They listened to Chamberlain's words in their stylish mess while bar stewards served them beer in pewter mugs. The mood, recalled Peter Townsend, was 'grim and solemn'.[4] Yet once the announcement came 'the tension broke. The fatal step had been taken ...' Caesar Hull, a South African, 'was the first to rejoice. "Wizard!" he kept repeating ...'

They went back to their aircraft 'waiting for the English sky to blacken, as Goering had promised it would, with hordes of his bombers. But only flaky white clouds sailed across England's sky ...'

There was a similar reaction at Cranwell. Tim Vigors was one of about fifty cadets gathered in the college ante-room. When the fatal words were spoken 'as one man we jumped to our feet cheering with excitement. There was not one amongst us who would not have been bitterly disappointed had the declaration of war not been made.'[5]

Every fighter pilot and bomber crew member believed that he would be at the forefront of a battle that would in all probability start immediately. In the words of the historian John Terraine they were holding what in medieval times was called 'the right of the line', that is 'the vanguard' and 'the place of greatest danger'.[6] Britain's long-term security still depended on the Royal Navy. The immediate danger, though, was from the air and the 'knock-out-blow' that had immediately flashed into Slessor's mind when he heard the sirens wail.

That thought had been followed by another: 'I wondered [he wrote years later] how my Service was going to come through this ordeal – wondered even whether it was going to be safe to be seen about in an RAF uniform after the next few days.'[7] He remembered an episode he witnessed as a young officer in the Royal Flying Corps based at Sutton's Farm in Essex, close to London. It was the early autumn of 1915 and the capital had been under repeated bombardments by Zeppelin airships. British aircraft and artillery seemed incapable of stopping the attacks and people were frightened and angry. Having failed to shoot down a raider the previous night, Slessor was driving through the East End in a lorry towing a trailer laden with aircraft components when he ran into trouble. 'As we entered the Mile End Road with our headlights on [he wrote] there were angry cries, and we were mobbed till we had to pull up and get a policeman to stand on the step on either side of the driver's seat of the tender, to get us through at all.'

In fact, Britain's air defences were in a much better state than they had been a quarter of a century previously. Of the three operational commands, Fighter Command was by far the best equipped and organized to carry out its task. Thanks to the political decision taken by civilian amateurs in 1938 to overrule the Air Force professionals and switch the focus of the rearmament programme away from bombers, the fighter squadrons were in reasonable shape to face an onslaught. An efficient defence system was coalescing. Through the summer of 1939 fighter squadrons traded in their biplanes for Hurricanes and Spitfires, future supplies of which looked secure. Having lagged behind for five years, Britain was about to overtake the Germans in aircraft manufacture and would outproduce them by 47 per cent in 1940.[8] The opening of a new Rolls-Royce shadow factory at Crewe to supplement the works at Derby ensured there would be no shortage of the Merlin engines that powered the fighters. The airfield building programme begun in 1935 provided a line of fighter bases strategically placed from Wick in the far north of Scotland to Exeter in the south of England which shielded all possible enemy approaches.

By the summer of 1939 there were twenty Chain Home radar stations covering the upper airspace which could identify aircraft at a distance of between fifty and 120 miles, stretching from Portsmouth to Scapa Flow. The coverage was soon to be improved by the addition of Chain Home Low stations which picked up low-altitude raiders. There were enough pilots to fly the fighters, though events had moved too quickly for there to be a comfortable manpower reserve. The main deficiency was in the quality of training.

Flying training never managed to keep pace with the great increase in manpower. In 1934 the RAF trained about 300 new pilots. In 1941 it trained 22,000 from all over the empire.[9] To give proper instruction that would keep them abreast of rapidly changing aviation technology required schools, instructors, practice aircraft and instructional aids. A scheme to provide all this was drawn up by Arthur Tedder during his 1934–6 stint as Director of Training. The programme involved capital investment and big ongoing costs which successive governments rejected. Rearmament was, after all, conceived as a temporary measure, an essentially political policy aimed at deterring Germany. There was no intention to build up and maintain an outsized Air Force in perpetuity. The result was that, in order to produce the numbers required within the budget allowed, course times were repeatedly cut and vital aspects of air warfare were inadequately taught.

Fighter Command was probably the least affected by the flaws in the training programme. Unlike Bomber Command it needed only one trained man to operate most of its aircraft. Nonetheless, its pilots were still ill prepared for the sort of war they would have to fight. They received no instruction in tactics at flying school. Instead they learned them from more experienced comrades in exercises when they arrived on their operational squadron. In the absence of real experience instruction was based on conjecture. The drills that were taught would turn out to have little connection with the reality of air fighting. There was an obsession with formation flying which turned out to be of limited military use. Once in action, pilots were supposed to respond to different situations by following different styles of attack, 'Number One', 'Number Two', etc., which relied on their target flying straight and level and taking no evasive action.

Contact with the enemy quickly revealed the chaos of combat which made nonsense of the air-display precision of the training manuals. Remarkably little trouble was taken in teaching pilots how to shoot. Gunnery played a small part in the curriculum and in the early part of the war pilots could arrive on front-line squadrons without having fired their guns while in flight, and most had only minimal experience of night flying.[10]

It would be nine months before Fighter Command was in heavy action. Despite all the foreboding about the 'knock-out blow', the Germans were in no hurry to try and land one. Hitler's offensive plans did not involve Britain at present and he was still hopeful of avoiding a clash if possible. This created a blessed hiatus that allowed pilots to bond with their aeroplanes and fit into the squadron team.

It was Bomber Command that suffered most from the weakness of the training set-up. Its failures further undermined the squadrons' ability to carry out the vital role that had been decreed for them. They started the war with stopgap aircraft that were incapable of launching the mass, long-range raids that were envisaged in the Air Staff's counter-offensive strategy. Even if the Stirling, Halifax and Lancaster had been available at this stage, the crews would not have been able to fly them efficiently.

The training they got for their existing aircraft was inadequate. The Wellington, Hampden, Blenheim and Whitley monoplanes were considerably more complicated than the biplanes they replaced and needed a high level of skill and teamwork from those who operated them. In 1934 it was unusual for an aircraft to carry more than one man in addition to the pilot.[11] By 1942 crews of four, five, six or seven were common. The aircrew instruction in place in the transition period from peace to war did not come close to creating the level of ability required.

Pilots were fledged at flying training schools which were supposed to transform them from absolute beginners into fully formed military aviators ready to take their place in the front line. The optimum course time was originally set at a year, then, when this proved unrealistic, reduced to nine months. When in 1937 it was decided that larger bombers would need two pilots to cope with long-range missions, the extra demand cut the training time to six months.[12] Adjustments were made, such as farming out 'ab initio' training to civilian flying schools under contract to the Air Ministry. However, the need to churn out pilots meant the standard reached was, in the words of the RAF's internal account, 'barely essential'.[13] Things began to change in May 1940 with the introduction of Operational Training Units (OTUs) that were supposed to fill in the gaps in training so that crews arrived on their squadrons properly prepared for action. But it was not until 1942 and the so-called 'New Deal' that aircrews finally received the time and attention they needed to reach efficiency.

In the meantime, in the RAF's own judgement the need to produce the maximum output meant that in the run-up to war 'practically none of the increased training requirements which

[new] technical developments called into existence were met by schools during the years of expansion'.[14] Cockpits came with a plethora of instruments and controls. Although 'advanced trainers for efficient instruction' were needed, 'the supply of these aircraft was slow and scanty'. Night flying, and flying on instruments only were now vital skills yet 'only rudimentary instruction ... could be given for lack of facilities and time'. The conclusion was that a pilot emerging from flying training school in 1939 had learned little more than a pilot graduating in 1934 when Hitler was still a curiosity.

The debate about how many pilots were needed to fly a long-range aircraft was not resolved until 1942 when it was finally settled that one was enough. The indecision was symptomatic of the confusion about aircrew roles. Long flights clearly required expert navigation. Yet until 1942, when the specialist aircrew category of 'navigator' was introduced, the job was allotted to the second pilot in a large aircraft or the observer in a smaller one.

Neither would have had any advanced training in navigation. Despite its centrality to the prevailing orthodoxy of bombing primacy, the subject was badly neglected. Before the war wireless-equipped aircraft depended on position-fixing signals from ground stations to find their way. These were useless over enemy territory and navigators had to use dead reckoning: following a course by means of sextant sightings of the sun or stars or landmarks below and setting them against speed and wind strength. Over a blacked-out landscape in skies that were frequently thick with cloud the margin of error was enormous. Four months before the war began a daytime practice exercise led a senior Bomber Command officer to report that 'dead reckoning navigation by day when above cloud could be expected to bring an aircraft only to within about fifty miles of its target'.[15] Poor navigation rendered useless much of the bomber effort in the first years of the war but senior officers never seemed to give the problem the urgent attention it deserved. 'Dilatory discussions about the need for technical aids such as radar and the Air Position Indicator did take place from time to time,' wrote the authorized historians of the strategic air campaign against Germany, Sir Charles Webster and Noble

Frankland, 'but a general inertia overcame all significant progress.'[16] It was only in the autumn of 1941, when Winston Churchill demanded action after seeing photographic analysis that revealed the shocking inaccuracy of much bombing, that things changed.[17]

An important, but untested, theory that had taken root at the Air Ministry maintained that on sorties over enemy territory, bombers flying in formation would be able to defend themselves with their on-board guns. If true, this would seem to demand a high level of competence in the airmen manning them. Before the war, the job was done by ground crew members for whom flying was a second-ary duty and who returned to their regular trades when not in the air. The category became full-time in 1939 and from May 1940 air gunners along with wireless operators were upgraded to the rank of sergeant.[18] However, as the RAF narrative records, 'during the first two years of the war, none of the non-pilot aircrew training was particularly satisfactory. Navigation training was hampered by war-time conditions, as well as lack of equipment: gunnery training suffered from lack of suitable aircraft and equipment: and in neither case were the instructors well suited to the work they had to do.' It was left to the OTUs to try and repair the deficiencies.

Shooting school

All these weaknesses were well known to those at the top of the Air Force. They had been pointed out with undiplomatic persistence by Edgar Ludlow-Hewitt, who took over Bomber Command in 1937. Ludlow-Hewitt was another member of the Air Force's upper-echelon awkward squad, 'far and away the most brilliant officer I have met in any of the three Services', according to Arthur Harris, his temperamental antithesis and not a man given to gushing compliments.[19] He was the son of a clergyman who left the Army to join the RFC, fought bravely on the Western Front and rose quickly in the post-war service. He was one of the few officers in the upper ranks who felt the need to maintain their flying skills.

Ludlow-Hewitt saw expansion as a trap. Numbers might grow but quality would inevitably plunge. He argued persistently that a smaller but war-capable force was much better than the larger but unprepared one that was in the making. As war approached his warnings became increasingly unwelcome. The attitude of the Air Council – the supreme body of the RAF which brought together the Secretary of State and senior officers and officials – was that it was an unfortunate inevitability that expansion would bring a reduction in efficiency. Like the head of the other commands, Ludlow-Hewitt would just have to play the hand he had been dealt.

His frequent warnings seem to have been dealt with piecemeal, or in some cases ignored. At a meeting of the Air Council on 18 July 1939 the Secretary of State, Kingsley Wood, insisted that a letter from Ludlow-Hewitt that had been lying around unanswered for two months be dealt with forthwith as it amounted to 'an indictment of the Air Council and Air Staff'.[20] The reaction of the CAS Cyril Newall was brusque. In his view, the document was a back-covering exercise, 'written with the object of putting on record certain unavoidable shortcomings due to expansion'. Ludlow-Hewitt was 'trying to clear himself in the event of catastrophe'.

The exchange of letters that followed failed to pacify Ludlow-Hewitt. A fortnight later Newall told the Council that the latest communication from him 'contained a very serious statement which might even be taken as meaning that in the event of war [he] would not be prepared to fight with his present equipment'.

Ludlow-Hewitt was summoned to air his concerns at a special meeting, at which he told the Council that he was worried about the poor level of gunnery, the lack of adequate training the flying schools were providing before crews reached squadrons and the absence of proper bombing ranges. All of these complaints were wearily familiar. Only a fortnight before he had written to the Air Ministry that 'as things stand at present the gunners have no real confidence in their ability to use [their] equipment efficiently in war, and Captains and crews have, I fear, little confidence in the ability of the gunners to defend them against destruction by enemy aircraft'.[21] His insistence that operational squadrons should be removed from the first line to train flying school graduates up to combat standards was already causing serious friction. The need for proper bombing facilities was a hardy perennial of staff meetings (the lack of action was blamed on the strength of local opposition and the fact that non-populous areas tended to be full of mountains and bogs, though, as the Air Ministry mandarin Sir Maurice Dean later pointed out, there was no shortage of empty desert in the empire in which to place experimental facilities).[22]

What is most striking is the last item on Ludlow-Hewitt's list. According to the minutes of the meeting he 'stated that the question he wished to raise here was a very big one; the question of what type of bombing was most effective. It could not be decided of course around a table. Extensive experiments would be necessary and it was the importance of initiating these without delay which he wanted to stress.'[23] He went on to give an elementary tutorial on the relative merits of high-level and low-level bombing.

The discussion about which approach was best had been going on continuously since January 1934 when the Air Ministry had set up a bombing committee. Yet now, five and a half years later and with the outbreak of war a month away, the argument had got no further and no practical work had been done to decide an operational issue of fundamental importance.

It is possible to sympathize with the Air Council's argument that the hectic pace of expansion meant the unavoidable cutting of many corners. What is less easy to understand is why, in the light of the mass of negative evidence, they persisted in overestimating

Bomber Command's capabilities and exaggerating what it could achieve. It was perhaps a matter of self-preservation: facing reality would have resulted in a devastating loss of face and undermined the commanding position the RAF had staked out for itself in the political and military landscape.

The Air Staff entered the war with a list of objectives that had no possibility of being achieved. Their 'Western European War Plans' was a fantastical document establishing a schedule of action to bring Germany to its knees. The first step in the bombing campaign was a bid to pre-empt the 'knock-out blow' by attacks on 'the German Air Striking Force and its maintenance organisation (including aircraft industry)'.[24] Next would come military road, rail and canal communications. After that the effort would concentrate on obliterating Germany's war industry in its heartlands in the Ruhr, Rhineland and Saar and knocking out oil installations.

It was fortunate that events conspired to prevent any attempt to carry them out. Instead, offensive operations focused almost entirely on German warships lying in or near their North Sea bases, an objective that came twelfth in the War Plans list of priorities. There were several reasons for this restraint. At the declaration of war President Roosevelt had appealed to the main belligerents to undertake not to bomb cities or launch any air operations that endangered civilian lives. Britain and France agreed immediately, Germany two weeks later. The Chamberlain government was anxious to comply. The French if anything outdid their allies in their dread of doing anything to provoke the Germans into doing to Paris what they had done to Warsaw.

Slessor wrote after the war that, even before the fighting began, recognition of the true position had dawned on the Air Force high command: 'It became more and more obvious as war came nearer that the force likely to be at our disposal in the next few years ... was sadly inadequate to our needs, whether in technical performance, hitting power, training or ability to sustain operations in the face of war wastage of aircraft and crews. The expression "conservation of the bomber force" began to take its place in our thinking, and by the outbreak of war had become a determining factor in policy ...'[25]

That cannot have been how it felt to the crews operating in the opening days of the air war. The first proper sortie provided a tragic illustration of many of Bomber Command's weaknesses. At lunch-time on 4 September, Flight Lieutenant Ken Doran was waiting by his Blenheim at Ipswich civil airport with four other crews of 110 Squadron. They had moved there from their base at Wattisham in the expectation of action. Doran was an adventurous twenty-six-year-old who after leaving St Albans School had done a stint as a private in the Army before quitting to join the RAF on a short service commission. The tension of waiting was broken by the arrival of some 'gen'. Units of the German fleet had been sighted 'but weather in the Heligoland Bight, it appeared was bloody, and the only attack possible would be a low level one'.[26] A reconnaissance flight had spotted warships lying near Wilhelmshaven and further north off Brunsbüttel at the mouth of the Kiel Canal. Fifteen Blenheims and fourteen Wellingtons from a variety of squadrons were ordered off to attack.

The Blenheims of 110 Squadron had been carrying 500lb Semi-Armour Piercing bombs but for some reason a decision was made to replace them with General Purpose bombs with an eleven-sec-ond-delay fuse. Then 'at last everything was ready and the final briefing had been given by the Station Commander, who finished up with these words to the rear gunners: "Don't shoot till you see the whites of their eyes."'

Each squadron was to make its own way to the target area. There would be no fighter escort to protect them. Ludlow-Hewitt had suggested their desirability in August 1938 but the Air Ministry was unenthusiastic. They stuck to the view that existing fighters did not have the range to cover long-range missions and, even if they did, when they broke off to do battle with attacking fighters the bomber force would anyway be left undefended. Nor could they take comfort in armour if they came under fire. The Air Staff had opposed installing steel plating as it 'reduced the weight of the bomb load'.[27]

They took off at teatime. Navigators got a fix on their position from the last ground station they passed before crossing the coast. Then they were on their own, out over the North Sea with their maps and compasses and calculations of wind speed, operating on a system known in the service as 'by guess and by God'.

It was not long before they hit the weather. 'The Met forecast was only too accurate,' remembered Doran who led the attack.[28] 'A solid wall of cloud seemed to extend from sea level to about 17,000 feet. We obviously had to keep down below it to have any chance of finding our target so we went down to sea level and flew in and out of cloud between 50 and 100 feet.' In the disorientating greyness where sea and sky merged indistinguishably the great danger was of ploughing into the waves. There was nothing on which the observers could get a bearing. Then 'suddenly a couple of barges appeared out of the murk and vanished. At the same time we got our first sight of the German coast.' After 'a bit of feverish map reading' they realized that they were on the approach to the Schillig Roads that led into Wilhelmshaven. 'By an incredible combination of luck and judgement we were bang on our track.' The gods were smiling. The cloud lifted to 500 feet and they saw a large merchant ship. Just behind it lay the *Admiral Scheer*, one of the Kriegsmarine's pocket battleships, as well as a cruiser used as a training ship, the *Emden*. It was anchored in shallow water near the bank and protected on the landward side by a balloon barrage.

Before taking off they had decided that the five aircraft would attack in two sections of three and two, arriving from different angles, and pass over the target within the eleven seconds before the bombs exploded. Doran 'decided to make our attack slightly across the fore and aft line of the ship and make our getaway by a sharp turn to port to avoid the balloon barrage'.

They climbed to 500 feet and swooped in a shallow dive. As they approached they saw 'the matelots' washing hanging out around the stern and the crew idly standing about on deck. It seemed as though we had caught them literally with their pants down.' At first the sailors seemed to think the aircraft were friendlies, but 'when they realized our intention was hostile started running like mad'.

Doran led the first section into the attack. His Blenheim 'dropped its bombs bang amidships'. The crew were now working the anti-aircraft guns and the barrage was supplemented by onshore flak batteries which 'kept us pretty busy carrying out evasive measures'. The bombs from the second aircraft undershot by ten yards and exploded in shallow water under the ship. The pilot of the third aircraft reckoned he would not be able to get over the *Scheer* before his bombs exploded and dropped them on 'another target'. The second section of two aircraft was led by Flying Officer Henry Emden. He apparently decided to switch targets and go for the cruiser which shared his name. On the approach his aircraft was hit by flak and crashed into the *Emden*, killing nine sailors as well as all four of the Blenheim crew. This was the only damage inflicted on the Germans. The two bombs landed on the *Scheer* bounced off the armoured deck and then failed to explode.

The operation would prove shockingly expensive. Five Blenheims from 107 Squadron managed to locate the cruiser *Admiral Hipper*. In the ensuing attack, four of them were shot down. At Brunsbüttel, Wellingtons from 9 and 149 Squadrons arrived to find warships in the water but fierce anti-aircraft fire and bad weather meant that only one crew claimed a possible hit and two of the attackers were shot down. The tally for the day was seven aircraft lost, nearly a quarter of the force. Twenty-four men were killed, and two survived to be taken prisoner.

Ten aircraft in the force turned back after getting lost. Due to navigational error two Wellingtons missed Germany altogether and flew on to the Danish town of Esbjerg 150 miles to the north of the target area, dropping bombs that killed two people.

Despite the poor beginning, Bomber Command stuck with the same methods for the rest of the year. Senior officers were reluctant to abandon the idea that the bombers' on-board guns should be able to pump out enough defensive fire to see off attacking fighters. There was plenty of evidence from gunnery training school to make it clear that this was not the case. The standard of shooting accuracy was abysmal – not due so much to the incompetence of the gunners as to the fact that it was extremely difficult to connect with a fast and manoeuvrable aeroplane. Even in 1942, when air gunner Eric Banks was doing his training at Barrow-in-Furness he was surprised to find that when it came to the air-to-air firing at slow-moving towed drogues a hit rate of 'anything above four per cent or five per cent was regarded as a good score'.[29] A year later Norman Lee passed out successfully from the Elementary Air Gunnery School at Bridlington with an average score of 2.4 per cent.[30]

To acknowledge this fatal deficiency would have meant abandoning daylight operations, and with it any chance of hitting targets with any accuracy. The truth was exposed on two disastrous operations in December. On 14 December five out of twelve Wellingtons from 99 Squadron on a search for shipping off Wilhelmshaven were destroyed by flak and fighters. Four days later, while on a similar mission, twelve Wellingtons out of a force of twenty-two which reached the target area were shot down, most if not all of them by fighters. The notion of the self-defending bomber formation was now dead and from then on most operations would be conducted at night.

In this period, Bomber Command lost sixty-three aircraft and 171 men in operations over enemy territory. Even more aircraft had been destroyed in training exercises – sixty-nine with the loss of eighty crew. Most of the aircraft, including the training losses, were the most modern in service – Hampdens, Whitleys, Wellingtons and Blenheims.

This hardly seemed in line with a policy of 'conservation of the bomber force'. Crews were sent off on risky missions in the knowledge that likely results were pathetically small. The Blenheims that attacked the *Scheer* had no chance of sinking her. They had a payload of only 1,000lb. The bombs they carried were ineffective and underpowered with high explosive making up only 34 per cent of the overall weight.[31] They were unlikely to do much more than scratch a heavily armoured capital ship, even if they managed to explode. A significant proportion did not. Of the medium-capacity bombs dropped on south-west Germany in 1940–41, about 40 per cent were duds. [32] Clearing away the rubble of Cologne after the war, more than 10,000 unexploded Allied bombs were discovered.[33]

A proper bomber offensive would not be possible until the arrival of the big four-engine heavies and that was still at least two years away. Despite the costly debacles of December, attempts to hit German shipping continued intermittently until April 1940. Crews were ordered to stay away from the German coast and use cloud cover where possible, but no vessels were sunk. Most Bomber

Command sorties were night-time excursions to drop anti-Nazi leaflets over German cities, an activity which rated only fourteenth in priority in the Western War Plans. Six million leaflets were dropped in the first operation alone, declaring that 'this war is as repulsive to us as it is to you' but warning Germans 'not to forget that England, once forced into war, will wage it unwaveringly to the end'.[34] Neither this, nor the many millions more which fluttered down in the years to come, produced any discernible results. Nonetheless the operations, which often doubled as reconnaissance missions, were useful. New distance records were set and crews got vital experience of night flying and navigation. They were rarely troubled by flak or fighters, an encouraging but surely temporary state of affairs, which weighed in the decision to switch the main bombing effort from day to night.

The main enemy in the brutal winter of 1939–40 was the weather. On the night of 27 October 1939, a force of Whitleys was sent off to drop leaflets over Munich, Frankfurt and Stuttgart. None of them was equipped with de-icing equipment or cabin heating and the electrically heated flying suit had yet to come into service. As they climbed into cloud, they slowly became encased in ice. A post-operational report recounted how on one aircraft 'crystalline ice formed on the leading edges of the wings, over the gun turrets and on the cabin windows. The front gun was frozen up and rendered useless. The aircraft's trimming tabs were jammed by ice and the dustbin turret stuck about a third of the way down its travel … after two and a quarter hours in the air the oxygen supply in the cabin was exhausted. Some of the crew occasionally banged their heads on the floor or navigation table as a relief from the feeling of frost-bite and [lack of] oxygen.'[35] On the return journey 'the icing became worse and the rear guns now also froze, lumps of ice flew off the airscrews, striking the sides and nose of the aircraft'. The Whitley nonetheless managed to struggle back and land at a base in France.

When opaque ice blotted out the windscreen and instruments of another Whitley the captain gave the order to bale out. The rear gunner, whose intercom had failed, stayed on board unaware that he was alone. The pilotless bomber duly crashed with the gunner still inside. In a quirk of fate that would bear endless repetition in pub and canteen, he staggered out of the wreckage having suffered only a few burns and bruises, convinced that his crewmates had been incinerated in the flaming debris.

The relative inactivity of Bomber Command during the Phoney War was a relief to its chief. Ludlow-Hewitt had seen nothing to change his gloomy view of its immediate prospects, and opinion that as much time as possible was needed to build up strength and competence. His caution, candour and pessimism made his continued tenure impossible. His replacement was Charles Portal, the dominant figure in the RAF story for most of the rest of the war.

'Peter' Portal, as he was known to his peers, would lead the Air Force until victory, making him the longest serving of the wartime chiefs. According to a contemporary, Hugh Walmsley, he was 'a brilliant pilot, a brilliant staff officer and a brilliant commander'.[36] He was short with a large head, bright, appraising eyes and a prominent nose. He went to Winchester, a brainy boy at a brainy school, and was studying at Christ Church, Oxford, when the war broke out. He ended up in the RFC and was taken under Trenchard's wing. After the war he was sent to the RAF Staff College established at Andover to hone the minds of the brightest young officers then given command of 7 Squadron, a bomber unit, based at Worthy Down. Portal was quiet, in a service that tended to be boisterous, and disapproved of self-publicity. He was nonetheless obsessively competitive. He acted as bomb aimer in the annual Lawrence Minot bombing trophy and won it twice. A contemporary, William Yool, remembered how when the squadron was assigned to one side in army manoeuvres on Salisbury Plain, Portal flew as observer with one of his pilots. 'On a night of blinding rain and poor visibility they effectively ruined the manoeuvres by flying around the area at a low height in a Virginia, pinpointing the "enemy" units so accurately with the aid of an Aldis lamp that Portal's side had a complete picture of the enemy's dispositions. Some of the soldiers were not amused and complained that it was not war.'[37] He liked to win at everything. When commanding RAF forces in Aden in the middle 1930s he took up sailing. On Wednesday afternoons, the wife of a colleague remembered, he would race dinghies with the senior naval officer, and beat him every time. The pair would then swap

The incarnation of the Air Force ethos. Guy Gibson and crew at Scampton in July 1943, two months after the Dams Raid. It was the zenith of Gibson's career and the threatening Lincolnshire sky seems to hint at trouble ahead.

Hugh Trenchard inspects men of the RAF Regiment. Though long-retired, the 'Father of the Royal Air Force' continued to exert strong influence, directly and through former protegés.

When war came, it was the RAF that recruits flocked to.

While the WAAF offered women the prospect of fulfilment and adventure. These are camera gun technicians.

Hugh Dowding with some of his Fighter Boys (Douglas Bader at right) at the war's end. The Battle of Britain fixed the RAF permanently in the nation's affections.

Much more than a wonderful fighter. The Spitfire would become an eternal symbol of graceful defiance.

Some of the Few. George Barclay (second from right) with 249 Squadron comrades.

'The beau ideal of the Fighter Boy.' Like many survivors of the battle, Paddy Finucane would be sacrificed by Douglas and Leigh-Mallory's policy of cross-Channel raiding.

'Sawn-off Lockie.' Eric Lock, one of the highest-scoring aces of the battle, drawn here by Cuthbert Orde, was another victim.

ORDE
14 July 1941

The youngest of the wartime service chiefs, 'Peter' Portal was also the most impressive: brilliant, driven and extraordinarily self-possessed.

Bomber Command's stout overlord. Arthur Harris looking unusually reflective.

The supreme instrument of the bombing cult. With the AVRO Lancaster, the RAF could finally deliver on its promises.

Flying in a bomber was the aerial equivalent of fighting in the trenches. In the spring of 1942 aircrew prepare to board a Short Stirling. More than 55,000 would die.

The Vickers Wellington served from the first day of the war to the last over land and sea. Nearly 11,500 were built – more than any other British bomber.

Architects of victory.
In North Africa and
Italy, Arthur Tedder
(top) and Arthur 'Mary'
Coningham (bottom)
would forge the tactics
that put air power at the
centre of Allied success.

boats and Portal would beat him all over again.[38] His real passion was hawking. The fascination began when he was a young boy and lasted until work prevented him from pursuing it with the intensity that he felt it required. Nobody failed to notice that Portal, with his keen, dark eyes, deep-scored cheeks and great, beak-like nose looked remarkably like the birds he loved.

While serving as Chief Flying Instructor at Cranwell in the early 1920s he kept twenty-four merlin and peregrine falcons, training them, fussing over their diets and nursing them when they became ill. Between mid-July 1921 and the beginning of February 1922 he took them out on 127 occasions, noting every detail of the hawks' performances in obsessive detail. One of his favourites was Rattle, 'a beautiful hawk to look at and a fine flier. Did not take to partridges at once. Kills pigeons well.'[39] Each success was celebrated. The total bag for the season was 187 larks, 162 partridges and ten 'various'.

Falconry requires an unemotional acceptance of the beauties and cruelties of nature. The pleasure comes in watching a bird you have raised from young doing what it is supposed to do supremely well, that is, spotting its prey and driving it upwards in ever-widening circles until it has gained the height advantage. Portal described vividly in the college magazine what happened next: 'After a few more mighty strokes his wings shut close and he hurls himself with truly appalling speed, down through the sunlit air ... "Whack!" The sound of the blow is carried back to you. Leaving a little puff of feathers hanging in the sun, that luckless partridge drops to earth like a stone ...'[40] For all his urbanity Portal had an air of the hunter about him and always accepted the atavistic realities of existence. The quiet manner hid a broad streak of ruthlessness. He shared this outlook and disposition with Arthur Harris, his successor at Bomber Command, ensuring that it would maintain its posture of all-out aggression until the last days of the war.

On 9 April 1940 the Germans made their long-awaited next move. For the Air Force, the invasion of Denmark and Norway brought more losses with no significant results. RAF aircraft were sent off to try and bomb the ships ferrying men and supplies and to attack Luftwaffe bases covering the invasion. The bombers were operating beyond the range of fighter cover and were extremely vulnerable to the attentions of the Messerschmitt 109s and 110s. Pilot Officer Tony Smyth had moved with 214 Squadron up to Lossiemouth in the north of Scotland a few days before the invasion and had already seen fighters shoot down two Wellingtons from his sub-flight while on a shipping search off Denmark. At last light on 11 April he flew as second pilot to Flight Sergeant 'Darky' Powell, a pre-war regular, to attack Stavanger airfield from where transport planes were ferrying German troops forward. 'It was quite fine when we came to the first islands off the coast with their white light-houses and farms turning pink in the light of the setting sun,' he recalled.[41] 'It was very beautiful and I longed to revisit it in more peaceful times.'

These thoughts were interrupted when 'suddenly the air gunner in the astrodome called out "fighters one mile to port beam!"' The ribbons of red incendiary fell away harmlessly and after overshooting the airfield the first time they turned back to try again and flew into 'a real fireworks display with streams of tracer bullets flying in all directions ...' Two more attempts were thwarted by intense anti-aircraft fire and the presence of radio masts. Before they could try again Smyth looked over to see a Wellington piloted by Pilot Officer F. E. Barber engulfed in a sheet of flame. He had time to remember that the wireless operator was a leading aircraftman called Westcott whose father was a policeman in Worcestershire near Smyth's home, to whom he gave a lift to and from the base when the flight was granted leave. Then there was 'an almighty explosion in the cockpit with a flash of light that left us temporarily blinded and the plane leapt upward and then dived towards the harbour'. A 20mm shell, from a fighter or anti-aircraft gun, had exploded on the side of the cockpit, and two more hit amidships and in the rear turret. Powell was wounded in his left side but still capable of flying and the rear gunner was bleeding heavily from his thighs. Smyth, who had been saved from serious injury by the parachute buckle on his shoulder, bandaged the gunner and administered morphine while Powell jettisoned the bombs, announcing, 'I've had enough. I'm going home.'

They flew back into the sunset, with Smyth on the lower deck, pushing back on the control column to ease the weight on the pilot's arms. The pilot's compass had been smashed and they had only a small compass from the dinghy emergency pack to guide them. Somehow they made it to Kinloss 'with Darky still flying magnificently', a feat for which he later received the Distinguished Flying Medal. After seeing the crew into hospital Smyth collapsed, reflecting that 'in three weeks, of the eighteen aircrew in my sub-flight, twelve were dead, five were in hospital and I alone was on my feet'.

The cost to Bomber Command of the Scandinavian foray was nearly forty aircraft lost, 132 aircrew dead and twenty taken prisoner. The results were negligible. Fighter Command did not fare any better. After Allied troops were landed in central Norway in a doomed attempt to hold the Germans, fighter squadrons flew off from Royal Navy carriers and set up makeshift bases on frozen lakes from where they launched heroic attempts to provide the ground forces with some protection. The odds were hopeless and the squadrons lacked supplies, spares, communications and even shelter. Sergeant Richard Earp, an ex-Halton boy, flew Hurricanes with 46 Squadron from a makeshift airstrip of 'coconut matting and wire netting' alongside a fjord at Skaanland.[42] He slept in a tent on the ice with six others. 'All I had was a groundsheet and two blankets,' he remembered. 'You couldn't sleep ... It was terribly bloody cold.' In the week he was there he 'never saw anything or hit anything'. When the inevitable withdrawal was ordered, Skaanland was ablaze with crippled aircraft and fuel dumps, set on fire to deny them to the enemy.

Earp left Norway on a trawler. Ten of his comrades managed to land their Hurricanes on the carrier *Glorious*, a feat which was supposed to be impossible for a heavy monoplane. Lighter Gladiator biplanes from 263 Squadron were already embarked. The following afternoon the German battlecruisers *Scharnhorst* and *Gneisenau* intercepted *Glorious* and two destroyer escorts as they sailed for home. Two hours later, all three Royal Navy ships were sunk with the loss of 1,519 lives. Only two of the Air Force men aboard survived. So ended a costly ordeal that brought little in the way of compensatory knowledge or experience. It was, however, only the prelude to another passage of painful failure.

The German attack on the Low Countries and France on 10 May was to reveal yet more weaknesses in the Air Force's preparations. In the years between the wars little time had been spent on working out how aeroplanes could work in effective co-operation with troops on the ground. Air Staff officers, notably John Slessor, understood the importance of integrating air and land power. However, the primacy of the bomber doctrine and the scarcity of resources meant that little progress was made. Overseas, the Air Force and Army had worked together in small policing operations against primitive rebels. Back at home relations were often strained as airmen resisted what they saw as the soldiers' unreasonable demands to divert resources their way.

The tactical and strategic relationship between Air Force and Army faced its first big test in modern warfare conditions when, a few days after the start of the war, the RAF accompanied the British Expeditionary Force (BEF) across the Channel.

The British Air Forces in France (BAFF) were divided into two formations. The Air Component of the BEF, based in the Nord and Pas de Calais, was made up of five squadrons of Westland Lysanders, robust but slow, high-wing monoplanes with fixed undercarriages, and a single rear-mounted machine gun, which were tasked with tactical reconnaissance and artillery spotting. Four squadrons of Blenheims would carry out strategic reconnaissance up to the Rhine. Four Hurricane squadrons were assigned to protect the troops and the Lysanders, which could be reinforced from Britain when the balloon went up.

The Advanced Air Striking Force (AASF), based at Reims, had ten squadrons of Battles and Blenheims, charged with supporting the ground troops by attacking the German advance, preferably at choke points like bridges and road junctions. They were to be covered by two squadrons of Hurricanes, which again would be reinforced when hostilities began.

Blenheims carried a small bomb load but were at least reasonably fast. Battles were now recognized by aircrews and commanders alike as practically useless, slow and poorly defended and 'absolute death traps' even to the eyes of a very junior pilot like Tony Smyth.

Their utter helplessness against fighter attack was established in the first weeks of the war when five Battles of 150 Squadron were sent on a reconnaissance mission twenty miles the other side of the Franco-German border. Four were shot down by Me 109s and the fifth damaged beyond repair.[43]

Neither aircraft was designed for ground support work. The Luftwaffe had Junkers 87 Stuka dive bombers, which were used as aerial artillery to pound enemy defences as the Wehrmacht's tanks thrust forward. The RAF's focus on strategic bombing had left no room for the development of a British dive bomber. Existing aircraft were thought to be technically incapable of dropping bombs from a steep angle. There was talk of fitting aircraft with air brakes which might make dive bombing feasible or developing shallow dive bombing tactics but neither option was properly investigated or pursued.[44]

Thus, the choices were high- or low-level bombing, both of which brought considerable disadvantages. At heights of 15,000 feet and above the chances of hitting a small target like an advancing column, bridge or train were very small. Going in at a few hundred feet greatly increased accuracy but also vulnerability to flak. All this was understood by the Air Force chiefs. In January 1940 the operational instructions issued to commanders in France and presumably based on observation of the Polish campaign stated, 'Bomber aircraft have proved extremely useful in *support* of an advancing army, especially against weak anti-aircraft resistance, but it is not clear that a bomber force against an advancing army, well supported by all forms of anti-aircraft defence and a large force of fighter aircraft, will be economically effective.'[45] The events that followed the arrival of *Blitzkrieg* in the West proved the accuracy of this euphemistic assessment.

On 10 May, the massacre of the bombers began. The BAFF commander, Arthur Barratt, ordered the first aircraft off at noon to try and stem the German columns pouring across the Belgian border. By evening twenty-four Battles had either been shot down by fighters or the mobile artillery batteries that trundled alongside the advancing troops or otherwise destroyed on the ground. Another twenty-four light bombers were lost the following day. By 12 May the

Germans were across the River Meuse near Maastricht and had secured bridges across the Albert Canal to the west of the city at Veldwezelt and Vroenhoven through which they could channel forces on to Brussels. The bridges were strongly protected by flak batteries and machine guns and fighters were on hand to deal with any interference. That morning at the grass airfield at Amifontaine near Laon that they had occupied since the previous December, a call was made to the crews of 12 Squadron for volunteers to attack the bridges. By now everyone knew the likely outcome but every man stepped forward. In the end the first six on the duty roster were chosen. The raid was led by a twenty-one-year-old Flying Officer Donald Garland. He had been born in County Wicklow in the Irish Republic. His parents moved to London and he went to Cardinal Vaughan Memorial School, a Catholic direct grant college in Holland Park. He left at seventeen, working for a while in an insurance office before signing up for a short service commission. He was one of four brothers to join the RAF, none of whom would survive the war.

In the end five Battles took off from Amifontaine as one was held back with wireless trouble, a development the crew must have been profoundly thankful for when they learned what happened next. Garland led one section, Flying Officer N. M. Thomas the other. Before setting off they had a 'rather heated discussion' about tactics.[46] 'Garland was determined to carry out a low-level attack thinking it not only the best form, but the safest,' wrote Thomas who preferred a high approach and tried to persuade him to do likewise. 'My parting words were "it will be interesting to see the result, and may we both be lucky enough to return."'

As the formation approached the bridges they were met with a blizzard of flak and machine-gun fire and set upon by fighters. Garland hurled the Battle through it all, swooping down to deliver a bomb which damaged but did not demolish the Veldwezelt bridge. His aircraft was destroyed in the effort. Ablaze from stem to stern and trailing a great banner of black smoke, it smashed into the ground near the village of Lanaken killing him, his observer Sergeant Thomas Gray and the wireless operator/gunner, Leading Aircraftman L. R. Reynolds. Garland and Gray were both awarded the Victoria Cross, the first RAF men of the war to win it. The manifestly unjust criteria that the Air Force applied to determine gallantry awards meant that Reynolds was not. As a mere WOP/AG he was deemed not to have been in a 'decision-taking' position and could not share the credit. Only one of the five Battles made it back to base, the others falling to flak and fighters.

Another twenty-nine bombers were destroyed that day but the orders remained the same and the appalling losses seemed to do nothing to dent the resolve of commanders to order further attacks or the crews to carry them out. At mid-afternoon on 14 May Leading Aircraftman Len Clarke, a WOP/AG, flew off with his crewmates to attack bridges over the Meuse near Sedan with four other Battles from 12 Squadron. His pilot was Sergeant Reg Winkler an ex-apprentice. The observer Sergeant Maurice 'Bish' Smalley and he had joined the RAF as part of the expansion programme two years before. Amifontaine, where the airmen lived in tents and a single Nissen hut, had so far escaped attack but as they climbed to 6,000 feet there were signs everywhere of the Luftwaffe's power. Clarke saw 'bombed trains, burning buildings, halted road convoys meeting streams of refugees …'[47]

As they approached Sedan they ran into concentrated flak and from his position behind his single Vickers machine gun he spotted Messerschmitt 109s closing up from behind. Almost at once one of the bombers faltered and started to smoke, victim of the ground flak, then fell away, jettisoning its bombs as it dived. He later learned that it managed to limp back to base, the only one to survive the trip. Soon, Clarke's aircraft 'began suffering damage. Several holes [appeared] in the wing upper surfaces although luckily the fuel tanks seemed to escape. One shell passed through the starboard wing between the bombs and the flare racks exploding above.'

The target was an old stone bridge on the edge of Sedan. 'On reaching the target we followed the leader into a dive, Reg pushing the nose down steeply, so much so that I queried over the intercom whether he was all right.' When the pilot levelled out he could 'see dust and smoke straddling the river. Houses were already burning on one side of the river by the old bridge.'

They were coming in at about 2,000 feet behind the lead aircraft when it took a direct hit from an anti-aircraft shell and it plunged to the ground showering debris. Astonishingly, one of the crew, the wireless operator AC1 J. D. Wright, survived. Then it was their turn. A shell struck the nose, destroying the Battle's sole engine. Clarke felt 'a heavy thud which threw the aircraft upwards. Smoke, oil and glycol [engine cooling fluid] poured back and flames swept upwards into Reg's cockpit.' The aircraft was still just controllable but they were losing height rapidly. I asked Reg whether he could get it down but at once he gave the order to bale out.' Clarke 'went out first, Bish giving me a final push over the side and I experienced that unique sensation of falling into a bottomless pit before being jerked into silent downward flight'. Looking around he saw their Battle slant into a final doomed dive and in the distance his two crewmates floating safely down. He landed heavily, just avoiding a ducking in a channel that fed the Meuse. As if to rub in their dominance, as he 'gathered myself together, a dozen Bf 109s [Messerschmitts] flew overhead'. Clarke, Winkler and Smalley were taken prisoner and spent the rest of the war in prisoner-of-war camps. Six of their 12 Squadron comrades died in the attack. Forty-seven bombers were destroyed that day in attacks on the Sedan bridges. Thirty-three of them were Battles. The seventy-three men who were killed died in vain for their sacrifice had no appreciable effect on the German advance. In twelve days of fighting, from 10 to 21 May, the AASF was all but wiped out.

The France-based fighter squadrons and those that flew across the Channel to help them struggled heroically to blunt the Luftwaffe's attacks but even having had nearly nine months in which to prepare they were still fighting under great disadvantages. Command and control was minimal with little or no radar cover to warn of enemy movements. Briefings were non-existent and fighters usually encountered the Luftwaffe by chance. Operating in threes and sixes they were almost always outnumbered. 'Well another day is gone, and with it a lot of grand blokes,' wrote Flight Lieutenant Ronnie Wight of 213 Squadron to his mother on the evening of 31 May.[48] 'Got another brace of 109s today, but the whole Luftwaffe seems to leap on us – we were hopelessly outnumbered. I was caught napping by a 109 in the middle of a dog fight, and got a couple of holes in the aircraft …'

Despite the crippling handicaps they acquitted themselves magnificently, managing to destroy or badly damage 364 German aircraft. Of the 452 Hurricanes sent to France only sixty-six returned to England. Of the 386 lost, 178 were left behind in the retreat, most having first been set on fire. The figure would have been yet higher had it not been for Dowding's courage in opposing Churchill over French demands for reinforcements and reluctance to allow any more of his precious fighters to be sacrificed in a cause that was so obviously lost.

The sedate Lysanders of the Army Co-operation Squadrons never had a chance to do their job. 'Their performance ... was inadequate and the tasks they were set were impossible,' wrote Christopher Foxley-Norris of 13 Squadron.[49] 'After quite a short period of fighting, my own squadron had lost all its serviceable aircraft and those of us who survived joined the pathetic rabble of refugees fleeing westwards ...'

Fighter Command's attempts to cover the Dunkirk evacuation brought more serious losses. Much of the air fighting took place out of sight of the troops and the legend sprang up among them that the RAF had let them down. It was a lie. 'I believe the BEF troops were booing the RAF in Dover the other day,' wrote Ronnie Wight to his mother. 'If anyone says anything to you in the future about the inefficiency of the RAF ... tell them from me we only wish we could do more. But without aircraft we can do no more than we have done – that is our best ... I know of no RAF pilot who has refused combat yet – and that sometimes means odds of more than fifty to one.'

The RAF operated in France in an atmosphere of unreality and wishful thinking. An echo of it is heard in an anecdote told by the New Zealand officer Arnold Wall, who, after losing an eye, was no longer fit for flying duties and was commanding a component depot near Amiens. One day he was told to expect a visit from Trenchard who was touring RAF facilities. He found him 'a bit hard of hearing, but only slightly so – extremely affable'.[50]

After lunch in the mess, Wall recorded, the great man 'drew me over to a map of North West Europe that we had pinned up on the wall. During the morning I had been skiting a bit about our mobility – we had proved we could get the show on its wheels and away within an hour of a movement order, and Boom led off with this.

'"You say you can be on the move at an hour's notice. That's good. Now tell me where you'll be moving *to*?"

'Who the hell knew that? But one had to say something, and the best I could think of was "wherever Component HQ tell us to move, sir."

'"That's not what I hoped you'd say." He sounded very serious, and all I could think of was to ask, "what should I have said, sir?"

'"I hoped you'd say 'Forward! Forward into Germany!'"

'I was disappointed in the dear old man for I thought this was a damned silly thing to say.'

The RAF's record for the first nine months of the war was largely a story of failure. The experience did not produce any fundamental re-examination of overall strategy. A committee was set up to report on the debacle in France. It was chaired by sixty-one-year-old Air Chief Marshal Sir Robert Brooke-Popham, an old-school officer who stated at the outset that it was not his intention to 'allot blame or spread whitewash'.[51] The RAF's overall performance and the appalling losses sustained in men and machines were never analysed. The tone was relentlessly positive. 'With very few exceptions the whole of the personnel interviewed were cheerful, confident and ready to do anything,' he wrote. 'Where any signs of depression existed it appeared to be mainly due to the failure to obtain any obvious results.' He was full of praise for the airmen's initiative and disregard for the 'pernicious [peacetime] doctrine of "safety first"'. In all it was 'very gratifying to see the refreshing breeze of living dangerously once more ventilating men's minds'. He could even find something nice to say about the Battles, which he believed would 'still be able to do good work' in the event of an invasion.

Years after the war senior officers were reluctant to accept that there might have been alternatives to the course of their actions in this first phase or that less costly methods might have been used to determine what was feasible and what was not, in the largely unexplored sphere of modern aerial warfare. The willingness to endure heavy losses in the knowledge that they brought negligible results was sustained in the night-bombing campaign that began in earnest later that year. 'We had to feel our way towards the development of tactics and technique that we felt sure would in the end produce results,' explained John Slessor, who took over 5 Group of Bomber Command in May 1941.[52] 'The lessons we learnt could, I am afraid, have been learnt only in the grim school of actual war experience.'

Unsurprisingly, some of the guinea pigs saw things differently. Many of those who died in the opening passage were pre-war professionals, part of the core around which the civilian air force would have to be built. 'They were proving and disproving the basic doctrines by which air warfare had to be fought, but far too few of them lived through those first few months to practice themselves the lessons they had learned,' wrote Christopher Foxley-Norris, who, having survived the French disaster and the war, ended up an air chief marshal.[53] 'The manner in which the RAF's professional manpower ... was frittered away before the war had even started for most of the participants was tragic, criminally tragic. But nobody seems to have admitted responsibility for the mistakes made or been penalized in any way for them. Reputations survived, even when aircrews did not.'

7

The Battle

On 10 September 1940, Pilot Officer George Barclay of 249 Squadron described to his parents ('darling Mummie and Far') a patrol he had flown over the Thames Estuary in his Hurricane a few days before. 'It was a grand day and from 15,000 feet the view was so delightful that one was tempted to sit there and admire it instead of searching for the Hun,' he wrote.[1] Barclay knew the landscape beneath his wings very well. He had grown up in Great Holland on the Essex coast where his father was vicar. He picked out Westgate-on-Sea which brought back memories of his old prep school, Hawtrey's, and 'flying model aeroplanes on the cliff'.

> Then there was Burnham-on-Crouch, where Norman, Eddy and I became 'photographer's assistants' for a day … and there was Rochester and I thought of Aunt Chris's former home (and 'Tuppence!') and the Archdeaconry. Then right on the horizon I could just see Clacton and in the haze I could just make out where Great Holland ought to be, though I couldn't see it.

He was hauled back to reality by the sight of the balloon barrage below and the great sprawl of London which he was there to defend. He 'spent the next several minutes searching the sky for Huns and checking over the cockpit instruments' when 'over the wireless came a shout: "Hullo leader, Messerschmitt 109s behind us in the sun …"' In the 'scrap' that followed Barclay managed to shoot down one Me 109. He then climbed to attack a formation of bombers and 'did a head-on attack on the leader. As I broke away my ammunition gave out, but I saw one of the leader's engines smoking. Now I couldn't see anything as oil was pouring out of the engine onto the windscreen and ... gave signs of packing up altogether.' Deciding he would not make it to his base at North Weald he 'made a successful crash landing in a field about five miles away ... quite OK and the Hurricane not much damaged'. He waited for some soldiers to arrive to guard the machine and arrange a lift back to his squadron. In the meantime, 'the whole local population had turned out to have a look'.

He got back just as the 249 pilots were taking off to intercept another raid but there was no serviceable Hurricane for him to fly so he 'sat in an air raid shelter and listened to two waves of Hun bombers go over after dropping bombs on London'. Signing off the letter he apologized for the central role he had given himself in the account: 'I'm afraid it's all about me but of course the rest of the squadron did their stuff and went off again after rearming.'

Barclay's account brings home vividly the intimate nature of the Battle of Britain. The pilots were looking down on the places and people they were fighting for. Looking up, the population had a grandstand view of the exploits of their champions. It was the first time in English history that a clash of almost incalculable importance had taken place under the eyes of the nation. Fighter Command's victory was a turning point in the war. It was also a defining passage in the RAF's own history.

The Battle of Britain had been given a name and invested with a significance several weeks before events began to unfold. The name was supplied by Winston Churchill in his speech to the House of Commons on 18 June 1940, in which he also set out what was at stake – no less than 'the survival of Christian civilization ... our own British way of life and the long continuity of our institutions and our Empire'.

As an attritional struggle it lacked a clear-cut beginning, climax or end. The shape that it took on was imposed retrospectively. The official opening and closing dates were set, after some deliberation, by Fighter Command's C-in-C Hugh Dowding in his despatch, submitted in August 1941. He decided that the Battle began on 10 July and ended on 31 October. The timeline was, he admitted, a matter of opinion as 'operations of various kinds merged into one another almost insensibly'.[2] The Air Ministry's own account, published by the Stationery Office at the end of 1940, chose 8 August as the beginning.

For the airmen and the civilian onlookers, the event had no neat contours. Some pilots maintained that it was only subsequently that they thought of themselves as having taken part in the Battle of Britain.

When Churchill announced its debut, he assured his audience that it would end in victory. In the fighting of May and June the RAF had 'proved itself far superior in quality both in men and in many types of machine to what we have met so far'. Despite the disadvantages of operating from foreign soil the Air Force 'had still routinely managed to inflict losses of two-and-a-half to one'. The results were even better over Dunkirk, where, he claimed, 'we undoubtedly beat the German air force which gave us mastery locally in the air and we inflicted losses of three or four to one'.

In the next round of the contest, the RAF would enjoy all the benefits of operating from their home ground. In addition, he told the House, 'our fighter air strength is stronger at the present time, relatively to the Germans who have suffered terrible losses, than it has ever been'. He now looked 'forward confidently to the exploits of our fighter pilots who will have the glory of saving their native land, their island home and all they love from the most deadly of attacks'.

The factual claims in the speech were for inspiration not information. The true loss rate for the Battle of France was more like one-to-one. His account of the air war over Dunkirk was similarly exaggerated. He also misled the country about the favourable balance of fighters. The waste of men and machines in France had been prodigious. At the start of July, the Luftwaffe had at least 760 Me 109s against Fighter Command's 591 Hurricanes and Spitfires. On the other hand, aircraft production was at last running smoothly, there was a reservoir of pilots waiting to fill the gaps in the ranks, albeit only partly trained, and a radar-directed early warning system that on paper at least looked effective.

His reference to the psychological advantage of operating from the home base seemed justified. It made a difference that the pilots were fighting to defend British rather than French families and homes. There was also the significant practical benefit that pilots who were shot down and survived would live to fight again, sometimes only a matter of hours after they baled out or crash-landed.

A clinical assessment – the sort employed by revisionist accounts written decades after the event – might rightly conclude that the RAF had no excuse for not winning the Battle of Britain. But the issue would not be decided simply by numbers and equipment. The Battle of France had proved that. The French had strong fixed defences, an enormous army and a sizeable air force, albeit equipped with second-rate aircraft, and they too were fighting for their freedom, honour and loved ones. Yet they had collapsed with astonishing speed. Morale had played an important part in the story, and, as the airmen who lived through the catastrophe observed with pity and sometimes contempt, backbone was in short supply among French soldiers and airmen in May.

The RAF had outperformed the Armée de l'Air, in combat and in resolve. In defending France, it sustained great physical damage. The battles in the skies over Flanders bore some similarities with those the airmen's fathers and uncles had fought on the ground below, only twenty-odd years before. Like them, they had been thrown, again and again, into sacrificial assaults that brought no results, by men who seemed devoid of imagination and lacked the moral courage to call a halt.

Even with all the advantages of defence, would those who had survived one holocaust be willing to face another? And how long could those who had yet to be tested be able to endure an onslaught from a Luftwaffe which, whatever Churchill said, was still immensely strong and roaring drunk on victory? Morale was a vital factor in the Battle of Britain, not just for the Fighter Boys, as the pilots soon became known, but for the British people. At the end of a summer of shared dangers, the two had been fused together in mutual affection and admiration and the RAF was fixed at the front and centre of the British war effort.

Despite the complacent tone of Brooke-Popham's analysis of the air battles of May over France and Belgium there was good reason to worry about the possible effect of the debacle on Fighter

Command's pilots. The squadrons returning from France brought back some grim tales of chaos, incompetence and pointless losses of men and machines. The hardest hit unit was 85 Squadron, which got through twenty-five Hurricanes in a matter of days. It was the physical losses that mattered more: seven pilots killed, five wounded and one taken prisoner (the standard squadron strength averaged around twenty pilots). Next hardest hit were 3 and 87 Squadrons, each of which had six pilots killed, with a further six wounded between them. It was not just a matter of filling the gaps. The trauma had the potential to undermine each unit's identity and fighting spirit.

Concern about aircrew 'waverers' began to surface in the lull between the fall of France and the start of the Battle of Britain. The subject was first aired at the Air Council meeting of 10 July when the Air Member for Personnel described the arrangements in place for dealing with 'officers who had lost the confidence of their COs in their resolution and courage in operational flying'.[3] Air Marshal Edward Gossage reported that the current practice was for them to be posted to non-operational units where they worked as ferry pilots or towing targets for air gunnery practice. By September the mood had hardened and the Council decided there would be 'no rehabilitation or continued employment on flying duties' for waverers.[4] By November they had become official pariahs. Henceforth they were to be stripped of their pilot's, observer's and air gunner's badges and reduced to the ranks and their documents stamped with the letter 'W'. A new designation of their condition made an appearance. The Council noted that 'the delinquency was not cowardice but lack of moral fibre' – soon to be abbreviated to the notorious 'LMF'.

The tough line taken by the Air Staff seems more revealing of a rather ignoble lack of confidence in their own men than of any serious problem with morale. There is little evidence, official or unofficial, that 'waverer' cases were widespread. If anything, the opposite was the case. The men who went into battle with the Luftwaffe that summer seem to have been remarkably unaffected by the precedents set in Norway and France and the doubts that sometimes surfaced about the competence of their superiors failed to dent their devotion to duty.

It was not as if they did not know what to expect. Of the twenty-five Hurricane and Spitfire squadrons in 11 Group (which covered the approaches to London and where the fighting would be fiercest) at the start of the Battle, nineteen had been in action in France or over Dunkirk. Twelve had experience of both.

Trying to analyse the elements that made up the strength of the pilots' resolve is difficult, partly because of the absence of contemporaneous data. Most participants' accounts were produced after the event and are inevitably coloured by hindsight and the narratives and attitudes that prevailed at the time of writing. The Fighter Boys left little behind in the way of letters and diaries. Either they were out of the firing line and had nothing much of significance to record, or they were in the middle of it and too busy or exhausted to pick up pen or pencil at the end of a day's fighting. However, enough of this historiographical gold dust has drifted down to us, usually brief lines favouring fact over feeling, set out in Letts wash-leather diaries or on pale blue writing paper headed with the RAF crest, to give a glimpse of the way it was in those crowded months.

One striking aspect is the almost total absence of comment about significant political and military events that take place beyond the writer's horizon. George Barclay's diary was unusual in mentioning 'all sorts of discussions' involving the 'Station Commander, the CO, "Jersey" (a Pole) and the pilots' on 'the war, the Air Force etc'. Their main concerns were about the complacency shown by politicians and the public about the task ahead. The conclusion was 'that we shall eventually win this war, but it will be the hell of a job and more so unless we pull ourselves together'.[5] Barclay was at the sophisticated end of the Fighter Boy spectrum, coming from a long line of well-educated and distinguished soldiers and churchmen and joining the RAF from the Cambridge University Air Squadron.

In almost all the other testimonies, the historical landmarks by which we gauge the progress of the war do not seem to have been much noticed by the pilots. For all the titanic importance that Winston Churchill has assumed in our understanding of the story, he did not loom large in the Fighter Boys' thoughts, for no one in these documents mentions him. Nor did the causes of the war or the underlying ideologies.

When the bombing of London began in earnest on 7 September Denis Wissler, a nineteen-year-old pilot with 17 Squadron, was moved to write in his diary: 'What complete swine these Jerries are.' Six days later, as the Blitz continued, the entry reads 'God damn and blast Hitler'.[6] Wissler was intelligent but uncomplicated, a product of Bedford School, which provided the RAF with many officers, and had joined on a short service commission a few weeks before the war started. George Barclay, who knew Nazi Germany from two trips there during school holidays and studied the language, made only one reference to the nature of the enemy when he recorded the verdict of one of the squadron's discussions: 'one German is nice, two Germans are swine'.[7]

Their emotions were focused inward, on family and friends, spreading wider to embrace service chums, the squadron and the RAF. If there is any higher sentiment on display it is a mild patriotism, not overt or noisy, rather a barely articulated assumption that Britain is a good place with values that are worth fighting and dying for.

By the summer of 1940 the dilution of the old pre-war RAF elite was well advanced. Rapid expansion meant squadrons were manned by men drawn from a wide swathe of backgrounds and from the length and breadth not just of Britain but its Dominions. As such the Air Force could, and frequently did, claim to be a representative social and geographical distillation of the nation and empire. Of the 2,340 pilots and 594 other aircrew who flew in the Battle of Britain, 1,129 joined as regulars, the biggest category (665) serving on short service commissions. Reservists made up 1,436 of the total, the great majority of them being the 1,199 men from all walks of life who joined via the RAFVR. There was also a significant contribution from the Dominions (127 New Zealanders, 97 Canadians, 29 Australians) and defeated European nations, led by Poland and Czechoslovakia, as well as adventurers and idealists from America and Ireland. It was therefore the 'citizen' element of the Air Force that made up the largest component.

The great stream of manpower that poured into the RAF at the start of the war arrived from a dozen different directions. It sounded like a recipe for turbulence. At the smaller, more manageable level of a fighter squadron, the channelling process was quite smooth. The organization proved efficient at taking the variegated human material, blending from it a powerful institutional identity and giving it a strong *esprit de corps*.

Fighter squadrons were small, about the size of an Army company, with about fifteen to twenty pilots supported by eighty or so ground and administrative staff. The scale allowed a sense of belonging, creating an emotional tug that could rival that of family. 'I returned from ten days leave today,' wrote George Barclay in his diary in the autumn of 1940. 'I've had a grand time and an excellent change … But all the same, it's very good to be back with the squadron.'[8] A few weeks later he remarked again after a shorter break that 'even after forty-eight hours it's good to be back …'

Denys Mileham was heartbroken to be posted away from 41 Squadron four months after joining it in September 1940. 'Pretty sick about being here,' he wrote to his parents from Grangemouth where he was now an instructor.[9] 'This is a lousy station after Hornchurch.' Things had not improved a few weeks later. 'I hate this place more every day … I wish I could get back to my old squadron.' Among his personal effects collected after his death in action shortly afterwards was a card from his old CO Don Finlay, well known as an Olympic hurdler before the war, who trusts he is 'still showing the squadron spirit'.

Barclay had been at Stowe and Mileham at Berkhamsted, both public schools. For the many pilots with similar backgrounds squadron life must have felt familiar. There were the same close friendships, occasional rivalries, and emphasis on boisterous, communal fun that they had known in the classrooms, dormitories and playing fields of their boyhood. This was the atmosphere that prevailed in the officers' mess and, even though one third of the airmen who took part in the Battle of Britain were sergeants, the outlook that coloured the fighter squadron identity.

In the world evoked by the letters and diaries drink plays a multiple role: as a lubricant for jollity, a salve for frayed nerves and, in dark moments, the water of oblivion. But mostly alcohol was associated with fun. Drinking sessions on the station often ended with impromptu games of rugby and the forceful removal of trousers. 'A

Denys Mileham

bit of a party in the mess,' wrote Denis Wissler on 2 July. 'Everyone in sight was debagged, me included.' He had been up since three that morning so decided to call it a night at 10.30 as he had 'the prospect of getting up again at 3'.

It was sometimes said after the war in the pilots' defence that their boozy image was misleading and that the beer that was their drink of choice had been so reduced in strength by wartime regula-tions as to be barely intoxicating. Whatever it was Wissler drank seemed to do the job – or perhaps he had a weak head. 'Went out on the piss tonight but [I am] more or less OK tonight [sic] as I write this' is the diary entry for 13 March when he was finishing his train-ing at Sutton Bridge. Three days later he 'had a drinking party with some of the instructors and really they are all damn good chaps and of course I couldn't hold the pace and I got a bit pissed'.

Unsurprisingly, his intake increased at particularly stressful times such as the latter part of April 1940 when his then unit, 43 Squadron, was standing by to be sent to France. Having survived a fortnight of hard fighting in conditions of utter chaos, he made a perilous journey back to the squadron base at Debden. There he 'got a shock' when he was summoned by the CO and told he was being transferred immediately to 17 Squadron, based at Kenley, south of London. Some friends went with him part of the way to have a farewell drink.

'We managed to get two hours in town and I had dinner alone at the Troc,' he wrote on 8 June. 'I really got completely plastered and was put to bed at Kenley by the Wing Commander there.' This saintly figure – probably the station commander Tom Prickman – then 'woke me up at 3.30 with some Alka-Seltzer, brought me his bath robe and had already run my bath'. The reason for the early start was that he was due for his first operation at dawn, flying back to France and Le Mans aerodrome with another 17 Squadron pilot, Count Manfred Czernin, to help cover the last stage of the withdrawal. Wissler was in the thick of the Battle of Britain from the end of July when drinking references fade away to be replaced by accounts of the relentless fighting.

But even the strain of being in action daily did not deter the pilots from enjoying themselves whenever the opportunity arose, and a restorative whiff of oxygen to take away the hangover did not always do the job. In an undated entry in his diary George Barclay described being scrambled one morning and trying 'to take an intelligent interest but my mouth was like the bottom of a birdcage as the result of last night's party …'

Fighter Boys loved the 'flicks' and would watch any movie the local fleapits had to offer, even if they had seen them before. The prospect of a dance was always welcome, especially if there was a healthy ratio of women to men. 'Our squadron dance took place in the village hall at Steeple Bumpstead and it was a grand success,' 73 Squadron's unofficial diarist Pilot Officer Charlie McGaw recorded on 24 September.[10] 'Fifty WAAFs from Debden arrived by devious routes. The bar was so popular during the evening that it soon ran out of refreshments.' The presence of danger added a frisson for 'as the dance finished at 22.30 hours our friend the enemy passed over-head and loosed a salvo of bombs some miles away but close enough to cause a certain amount of twittering in the feminine ranks'.

The dances were segregated with officers and other ranks holding their own events. There was, though, a certain amount of social overlapping. At Debden, the sergeant pilots of 17 Squadron held a regular Sunday night dance at which the station band, all pre-war professionals, played. It was by invitation only and officers were gratified to be asked along.

On the whole, though, at this stage of the war it was still the officers, almost all of whom were steeped in the hearty traditions of the British public school, who set the tone. It did not matter that some of the sergeant pilots came from similar backgrounds. Possession of a commission created a distinction. It is revealed unconsciously in these letters and diaries where officers are usually referred to with Christian names or nicknames attached, NCOs only by their surnames. Officialdom recognized that, in an all-out war, some credit had to be given across the board. Nonetheless the achievements of the NCOs did not get the same attention as that devoted to the feats of the officers. When Cuthbert Orde, an artist who had flown with the RFC in the First World War, was commis-sioned by the Air Ministry to draw the portraits of some celebrated Fighter Boys, only ten of the 163 who were selected to sit for him were sergeants. The exercise resulted in a book. All but three of the sixty-four rather pedestrian portraits printed were of officers.

Perhaps too much can be made of these details and it may be that conventional formalities of expression of the time disguise the degree of fraternization. In the 72 Squadron diary, the sergeant pilots listed at the back have nicknames ('Duffy' Douthwaite, 'Snowy' Winter, etc.) while 73 Squadron's shows socializing together was unremarkable. The entry for 21 September records how, on hearing that Sergeant Maurice Leng had been invited to an Army officers' dance in Saffron Walden, 'Pilot Officers Langham-Hobart, Rutter, Hoole (the engineer officer) ... decided that [he] needed support'. They set off with Leng and two other sergeants, Herbert Webster and Robert Plenderleith, and 'in spite of the fact that immaculate army types eyed their polo-neck sweaters askance, a good time was had by all'. Leng maintained after the war that 'there was no sort of officers vs sergeants ballyhoo. We were all in the same boat and there was marvellous camaraderie.'[11] The distinction was anyway usually a temporary one. Leng was commissioned in April the following year and virtually every Battle of Britain sergeant pilot ended up an officer.

Whether you wore stripes on your arm or pips on your shoulder there were governing codes and attitudes that bound the squadron together. The pervading mood was a studied cheerfulness and an *a priori* determination to make light of bad situations by understatement and attempts, no matter how feeble, at humour. Form dictated that brushes with death were to be treated as a joke. Denys Mileham passed on the news that James MacPhail, a boy he had trained with and who had come to lunch at the family home in Boxmoor, Herts, 'was shot up three days ago and had to leap out. He landed, by parachute, in a thorn bush, and is suffering from a sore bottom.' He must also have been badly burned for the records show he received plastic surgery treatment at the Queen Victoria Hospital, East Grinstead, and was one of Archibald McIndoe's 'guinea pigs'.

Barclay recorded how 'Butch Barton had to bale out when the squadron attacked some [Dorniers]. He landed quite OK and was brought back in an army car. The army couldn't make out why everyone just stood and laughed when Butch arrived, taunting him with the jibe, "shot down by a bomber!"'

If this insouciance was an act, it was remarkably well maintained. On 7 September Pilot Officer Bob Rutter of 73 Squadron wrote from St Andrew's Hospital in Billericay, Essex, to his CO Squadron Leader Maurice Robinson. Rutter was recovering from a bullet wound to his ankle, after being forced to bale out while flying alongside Robinson two days before. The letter is worth quoting in full.

> Although only slightly damaged, it appears that I shall be out
> of the show for some little time ... I followed you into the first
> attack, went into echelon and tackled the bomber to your right
> 'à la No 5 attack'! Smoke poured from his starboard engine and

as I broke away the engine was well ablaze. Turning for an attempt on the second one I noticed several 109s below. Next there was a sharp cracking as several bullets came through the floor from underneath and in front, presumably fired by the latter. I dived sharply out of trouble, as oil came spurting from the engine and covered the dashboard. The engine seemed to be running fairly well, so having wiped some of the oil from my eyes and the altimeter I noted that I was down to 5000 feet and looked round for a likely forced landing field.

The next minute there was a loud explosion from the engine followed by smoke and as I couldn't by then see anything much, baling out seemed the best course.

The machine crashed in a field and I touched down in a beet field, reached the road and was picked up some five minutes later by an ARP Warden who took me to his house. An Army Major and MO [Medical Officer] soon arrived and applied field dressings, whilst I knocked back a treble brandy, afterwards driving me here.

After an X-ray and a shot of gas I awoke to find a foot swaddled in bandages, a splint and the 'verdict.' One bullet was extracted, another went in and came out again and a bone was splintered. The wounds ought to heal in around a fortnight when the foot goes into plaster for a month so that's that.

I'm wondering how the squadron came through and whether you've had any further joy. Should you be too busy to drop me a line, will you please ask one of the boys to do so …

After asking for some personal items to be sent on he finished: 'Everybody here is thoroughly spoiling me, which is very unfair considering the Squadron is roughing it and carrying on, especially as it's due to my stupidity in getting shot down.' He signed off 'wishing you all the best of luck and good hunting and hoping to hear of your future successes'.[12]

The letter illustrates many of the virtues and qualities of the Fighter Boys: good-humoured, modest, polite but also cool, factual and competent. The apologetic and duly deferential tone towards his CO, while correct, was at odds with the facts. Rutter celebrated his twenty-first birthday two days before being shot down. However, he was far more experienced than Squadron Leader Robinson. He had fought throughout the Battle of France and was one of the last pilots to leave, flying from Nantes on 18 June. He had since been in the line with the squadron throughout the Battle of Britain. Robinson, a thirty-year-old Cranwell graduate, had done no operational flying until he took command a few weeks before.

Death's frequent appearances in these contemporary accounts are treated with routine solemnity that gets more perfunctory as time passes. On 29 September Barclay told the story of how Sergeant Edward Bayley, who flew as his number two in Red Section, 'vanished and apparently running short of oxygen ... lost consciousness and dived straight into the ground, knocking down two cottages and unfortunately three people were killed ... in peacetime it would have been a major tragedy. In war it is nothing. *C'est la guerre* ...'[13] Three weeks later, writing to his sister Mary he could not resist telling her to date he has '4½ Huns to my account as "destroyed" ... added to this I have three "probably destroyed" and six "damaged"'.

He went on: 'I suppose it sounds as if we are having a grand time – well I suppose we are really – I'm realizing an ambition, but it's a bit tough to see fellows wiped off one by one. There are only four officers in the squadron, myself included, who have come through September absolutely unscathed.' Four of his fellow pilots had been on the same course with him at Cranwell, which was turned into an OTU at the start of the war. 'I am the only survivor,' he wrote. 'Two ... are dead and two wounded. But it's remarkable how hardened one gets to people not coming back.'

Death was democratic, reaching out to claim the best pilots with the same even-handedness as it did the mediocre. Richard Lee was one of the dominant figures of 85 Squadron, bold, lively and handsome. As a Cranwell graduate he was destined for the top of the service. Denis Wissler came across him in France where Lee's reputation was made. 'Dickey Lee returned today after having crashed in German occupied Belgium and escaped in civilian clothes,' he wrote on 13 May. Six weeks later back at Debden he noted that 'Dickey Lee came down today with [his newly awarded] DSO and DFC which looked very nice. He is off flying at the moment recovering from a wound in the leg but he looks very cheerful.' Then, on 18 August, a day of huge battles, a simple entry: 'Dickey Lee ... was lost this afternoon.' Lee's end befitted his warrior spirit, shot down in the late afternoon while charging into a formation of Me 109s thirty miles off the coast of Essex.

Characters who were the life and soul of the squadron jollifications were one day no longer there. Oswald Pigg, a pre-war short service officer from Newcastle upon Tyne, features regularly in the unofficial history of 72 Squadron, based on the diaries of one of its pilots, Robert Deacon Elliot. 'That night [3 June] the whole Squadron was entertained by the Chief Constable of Gravesend in the Police Club,' reads one entry.[14] 'Transportation was a problem quickly resolved by the Gravesend Fire Chief who provided us with one of his fire engines. We swarmed onto this huge red brute – with Oswald Pigg as officer i/c Fire Bell – which he rang continuously all the way home, and in doing so brought the whole camp to a state of readiness ... the rest is a blank.'

Then, on 1 September, when the squadron was operating from Croydon: 'At 0955 we were scrambled – Squadron strength – and soon in the thick of it again. Enemy aircraft were everywhere it seemed. A terrific scrap with Me109s and once more we suffered a setback. F/O Oswald Pigg missing – and many days later confirmed killed. He was found buried under his Spitfire in some remote wood in Kent. A most cheerful fellow and an aggressive fighter in the air. He had a sister in the WAAF ...'

There was little time and no purpose in dwelling on these things. Occasionally, though, melancholy thoughts intruded. On 6 August Denis Wissler recorded matter-of-factly the death of Pilot Officer Henry Britton who 'returned to Debden after circling this 'drome [Martlesham] after taking off on patrol and later while testing he stalled in a turn and crashed and was killed'. Four days later, though, he was forced to reflect on the event. 'Had the day off,' he wrote. 'I attended P/O Britton's funeral and it was the most harrowing affair I have ever come upon.' The lesson was that life was too short to cry.

'I had a good time in the evening when I went to Cambridge to see a flick and then went to an Indian restaurant and had a fine curry, getting back to Debden at 12.30 approx.'

The airmen were sustained by the same thought that every soldier and sailor carried into battle with them since warfare began. The man standing next to you might be killed. But you, somehow, would survive. 'I feel invincible in the air,' wrote George Barclay. 'Probably experienced and older people would call it gross overconfidence, but I'm sure the average pilot is invincible in his own mind until he gets beaten up.'

They were also driven by a desire to succeed, for themselves, the squadron and the nation. Churchill had established the burden of responsibility resting on their young shoulders. The message was reinforced early in June by a letter from Dowding addressed to 'My Dear Fighter Boys'. After telling them how proud he was of their performance in northern France he spelled out the task ahead: 'I want you to know that my thoughts are always with you and that it is you and your fighting spirit which will crack the morale of the German Air Force and preserve our Country through the trials which yet lie ahead.'[15]

Fighting spirit on its own was not enough. A very specific sort of skill was needed in aerial combat. To shoot down an enemy aircraft a pilot had to manoeuvre into position, hold the target in his sights or calculate the angle at which he needed to deflect his bullets for the victim to fly into them, then keep the fire hosing into the fabric of the aircraft long enough to kill the captain or hit a vital part. It required a certain ruthlessness and detachment as well as outstanding dexterity and physical toughness. Attacks on bomber formations were usually followed by dogfights as the escorting fighters intervened. The dives and tight turns of these combats had alarming physical results. Steep turns caused the pilot to black out. The centrifugal forces made the blood feel as heavy as molten metal and gravitational pull of seven 'g' meant a man normally weighing 180lb now weighed 1,260lb.[16]

To succeed required not just flying ability but exceptional determination. Denis Wissler did not regard himself as a particularly good pilot and his diary is touching in its frank depiction of his shortcomings, disappointments and frustrations as he struggled to get off the mark. Mechanical problems with his aircraft or the vagaries of the duty roster meant that for one reason or another he never seemed to be flying when the squadron had a good day. Much of July was spent operating out of Debden and Martlesham Heath carrying out routine shipping patrols over the Channel and responding to 'flaps' which produced no action. Days went by without an enemy aircraft being sighted. His first combat of the Battle of Britain was an unsatisfactory affair. On 27 July while patrolling with his flight commander Alf Bayne and Harold 'Birdy' Bird-Wilson they encountered a Heinkel 111 being 'half-heartedly attacked by Spitfires'. They joined in, making 'a head-on attack and then an astern attack, pieces and oil coming out in all directions. The enemy aircraft slowly went down to the water. I thought it was trying to get away low down and made another head-on attack. This time it went into the water.' He watched as three crewmen climbed out into a dinghy then 'called up over the R/T for a boat to be put out'.

Wissler's flat account does not suggest he regarded this as a glorious encounter. It was not until 25 August, when the squadron was operating out of Tangmere and the Luftwaffe's assault on Fighter Command airfields was raging, that his doubts about himself seem to drop away and the tone changes to that of a competent and confident young warrior. 'This was a hard day being at 15 minutes and readiness the day long,' he wrote. 'At about half-past seven we had a hell of a scrap over Portland in which about 100 [aircraft] were engaged. Flt Lt Bayne made an attack below and astern quarter, the Me110 whipped up in a stall turn and I gave him a long burst while he was in a stalled condition. It fell over and went down. I then went on my own and made a Me110 break formation. I gave it another burst and it went down towards the sea.' Success tasted good. Five days later a rumour went around that the squadron was to be taken out of the line and posted to Northern Ireland. 'I hope not', reads the scrawled diary entry.

George Barclay's eagerness can be measured in his frustration and annoyance on the occasions when he checked on the 'state board' which listed the pilots who would be operating that day and the level of readiness (an hour, fifteen minutes etc.). 'I was off the state in the morning and was very angry ... because of it,' he wrote on 2 September. Three days later he was 'off the state again today worst luck'.

Barclay was an excellent pilot who loved flying. He had absorbed his father's creed and was a committed Christian. His beliefs did not blunt the unwavering hostility towards the would-be invaders whom he despatched with satisfied efficiency. In September, he destroyed at least two Messerschmitt 109s and Dornier 17 and Junkers 88 bombers as well as sharing a Dornier 215. His descriptions of the battles are unemotional. 'There was a good scrap over the Channel about eight miles off Folkestone,' he wrote on 15 October. 'I got a "probable" 109. He flew straight across my bows – I gave him a long burst and he went over on his back and went down seemingly out of control. I continued to fire at various deflections and he streamed glycol.' He had to break off when he was set upon by seven 109s but 'they were quite easy to evade so low down (5,000 feet)'. It must have been a hectic few minutes but he nonetheless enjoyed the flight back to base: 'It was fun skimming ... over Kent at 800 feet below cloud. Had a wonderful view of Canterbury Cathedral ...'

Barclay did not disguise his aggressive instincts and delight in victory. 'I saw five 109s at about 2000 feet streaking for home and pulling the plug gave chase,' he wrote on 7 November. 'I caught them and had a dogfight with one. Eventually he went into a climb and I saw that his engine had stopped. Whoopee!'

Contemporaneous accounts like this confirm the pilots' subsequent assertion that they felt they were attacking machines rather than men. One November afternoon curiosity took Barclay to view a Dornier 17 that had been shot down nearby. It was a curiously unaffecting experience. 'There were bits of German everywhere, but so mangled that it wasn't as gruesome as one would have thought – the toes of one foot rather put me off, but in the failing light it didn't look too human.'

Success was regarded as collective as much as individual, a cause for celebration by the entire squadron as well as the victorious pilot. Barclay recorded how when a batch of decorations were announced to four squadron members 'great jubilations and a most monumental party was the result', starting at an Epping pub, the Thatched House, which was only two miles from the base, before moving on to the mess. Boasting and line-shooting on the other hand were distinctly bad form. Denis Wissler recounted the reaction to a press interview given by a 17 Squadron pilot, Count Manfred Czernin, who, though born in Berlin, the son of an Austrian diplomat, had an English mother and had been educated at Oundle public school. 'Czernin has been shooting a grand line in the Daily Sketch about his dog and the number of enemy he has shot down,' he wrote on 2 August. 'It is treated with derision up here.' The temptation to mock led some of the pilots to write to the paper claiming the Count had been too modest and his true score was not eight enemy aircraft but eighteen.

The cult of understatement was so strong that pilots could not even admit in the privacy of their own diaries to any satisfaction when their efforts were recognized. On 12 November Barclay recorded: 'I was awarded the DFC – this morning the Wing Commander announced it. I don't feel I deserve a medal and I feel still less like the dashing type one imagines wins medals!' He spent the following morning at work on his tunics, 'sewing, sewing, sewing', not just the purple and white DFC ribbon but the stripes to mark moving up a rank to flying officer.

Collective pride was matched by an unwillingness to advertise failure. Not every pilot was a hero, but one has to look hard for evidence of dereliction of duty. 'The squadron ran into some 270 E/A [enemy aircraft],' Denis Wissler wrote on 19 August, 'P/O Solomon being shot down. FO X led his section back as soon as he saw the enemy and Sgt Y broke away and came home from the CO's section.' Underlying the reticence, perhaps, is the understanding that only another fighter pilot could have of how much resolve it needed to persevere, and the sympathy for those who faltered that went with it.

Congratulating Paul Richey after the publication of Fighter Pilot, a brilliant first-hand account of the fighting in France, his old 1 Squadron comrade Mark 'Hilly' Brown wrote: 'I like the way you have been so kind about the whole thing, Paul. Anyone who turned out dead-beat was left completely out and everyone's faults or shortcomings completely ignored. The squadron's history is now written as it should be.'[17]

There seems to have been little feeling among the pilots that they were operating inside a much bigger and steeply hierarchical structure. Identity and loyalty was focused on the squadron but extended to the other fighter units they fought alongside. Senior figures made appearances from time to time. Trenchard invited himself on a tour of fighter bases in June and gave the young pilots the benefit of his First World War wisdom, assuring 72 Squadron that 'there was no doubt in his mind that we would win through again'.[18] The 12 Group Commander Trafford Leigh-Mallory and 11 Group's C-in-C Keith Park visited frequently. Even 'Stuffy' Dowding took time from his crushing responsibilities to go to 249 Squadron to buck them up with the welcome news that new Mark II Hurricanes with improved Merlin engines and 20mm cannon instead of .303 Brownings for armament were on the way. These events merited only fleeting mentions. Denis Wissler recorded the arrival of the Duke of Kent to Tangmere in the middle of the desperate battles of late August for which the pilots had to line up for inspection at their dispersal huts just as they were ready to take off: 'He however only shook hands with us and asked how long we had been in the service and the squadron.'

The battlefield the pilots was fighting in was enormous – the whole realm of the skies – and the experience was essentially a lonely one. Once in combat, fighter pilots were on their own for it was impossible for a commander to control the actions of his men. Each had to respond to events, usually at lightning speed, with his own instincts and judgements. By contrast on the ground life was intensely collegiate, focused on the squadron and the base with little sense of a connection to the vast Air Force organization beyond the camp gates.

In these circumstances, the role of leaders took on a particular importance and their faults and qualities could have a considerable effect on levels of efficiency and morale. A popular and respected CO boosted spirits. Ronny Lees, the thirty-year-old Australian-born commander of 72 Squadron and a pre-war RAF professional, was a genial, fatherly figure to his men, making Robert Deacon Elliot 'feel very much at home' when he turned up as a raw RAFVR acting pilot officer at a snowbound Drem in Scotland in December 1939. He was also efficient, spotting fatal gaps in his pilots' training and trying to fill them. In the spring of 1940, while many squadrons were still pursuing the pre-war obsession with tight formation flying, he concentrated on night flying and air-to-air live firing practice, both hideously neglected in the pre-squadron training curriculum.

In the Dunkirk fighting, the squadron was based at Gravesend and Lees led from the front, destroying a Junkers 87 on 2 June. Then, wrote Deacon Elliot on 21 July, came 'a very sad day for the Squadron. News of the CO's posting to 13 Group Headquarters as Wing Commander operations came as a shock to us all … it was difficult to envisage the squadron under any other's command … his dynamic leadership, both on the air and on the ground, his deep understanding and the fine example he always set endeared him to officers and men alike.'

Lees was given a true Fighter Boy send-off, debagged after a scrum in the Schooner pub at Alnmouth, near the base at Acklington. The choice of replacement was one that, once again, caused wonderment at the mental processes of the Air Ministry personnel department. Squadron Leader Anthony Collins was another pre-war regular, whose last experience of operations had been against tribesmen in northern Iraq in the early 1930s. According to Deacon Elliot, 'he was a photographic expert and … came straight to the Squadron from his office in the Air Ministry, having not flown Spitfires before'. Elsewhere his previous appointment is listed as 'Officer i/c Photography at Coastal Command, Lee-on-Solent'.[19] Either way, 'we all thought this was not a very prudent move by higher authority nor was it fair on either the individual or the squadron'.

On 31 August, the squadron moved to Biggin Hill and were in action later that day. It was Collins's first operational mission and he was shot down, crash-landing near Hawkhurst. Although 'very shaken he came back for more'. A few days later he was in trouble again after a combat with Messerschmitt 110s over Herne Bay. He was wounded in the knee and hand and did not return to the squadron after treatment. Meanwhile, Ronny Lees had chosen to spend a week's leave flying with his old comrades. The fact that he too was shot down on the same day in combat south of Dungeness was evidence of the truth that experience only provided limited protection in the kaleidoscopic violence of air combat.

Some commanders managed to create a family atmosphere in the unit. Having a wife helped. At 73 Squadron, the diary notes, 'Mrs Robinson, the CO's better half, has got us adopted by a knitting circle.' She also 'collected all our "smalls" and took them off to launder them', and the following day 'brought our laundry back, beautifully done'. Station commanders like Victor Beamish at North Weald and Dick Grice at Biggin Hill imposed their big personalities on those they led, inspiring, cheering and sympathizing with pilots, ground crew, WAAFs and administrators alike.

Some leaders, though, seem to have made little impression. Denis Wissler barely mentions his first CO, Ralph MacDougall. When he was posted away to be a fighter controller on 17 July, he decided 'first impressions' of his replacement Cedric Williams 'are not good'. Williams was thirty years old, a Cranwell graduate who later returned to the college staff and seems to have moved to his new command from a post in the Air Ministry Directorate of Intelligence without any direct experience of the air war to date.

Wissler noted a few days later following a session of 'practice attacks' that 'the CO had never done them'. A few weeks later he records grumpily that after a day involving several patrols and 'flaps' 'the CO had the bright idea of doing attacks at 9.15 [p.m.]'. 'They were a failure and the CO lost us, what with darkness and mist. We did not get back until 10.15 [7 August].' On 25 August comes the laconic entry: 'SL Williams lost. Wing shot off.' He went down in the sea after launching a head-on attack on a Messerschmitt 110. By then his determination and keenness had brought some reward. Before he died he claimed a Dornier 17 and a Junkers 88 destroyed.

The upper levels of Fighter Command seem wisely to have made little attempt to interfere with the raw tactical conduct of the battle and left it to the pilots themselves to devise a methodology based on reality instead of theory. Carefully constructed pre-war drills, though, continued to be practised almost to the end of the summer. In the meantime, the pilots worked out their own tactics. In late

September, as fighters began to operate in wing formations, George Barclay described getting together with 46 Squadron to devise a system where one squadron was flanked by two sections of the other weaving protectively alongside. A few weeks later they agreed on a drill to 'work in sections of four and break away in pairs if attacked by 109s'.

The pilots, though, had no control over how, when and where they went into battle. Their daily lives were completely ruled by the decisions made by the officers who directed the squadrons' response to raids from the sector ops rooms. The relationship between controllers and pilots was tense. The contemporaneous accounts brim with exasperation. In mid-September, the 73 Squadron diary announced that 'faith in the ops room which continues to give "scramble" orders while still calling the squadron to "readiness" is dwindling. Soon we will be getting "scrambles" when we are on leave! That is if we ever get any leave!!'

The overcautious ordering of alerts meant that a pilot's day could stretch from 3 a.m. to 10 p.m., hours that were spent sitting around dispersal where the aircraft were parked and doing little or no flying but nonetheless simmering in a state of anticipation that did not allow the real rest that they all desperately needed.

By 4 July Denis Wissler was complaining that he had been 'up at 3 again this morning. I am getting a bit tired of seeing the dawn break … we are now sleeping at the dispersal hut in order to get a little more sleep.' A month later things were no better: 'We went over to Martlesham today and did quite a bit of flying,' he wrote on 6 August. 'We did not see any Jerries though we chased some invisible ones. We were at readiness again until well after dark. Blast operations.'

Worse was when the instructions given by control either failed to put the squadron in a good attacking position or left them danger-ously exposed to the enemy. On 23 September 73 Squadron's day got off to a bad start when they were served an inedible mess of 'mince' for breakfast. They were then ordered to take off from Debden and join up with 257 Squadron at nearby Castle Camps to intercept a raid. They were to be covered by 17 Squadron, also at Debden, but they 'failed badly in their necessary task, and aided by what can only be described as crass stupidity on the part of Ops, the squadrons were broken up by Me 109s'.

The debacle – 'for debacle it was' – began when, while patrolling at 20,000 feet, the squadrons were ordered to come down to 10,000 feet, thereby losing the advantage of height. James Smith, the Canadian pilot officer who was leading the patrol, 'promptly and wisely questioned this but the order was confirmed, so being left no option he began to go down'.

> Disaster then came among us. At 17,000 feet when 17 Squadron had left the tail completely uncovered, Me 109s ... hurtled down from the sun and the formations went over like ninepins. The first news the ground staff had ... was the arrival of Sgt Webster, seething with rage and with machine well bullet-marked. One bullet had struck an ammo tank in the port gun bay and exploded a belt of rounds and weakened the wing struts ... of the twelve machines which had taken off only eight returned ...

Miraculously, all the pilots survived, two ditching into the sea, one crash-landing and one baling out, though two were severely burned. The incident served to further reduce the squadron's already diminishing reserves of enthusiasm and energy.

The diary reveals a pattern of initial eagerness gradually being eroded by the endless grind of action. At the beginning of September 73 Squadron was based at Church Fenton, out of the front line of the battle and chafing at the bit. 'Nothing ever seems to happen to us these days,' lamented Hugh Eliot, who was by then the squadron 'Venerable Bede' charged with chronicling their story. 'There are still rumours and hopes of a move towards the South but the days pass and it never comes.' The following day 'everyone's spirits rose a mile today when the news came to stand by for a temporary move to Duxford'. It was not to be but two days later they were installed at Debden and in action within a few hours. 'The Hun came over at 1300 hrs and we were after him like a shot,' reads the entry for 5 September. This first encounter was a painful one. The diary claims one enemy aircraft damaged and one 'probable' but the likelihood is only one Heinkel 111 was hit and managed to make it back to its base in France. Four of the squadron's aircraft were shot down, including that of the CO, Maurice Robinson, and Sergeant Alexander McNay was killed, though his death was not confirmed for several days. However, the following day the diary's cheerful note was maintained: 'Another bright day and everyone looking forward to more hunting.' The upbeat commentary continued as the squadron's performance improved 'with everyone ... elated by our success'.

The mood started to change on 14 September, 'our blackest day', when four aircraft were shot down, one of them in a friendly-fire clash with a Spitfire, and a pilot killed. Clear skies and good visibility became much less welcome. It was cloud and mist that they were now longing for. 'Glorious "pilots weather" today', reads the entry for 19 September, 'raining like blazes and blowing half a gale'. But the following day 'our luck did not hold ... and the morning turned out bright if somewhat windy.' Eight days later comes the complaint that 'this weather will persist in being cold and sunny. No rest for the wicked.' By 2 October there is no pretence at enthusiasm. 'As the day dawned windy and misty our hearts cheered as we said, "Ah, real pilots weather at last" but it was spoken too soon and the sky cleared by 11.' The sentiment was shared by Denis Wissler on 13 October: 'The weather again today was clear and bright,' he wrote. 'Oh for some clouds and rain.'

The diminishing appetite for danger does not seem to have been primarily the result of mounting fear or fraying nerves. Pilots would say after the Battle that they were frequently terrified but this is not particularly apparent in what was written at the time. Wissler's diary is candid but there is only one reference to feeling fear in the air; and that was when he flew into flak while patrolling over France on 12 June ('most terrifying') rather than during a dogfight. He had another 'most terrifying' experience on 11 September, this time during a visit to London where he was caught in the nightly Blitz.

George Barclay wrote that 'the worst part of the job is the few minutes before we actually get scrambled – when we know we are going off shortly. Once we are in the air, everything is OK.' He was on the ground at North Weald on 3 September when the tannoy warned of approaching hostile aircraft and ordered everyone to take cover. He 'hopped into the shelter and almost immediately hell was let loose. 250 bombs were dropped – the noise quite unbelievable and it seemed as if we were bound to get hit by at least one. The noise was utterly terrifying whilst it lasted …' He emerged 'to see the aerodrome enveloped in a vast cloud of smoke and dust'. He concluded 'if bombs are going to be dropped – give me an aeroplane every time'.

The Luftwaffe assault was directed at civilians and airmen alike and the pilots were well aware that the danger was shared by everyone. Two of Barclay's uncles, one an Anglican missionary, were killed when a bomb struck Church House in Westminster on 14 October, close to where Wissler's parents lived in Dolphin Square.

Barclay had been impressed by the sang-froid of the base personnel when the Luftwaffe struck, noting that 'the WAAFs took the bombing as staunchly as did the men'. The stoicism and devotion to duty the pilots saw around them and on their trips up to town left them in no doubt that they did not have a monopoly on courage and resolution.

The most insidious enemy of morale was fatigue. The references to exhaustion become a trope of Wissler's diary as the days pass and the Germans keep on coming: 'We are all awfully tired tonight' (5 July); 'I shall sleep very well tonight given half a chance' (23 July); 'God were we tired this evening' (25 July). Once while flying a patrol he 'felt very tired going round and round and only just managed to stop myself dozing off'.

George Barclay described in an undated, barely punctuated entry written in a scrawl that gives it a pungent immediacy of being woken at 4.30 a.m. in the dispersal hut, climbing into his Irvin fur-lined flying suit and taking down the blackout on the window to see a lovely autumn morning with a duck-egg-blue sky half covered with high cloud. 'John came and looked over my shoulder: "Another bloody fine day," he said with disgust … now a fine sunny day meant flying, flying, flying and terrific tension all day gazing endlessly into the burning sun to see what wily Hun was lurking there …'

He walked out 'almost asleep' to his Hurricane and went through his checks: tanks full, trail trimming wheel neutral, airscrew fine pitch, directional gyro set, gloves in their compartments, helmet with oxygen and R/T leads connected: 'in fact as I liked it, everything set for a quick getaway'. He went back into the hut to find his friend Tom Neil fully dressed but 'fast asleep in a deckchair, his head lolling on his yellow Mae West'. He lay down on a bunk and 'immediately became unconscious as if doped ...' He woke 'with a terrific start to see everyone pouring out of the hut, putting on Mae Wests, silk gloves ... I could hear the telephone orderly repeating "Dover – 20,000. Fifty plus bandits approaching from South East." Percy shouted scramble George, [you] lazy bastard and automatically I ran out parachute on, pulled into cockpit by crew who had already started up the engine, straps, helmet, gloves, check the knobs, taxi out, get into right position in my section and take off. I put the R/T on and only then do I wake up and realise l am in the air flying No 2 in Yellow section.'

In these hectic conditions there was no time to brood. It was in the slack time that the doubts surfaced and the glooms descended. Denys Mileham strayed from the habitually optimistic tone of his letters home to admit, shortly after his return from France in June: 'The strain of everything is almost unbearable at times. I have lost so many friends ...' At about the same time Denis Wissler confided to his diary: 'Oh God I do wish this war would end.' It was another three months, though, before he admitted to feeling 'very depressed tonight. I don't know why, just a passing mood.'

Aided by the entries in his diary, Robert Deacon Elliot later tried to analyse the emotional journey the Battle had taken him on. 'Looking back over the past weeks of intensive activity in the South I vividly recall that my reactions went through three most distinctive phases,' he wrote. 'The first being one of exhilaration; the intense excitement of mixing with the enemy and the determination to shoot something down. Then oneself having been shot down a time or two, and shot at on countless occasions, became a little more wary with more emphasis on trying to stay alive ... Finally, towards the end and during the days before we moved North again, every mission was the same to me. I did not really mind or care whether or not I survived. Perhaps in this I was not alone. I'm not being smug in thinking these reactions were unique. I'm sure they were not.'[20]

Survive he did, both the Battle and the war, remaining in the RAF and retiring an air vice marshal. Denis Wissler did not. He was shot down off the Essex coast while attacking Junkers 87s on 11 November, just after getting engaged to Edith Heap, a WAAF he met at Debden and with whom he fell immediately in love. George Barclay made it through but only just. On Friday 29 November, during a routine patrol over Kent:

> Suddenly four explosions down my right-hand side. I realized they were cannon shells and as I whipped into a left hand turn … two more explosions and something hit me hard in the right leg but it didn't hurt. I felt waves of hot air and the Hurricane went into a spin from which I couldn't recover so I decided to bale out. All this of course in a couple of seconds. Back with the roof, straps undone and lean out and push with feet on dashboard – no result – back into cockpit, undo oxygen bayonet connection and try again. This time I'm out straightaway and fell forward over the leading edge missing the propeller by inches![21]

As he tumbled out, he was face upwards and noted the presence of one of his boots falling above him. '[I] began to spin to the left as I lay on my back, ever faster until it became unpleasant. Meanwhile I felt for the rip-cord with both hands.' As soon as he found it he was 'quite happy and settled down to the novel sensation of dropping through space, but the spin had become unpleasantly fast to the left so I put out my right arm and gradually slowed up'. He tried to turn onto his front but 'was quite helpless … I eventually succeeded by drawing up my legs and I slowly rolled over but couldn't see the ground owing to the wind in my eyes.'

Looking up he could see his Hurricane 'spinning furiously directly above me and as I watched a large puff of white smoke shot out of it as if there had been an explosion inside. But I was so enjoying myself, nothing seemed to matter in the least.' Feeling he had delayed the drop quite long enough, he pulled the cord and 'the parachute streamed out between my feet and there was a small jerk followed immediately by a pretty severe jerk which … caused me to do a complete somersault and my second boot came off, and there I was, dangling in complete silence at about 2,000 feet.'

He was lucky not to be obliterated by his Hurricane which hurtled past and 'spun in', bursting into flames. He made a good landing in an apple orchard and was soon surrounded by locals who put him in a car which took him to Pembury Hospital in Tunbridge Wells. He calculated he had fallen about 18,000 feet before his parachute opened – pilots were told to delay pulling the cord for as long as possible to reduce the risk of colliding with friendly aircraft or being shot up by the Germans, an occasional additional hazard.[22] The descent was witnessed by Miss Christina Barclay, an elderly relation who lived near the hospital. A week later he visited her to celebrate his twenty-first birthday.[23]

By then, all chronologies agreed, the Battle was over. The great armadas of bombers were no longer seen in daylight and the Luftwaffe effort had switched to the night-time Blitz that would persist until late the following spring. It was an ordeal, but it did not feel like the prelude to invasion.

In no time at all the victory was mythologized. The legend was built while the fighting was still raging. The Air Ministry promoted vigorously Fighter Command's achievements. Pilots made evening broadcasts on the BBC during the Battle and continued to recount their exploits on the airwaves for months afterwards, reading out scripts written for them by Air Ministry hacks in a curious Hollywood-tinged style. Some of the propaganda effort was directed across the Atlantic, in keeping with Churchill's strategy of trying to persuade the United States that Britain was a worthwhile ally. On 13 July, pilots at Debden were ordered to carry out aerobatics for the benefit of a visiting team from *Life*, the American photo magazine with a circulation of nearly twenty million. The material arrived too late for a long article in the issue of 15 July which announced that 'the preliminaries of the Battle of Britain have already begun' and declared 'above all ... the 300,000 men of the Royal Air Force are the real shield of England'.

On the stout foundations of the Battle, the Air Ministry publicists built an image and a story that would endure when press cuttings were forgotten. A team of writers, artists and photographers was sent out to tour the bases gathering material for books.

In 1941 Cecil Beaton produced a record of all aspects of the RAF which came with a written commentary, but in the preface it was Fighter Command that moved him to rapture. 'Never before have battles been fought six miles above the surface of the earth at a speed of over three hundred miles an hour,' he wrote. 'Never before has it happened that the English hero, who, having shot down a German, has in turn immediately afterwards himself been shot down to return home by Tube, feeling, as he says, "rather depressed."' He concluded: 'A new model of men has been cast. The feats of their bravery haunt us, they baffle us, and satisfy completely the spirit of romantic daring inherent in our island race ... part of the sailing tradition and feeling of freedom and adventure that is the heritage from Drake ... and the Englishman who enjoyed drifting along with the breezes in his boat at four knots an hour is the father of the boy who now wishes to beat the winds in his Hurricane.'[24]

The war had already produced one RAF film, *The Lion Has Wings*, rushed out in the first months to reassure the public that the Air Force was well able to protect the nation from aerial attack. It was a mixture of documentary and with filmed reconstructions (some of it footage from MGM's abandoned *Shadow of the Wing*) and skilfully edited actuality. It was 'a hodgepodge' according to Michael Powell who worked on it, and looked distinctly dated by the time it appeared, as well as inaccurate.[25]

The Battle provided a wonderful basis for something more lasting and worthwhile. The British film industry rose to the occasion with *The First of the Few*, a much more subtle affair which approached the saga through the parable of R. J. Mitchell and the Spitfire. The plot, which did not handicap itself with too close an association with hard fact, presented the designer as a lone genius who overcame characteristic British indifference and sloth to provide the nation with the means of salvation. The Spitfire is a symbol of a more positive manifestation of Britishness – small, perhaps, but beautiful and powerful, and determined and deadly when its freedom is threatened. The photography of Mitchell's masterpiece in flight is accompanied by music by Vaughan Williams to add to the impression of airy joyfulness. Leslie Howard, an established romantic star in Britain and Hollywood, drove the enterprise, producing and directing and taking the starring role. It also featured David Niven who had generously overlooked the slights he had received at the hands of the RAF to appear as a station commander. Combat footage was cut in with staged take-offs and landings and ground scenes using Battle of Britain pilots and a staged dogfight between Spitfires and a captured Heinkel 111. *The First of the Few* did not appear until the summer of 1942 and was loved by the public and critics alike ('a tribute and a record true', according to the *Daily Herald*).[26]

By then the Battle of Britain was officially embedded in the national story. In September that year King George VI led a service of thanksgiving in Westminster Abbey, starting a tradition that lasts to this day, and plans were announced for the construction of a memorial chapel there, the first of many monuments to the pilots.

Nothing like the Battle would ever happen again. Soon after its end changes at the top of Fighter Command ensured that henceforth the Fighter Boys would be fighting a very different war. In an impressive display of ruthlessness, the new Chief of the Air Staff, Charles Portal, shunted Dowding aside, though he had made it clear he was eager to stay on. He was replaced by Sholto Douglas, Deputy Chief of the Air Staff, who was heavy-set, self-regarding and ambitious. He had made Dowding's life difficult during the toughest weeks of the fighting by supporting the 12 Group commander Trafford Leigh-Mallory's advocacy of massed 'Big Wing' formations over the smaller numbers and defensive approach favoured by Dowding and the 11 Group commander, Keith Park.

The Battle of Britain was a defining moment in the history of the RAF, as it was for the nation. Success brought the service its own cherished victory, one that rang with the same historic resonance as Trafalgar and Waterloo. Those battles came with the names of Nelson and Wellington attached to them. Uniquely in British history, this one belonged not to an individual but a group. The country owed its salvation to the Air Force and in particular the young men of Fighter Command. There was little time to savour the victory. One challenge was immediately replaced by another, in which the prospects of success were far less promising.

8

Fighting the Night

One night in the early summer of 1941, the men of 151 Squadron crowded into the guardroom of their base at Wittering to examine a German airman who was the sole survivor from a bomber that had just been shot down. 'We all gathered round to have a look at him,' wrote Pilot Officer Harry Bodien to his sister Vina.[1]

'He was a dirty looking bugger with close cropped hair and only stood five feet nothing. The CO is not friendly with Huns and made the interpreter ask if he got his two Iron Crosses for bombing women and children. That rather shook him but he was shaken a lot more when he was told we were going to shoot him at 5 o' clock in the morning.'

The letter was written when nightly raids on British cities were fresh in everyone's memories. The harsh tone fitted the grim struggle that the RAF had been waging all winter.

The aftermath of the Battle of Britain brought no sense of euphoria. Its ending was scarcely perceptible, for as one threat faded another arrived. It would take different skills, qualities and technologies to confront the new danger. Even before 15 September, the climax of the daytime battle, the Luftwaffe had opened a new front. On 7 September, the systematic bombing of London began. The capital was attacked on fifty-six out of the following fifty-seven days, from October mostly after dark. In November, the Blitz was extended to industrial cities in the Midlands, then, as German strategy focused on cutting Britain's transatlantic lifeline, on major ports. The Blitz hit civilians in a way that the Battle of Britain had not. More than 40,000 men, women and children were killed and a million houses destroyed. The suffering was felt in virtually every big population centre. Before it ended, the inhabitants of Belfast, Bristol, Birmingham, Cardiff, Coventry, Glasgow, Hull, Liverpool, Manchester, Newcastle, Portsmouth, Plymouth, Sheffield and Swansea had heard the wail of the sirens, run for shelter and cellar, felt the thud of falling bombs and emerged to see their old familiar streets, shattered and smoking.

The pre-war neglect of night-flying training and lack of research into the question of how to intercept raiders in the dark were laid bare by the Luftwaffe's switch to a night offensive. Initially, the heroes of Fighter Command were mostly powerless to stop the continuous incursions and the bomber fleets had the run of the skies.

Radar offered a solution. However, in the run-up to the war, Britain's first priority was a warning system to alert defending fighters to attacks from the sea, which the Chain Home radar stations did with great success. There had not been time to build a network that looked inland so that once a raider crossed the coast it could only be tracked by the eyes and ears of the Observer Corps, a situation that Churchill described as 'a transition from the middle of the Twentieth Century to the early Stone Age'.[2] Work was underway to create an all-round terrestrial radar network, as well as developing miniature sets that could be carried in aircraft, but it had not got far when the German focus shifted.

Only eight squadrons specialized in night fighting. They flew in Blenheims which were too slow to catch the bombers they were supposed to destroy and whose Mark I Air Interception (AI) radar had a range of only two miles. From October, regular Fighter Command squadrons were told to concentrate on night flying. However, their main function at first seems to have been to try and reassure those on the ground that something was being done to protect them. Any impression of security was, as the Air Ministry well knew, illusory. In the first ten weeks of the Blitz the Luftwaffe flew 12,000 night sorties, mostly against London. Eighty-one enemy aircraft were destroyed, most by guns and only eight by fighters. This equated to a very light loss rate of less than 1 per cent, placing no strain on replacement of men or machines and allowing the Luftwaffe to carry on indefinitely.[3]

The first the men of 264 Squadron heard about their new role was when they received a visit from the commander of 12 Group, Trafford Leigh-Mallory. The squadron had been badly mauled in the hectic fighting of late August while operating out of Hornchurch. They flew the Boulton Paul Defiant, a hybrid fighter which was reasonably fast and manoeuvrable and had a four-gun turret mounted behind the cockpit. It achieved some success shooting down bombers but the turret's field of fire was severely restricted. Against Messerschmitt 109s it was extremely vulnerable, and defenceless when attacked head-on. After losing eight aircraft within three days at the end of August, 264 were withdrawn to lick their wounds at Kirton-in-Lindsey in Lincolnshire. Such was the weight of casualties that the most senior pilot left alive and uninjured was a twenty-year-old pilot officer, Sam 'Tommy' Thomas.

The crews were not very impressed by their VIP visitor. One of the pilots, Desmond Hughes, recalled a 'somewhat pompous and over-weight' figure who sat in a deckchair in the warm sunshine with the pilots and gunners at his feet and delivered a pep talk.[4] He finished by ordering them to be ready for night operations by the time the next full moon period arrived. The instruction confirmed that, henceforth, the main fighter effort would be conducted in darkness not in daylight. The reference to moonlight was acknowledgement that, in confronting the night raiders, the crews would have no electronic aids to guide them and would have to rely on their eyes.

It was a situation they had been given virtually no preparation for. 'It was a new way of life altogether,' wrote Hughes. 'Gone were the endless days of fluctuating states of readiness; gone the frenetic scrambles ... gone the dog-fighting.' but also 'gone the constant peril of being jumped by 109s'. The main enemies were the darkness and the weather which would 'kill more night fighter crews than the Luftwaffe air gunners ever did ...'

Flying in darkness was counter-intuitive. It meant placing utter reliance in what your instruments said, rather than on what your senses told you. Learning this rule was essential to survival. Shortly after dusk on a moonless night Hughes watched 'one Defiant take off and instead of climbing straight ahead, go into a slow turn to port. It got no higher than 150 feet before it began to lose height again and flew into the ground, exploding into a ball of flame.' The pilot, Derek O'Malley, and New Zealand-born air gunner, Lauritz Rasmussen, were killed. O'Malley was a lawyer who joined the RAFVR before the war and at twenty-nine was a comparatively old man by Fighter Command standards. He was nonetheless inexperienced and the episode taught Hughes that you 'just had to establish a sustained rate of climb on your instrument panel before going into a turn of any sort'.

To the crews of 264 Squadron it seemed that the extra hazards involved in their new work were not appreciated by their superiors. Early in October they moved south to Luton and there was another visit from the brass. It was a dark evening and the sky was completely covered by low cloud. Taking off was relatively straightforward and once above the clag they could operate as normal. But with no radio link to the ground, no electronic beacons and only feeble runway 'glim lamps' to guide them in, there would be almost no chance of putting down again safely. 'Tommy' Thomas, now promoted to flight lieutenant, was still leading the squadron. He had told the local ground controller the situation and Desmond Hughes and his air gunner, Fred Gash, who were one of the duty crews, settled down expecting a quiet night. Then,

a couple of hours after dark and without any advance warning, a car drew up outside our dispersal hut and a tall, brooding figure emerged. He asked a passing airman who was in charge and was told 'Flt Lt Thomas, sir.'

'Tell him that the C-in-C is here and wants to talk to him.'

Off ran the airman and soon 'Tommy' was out at the car saluting smartly.

'This is a fine airfield,' said Air Chief Marshal Dowding, gazing out towards our glim-lamps. 'How many aircraft have you got in the air, Thomas?'

'None sir! Until this low cloud lifts, we would lose any aircraft we scrambled. We can take off OK but there's nowhere to land afterwards – we would have to bale out.'

'But Thomas … there are some Huns airborne. We should be after them. Why can't you land somewhere?'

According to Hughes, Thomas then 'gave the C-in-C a detailed account of the problems: single channel short-range RT [radio-telephony], no direct link between scrambled aircraft and Luton; inaccurate sector fixing [direction from the controller]; quite inadequate weather conditions of one mile visibility and low cloud; no RT homer on the airfield, hills in the vicinity with cloud right down on them etc. etc.'

Dowding 'listened in silence, his expression growing grimmer all the time. When "Tommy" had finished, he growled: "I didn't come here to listen to a list of complaints, Thomas" and stumped off to his car.'[5]

Hughes was an upstanding man, modest and patently honest, who rose to the rank of air vice marshal and commanded the Cranwell cadet college, and there is no reason to doubt the story. Another officer left an account of how pilots were sent off in hopeless conditions with no chance of success and every possibility of disaster in order to build the fiction that air cover extended throughout the hours of darkness. Flying Officer Trevor Wade of 92 Squadron recalled patrols that were essentially 'a case of showing the flag to the locals, who no doubt got some satisfaction out of hearing a couple of Spitfires screaming overhead, even if the screams were brought about by our endeavours to get out of our own searchlights and subsequent AA fire'.[6]

It did not pay to be too frank about the difficulties. Hughes claimed that as a result of his youthful candour, Thomas received an adverse report from Dowding which 'stayed on his personal file and badly affected his promotion prospects for some two years after'.[7] Dowding's impromptu visit 'did nothing to cheer up 264's aircrew, frustrated as they already were by their inability to get at the German raiders'.

On 15 October 1940, Hughes and Gash did something to raise their spirits. It was a cold night but there was very little cloud and the moon was full. The pair scrambled just after nightfall and were given a patrol line just inside the Essex coastline on the Thames Estuary. They were flying at 17,000 feet when Hughes spotted a condensation trail, silvery in the moonlight, and set off in excited pursuit. It was only after three circuits without sighting the enemy that he realized he was chasing himself. He returned to base 'in disgust and embarrassment' but a few hours later was sent off again, patrolling the same area. The night was brilliantly clear now and they could see ominous whitish patches covering parts of London: smoke from another Blitz. He was 'just about to think, "Ah well! Another hour of watching the bombs fall and not being able to do a damn thing about it" when I saw something move across the stars and turned gently towards where I had seen the movement.'

He noticed a 'dark shapeless blob' which 'slowly grew into a long black line and then I picked up the incandescent glow of an exhaust. Shouting "Tally Ho!" on the RT, I turned gently back to starboard, throttled back a little and slid into wide formation on what was clearly a twin-engine aircraft. As I dropped down a little below it, some fifty yards on its beam, the unmistakeable wing-plan of a Heinkel 111 was revealed. I told Fred to open fire and he made no mistake. A long burst with the de Wilde [incendiary bullets] twinkling brilliantly on its starboard engine and the Heinkel was a mass of flame. It slowly turned over to port and went down in a steep dive, trailing a plume of fire as it went. I started to follow it but it was obviously finished and I eased out of my dive. It crashed in open country with a mighty explosion ...'

These sorties were very different from the daytime operations of the summer. In the Battle of Britain squadrons operated as units. On being scrambled pilots ran to their machines and took to the air together, lining up in loose formation behind a commander who led them into combat as a group. The order did not survive more than a few seconds once the fight was joined, breaking down to a mêlée of individual actions. Nonetheless, these operations started as team efforts, and the feeling of camaraderie boosted confidence and the desire to be seen to do well. Night fighters were mostly lone wolves. In 264 Squadron, virtually all patrols were by single aircraft, except occasionally at dusk when a pair might operate together, separating when the light failed.

The accounts that the participants left seem rather cold and clinical compared with the testimony from the Battle of Britain. There was no talk of chivalry now and, for some at least, it was the man as much as the machine that was in their sights. Harry Bodien was a Halton apprentice who trained as a pilot and flew with Coastal Command before wangling a transfer to fighters at the end of 1940. In early 1941, aged twenty-five, he was flying Defiants with 151 Squadron. He explained his reasons in one of his remarkably frank letters to his married older sister, Vina, in which he discussed everything from his bowel movements to his sex life. 'There have been several things that have happened in the last two years or so that make it imperative that I get right at those Huns,' he wrote.[8] 'It's not hate but a combination of little things that have affected me.'

Like many airmen, Bodien appears to have taken the Blitz as a personal affront. It produced a double sense of outrage; both at the violation of the cities and the RAF's inability to prevent it. He approached his work with a cold fury, itching to get into action whenever possible and recording his successes with unapologetic pride. There were quite a few: eight kills and one probable by the summer of 1941, which were recognized with the award of a DFC. The citation states that 'on one occasion, despite having trouble with his own aircraft, [he] kept up a series of attacks on an enemy aircraft for some forty-five minutes and finally destroyed it'.

Bodien described the episode in detail to Vina. He came across his victim while patrolling north of Wittering. In his account the Heinkel 111 takes on a human identity. 'We opened fire and knocked some good lumps out of his belly but as he had dropped all of his bombs he didn't explode,' he wrote. The enemy gunners returned fire vigorously, hitting the Defiant's turret, destroying one gun and putting two of the other three out of action.

Bodien had to break off while the gunner struggled to get the damaged Brownings working again. The slow progress made him lose his temper and he 'yelled at the gunner if he didn't get his guns firing I'd kill him and after a while he said they were OK'. Then he went in again and 'got in a good squirt that killed the bottom gunner ...' The duel continued until they crossed the coast. The Germans appeared to have given up, for the Heinkel turned back towards land with its navigation lights switched on. It made no difference and Bodien moved in for the *coup de grâce*. 'I slid up in front of his port wing and told the gunner to kill the pilot from about five yard's range. He did this and the Heinkel dived straight into the sea where she burnt for a bit ...'

Bodien's passion for the fight was matched by his detachment when considering the results. A few months earlier he and his gunner shot down a Dornier which crashed ten miles from the base. The following morning, he 'went out and had a look at what was left. There was a lot of meat strewn around, and five people were in it because nine feet were found. I took a gun, a quick release from one of the parachutes and a few scraps from the wireless operator's log, including a photo of the bloke in his identity card showing him to be nineteen years old and a photo of his girl. Not bad either, tho' I don't expect she would like me very much.'

Bodien was a pre-war professional, who prided himself on his skill and toughness and could be scathing about the influx of novices. While at the Sutton Bridge OTU he complained to Vina about the 'sprog pilots straight from flying school' who were 'new to blood' and 'get on my nerves with their nattering' about the crashes, deaths and injuries that were part of the training experience.

For those without hundreds of hours of flying time logged, the darkness produced bewildering sensations which were not there in daylight. Roderick 'Rory' Chisholm's account of his first operational flight with 604 Squadron, a specialist night-fighter unit equipped with Blenheims based at Middle Wallop in Hampshire in August 1940, reveals the huge mental effort involved in simply trying to keep the aeroplane in the air. He had orders to patrol along a line near Bristol that would be marked out by flares on the ground.

The patrol was a mixture of nervous tension and great exhilaration. Bristol was being Blitzed 15,000 feet below me. I saw bombs explode and anti-aircraft fire and plenty of fires, but since I was never sure of myself, or of the attitude of the aircraft or my own position, this patrol was of no potential value to our night defence. The situation as far as I was concerned was never under control, and when I was told that a 'bandit' was reported at 'angels ten' passing Point Four of my patrol line and asked whether I could see anything I had to say that I could see nothing. I was unable to take much notice of what was going on outside because all my attention was concentrated on trying to keep [the] aircraft on an even keel. My nervous grip on the controls always tended to unsteady it by making over-corrections, and when I could relax temporarily having won the advantage over gravity (the dreaded Isaac) for a moment, I would be looking down for the flares which marked the patrol line. Gravity would then get the upper hand and I would again have to pore over the instruments until they danced before my eyes. And so it went on until I was told to come home.[9]

In this world of solitude and disengagement the chemistry of the crew became a vital factor in morale and success. Desmond Hughes was first paired with a New Zealander who, though a 'sound enough gunner ... was stolid to the extent of being monosyllabic and devoid of any sense of humour'. Then, when crews were switched around, he received Sergeant Fred Gash in his place. They hit it off immediately and the partnership would endure for eighteen months. They were both unpretentious, good-natured and conscientious with a quiet but strong sense of duty and patriotism. Hughes was from a prosperous, well-connected Ulster family. He was studying law at Cambridge, where he was a member of the University Air Squadron, when the war broke out. Gash was brought up in Manchester, son of a textile factory manager, and went to the prestigious Manchester Grammar School, leaving at seventeen for a job in a printing works. Both had fallen in love with flying following a ten-minute flip at an air show. Gash joined the Lancashire Aero Club and gained his pilot's licence but such was the rush of volunteers that when he turned up at Manchester Town Hall on the first day of the war to apply for the RAF he was told that the only vacancies left were for air gunners.

Each had complete faith in the other. Many years later Gash recalled how the fact that he had such 'confidence in my pilot' was one reason why, though the squadron suffered dreadful losses, 'the thought never crossed my mind that I was not going to come back'.[10] They made a winning team, accounting for at least five enemy aircraft between them. Gash believed they could have shot down many more. He remained a staunch defender of the Defiant's battered reputation and felt that it was poor tactics rather than design deficiencies that were responsible for the heavy losses. 'We should have been used to attack the German bombers solely while the Spitfires and Hurricanes took care of the German fighters,' he argued. 'It was the fighters that knocked the hell out of us, not the bombers.'

Through the winter of 1940–41 great ingenuity went into bluffing and confusing the raiders. Colonel John Turner, late of the Air Ministry's works and buildings department, was brought out of retirement to lead a brilliant deception campaign, building scores of dummy airfields code-named 'Starfish', complete with flare paths and landing lights which tricked hundreds of raiders into dropping their bombs on empty countryside. Electronics experts were soon at work interfering with the German 'X-Gerät' radio beaming system so that attacks were directed away from their targets. These stratagems were surprisingly effective. But a really effective counter-offensive needed the same combination of technology, married to a command and control system, that had brought victory in the Battle of Britain. It began to take shape with the arrival of improved on-board radar and ground tracking stations. The stations were equipped with revolving radar arrays which gave 360-degree cover and the system that evolved from them was known as GCI (ground-controlled inter-ception). Once an incoming aircraft was detected, a night fighter equipped with an airborne interception (AI) set was given a course to home in on it, and with luck to shoot it down. Success did not come easily. The first AI sets were crude and it needed much practice for the operator to gain the skill to use it effectively.

The process was slow and frustrating but by the beginning of 1941 it was clear that the potential existed to tilt the course of the battle. A remarkable air warrior was at the forefront of the fight. John Cunningham combined a deep theoretical and practical knowledge of aeronautics with extraordinary piloting skills. After Whitgift School in the outer suburbs of south London he was taken on as an engineering trainee by de Havilland's, the great pioneers of British aviation and still under the energetic control of its founder, Captain Geoffrey de Havilland. Cunningham not only designed aircraft but tested them. The company base was at Hatfield, just north of London, and he flew at weekends with 604 Squadron, an Auxiliary unit based not far away at Hendon. In July 1940, 604 was moved to Middle Wallop to concentrate exclusively on night operations. GCI was being developed in the sector but by the autumn no one had managed to shoot down a bandit.

With the arrival of Beaufighters at the end of September, the squadron's fortunes began to change. The 'Beau' lived up to its name. It was big, powerful, streamlined and handsome and its twin Merlin engines could push it along at 335mph. On the night of 19/20 November, Cunningham took off on patrol with Sergeant John Phillipson who had been a ground radar operator before volunteering for aircrew. To reach targets in the Midlands, the raiders had taken to approaching from the south-west across a broad stretch of the Channel and the Beaufighters of Middle Wallop were well placed to interdict them as they came in from the sea. When the first blips blossomed on the cathode ray tube in the GCI station controlling operations at Sopley, near Bournemouth, Cunningham was vectored on to one of the intruders.

His natural distaste for drama meant he left behind only a sparse account of what was a historic moment. Seeing a concentration of searchlights glowing on the underside of clouds, he headed towards it. Then Phillipson announced that he had got a solid contact. It was now his job to steer his pilot towards it, watching the screen and calling out the adjustments. Eventually, as Cunningham told his biographer, he saw 'a cluster of stars which seemed to be moving in a different direction from the others and as he did a dark shape formed around them, only to fragment as [I] looked directly at it. Climbing a little closer, a silhouette took shape.'[11] He manoeuvred the Beau underneath the aircraft and identified the bulbous, glazed nose and broad, tapered wings of a Junkers 88. The Beaufighter carried four 20mm Hispano cannon in the nose, enormously destructive if brought to bear accurately. Cunningham got in close before opening up. The Ju 88 tipped over and dived straight to earth, exploding spectacularly on impact.

His feat was emulated a few nights later by the squadron CO Mike Anderson and thereafter the pattern was of gradual success, accelerated by the arrival of improved Mark IV AI radar. In April 1942 night fighters shot down forty-eight raiders, while anti-aircraft fire brought down thirty-nine. In May, the figures climbed to ninety-six by fighters and thirty-one by guns.[12]

Even with the change of fortunes, night fighters could not claim the credit for beating back the German night Blitz. In May 1941, the Luftwaffe's losses were still a sustainable 3.5 per cent of sorties. It was external events that brought the offensive to an end. In June, Hitler invaded Russia and the Luftwaffe was needed elsewhere.

By then the nocturnal aces were well established in the public mind as a new cast of Air Force heroes, with John Cunningham and his regular AI operator Sergeant Jimmy Rawnsley its stars. One night they were called on to perform for the King when he turned up at Middle Wallop just before the first patrol set off. In the course of chatting to Rawnsley, His Majesty asked how many aircraft he had downed. When he replied 'nine', the King requested that he get another one for him that night. The royal party began by watching events unfold on the screens of the Sopley GCI Station, a primitive establishment comprising a caravan and cluster of huts, over which a large antenna swept in 360-degree rotation. It was driven by a pair of airmen, hidden in a shack, pedalling a contraption like a tandem bicycle.

As the action moved closer it was suggested that the King move outside for the finale. By now Rawnsley had brought Cunningham into an ideal attacking position. The raider was still unaware of his presence when the cannons opened up. According to the account Cunningham gave his biographer, 'the crescendo of the guns opened the final act as [I] pulled away to avoid hurtling wreckage. A flickering glow lit the inside of the Heinkel ... and its wheels dropped down, the hydraulics shot through. Flying alongside [we] watched the glow expand through the skin as engulfing flames took over. Mortally wounded, the He III shuddered, and curved over into a steepening dive, flames streaming behind.'[13]

These feats were seized upon by the RAF's publicity machine which was anxious to continue promoting the Air Force as protectors and defenders, as well as to provide some evidence that the Luftwaffe were not able to attack with impunity. There were

'Cat's Eyes' meets the King

difficulties about how much could be said because of government reluctance to reveal the existence of the still secret AI technology. Cunningham, whose virtues included extreme modesty, had no choice but to accept the absurd role that the publicists cast him in. He became famous as 'Cat's Eyes Cunningham' whose amazing prowess at shooting down Germans in the dark was the result of phenomenal eyesight, enhanced by a diet of carrots.

Despite the battering they were receiving at the hands of the Luftwaffe, the public's fascination with and admiration for the Air Force seemed unaffected. The government kept a close watch on the state of civilian spirits. The Home Intelligence division of the Ministry of Information was charged with monitoring national morale and produced weekly reports based on data from a variety of sources including the Mass Observation network. From the outset, the public seemed to accept bombing as an ugly new fact of wartime life 'which if it cannot be cured must be endured'.[14] The bulletin for the week 11–18 December 1940 stated that 'in the Southern region, people are reported to be getting a little tired of the slogan "Britain can take it"'.[15] However, nowhere during the Blitz period is there any direct criticism of the men of the RAF. One respondent in a Mass Observation survey – 'the inhabitant of a Southern port, much blitzed' – remarked sourly: 'we hear a lot about their activities, but I have never seen an RAF fighter about when the air over our city has been thick with German bombers'.[16] But people seemed, rather, to blame pre-war politicians for not giving the Air Force the right equipment to face the threat than the airmen themselves, and to accept that an antidote might take time to arrive.[17]

The Battle of Britain effect, which raised the reputation of the whole service to stratospheric heights, would carry the Air Force through many setbacks and persist to the end of the war. The Air Ministry's Public Relations Directorate understood the need to keep the memory fresh. Shooting of *The First of the Few*, the first film version of the epic, began early in 1941. The film's producer, director and star Leslie Howard, internationally famous after playing Ashley Wilkes, the upstanding Southern gentleman who lost out to Clark Gable's caddish Rhett Butler in the competition for Vivien Leigh's Scarlett O'Hara in the great box office hit of 1939, *Gone With the Wind*, decided to lend authenticity to the flying scenes by using half a dozen real pilots including Brian Kingcome of 92 Squadron. The Fighter Boys were treated like kings. Kingcome recalled that the work itself was undemanding, calling for 'little more than lolling about in flying clothes in a fake dispersal hut, going outside to look sombrely skywards from time to time, and delivering such daft lines as, "Good luck – they'll need it," to cue in stock shots of Spitfires and German bombers flying overhead'.[18] One image of a pilot's gloved thumb jabbing at the control column gun button would be used in countless documentaries thereafter, cutting away to footage of an enemy aircraft going down in flames. It was Kingcome's proud boast that the 'thumb on the firing button, which must have been seen by more people than any thumb in history' belonged to him (it can still be seen in the video display accompanying the Spitfire suspended in the main hall of London's Imperial War Museum).

After their day's labours, they returned to the Savoy Hotel where Howard had put them up. For Kingcome the whole experience was 'a joyous interlude and a marvellous break from airfield routine. I hardly remember when I enjoyed myself more.' At the end of each day's shooting the pilots were taken on a round of 'London's best clubs and pubs, no expense spared …'

Word soon got around the London area fighter stations and the actor-aviators noted the remarkable number of comrades who '"just happened" to be passing the Savoy as we were setting forth on our nightly expeditions'. They frequented the old Fighter Boy favourites, clubs like the 400 in Leicester Square, 'whose dimly lit dance floor and seductive music were excellent backdrops for young men in uniform trying their luck with the "I'm off to war tomorrow and may never come back" routine'. Then it was on to the Bag O'Nails in Kingly Street, Soho, a 'far more raucous affair where serious boozing took priority'. They finished with a nightcap or two at the hotel while Leslie Carroll and his Savoy Orpheans played the evening out.

Howard further demonstrated his gratitude by providing some illicit entertainment which he thought the young pilots might appreciate. Kingcome recalled that 'after much sly nudge-nudging and wink-winking and many taps to the nose, we were informed that a special treat had been laid on for us – one of "those" films. It required to be shown in great secrecy after the studio had finished the day's work and everyone else had gone home.' At the appointed hour, they sidled embarrassedly into the private projection room led by Howard himself and the fun began. It was called A Walk in the Woods and looked as if it had been shot in the 1920s. The action began 'with a car being driven along a woodland track by two pretty young women, who very soon decided to stop and take a walk in the woods – so justifying the title though from this point on, justifying the title ceased to be of any central concern. The young women pointed upwards at the sun and, with suitably histrionic gestures, indicated how hot it was today. This gave them the cue to begin to take off their clothes …'

Meanwhile, 'visible to the audience but unbeknown to the girls, a shady-looking young bounder lurked amid the trees. One glance at his waxed moustachios and sleekly oiled hair had been enough to make us suspect that he was not there just to study botany …' From then on 'it was all go, but projected as it was, with a jerky speeded-up action to match wildly exaggerated gestures and expressions which passed for acting in early movies, the effect was achingly funny'. As they split their sides, the pilots could only hope that they had not caused offence to their well-meaning host.

In the lonely period between the fall of France and the fundamental changes to the strategic game brought about by Operation Barbarossa and Pearl Harbor, the maintenance of national morale was of profound importance. Any sign of progress, any glimmer of hope, was to be magnified to maximum proportions, even if the picture that resulted bore little resemblance to reality.

The Prime Minister's tone shifted in the autumn of 1940 from ringing defiance to the promise of retribution and ultimate victory. On the first anniversary of the war he declared in a memo to the Cabinet: 'The Navy can lose us the war but only the Air Force can win it ... the Fighters are our salvation ... but the Bombers alone provide the means of victory.' The public was soon being assured that, although bombs were falling around them, over the horizon even worse things were happening to Germany. In a speech in the House of Commons he asserted that 'night after night, month after month, our bomber squadrons travel far into Germany, find their targets in the darkness by the highest navigational skill, aim their attacks ... with deliberate, careful precision, and inflict shattering blows upon the whole technical and war-making structure of the Nazi power'.

By now the conceptual underpinnings of the pre-war plans for the bomber offensive were trembling under the weight of operational realities and the difficulties of striking effectively were all too apparent. The Air Staff still clung to the belief that performance would eventually catch up with the montage that was being concocted. The real situation was too painful to divulge. After the failures and crises of 1940, neither politicians, nor the public, nor the Air Force itself were in a mood to confront the truth. Instead, illusions were fostered in the cause of maintaining morale. Bomber Command told Group Headquarters that 'full publicity should be given to our bomber operations in the fullest and most attractive light'.[19]

Everyone played along. Newspaper and magazine reports, BBC broadcasts and official announcements all presented the bombing effort as a story of continuous and growing achievement in this period, a narrative that was diametrically opposite to the truth. Initially at least, the fiction was relatively easy to maintain. Unlike the Battle of Britain, all the action took place out of public view. Official bulletins were backed up by accounts by participants. A typical one 'by a flying officer of a heavy bomber squadron' described a raid on Berlin in September 1940, one of a series ordered in retaliation for the bombardment of London.

'We found our targets without difficulty. It was a gas generating plant only a few miles from the centre of Berlin ... when the bombs burst, there were four huge explosions across the works ... it reminded me of a scene on the films ... two huge fires started and huge tongues of flame leapt up, then dense smoke ... the bombs had fallen about fifty yards apart. Almost immediately the fires and the explosions seemed to link up and for a distance of 200 yards through the works there was this great mass of flames ... we circled round and watched the fires blazing up. The rear gunner I remember, shouted: "Oh Boy, it's terrific."'[20]

In tandem with these accounts came reassurance that what the public was being told about the Air Force's activities was actually true. At the same time as the report above was made, Macdonald Hastings asked *Picture Post*'s millions of readers: 'Can we believe the claims of the RAF? Are our bombers any more successful in raids over Germany than the German bombers over Britain?' The comforting answer was that the official version was accurate. He based the conclusion not on the word of the authorities but what he said was the rigorously checked testimony of the airmen themselves.

'Our bomber crews who night after night fly over Germany, say that the official communiques claim only a fraction of the destruction which the RAF heavy bombers are working on Germany's war economy,' he wrote.[21] 'When they come back from a raid, the Bomber crews are interrogated by Intelligence Officers who wouldn't believe we'd won the war unless they saw the Armistice signed with their own eyes ...' He described the process by which the debrief material was passed up to the Bomber Group headquarters 'which suspects even Intelligence Officers' reports. Group Headquarters pass on a revised account to Bomber Command, who are careful to modify any claim which might imply a tendency to boast. Bomber Command in their turn send a report to the Air Ministry ...'

The report was an early exercise in explaining to a mass audience the character, purpose and methods of Bomber Command. It was spread over seven pages and illustrated by sixteen excellent black and white photographs. Hastings was not an Air Ministry stooge. Nonetheless, the article must have pleased its readers in Adastral House. It presented bombing operations as they would like everyone from the Prime Minister down to see them.

The piece was based on a visit to 214 Squadron, equipped with Wellingtons and based at Stradishall in Suffolk, and appeared just as the Blitz began. Hastings described a routine that would soon become implanted in the minds of the British public; the initial briefing revealing the target and setting the number of aircraft on the trip, then the first preparations; plotting courses, testing engines, loading fuel and bombing up. In the afternoon came the final briefing with specialists giving the weather forecast and latest intelligence on enemy defences. There was a break for supper before the crew climbed into their flying gear and headed out to the aircraft. The report underlines approvingly the collective and unhierarchical spirit of the enterprise: 'Each aircraft has a crew of six men,' Hastings wrote, 'two pilots, navigator, air observer, wireless operator and rear gunner. There is no rule as to which are officers and which are not. Sergeant pilots are sometimes captains of aircraft in which officers are rear gunners. The ranks mix together on terms which are among the most pleasant features of Air Force life.'

It is made clear that Bomber Boys and Fighter Boys are different sorts of heroes, for 'the men who fly night bombers are quieter and more serious than the fighter pilots. Their responsibility is heavier; the technological knowledge required of them is more complicated and the physical strain is more prolonged. The fighters are in the air, at most, for a few hours ... the bombers are out all night, steering their course with cold deliberation, through the blackness, studying their maps, puzzling out the direction of their target, and taking everything that the enemy likes to throw at them.'

Back at base the staff grab what rest they can before awaiting the return. There are anxious moments when an aircraft is arriving, but 'more often than not ... all our aircraft return safely'. The piece dwells on the rigours of the debriefing process which, he claimed, 'the crews will tell you [is] the worst part of the trip'. The intelligence officers inquire carelessly if they've had a good trip. 'The crew, true to the Air Force tradition of modesty, reply in an off-hand way that it was "very nice" or "not so nice"'.

Then 'they get down to brass tacks. What time were you over your target? How did you know it was the target? Did your bombs hit the target? What height were you? If you were as high as that, how did you identify the target?' The description of the night's work ends with a detail that would stick forever in the mind of civilians suffering the privations of rationing: a plate of bacon and eggs.

The impression given by the article is of calm, resolute efficiency producing solid results. 'If the bombers have done their job – and they usually have – they have brought back evidence that a specific object has been raided.'

He continued: 'that's the difference between German bombing methods and ours. The Germans pin their hopes on mass destruction; we count any bomb which fails to hit a predetermined military objective a wasted bomb. It is not merely a matter of the rules of warfare. It is sound common sense. Killing civilians and blowing up their homes won't win the war. But the systematic destruction of the enemy's internal economy will, in time, paralyse his armies.'

Hastings went on to claim that the RAF was superior to the Luftwaffe in navigational skill and the quality of its aircraft, bombs and bomb sights. The truth was that 'both the Luftwaffe and the RAF know that one side is claiming too much and the other too little. The Luftwaffe must think that the RAF is mad.'

Coming as it did as Londoners were feeling the full weight of the Luftwaffe's nightly bombardments, the article was obviously intended to promote the idea that Germany was suffering, too, though the RAF's campaign was aimed strictly at legitimate military targets. Woven into the text is the Air Ministry credo that it is the work of the bomber squadrons that will prepare the ground for victory.

As a reflection of what was going on at the time, the piece is wrong in almost every respect. To what extent was the propaganda believed? Ministry of Information-commissioned surveys reported scepticism. 'Many ... particularly inhabitants of the blitzed cities, doubt whether our bombing is as effective as it might be,' concluded one in mid-March 1941.[22] The effort to claim the high moral ground with claims that British bombs were aimed only at 'pre-determined military targets' appeared to be wasted on a population comfortable with the idea of retaliation in kind. 'Public feeling in favour of reprisals continues to be strong,' declared the Home Intelligence report for the last week in March 1941.[23] 'The moral aspects of the problem are now almost entirely discounted. Personal experience has made the inhabitants of blitzed towns believe that attacks on the centres of population is "a paying military proposition" and they demand that we should apply the lesson to Hamburg and Berlin.'

The men directing the bombing campaign had come to the same conclusion some months before. Shortly after the *Picture Post* article appeared, the Air Staff accepted that the precision attacks on strategic targets it had promised were unattainable with its current resources, and other means would have to be used if air raids were to have any effect at all.

A directive issued to Charles Portal, briefly chief of Bomber Command between April and October 1940, on 21 September reaffirmed that war industry targets and particularly oil storage plants remained the 'basis of our longer term offensive strategy'. However, in the meantime, Portal was told to broaden the scope of attacks to include Berlin, even though it contained no priority targets. The aim was to cause 'the greatest possible disturbance and dislocation both to the industrial population and to the civil population generally in the area'.[24] Portal needed no encouragement. He had already proposed raids in retaliation for the London Blitz on industrial towns like Essen in the Ruhr, 'the whole of which can for practical purposes be regarded as a military objective'.[25] In the next few weeks the pretence that Germany could be fatally undermined by pinpoint attacks on high-value industrial targets would be abandoned, to be replaced by the belief that it was more realistic to attack whole towns and with it the morale of the German people. At the end of October, Portal's successor, Richard Peirse, received precise instructions from the Air Staff directing him to carry on aiming at oil targets but in adverse weather conditions to switch to attacks on Berlin or towns in central and western Germany. He was urged to adopt the tactics that the Luftwaffe was using so effectively in Britain and open the raid with an incendiary bombardment, then bombing on the fires 'with a view to preventing the firefighting services from dealing with them and giving the fires every opportunity to spread'. So it was, wrote the authorized historians of the strategic bombing campaign, that 'the fiction that the bombers were attacking "military objectives" in the towns was officially abandoned. This was the technique which was to become known as area bombing.'[26]

This fundamental change in the direction of the bombing campaign coincided with an important reshuffle at the summit. On 24 October 1940 the Chief of the Air Staff Cyril Newall was defenestrated and Portal installed in his place. Newall had been a marked man for some months. His appointment to succeed Edward Ellington in September 1937 had come as a surprise, particularly to Dowding and Ludlow-Hewitt, who both fancied their chances. As the man overseeing the frantic preparations for war with Germany he inevitably took the blame for the major weaknesses revealed by the shock of combat. By the time the Battle of Britain was over he had lost the confidence of Churchill and gained the enmity of Lord Beaverbrook whose dynamic work as Minister for Aircraft Production still left him plenty of time for intrigue. Trenchard, fearing that Newall had abandoned faith in the bomber doctrine, joined the conspiracy against him and, at the age of fifty-four, Newall was despatched to the side lines as Governor General of New Zealand.

In truth it was time for him to go. He was worn out and by 1940 'an absolute bag of nerves' according to his then assistant Sholto Douglas, incapable of imposing grip and vision when the RAF desperately needed both.[27] He did not shrink from wielding the axe when he thought it was necessary, getting rid of Ludlow-Hewitt earlier in the year and making an unsuccessful bid to remove Dowding. Portal's appointment came as no surprise. He was the obvious choice and his tenure remained secure until the end. Under Portal, the primacy of strategic bombing was assured, even if the methodology changed. He did not think it necessary to spell out the new emphasis on 'area bombing' to either the public or the crews.

The men of Bomber Command carried on as before, buoyed up with the belief that they were engaged in a quasi-scientific process of dismantling the German war machine. Teddy Fry was a sergeant pilot, a trainee estate agent in Sittingbourne, Kent, before the war who joined the RAFVR in July 1938. He was one of the men Hastings observed on his visit to 214 Squadron for *Picture Post*. His letters reveal a pride in what he and his comrades were doing and apparent enjoyment of his work.

In the summer of 1940 he made several sorties to the Ruhr as well as taking part in a short-lived and unsuccessful effort to turn large German forests into blazing infernos by showering them with incendiaries. Fry was eager to hit Germany where it mattered. 'I've at last done a real trip,' he reported in a letter sent on 2 September to his widowed mother Eva and sister Elizabeth at their semi in Sidcup.[28] 'Nothing worth the DFM or anything ...'. But it was my first trip there – Berlin. There and back 8 hours 20 mins flying ... really good trip. Made the other trips to the Ruhr [seem] like a practice flight.' Two weeks later the night Blitz was underway and Sidcup lay under the flight path of the raiders. Fry offered the reassuring thought that Hitler would not have it all his own way: 'Two can play his game and we are as good at it as him.' The tempo of operations had picked up and he was in a routine of 'work all night, sleep all day. You must do it – sleep and lounge about *absolutely* as much as possible. The more you rest, the more racket you can stand, and the more racket you can stand the shorter will be the war.'

In November, he wrote proudly to his sister to alert her to his part in a raid three nights before. 'Boy! did we have fun and games that night over Berlin.' He enclosed a cutting from the *Daily Telegraph* for 25 November. Citing an Air Ministry communiqué, it reported that the attack 'began shortly before eight o clock when the Putlitzerstrasse and Lehrter railway goods yards right in the middle of the city were bombed. Ten very large fires were started ... at the same time 1,000 incendiaries were dropped on the yards between the Potsdamer and the Anhalter railway stations.' An unnamed pilot described how, after an interval of a few seconds of his bombs being dropped, 'up went a whole lot of fires in the most amazing way … we were flying at a good height but the inside of our machine was lit up as though we had the electric light on inside'. He recognized the account as his own, 'word for word the report that I gave after the trip … I'm sending it because mother or yourself might like to hear about *some* of our exploits.'

By Christmas he had thirty-one trips under his belt. 'Just about time I got off,' he wrote. 'Still, with another four trips I get the record for the squadron. Rather tempting you know – should just be able to do it.' He fell just short for after two more trips he was moved to No. 12 OTU at Benson in Oxfordshire, presumably as an instructor. His efforts had won him a DFM. On 20 February, he wrote home to break the news and invite them to the investiture: 'Stand by you two for the 18th March at 10.15 at the Palace. Please don't say that you have nothing to wear or any other nonsense because you don't have to be a duchess or a glamour girl to be mother and sister to a DFM …' Teddy Fry never kept the appointment at the Palace. He was killed in a flying accident eight days later.

Despite the move away from futile attempts at precision to unfocused attacks on cities, the Air Ministry continued to foster the illusion that bombing was both effective and a relatively clean business. The Air Staff used the cinema to promote a rosy account of Bomber Command's achievements. *Target for Tonight* was released in August 1941. Every facility had been granted to the director and writer, Harry Watt, one of a new breed of British documentary film makers. The film mixed drama with actuality, using RAF air and ground crew, aeroplanes and bases to tell the story of a single night raid over Germany. The action focuses on a Wellington bomber, F for Freddie, and its pilot and crew drawn from all over Britain. The captain was played by Squadron Leader Percy 'Pick' Pickard, a pre-war regular with dozens of operations to his credit and filmed at Mildenhall. Such was the enthusiasm for the project that Richard Peirse, then Bomber Command's C-in-C, agreed to play himself.

Once again great emphasis is placed on methodical preparations and the dispassionate professionalism of all involved. The target is an oil storage complex in the Black Forest. The raiders take off at dusk and find the target without difficulty. Despite fierce flak they drop their bombs, but F for Freddie is hit and its wireless operator wounded. Somehow it staggers most of the way home, but seemingly on its last legs the pilot gives the crew the choice of baling out or remaining while he attempts a crash landing. They elect to stay and the captain gets them all down safely. At the post-op debrief the crew report that the first bombs fell short but that 'the last one started a major fire' producing 'black smoke, dullish red flames'. That is enough for the intelligence officer: 'Sounds like oil all right.' The raid has been a success.

The fictional nature of the story was disguised by the patina of documentary authenticity. *Target for Tonight* successfully competed with escapist feature films at the box office and even did well in America. According to Watt its success was due to its upbeat underlying message. 'Away back in many people's minds there had arisen the doubt that we could ever win,' he said.[29] 'Then came this film, actually showing how we were taking the war into the heart of the enemy and doing it in a very British, casual, brave way. It was a glimmer of hope and the public rose to it.'

The impulse to move onto the offensive was strong, even when it made little strategic sense. It was displayed in the use to which the fighter squadrons were put, once the Battle of Britain was over. Fear of an invasion persisted well into 1941. Then, in June, Hitler launched Barbarossa and the hinge of the war swung eastwards. The danger to Britain fell away, and with it the need to concentrate Fighter Command's resources at home. There were several obvious places in the vulnerable territories which acted as stepping stones between Britain and its eastern dominions where Spitfires and Hurricanes and seasoned pilots were badly needed. At the top of the list stood the Mediterranean theatre and Egypt where, following Mussolini's decision in June 1940 to jump into the war, the Army and Navy were now fighting the Italians. As we shall see in Chapter Ten, the RAF's Middle East Command initially had nothing like the numbers or equipment it needed to offer adequate support on land or sea. Fighters and men began to flow eastwards at the end of 1940, but with Hurricanes rather than Spitfires, and then early models. Weakness in the air undermined the chances of early success in the

Middle East and compounded the muddle and hesitation that marked the British effort in the first phase of the war.

The demand for modern aircraft was even more acute in the Far East. Following the fall of France, the Chiefs of Staff had decided that, with Britain now isolated and the Fleet badly needed elsewhere, the RAF would have to take prime responsibility for defending Malaya and Singapore, the citadel on which the security of Britain's Far Eastern territories and trade depended. Yet, when, seventeen months later, the Japanese erupted westwards, the Air Force that faced them was pitifully unfitted to offer any serious resistance. The Australian and New Zealand squadrons that made up the fighter force went into battle against the 'Navy Type 0' – known ever after as the 'Zero' – with the Brewster Buffalo. The American-made machine was as lumbering as its name suggested, taking 6.1 minutes to climb to 13,000 feet against the Zero's 4.3 minutes, and with a top speed more than forty miles an hour slower. Spitfire squadrons may not have saved Singapore – there were too many other factors conspiring in its downfall – but they might have bought time and reduced the dimensions of the catastrophe.

But none were sent. Instead, most of the fighters were kept at home and put on the offensive, mounting continuous cross-Channel operations over northern France. The decision is one that was questioned at the time, and nearly eighty years on the rationale for it has become no easier to understand.

The ostensible reason for going over to the attack was that it would keep the Germans off balance and teach them that the occupation of France would be challenged every day. It also reinforced the propaganda theme of 'hitting back'. There was a further supposed benefit in that the Germans would be compelled to keep fighters, anti-aircraft guns and radar in France for force protection instead of using them in their campaigns in Greece and Yugoslavia.[30] This was a dubious proposition and the risks involved were high. The new campaign meant that Fighter Command was effectively assuming the disadvantages of mounting operations over enemy territory that the Luftwaffe suffered in the Battle of Britain, without any likely compensating strategic reward. The German defences were as good as Britain's, and with the arrival of the Focke-Wulf 190 in 1942 the defenders had a machine that outperformed the attackers. Losses were bound to be high. And the lucky pilots who survived being knocked down knew that for them the war was over.

The switch to the attack was led by the new men at the top of Fighter Command. Sholto Douglas, by then deputy CAS, replaced Dowding at the end of November 1940 as C-in-C. At 11 Group, Keith Park made way for his old enemy Trafford Leigh-Mallory. The hasty departure of Dowding and Park so soon after victory would come to be seen as an act of ingratitude bordering on betrayal by Churchill. Douglas and Leigh-Mallory have been regarded as accessories to the crime. Leigh-Mallory was already tainted with accusations of disloyalty for his part in the 'Big Wing' controversy. But it is hard to see what would have been gained by keeping the old team in harness. Dowding had already had his tenure extended once and was exhausted. Park had been long in the job and was due another posting. Both were garlanded for their achievements and progressed to other, important jobs.

The charge that can be made against the newcomers is that they were proud and ambitious. They wanted to make an impact and the methods they chose with which to make their mark killed many good men and brought few results.

Douglas later claimed that the initial impetus for the policy came from Portal. He in turn had been influenced by an intervention from Trenchard, still energetically offering his counsel whether it was asked for or not. According to Douglas, Trenchard 'thought that we should now "lean towards France," and he advocated a system of offensive sweeps of fighters across the Channel which was along much the same lines as that used by us in our operations over the Western Front in the First World War'.[31] The enterprise was certainly stamped with the Trenchardian notion that it was essential to maintain a spirit of aggression, and that, as the official historians of the war wrote, 'powerful moral advantages would accrue as our pilots grew accustomed to exercising the initiative ...'[32] As with the bombing campaign, displaying the offensive spirit seemed to be regarded as an end in itself, almost regardless of the ratio between cost and effectiveness.

Operations broadly consisted of two main types. 'Rhubarbs' involved smallish fighter formations roaming over the French coast in the hope, as the Luftwaffe had hoped in the summer of 1940, that the defenders would come up to meet them and a battle of attrition would be joined. 'Circuses' were small bombing raids sometimes with very large fighter escorts, with a similar intention. The Germans were reluctant to play along. Between 20 December 1940 and 13 June 1941, cross-Channel operations resulted in fifty RAF pilots being shot down for a gain of fifty-eight enemy aircraft destroyed. These paltry results might have brought the unfortunate experiment to a close. But the German invasion of Russia intervened to give an ostensible strategic value to the exercise. The raids could be presented as a British contribution to the Russian war effort, by forcing the Germans to divert air assets away from the Eastern Front. In fact the effect was negligible. In the second half of the year, activity mounted, and so did losses. The scale of operations increased sharply, and this time the Germans felt compelled to respond. Official figures claimed that in the six weeks from the middle of June, 322 enemy aircraft were destroyed for British losses of 123 pilots. As the official history noted, however, 'the German day fighter force in Northern France was only some two hundred strong, and losses of the order claimed would have meant either its complete extinction, or its renewal from top to bottom'.[33] It turned out later that the true German losses were eighty-four. Whatever minor successes the campaign achieved were heavily offset by the human cost. More pilots were lost in 1941 on these exercises than in the Battle of Britain, and many of the dead were survivors of that struggle. Douglas and Leigh-Mallory's policy meant that seventy-five fighter squadrons were kept in the UK that would have been far better employed filling desperate needs in the Middle and Far East.

By going on the offensive, the Fighter Boys no longer had the comfort of fighting over their own territory to sustain them, and the terrors of combat were reinforced by anxiety about the journey home. Flight Lieutenant Stanley Meares of 611 Squadron, twenty-four years old and a pre-war SSC officer who nonetheless had little combat experience, described one adrenaline-soaked encounter in a letter to his parents on 29 June 1941. The squadron was escorting bombers on a Circus when he got caught up in a dogfight which he emerged from to find, as was often the case, the skies miraculously empty of aircraft.

'Being ... about fifty miles inside France, all by myself, I felt a little lonely and headed for home, but on the way back I passed right over the middle of St Omer aerodrome, which had two Me 109s patrolling it. I thought to myself that this was no place to start looking for trouble, and continued on my way.'[34] The Messerschmitts spotted him and Meares dropped to below tree-top level to shake them off. It did not work. He made a tight turn preparing to fight, but was horrified to see the 'Hun' turning inside him, gaining the firing advantage. He 'began to perspire a bit'. He could not climb away because the Messerschmitt would outperform him, nor dive as he was already flat on the deck.

'It struck me [he wrote] that I was fighting for my life which is the strangest of sensations. I knew with terrific clearness that unless I did something within the next split second I would be one of those who did not get home.' He pulled the stick back until it would go no further, blacking out for what seemed like minutes. When he came to again, 'I was flying about 20 feet behind the Hun, and he was obviously wondering where I had got to.'

In the dogfight that followed Meares gradually won the advantage and with the bit between his teeth pursued his opponent back to the aerodrome where he 'chased him down his hangars, in between them, over the flying field and back again. He was trying to get his ground defences to shoot me down, then in desperation he turned on his back at about fifty feet and I gave him a long burst and in he went ...' With his magazines empty he turned for home only to be bounced by another Messerschmitt. After another sweat-drenched tussle he threw him off and raced at ground level for the Channel. He crossed at Dungeness. 'I never knew how well I loved England until I saw her shores again,' he wrote. 'I had learned more about tactics and flying in twenty minutes than in all my flying years.'

Meares had been lucky, although his good fortune did not last. He was killed later that year in a mid-air collision in home skies.

Hundreds of others joined the ranks of 'those who did not get home'. From mid-June 1941 to the end of the year alone, Fighter Command lost 411 fighters over the Channel and the Continent.[35]

Among the victims of the new policy were several pilots who had been pushed into the limelight by the Air Force's PR men. Eric Lock was one of the most successful of the Battle of Britain pilots. He was born in Shropshire in 1919, into a family of farmers and quarry-men, attended a local private school and left at sixteen to work for his father. He joined the RAFVR in February 1939. He was posted to 41 Squadron just before the Battle began, without having ever flown a Spitfire. He opened his account with the Luftwaffe on 15 August, shooting down a Messerschmitt 110 and a Junkers 88. He ended the Battle with possibly twenty-six victories, making him the highest scoring Allied pilot of the campaign.

In late autumn, his fortunes began to change. He was shot down twice in November. The second time he had managed to destroy one Messerschmitt 109 before being hit by cannon shells from another. He was badly wounded in both legs and his right arm and the throttle lever of his Spitfire was severed, sending his aircraft racing away at 400mph. He left the attackers behind but was now too badly hurt to bale out. He brought the aircraft screaming down to 2,000 feet then switched off the engine and somehow managed to glide in to make a wheels-down landing in a field near Martlesham Heath in Suffolk. According to Cuthbert Orde, who heard the story from Lock when he did his portrait in 1941, 'for two hours he sat in his cockpit, bleeding from his three frightful wounds before rescue arrived in the shape of a couple of soldiers. He told them how to make a stretcher out of two rifles and an overcoat, and then was carried two miles, being dropped three times on the way, once into a dyke of water.'[36] He spent six months in hospitals and was oper-ated on fifteen times before going back on operations with 611 Squadron in June 1941. On 3 August, he was returning from a Rhubarb over the Pas-de-Calais when he spotted a German column and his wingman saw him dive to attack. After that he disappeared. No trace of him or his Spitfire was found.

Looking at the few photographs and the sketched portrait by Orde, which are all that is left behind, 'Sawn-off Lucky' is a dim figure to modern eyes. The few contemporary references shed little light on him. Orde remembered that while he sat to him he 'never stopped talking and he never stopped laughing – everything was a joke'.

Six days after Lock's downfall another famous name was brought down. The story of Douglas Bader, the legless veteran of Dunkirk and the Battle of Britain who overcame every obstacle, physical and bureaucratic, to get back in the air, made him ideal hero material, projecting an image of bulldog resolve that matched the face Britain wished to show to the world. His personality hardly fitted the prevailing Fighter Boy ethos; he was boastful and enjoyed the limelight, though the charge of line-shooting did not stick for his achievements were real enough. He lorded it over inferiors and cultivated those who could advance his cause. Fellow pilots tended to keep their thoughts about him to themselves. It was bad form to criticize and invited the charge of jealousy.

Bader revelled in combat. Having not been in the front line for much of the Battle, he seemed determined to make the most of the opportunities offered by the new campaign. In the spring of 1941 he was given command of a wing based at Tangmere at the foot of the Sussex Downs. From 24 March Bader flew sixty-two fighter sweeps over France. For Bader, war was a competition and he was always seeking to increase his score, which in the late summer stood at twenty, and inscribe his name in the record books. By then his squadrons were exhausted and his egotism provoked a near-mutiny. But with the backing of Leigh-Mallory, his patron and ally in the Big Wing controversy, Bader carried on. He finally came to grief on 9 August when he was shot up over northern France in disputed circumstances, baled out and was captured, to start a new phase of his wartime career as a spectacularly troublesome POW.

Of all the campaigns fought by the RAF in the Second World War, the fighter campaign over France was the most ill-conceived. It failed because there was nothing to win. It was obvious early on that gains were not worth the effort and losses and it settled down into a Trenchardian exercise in nurturing the offensive spirit in the mistaken belief that it would keep pilots up to the mark and sustain their morale. When the campaign was finally abandoned at the end of 1943 it had cost five aircraft destroyed for every German machine shot down.[37]

The sense of tragic waste hangs over this aspect of the air war as it does over the strategic bombing campaign. It is summed up by the brief story of Brendan 'Paddy' Finucane, born in Dublin to a father who fought in the 1916 uprising, who joined the RAF on a short service commission just before the war, and took part in the Battle of Britain. He was good-looking, clean-living, attending Mass each Sunday, and charming and easy with people high and low. His success in the air made him a natural for promotion by the RAF publicity machine. He was also singled out for his leadership qualities and in the summer of 1941, at the age of twenty-one, was the youngest wing leader in Fighter Command, operating over France from Kenley in Surrey. On 15 July, he led a 'Ramrod', a fighter attack with cannon and machine guns, on a German army camp near Étaples on the Channel coast in the Pas-de-Calais. The raid was timed for when German troops would be queuing for their midday meal. They crossed the Sussex coast at Pevensey Bay at 12.10 p.m. Finucane's wingman was Alan 'Butch' Aikman, a twenty-three-year-old Canadian, charged with eyeballing the airspace for German fighters.

At 12.22 p.m., as they whipped in at what seemed like wave-top height over the beach at Le Touquet, a light machine gun opened fire from a sand ridge, hitting Finucane's starboard wing. 'Immediately a wisp of white vapour streamed back from the damaged radiator,' wrote Anthony Cooper, Finucane's biographer. 'It was an extraordinary shot because the chances of a small calibre machine gun hitting a low flying Spitfire going at over 300 knots were minimal ...'[38] Aikman broke radio silence to report the damage to the radiator. Finucane acknowledged with a thumbs up and turned back to sea, apparently hoping to ditch. Aikman stayed with him. He watched as Finucane jettisoned the cockpit canopy. Before removing his helmet, he radioed a last message: 'This is it, Butch.' Trailing a stream of white coolant, the Spitfire ploughed into the sea and quickly sank. His end released a flood of heartfelt eulogies. 'We shall miss him greatly,' ran one. 'He was the beau ideal of the "fighter boy."' Another judged that 'as well as being a brilliant fighter pilot

… he had the true spirit of a crusader and a high purpose in all he did … I anticipated that he would turn out to be one of the greatest leaders we have ever had.' The first tribute came from Douglas, the second from Leigh-Mallory, architects of the very policy that had sent him to his death.

9

Ten Million Miles of Sea

Squadron Leader Tony Spooner, a much-decorated pilot and veteran of numerous perilous flights over the Atlantic and Mediterranean, wrote a poem that reflected the feelings of many of his comrades who served in Coastal Command.

> Fighters or Bombers? his friends used to say
> But when he said 'Coastal' they turned half away …[1]

The lines were often read at veterans' funerals, and the title – 'No Spotlight for Coastal' – seemed to sum up the unconsidered place they occupied in the war years; in the RAF's order of priorities, in the minds of the government and in the imagination of the British public.

It was Coastal Command's fate to be third in line for everything – resources, money, glory and attention. It operated far away from the public gaze and the nature of the work was repetitive and unglamorous and therefore harder for the propaganda factory to package. Yet its role in Britain's survival was at least as important as that played by Fighter Command, and its contribution to victory as significant as that of Bomber Command.

Unlike the others, it started the war lacking a clear role and simple, agreed objectives. It would take several years and much trial and error before its proper function became obvious and its squadrons were equipped with the right machines and technology to carry out their duties. The delay did not mean there was any slackening in the work rate. 'Constant Endeavour' was the motto given to Coastal Command, and it could not have been more appropriate.

The confusion over role and identity was partly the result of the Air Force's fractious and complicated relationship with the Navy. The Admiralty had never accepted the arrangement arrived at in 1924 by which aircraft and crews operating on Navy ships belonged to the RAF. In 1937 a compromise was reached in which control of all carrier-borne aircraft was returned to the Navy under the aegis of the Fleet Air Arm.

The deal did nothing to remove the fundamental incompatibility in the outlook of the services. At heart, the Admiralty continued to believe that logic and justice demanded that they should exercise full control over all air resources that directly affected the Navy's operations. The RAF, meanwhile, feared that ceding the principle would undermine, perhaps fatally, its hard-won status as an independent service.

The picture was made cloudier by prevailing strategic assumptions about how the war at sea would play out. The old charge that soldiers were always fighting the last war did not apply to the Admirals. Their plans and hypotheses suggested they had entirely forgotten it. Much of the naval effort in 1914–18 had gone into protecting the transatlantic sea lanes on which Britain relied for its survival. The main threat had come not from the powerful German surface fleet, which was neutralized after the Battle of Jutland, but from U-boats which in 1917 sank 6.6 million tons of Allied shipping, seriously weakening the country's ability to continue the war.

The danger had been overcome by a system of merchant convoys, protected by escorts armed with guns, depth charges and torpedoes. By then aircraft, too, were playing an important part and in November 1918 the Air Force had 285 flying boats and 272 land-based aircraft engaged in hunting U-boats. They managed to sink only seven enemy submarines but the deterrent effect was strong. The Naval Staff came to believe that 'the ideal was that a convoy should be escorted by at least two aircraft, one keeping close and one cruising wide to prevent a submarine on the surface from getting into a position to attack'.[2]

By the time the war started the wisdom had changed. Thanks to the development of 'Asdic', anti-submarine underwater detection, the Navy believed it could handle the threat without any need for heavy air support. Its main concern at the beginning was not the U-boats but the Kriegsmarine's squadrons of fast, heavily armed and long-ranging capital ships and pocket battleships which, once at large in the Atlantic, could savage Britain's supply lines.

So it was that in the joint discussions to design a co-operative air and sea organization, held between the Admiralty and Coastal Command, the emphasis was on defensive and passive tasks. The prime duty was to be reconnaissance: 'to assist the Home Fleet in the detection and prevention of enemy vessels escaping from the North Sea to the Atlantic', that is, the dreaded breakout of the surface fleet.[3] Next came the provision of air patrols to spot submarines and convoy escorts to scare them off in British coastal waters. Offensive operations were last on the list, the 'provision of an air striking force' and then 'mainly on the east coast'.

Despite the history of institutional wrangling, at the outset personal relations between Coastal and the Navy were good. Its chief, Frederick Bowhill, was a former sailor with 'sea water in his veins' who joined the RN in 1904, transferred to the RNAS in 1913 and started the First World War commanding the Navy's first aircraft carrier, HMS *Empress*, a converted cross-Channel ferry. He was no one's idea of a seadog, nor indeed of an aviator, with a bald pate, bulging eyes and shaggy red eyebrows that swept upwards across his forehead as if about to take flight. According to his successor Philip Joubert, the fierce impression they gave belied a 'puckish humour that solved awkward problems of prestige and smoothed ruffled sensitivities' – useful qualities in the circumstances.[4]

Joubert believed that Bowhill's 'wide knowledge of seafaring matters and his long experience in the flying service made him very well fitted to the control of the sea communications in war'. As a result he commanded the respect of the Navy. His successors, including Joubert himself, 'were not so fortunate. All of them had Army origins and as such were suspect ...' Nonetheless, though they might lobby persistently for greater air resources, the Admirals did not exploit wartime crises to pursue old claims. When, in the autumn of 1940, Lord Beaverbrook saw an opportunity to stir trouble with a dramatic proposal for Coastal Command to be handed over wholesale to the Navy, it was the opposition of the First Sea Lord, Dudley Pound, that effectively sunk the idea.

Joubert's one – inaccurate – criticism of Bowhill was that he harboured 'a grave suspicion of all scientists, and their works'. Service chiefs got used in wartime to being assailed by experts lobbying for a new gizmo that would supposedly win the war. Most of the innovations were useless but some did indeed turn out to have transformational powers. The breakthrough in the development of British radar, after all, emerged from initial research to test the validity of a 'death ray' that would kill the crews of hostile aircraft.

Joubert prided himself on understanding the crucial part that science would play in the war at sea, a struggle that Coastal Command would be in the thick of. Despite the Navy's initial breezy confidence, it would turn out to be just as much a life and death affair as the Battle of Britain, yet it would go on for years rather than months. The Battle of the Atlantic was waged in various forms from the first day of the war. Though a discernible turning point was reached in the middle of 1943, the U-boat menace persisted and the effort to protect the Allied oceanic supply lines by sea and air continued right until the very end. Everyone who mattered understood the immensity of the stakes. Yet there was never a systematic policy emanating from the government, or even from the Air Ministry, to give Coastal what it needed.

The struggle to keep the sea lanes open had many ups and downs. At the break of each false dawn there was a tendency to scale back the resources of the maritime air effort and divert them to other theatres. There was a perpetual clamour for men and machines from all branches of the service, but, with the bomber credo so deeply entrenched in the minds of the Air Marshals, it was Bomber Command's claims that carried the most weight.

At the start of the war the aircraft, armament and technical equipment with which Coastal Command was equipped were all pathetically inadequate for the tasks it was set. The situation would only get worse as the range of their duties grew ever wider. It was just as well that, at the beginning, its main responsibility was reconnaissance rather than offensive operations.

The Air Ministry issued specifications for a twin-engine reconnaissance/bomber in 1935. Two types were approved but one, the Blackburn Botha, turned out to be all but useless. At the outbreak of hostilities, Coastal's striking power rested on the frail shoulders of the Vickers Vildebeest, a lumbering, antediluvian biplane. Seaplanes were an essential element in the armoury, extending operational capacity to geographically difficult parts of the world and greatly reducing infrastructure needs. The excellent Sunderland, which carried a crew of thirteen, bristled with ten machine guns, had a range of nearly 3,000 miles and could stay airborne for more than thirteen hours, was due to be phased out and replaced with the Lerwick, another Short Brothers design. Like the Botha it proved to be a dud but when, in the spring of 1940, the Air Ministry turned again to the Sunderland, Short's Belfast factory was at full capacity churning out Stirlings for Bomber Command. Thus, Coastal's flying boat fleet in 1939 was supplemented by antique-looking Saro Londons and Supermarine Stranraers.

The unpreparedness of Coastal Command seems reprehensible now but it is easy to forget the enormous hurry in which the RAF went to war and the vast array of problems all services – but particularly the Air Force and Navy – faced with only limited resources from which to contrive solutions. There was not just a nation but an empire to defend and not one potential enemy but three, as Italy and Japan hovered opportunistically on the side lines. What is harder to justify was the later reluctance at the top of the Air Force to make a more intelligent use of available assets when it was clear that the Battle of the Atlantic was as crucial a struggle as the Battle of Britain had been.

New machines were on their way in the shape of Bristol Beaufort torpedo bombers, a happier result of the Air Ministry's 1935 specification, and 200 Lockheed Hudsons, ordered from the US in 1938, largely on the initiative of Arthur Harris against the furious opposition of the domestic aviation industry lobby. Until then, Coastal's backbone consisted of the ten squadrons equipped with Avro Ansons, a converted six-seater civilian passenger plane. The aircraft's reliability was reflected in its nickname, 'Faithful Annie'. Tony Spooner thought the 'dear, safe, wallowing Anson ... possibly the most viceless aircraft ever designed', but there were several crucial downsides.[5] It was slow, dangerous in violent manoeuvres and so short ranged that it could not get to the Norwegian coast – a vital area in the maritime war – and back. Guy Bolland, who in 1940 commanded Coastal's 217 Squadron, felt they were 'quite useless in any wartime role except a limited anti-submarine patrol to protect shipping'.[6]

At this stage, the mere sight or sound of any aeroplane was enough to cause any U-boat which had surfaced in order to vent the stale air from its hull and recharge batteries to make an immediate dive to safety. Tiger Moths, the game little biplane trainers that every RAF pilot knew from his basic training, were pressed into service on these 'scarecrow' patrols. The disruption they caused was valuable, but the German submarines had little to fear. According to Bolland, the Anson was 'both too slow and too fragile. The engines had to be started up by using a starting handle ... Its undercarriage was retractable but only after the use of another (collapsible) handle which took many turns to retract it after take-off and to lower it for landing. For waddling along from A to B it was fine, but the performance, bomb load and armament were totally inadequate and it was soon to be taken off front line duties.'

Bolland joined the RAF on a short service commission in 1930 after a career at sea as a junior officer in the Royal Mail Steam Packet Company. He transferred to Coastal on its creation and commanded the station at Pembroke Dock before taking over 217 Squadron in August 1940 and was by all accounts a popular and efficient commander.[7] The story of his time in charge gives a taste of the demands and hardships common to many of the command's squadrons in the first phase of the war.

217 was based at St Eval, a hurriedly constructed station on the north-west Cornwall coast, and was mainly involved in flying anti-submarine patrols over the Western Approaches to the Channel. The unit was in the middle of re-equipping with the Bristol Beaufort, a much more impressive aeroplane. Its twin Taurus engines made it the fastest torpedo bomber of the day and it was reasonably well defended with a machine gun in the wing and two mounted in a dorsal turret. The transition was difficult. Beauforts were much

harder to fly than the placid Annie. In the meantime, operations with Ansons continued.

With the arrival of German U-boats, followed by large surface warships, in the French Atlantic ports the scope of the squadron's work had widened. The Kriegsmarine now had direct access to the Atlantic sea lanes and the Admiralty inundated the RAF with demands for bombing raids on the ports of Brest, Lorient, La Pallice and Bordeaux. Bowhill responded willingly and Coastal squadrons were diverted into pinprick raids aimed at stalling the gathering threat.

Bolland's predecessor, Wing Commander L. H. Anderson, who had arrived on the squadron on I July 1940, was dismayed at the new orders. The Ansons with their fixed, forward-firing .303-in.-calibre machine guns, were laughably easy targets for the four squadrons of Me 109s defending the port. Their payload of four 100lb bombs would do little significant damage if by any chance they managed to deliver them. When, in mid-July, Anderson was told to launch a daylight raid on Brest, he refused to sacrifice his men in what he saw as a pointless exercise. He was removed from his command and, at a court martial in October, reduced to the rank of squadron leader.[8]

If Bolland's superiors believed that he would be more biddable they were soon disappointed. One of his first acts was to fit Vickers 'K' machine guns in the waist of the Ansons to provide them with a little added protection. However, when this reached the ears of Group Headquarters in Plymouth he was told that the modification was unauthorized and the guns would have to be removed. 'This was an order which I did not obey,' he recorded.

Bolland found that 'squadron morale was very low'. One of the factors determining a unit's state of mind was the degree to which its members felt that their actions made some contribution, no matter how small, to the war effort. The business of going back and forth over vast grey wastes of water, while struggling to keep fatigue and boredom at bay, often to return having seen nothing, did not bring any sense of achievement. Bolland wrote that after the war U-boat commanders 'made it plain in their memoirs how much they feared the mere sound of an aircraft and just the possibility of being seen', causing them to dive and disrupting their pursuit of their victims. However, 'those facts were not known to us at the time and it [was] impossible to persuade many of those who flew thousands of miles without a sight of the enemy that they were doing [anything] to win the war'.

Life on the ground that winter was unsettling with constant air raid warnings and occasional bombs landing on and around the base from raiders on their way back from plastering Merseyside. On 21 January 1941 a parachute mine landed on an air raid shelter, killing twenty-one of the base ground staff.

While the Beauforts were bedding in, Ansons kept up attacks on the Atlantic ports. When operating in darkness the fighters left them alone and they escaped relatively unscathed by flak so that in 200 sorties not a single aeroplane was lost. The crews noticed that the shells always seemed to burst some way ahead of them and concluded that they owed their survival to the fact that German gunners did not realize that the attacking aircraft were so slow and made a correspondingly exaggerated guess at the degree of deflection needed to hit them. Better aircraft only brought heavier casualties. In December 1940, the first month of night operations by the Beauforts, six machines and eighteen crew members were lost; this out of a squadron with a nominal strength of eighteen aircraft.

Admiralty pressure on the Air Force intensified with the appearance of the German battlecruisers *Scharnhorst* and *Gneisenau* in Brest in the early spring of 1941. They had joined the U-boats and the long-range Focke-Wulf 200 'Condor' maritime patrol and bomber aircraft in ravaging the Atlantic traffic, sinking 115,622 tons of shipping during their voyage south. They were constrained by the fact that they did not have the guns to tackle convoys which sailed with a battleship escort. That deficiency would be remedied with the arrival of their own battleship, *Bismarck*, which had finished its final sea trials and was due to dart through the northern seas to join them. The worsening situation brought a new call to arms from Downing Street. On 6 March 1941 Churchill issued his Battle of the Atlantic directive which ordered all available resources to 'take the offensive against the U-boat and the Focke-Wulf wherever we can and whenever we can'. When the German cruisers were confirmed as having docked at Brest on 22 March, an all-out air assault by Bomber and Coastal Commands began.

217 Squadron had already been involved in the effort to sink the cruiser *Admiral Hipper* which arrived at Brest in mid-February after two successful Atlantic sorties. The order to attack the port would trigger the premature departure of a second CO. Guy Bolland recorded how 'one day in March ... I had orders to send available aircraft to raid [Brest] in daylight. I was only too well aware how well-defended that was by guns and fighters. There was no possible chance of any of my machines getting anywhere near Brest, and if they were lucky enough to hit the ships, the damage they inflicted on the enemy would be negligible.' The chances of disaster were further increased by the fact that there would be no fighter escort to offer any protection over the target. He decided to take the drastic step of declaring that all his aircraft were unserviceable. Group Headquarters in Plymouth were immediately suspicious and queried the signal. Bolland recalled that 'as the day wore on C-in-C Coastal Command [Bowhill] came onto the phone demanding that I got some aircraft serviceable. The station commander at St Eval was not supporting me and I was out on a limb.'

Such was the pressure that he relented enough to make three Beauforts available, bypassing the station commander to warn Plymouth that 'this was a suicide order and I was dead against it as it would serve no useful purpose except to pander to the Navy's demand for action'. He told the Air Officer Commanding 19 Group, Air Commodore Geoffrey Bromet, 'that I did not expect to ever see any of my crews again and if this turned out to be true, to expect to see me in Plymouth that night'.

All three Beauforts were lost with only one of the twelve crew members surviving. Bolland kept his promise, turning up at the headquarters at Mount Wise that evening where he bearded Bromet and an unnamed senior naval officer. 'I told them as clearly as I could that the order to send young men to their deaths on useless missions was not on, and I did not think they could possibly under-stand what the defences of Brest were like.' He signed off with a suggestion that must have burned like acid: 'Perhaps it would be better if I could discuss this with someone on their staff who had fought in the war.'

For this insubordination Bolland was duly sacked. Unlike Anderson he was not subjected to court martial, and somewhat to his surprise found himself posted to the staff of the Commander of the Home Fleet, Jack Tovey, as Fleet Aviation Officer, handling liaison between the admiral and Bowhill.

The diversion of attacking ports did bring some results, in one case spectacular success. Bomber Command led the assault on the *Scharnhorst* and *Gneisenau* at Brest but it was a Beaufort of Coastal's 22 Squadron that did the most significant damage. On the morning of 6 April 1941, *Gneisenau* lay in the port's inner harbour having been moved there from dry dock the previous day due to the presence of an unexploded bomb delivered in an earlier RAF attack. The new position was spotted by a Spitfire from the Photographic Reconnaissance Unit and a strike ordered for first light.

Of the four Beauforts in the attacking force, only the one piloted by Flying Officer Kenneth Campbell managed to locate the target in the morning haze. Coming in low from seaward he would have seen before him, first, three flak ships bristling with anti-aircraft guns, then behind them a low stone mole that ran in from the west to curve protectively around the dock and five hundred yards beyond that the low bulk of the battlecruiser, hard up against the north wall of the harbour. More guns were clustered on the slopes behind the town, and other batteries sat on the two arms of land encircling the outer harbour. Within seconds of the Beaufort appearing every gun – a thousand weapons of all calibres – was in action. To hit the ship, Campbell had to drop his single torpedo just the other side of the mole. According to the official report 'coming in at almost sea level, he passed the anti-aircraft ships at less than mast height in the very mouths of their guns, and skimming over the mole, landed a torpedo at point blank range'.[9]

At that height and speed, he had no chance of clearing the high ground ahead and hauled the aircraft into a tight turn, thus presenting an unmissable target. The Beaufort plunged into the harbour in flames, but the torpedo ran straight and true, exploding beneath the *Gneisenau*'s waterline. The attack was followed by another Bomber

Command raid five days later, which killed many of the crew, and it would be eight months before the battlecruiser was seaworthy.

Campbell, of course, was dead, along with his crew, Sergeants J. P. Scott, the Canadian navigator, R. W. Hillman, the wireless operator, and W. C. Mullins, the air gunner. As the pilot and captain, Campbell was awarded the Victoria Cross. The others, in keeping with the practice of the time, were deemed to have played no part in the decision to press home the attack and got nothing. Campbell was a twenty-three-year-old Scot, born in Saltcoats, Ayrshire,

Campbell VC

educated at Sedburgh public school and Cambridge where he read chemistry and joined the University Air Squadron. What drove his extraordinary determination, what armoured him from the paralysing fear that the eruption of gunfire that met them must have provoked, we shall never know. In the photograph, from beneath his Air Force Blue side cap his steady eyes meet ours and tell us nothing.

The great Atlantic rendezvous of German surface ships never happened. In May, the attempted breakout by *Bismarck* came to a spectacular end when, after being battered by the shells and torpedoes of a combined naval task force, she went down 500 miles off Brest, with all flags flying. The episode provided some much-needed good news but also demonstrated that, used intelligently, combined air and sea operations could be devastatingly effective. Coastal played a crucial part in the battleship's demise. It was a Spitfire from the command's No. 1 Photographic Reconnaissance Unit, which on 21 May took the pictures from which *Bismarck* and its consort, *Prinz Eugen*, were positively identified as they steamed towards Bergen.

The following day a Fleet Air Arm Maryland dipped below the clouds blanketing the Bergen fjords to establish that they had now departed. Both Coastal and FAA reconnaissance aircraft dogged the battleship's steps as it passed through the Denmark Strait between Greenland and Iceland, and carried on the pursuit following the action of 24 May in which HMS *Hood* was sunk. When *Bismarck* shook off its shadowers on 26 May, it was a bold stroke by Frederick Bowhill that put them back on the trail. He ordered a patrol further south than the Admiralty reckoned the quarry to be. Coastal Command Catalina flying boats intercepted the battleship nearly 800 miles north-west of the haven of Brest and set in train the FAA Swordfish attack that slowed, and ultimately doomed, the battleship.

By now it was clear that the role allotted to Coastal Command at the outset was not ambitious enough. Its aircraft and crews would be better employed not just in reconnaissance and deterrent patrols but in an offensive role, hunting U-boats and destroying them.

The arrival of more and better aircraft and upgraded radar meant they were in a reasonable position to combine with the Navy to provide improved protection for the convoys and take the fight to the Germans.

Bowhill left in June 1941 to take over Ferry Command. On his watch, Coastal had undergone a quantitative and qualitative transformation. The nineteen squadrons it had started the war with had grown to forty. New aircraft like the US-manufactured PBY-5 Catalina seaplanes were almost as big as the Sunderlands and could operate 800 miles from base and stay in the air for seventeen hours. The flying boats were relatively spacious compared with most military aircraft but there was 'still less room in which to move than is to be found in a small fishing smack'.[10]

The Lockheed Hudson could be projected 500 miles with a time over the target area of two hours. Wellingtons and Whitleys ceded by Bomber Command could also spend two hours on station at that distance. The basing of a wing in Iceland in the late summer of 1940 opened the air umbrella wider, though a gap in mid-ocean still remained which could not be covered from either side of the Atlantic. There were some, though still not enough, long-range fighters to offer a degree of protection from the Condors and long-range Heinkels that reinforced the air offensive.

The men who flew the patrols had an identity which set them slightly apart. A disciplinary report noted that Coastal was 'a more stable command. The captains have earned their rank by long experience, and the crews as a whole are a more reliable and responsible type.'[11] Tony Spooner fitted the approving stereotype. In 1937 he had decided to try and become an airline pilot. The attraction was the pay and career prospects rather than any romantic attraction to flying. He had been an instructor before joining Coastal and had a strictly methodical approach to operations.

Steady types were needed in this unglamorous front of the air war. The report noted 'the isolated nature of many of the stations', far from the bright lights. Early in 1941 Spooner was based at Limavady, in Northern Ireland. The station was next to Lough Foyle, and he was able to vouch for the truth of the local saying that 'if you *can* see across the lough it's a sign that it's about to rain. If you can't, then it's raining already.'[12]

The work was tedious. As an official publication of the time put it, 'the chief enemy is not the German Luftwaffe or the German Navy, but boredom, which may provoke first inattention, then indifference. [The pilot] must spend hundreds of hours with nothing to look on but the expanse of sea and sky. "Wave, on wave, on wave, to West" stretches the vast monotony of the Atlantic Ocean. It may glitter in the noonday or lie devoid of light and colour in the hour after sunset; it may seem to crawl like the wrinkled skin of a beast or stretch in ridged and uneven furrows under the breath of strong winds; but it will be empty for hours.'[13] Protracted staring at the sea could prove fatal, sending the pilot into a trance and blinding him to the line between sky and water.

When disaster struck, as it all too often did, it was most likely to be caused by accident or error. It was hard to know, as the end came out of sight of ship or aircraft, witnessed only by the seabirds. On beginning his tour of operations with 221 Squadron flying Wellingtons over the North Atlantic, Tony Spooner noted how 'most of the losses remained unexplained ... crews went out and simply "failed to return." Perhaps an engine failed? Perhaps they got lost? Perhaps they flew into the sea deceived by their altimeters? Perhaps they got iced up, or ran out of petrol fighting engine ice?'[14]

The latter was a major hazard, 'our great enemy'. Whenever possible they tried to fly below the cloud base where icing was less likely, but when the weather made this too dangerous, they were forced to climb into the colder upper air. A chemical de-icing agent could offer protection to the wing and tail surfaces but rain soon washed it off. Propellers collected ice easily, as did the carburettor intakes of the engines. The drill in the case of the former was 'to make violent alteration in the revs per minute hoping to dislodge [it] by vibration and centrifugal forces'. In the latter it was to 'either try a full-power climb through the cloud to the clearer air on top or, as a last desperate remedy ... switch the ignition off – then on; the monumental back fire which resulted would with luck, clear the carburettor throat'. There was nothing they could do, though, to prevent ice encrusting the aerials which festooned their Wellingtons, emitting an eerie singing noise as they vibrated.

It seemed to Spooner that enemy action was the least likely explanation for disappearances, partly because it was obligatory to send an immediate 'ops flash' signal as soon as a hostile aircraft or vessel was sighted. A more dispiriting reason was 'the sad fact ... that neither 221 nor 502 Squadrons, [the sister unit] were finding the enemy, except on very rare occasions ...' Even if they did spot a U-boat, 'it usually was able to dive under the waves before the crew could drop their load of depth charges'. The figures bore out this judgement. In the first twenty-two months of the war, Coastal Command aircraft spotted 161 U-boats and attacked 125 of them. They managed to sink only two, and then with assistance from Navy craft.[15]

Philip Joubert took over command from Bowhill in June 1941 and, according to the official historian, made it his first task to 'develop the most effective operational technique for ASV aircraft, and in so doing to make the aeroplane at last a "U-boat killer"'.[16] ASV stood for air-to-surface-vessel radar, supposedly capable of locating U-boats on the surface and with a forward scan of twelve miles and a side scan of twenty. In its early forms, however, it was mainly of use as a navigational device, rather than as a means of pinpointing enemy submarines, and when the government's chief scientific adviser Sir Henry Tizard visited Limavady and asked the crews how many U-boats they had detected with it the answer came back 'none, or possibly one'.[17]

Fighting submarines was a mechanical, methodical business. The battlefield was vast, ten and a half million square miles of sea. The northern boundary lay inside the Arctic Circle and the southern on the Equator. It stretched in the east to the coasts of western Europe and West Africa, and in the west to the eastern seaboards of Canada, Newfoundland, the USA and Central America.[18] Finding U-boats in this wilderness meant catching them while they were leaving or returning from a hunting sortie, or as they tracked, or lay in wait, for a convoy. German cryptanalysts had partly penetrated the Navy's codes before the war began and also cracked those used by merchant shipping, which greatly helped the Kriegsmarine's commander Admiral Dönitz deploy his forces to maximum effect.[19] Much of Coastal's effort went into flying patrols in likely areas. This involved criss-crossing a designated grid for as long as the weather and fuel allowed until the 'Prudent Limit of Endurance' was reached.

If sighted, the patrolling aircraft had to get its attack in quickly for an alert commander could dive his boat in thirty seconds. On board the aircraft, a klaxon sounded action stations and bombs and depth charges were primed. There was often little to show for a successful operation except some mysterious debris. One report of an attack by a Sunderland 210 miles off Finisterre described how 'bombs were dropped within twenty feet when the submarine was at periscope depth and a large oil patch with air bubbles was observed. Later more bubbles appeared in the centre of the patch. After twenty minutes the oil patch extended with bubbles continuing to rise. The aircraft remained in the vicinity for three and a half hours ...'[20]

The crew of a Hudson, sent out from Iceland on 27 August 1941 after a patrolling aircraft from the same squadron attacked but failed to sink a U-boat, had the satisfaction of catching it just as it surfaced again. After it dropped depth charges 'the U-boat was completely enveloped by the explosions and shortly afterwards submerged completely'.[21] Two minutes later it reappeared and 'ten or twelve of its crew wearing yellow life jackets appeared on the conning tower and came down on deck'. The Hudson dived, 'firing all its guns it could bring to bear as it swept in tight turns around the submarine'. The crew then scrambled for the conning tower, re-emerging seven minutes later waving a white cloth, subsequently discovered to be the captain's dress shirt. Relays of aircraft then kept watch for eleven and a half hours until a naval trawler arrived to capture the prize.

The increasing success of the campaign was due to the greater number of better machines available, the improved quality of radar and the greater efficiency of depth charges, bombs and rockets. None of these were obtained without a struggle. Once again, the peculiar relationship that Coastal Command stood in, not just with the Navy but with the RAF itself, created special difficulties when it pressed for its fair share of resources.

Quite early in the war the Air Staff had accepted that the Admiralty should have overall control of joint air operations connected to the

Battle of the Atlantic. That meant Coastal Command was held in joint custody, with the RAF supplying men, machines and land bases while the Navy put them to work. It was a common-sense arrangement and the cogs, large and small, of the two services locked smoothly enough where they met in each of the command's operational areas.

The friction came at the top from the endless clashes between Admiralty and Air Ministry over resources. By the summer of 1941, Coastal Command had extended the protection it could provide to transatlantic convoys but a wide gap still remained in mid-ocean that was beyond the range of aircraft operating either from Britain and Iceland on one side and Newfoundland on the other. Aggressive patrolling to locate and sink U-boats was starting to have some success, but more machines and crews were needed to change the course of the battle decisively. The Admiralty naturally made repeated requests for very long-range aircraft to expand the air umbrella and maintain pressure on the submarines.

As Commander-in-Chief of Coastal, Philip Joubert supported the Navy 'with all my power', only to find that his own superiors were against him.[22] Requests for some of the new four-engine Halifaxes which began arriving on Bomber Command squadrons at the end of 1940 were ignored by the Air Ministry. In June 1941, a single squadron, No. 120, which was based in Iceland, was equipped with Consolidated B-24 Liberators supplied by America, which had the long legs to close the Atlantic gap. According to Joubert, Bomber Command only spared the aircraft from its 'private war with Germany' because 'their engines showed too much flame from the exhausts, and thus helped the enemy night fighters'. As detection technology improved very long-range aircraft like the Liberators turned out to be very effective hunters and killers of submarines, yet in February 1943 there were still only eighteen operating in the North Atlantic.

Coastal's bargaining power was diminished after the battle seemed to take a turn for the better in the middle of 1941. In 1942, another crisis developed. In March, more than 800,000 tons of Allied shipping was sent to the bottom, two-thirds by U-boats. There were similar losses in June and November. It seemed obvious to Joubert that some of Bomber Command's growing resources, in particular the Stirlings, Halifaxes and Lancasters arriving on the squadrons, would have to be switched to face the desperate threat looming in the Atlantic. His representations provoked more irritation than sympathy among those who were directing the larger shape of the war.

The reluctance to divert resources takes some explaining. No one could be in any doubt about the crucial nature of the struggle and the importance of Coastal Command's part in it. Dudley Pound, the head of the Navy, declared in March 1942: 'If we lose the war at sea, we lose the war.'[23] Churchill agreed with him, recording after it was over that 'the Battle of the Atlantic was the dominating factor throughout the war ... [everything] ultimately depended on its outcome'.

Why, then, the grudging responses, delivered with what felt like hostile relish by the likes of Arthur Harris, to Coastal Command's modest requests for the tools to do its job? The Air Marshals gave the outward impression of treating the Navy's needs sympathetically. Early in 1942 the First Lord of the Admiralty A. V. Alexander drew up a wish list for six and a half squadrons of Wellingtons, which were now being superseded by the 'heavies', to deal with increasing U-boat activity in the Atlantic. There was a further demand for two more bomber squadrons to be sent to Ceylon to help with the extension of the naval war into the Indian Ocean.

More memos fluttered across from the Admiralty carrying more requests. The response from the Air Staff seemed positive. The Secretary of State for Air, Archibald Sinclair, declared that it was the Air Ministry's duty to 'meet Admiralty requirements as quickly as possible', while Portal, the CAS, assured the Defence Committee that he and his colleagues shared the sailors' view 'that the present situation at sea calls for substantial assistance from the Royal Air Force'.[24] By this the airmen did not mean that they were in favour of any long-term transfer of resources away from the bombing campaign against Germany and towards the fight at sea. Sinclair was quick to point out that bomber squadrons would have to be re-equipped with ASV before they could carry out long-range reconnaissance duties, and by the time that happened aircraft that Coastal

Command had on order would have arrived and the deficiency made good. He added that the effort would anyway be 'largely wasted' as enemy targets were 'uncertain, fleeting and difficult to hit'.

The real motive behind the reluctance to give Coastal a higher priority was a determination not to allow the Air Force to be distracted from what it still passionately believed to be its true purpose: a strategic air offensive against Germany that would destroy its ability to wage war. The logic was that the Coastal Command effort was essentially defensive aimed only at preventing Britain from losing the war.[25] Only offence could bring victory, and that was the job of Bomber Command. It therefore followed that Coastal should get only the minimum resources necessary to avoid defeat.

The plethora of demands came at a particularly tense time for Bomber Command. A long period of heavy losses and consistent failure had forced it into a policy of conservation while it awaited better days. It was preparing to launch a new offensive, armed with bigger and better aircraft and a potentially game-changing navigational device called 'Gee', which raised hopes that the squadrons might at last be able to find their targets. By now Churchill and the government were losing faith in the Air Staff's claims for what bombing could achieve and the whole doctrine of the strategic air offensive was in danger of collapsing. Under a new commander, Arthur Harris, the bombers were being allowed another chance – quite possibly a last one – to live up to the role the airmen had claimed for themselves. Failure would mean humiliation, and the demolition of the RAF's arguments for its own independent existence. Most importantly, it would demonstrate that what it had presented as a broad thoroughfare to victory was in fact a dead end, thereby wrecking a fundamental premise of Britain's war planning. A breakthrough was imperative, but for the renewed campaign to have any prospect of success required the concentration of all Bomber Command's resources.

Thus, the reasonable tone that the Air Staff adopted when confronted with calls for assistance from the Navy and appeals for largesse from Coastal Command was not entirely sincere. Their minds were set on proving the truth of the Trenchard doctrine. If that meant inflicting a degree of hardship and raising the level of risk on other fronts, then so be it. They were convinced they were at last capable of bombing Germany effectively. By devastating the cities which supplied the Kriegsmarine with the wherewithal to sustain their war at sea, they would do more to win the Battle of the Atlantic than diverting effort to a defensive maritime role in which they had little expectation of success.

No one believed this more fervently than Bomber Command's new chief. Arthur Harris took over from Richard Peirse in February 1942. It was Peirse's bad luck to have held the job during a depressing period of international isolation and dismal results. Harris arrived just after the planets had undergone a momentous realignment. Thanks to Barbarossa and Pearl Harbor, Britain now had mighty allies and the technical and material difficulties that had crippled the bombing effort were coming to an end.

Ruthlessness, energy, ambition and a near-fanatical faith in the power of bombing made Harris the Air Force's most aggressive wartime leader. He had a laser intelligence and razor-edged powers of expression which he used to slash at anyone who dared to challenge his arguments and appreciations. Joubert learned straightaway that he could expect no help from Bomber Command's stout overlord. Within a few months of arriving Harris had created a buzz of success. Raids on the strategically unimportant but highly flammable old Hanseatic cities of Lübeck and Rostock gave substance to the claim that the Air Force was causing Germany real pain. At the end of May he launched the first Thousand Bomber Raid on Cologne. These were propaganda successes rather than serious blows to the German war economy but they reinforced Harris's faith that 'victory, speedy and complete, awaits the side which first employs air power as it should be employed'.[26] That meant throwing aircraft against German cities, not using them as a 'subsidiary weapon' in support of the Army and Navy.

Harris's hectoring voice echoed through Whitehall and Downing Street where Churchill's door seemed always open to him. In June, he called for the immediate return to Bomber Command of all the aircraft it had loaned to Coastal, for their absence from his order of battle was 'an obstacle to victory'. A few months later Churchill supported a move to prise two bomber squadrons seconded to Atlantic duties and send them back to Harris.[27] Harris also demanded the return of all bombers from the Middle East once the situation stabilized and the recall of all suitable aircraft and crews from Army Co-operation Command. According to one of the statistics, vivid but obscure of origin that he was apt to flourish, it took '7,000 hours of flying to destroy one submarine at sea ... approximately the amount of flying necessary to destroy one third of Cologne ...'

Would the Battle of the Atlantic have been won quicker if Bomber Command's men and machines had been thrown into the fray? The question burned fiercely from the beginning, spreading well beyond expert military and political circles, and was publicly aired in the House of Commons.[28] It has flared up frequently in the decades since. The debate is unresolvable. The truth is that the inter-war theories, policies and personalities of the RAF landed it in a place where there was little room for manoeuvre. Men, machines, training and doctrine all pointed in one direction, and that was to Europe and Germany. To change course so dramatically once the conflict was launched required a root-and-branch reorganization that needed to be both physical and conceptual. The timetable of war made the feat impossible. To construct an Air Force adequate to face all the challenges that Hitler threw up would have meant putting the clock back a dozen years.

To succeed, then, Coastal Command would have to adapt, to improvise, to analyse. Joubert sought solutions in science. Despite his disparaging remarks about Bowhill's alleged hostility to boffins, he inherited from him the brilliant brain of Professor Patrick Blackett who Bowhill had appointed as his Scientific Adviser in March 1941. Blackett, who went on to win the Nobel Prize in Physics, was sceptical about the value of strategic bombing and believed that priority should be given to winning the Battle of the Atlantic. He set up an operational research unit and recruited a star team to examine all aspects of the command's work. It was supplemented by scrupulous analysis of the pattern of U-boat activities overseen by the senior naval staff officer at Coastal, Captain Dudley Peyton-Ward, who valued every scrap of intelligence gleaned from crew reports, often debriefing the airmen in person.[29] The research resulted in the issue of precise tactical drills which offered the best chance of killing submarines.

Everything hinged on spotting and surprise. To stand any chance of damaging a submarine the hunter had to catch it unawares on the surface, for the window within which an attack might succeed was tiny. It took half a minute for a U-boat to disappear into the deep, where it was all but invulnerable, no matter how many depth charges were showered on the immediate area. Even the most fractional extension of the margins increased the possibility of success. Experiments showed that camouflaging the under-surface and sides of aircraft with white paint enhanced their invisibility against the pale skies of the North Atlantic, making the German lookout's job harder. From summer 1941, the livery of the Coastal Command aircraft operating in those latitudes earned them the nickname 'the White Crows'.[30]

Tony Spooner left Northern Ireland for a hair-raising spell in Malta, before eventually joining 53 Squadron to return to U-boat hunting. He was delighted by the improvements that had taken place in his absence. The 'greatest joy ... was to be given really effective radar. No longer were we to battle with the limited ASV Mark II. Now we had a circular screen which depicted the area around as a map orientated about our aircraft ...'[31] He was now flying a Liberator which 'could fly with one or possibly two engines inoperative', fitted with anti-icing devices and a radio altimeter which reduced the old danger of flying into the sea.

U-boats tended to remain submerged during the day when within aircraft range, surfacing at night to proceed more rapidly under cover of darkness. The arrival of enhanced ASV radar gave a little more point to night-time patrolling. Even if a conning tower showed up on the screen, the target needed to be lit up for a successful attack. Bowhill had backed an initiative by Squadron Leader Humphrey de Vere Leigh, labouring in a dull personnel job at Command Headquarters, to pursue the prospect of an ASV-directed searchlight mounted in the under-turret of a Wellington. Leigh was in his mid-forties and had served as an aviator in the RNAS in the First World War. He had no technical expertise but had developed his idea after chatting with returning aircrew about their operational frustrations.[32]

Experiments in May 1941 were encouraging and Bowhill referred the project to the Air Ministry. The dossier landed on the desk of Joubert, then an assistant to the CAS with responsibility for radio. But Joubert was pursuing his own night-illumination project, the 'Turbinlite', devised by Group Captain William Helmore to guide night fighters onto bombers. The aircraft carrying the Turbinlite had to work in tandem with another which would carry out the attack. The Leigh Light seemed more promising and, after taking over at Coastal, Joubert backed it. It still took a year before five Wellingtons from 172 Squadron were fitted with the new device. By the end of the war, Leigh Light-fitted aircraft had attacked 218 U-boats by night and sunk twenty-seven of them. The beam not only made the night day but tended to blind the German gunners as the attacker moved in for the kill. 'It was no wonder that nothing very dangerous ever came our way during this vital stage of the attack,' wrote Spooner. 'We were never hit once.'[33]

These improvements heaped yet more operational difficulties on the U-boats, forcing them to remain submerged as they made their way from the safety of their massively reinforced pens on the French coast to their hunting grounds. As was the way in the most technology dependent fronts of the war, dangerous innovation by one side stimulated counter-measures by the other. German boffins fought back with the Metox radar warning receiver necessitating a further refinement that tilted the odds back in the attackers' favour.

There was no great clash of arms that brought a decision in the Atlantic. Instead it was a story of huge and unflagging effort, both physical and mental, that brought only incremental advantages. Eventually the cumulative pressure told and by the middle of 1943 the joint operations of the Navy and Air Force had turned the tide. The continuing threat did not allow any relaxation of effort and Coastal Command was in continuous action not only in the Atlantic but across the world in every theatre where British troops were present. By the end of the war, by their own efforts, they had sunk 169 enemy submarines and seriously damaged another 111.[34]

For most of the time the crews on the air and the ground carried on their duties outside the glare of the propaganda limelight which played on their fighter and bomber comrades. The names and feats of outstanding warriors like Terry Bulloch, who sighted and attacked more U-boats than any other pilot, sinking four of them, and the New Zealand ace 'Mick' Ensor, are little known outside the ranks of the survivors. As John Slessor, who succeeded Joubert, remarked eleven years after the war, they 'certainly did not get their meed of public recognition at the time; nor have they since …'[35]

10

The Blue

On breaks from the desert, Sam Pritchard and his friends had a well-established programme of rest and recreation. They would 'collect four to six weeks' pay, then spend it within two to three days on good food, good drink and the best … accommodation available'.[1] Arriving in Cairo from his base at Gambut in Libya, the sergeant navigator from 216 Squadron would check into his hotel and 'luxuriate in the bath for about two hours from 9.30 am onwards, during which a hotel servant brought me a succession of cold Stella beers'. Then, 'dressed in my smartest bush jacket, immaculate slacks and "brothel creepers" I rendezvoused with friends at Groppi's or the Exmorandi Bar'. They lunched on 'wonderful fresh sea-foods, covered in sliced tomatoes, cucumber and other salads' washed down with more drinks. He then repaired to the hotel for a siesta before a servant awoke him by prior arrangement with a heart-starter of a raw egg mixed with brandy which rendered him 'suitably refreshed and full of beans for another rendezvous with friends and another night on the town'.

Three days of this was enough to empty his wallet and sap his strength to the point where he was 'sufficiently shattered and flat broke to return contentedly to my tent in the desert'. He found the sharp contrast between the dangers and hardships of life at the front and the fleshpots of Cairo strangely satisfying. The return to action 'felt like a 'period of spiritual atonement and asceticism. Never again in our lives would we relish the ambrosia nor taste the nectar in quite the same way once the "desert" component had been taken out of the equation.'

Pritchard was a nonconformist minister's son from North Wales. As for many of the British and Commonwealth and Allied refugee airmen who passed through the Middle East it was his first experience of 'abroad' and he was determined to make the most of it. Although he was only dimly aware of it at the time, as well as having a great adventure he was making history. The war in the desert would turn out to be a major evolutionary advance in the life of the RAF, in which its individual capacities and strengths were bundled into a powerful, coherent whole. Pritchard and his comrades were the instruments of a great achievement, albeit one that was a long time coming. In the Middle East, the Air Force became the essential element in the Allied war effort. In the campaigns in the Mediterranean and North African desert of 1940–43 air power came of age. It was the fulfilment of a long-proclaimed prophecy, though not at all in the way that Trenchard and his followers had envisaged.

The air war in the desert had its own particular feel. It was fought in a unique environment. Navigation was easy. There was bright blue sea on one side and sand and rock on the other. The battlefield was largely empty. Apart from bands of nomads and the inhabitants of coastal towns and villages, compared to northern Europe there were hardly any civilians to worry about. The landscape and environment had little meaning. When you landed, there were no family or friends on hand to give you moral strength, nor familiar streets, cinemas and pubs to remind you what it was you were fighting for. Nor was it the homeland of your enemies, just a way station on the long journey to the end of the war.

For the airmen, the fighting never stopped. In their role supporting the Army and Navy, there was always work to do. Later, some tried to romanticize the desert air war as something clean and chivalrous, an ennobling experience. The camaraderie that was forged between the Allied forces, whether airborne or earthbound, was real enough. So, too, were exhaustion, hardship and what the Australian fighter ace Bobby Gibbes called 'violent, terrible fear'. He was 'not afraid to confess to being frightened. I was almost always terrified.'[2] Nor did he shy away from admitting to feeling its awkward corollary; the joy of survival, revealed in a passage describing his mood immediately after a combat: 'The enemy has completely disappeared. You then collect the remnants of your squadron, count them hastily, then the fires burning below. Some of the fires … contain the mutilated bodies of your friends. But as you look down you have no real feeling other than … probably terrific relief that it is them and not you … as you fly back to your base, now safe at last, a feeling of light-hearted exuberance comes over you. It is wonderful to be alive …'

Britain needed desperately to hold on to the Middle East. If Egypt fell the Suez Canal would go with it. There would no longer be a direct route to the East and the resources of the empire, and the path to the oil fields of Arabia and Persia, on which it depended for a twelfth of its needs, would be blocked. As long as Italy stayed out of the military equation, Egypt was reasonably safe. On 10 June 1940, with France staggering towards collapse and Britain looking isolated and vulnerable, Mussolini declared Italy's entry into the war on the side of what he was confident were the sure-fire winners.

At a stroke, the strategic picture for Britain changed in a way that was every bit as dismaying as Germany's lightning conquest of Norway, Denmark, the Low Countries and France. A large Italian force was parked next door to Egypt in Libya. Deprived of the resources of the French navy, the British fleet now faced the sizeable and modern Regia Marina, alone. In the air, the Regia Aeronautica was equipped with machines that were as good as those the British could muster. The threat came from the south as well as the north. Large Italian forces were concentrated in the recently conquered territories of Abyssinia and Somaliland. The British garrison had also to contend with unfriendly neighbours in the Levant, in the shape of the pro-Vichy French forces in Lebanon and Syria. To complete the strategic horror show, Britain faced the prospect of the Balkans and Turkey falling to the Axis, thus completing their conquest of the entire northern shore of the Mediterranean.

Against this, the British could dispose only forces that, in the wry words of Denis Richards, were 'exiguous even by our own standards of military preparation'.[3] Reinforcing them and supplying them would present huge difficulties. There were yet more factors that further reduced the chances of success. In the early days, the theatre commanders of Army, Navy and Air Force were subjected to constantly changing orders from London as Churchill and the service chiefs struggled to meet new menaces which always arrived much more quickly than anticipated. The atmosphere of the solitary and desperate year from June 1940 to June 1941 seemed to incubate miscalculations. Chief among them was the decision at the end of 1940 to divert major resources away from North Africa to shore up Greece in its battle against first, Italy, then Germany. At the time, the top echelon of decision-makers agreed it was the sensible and proper thing to do. It soon became clear they had blundered, ensuring a debacle that set back victory in the Middle East by years.

The RAF's Middle Eastern Command bore great responsibilities and disposed minimal assets. It covered an area of four and a half million square miles including Egypt, Sudan, Palestine and Trans-Jordan, East Africa, Aden and Somaliland, Iraq and neighbouring territories, Cyprus, Turkey, the Balkans as well as the Mediterranean, Red Sea and Persian Gulf.[4] In June 1940, its commander-in-chief, Arthur Longmore, had twenty-nine squadrons to work with, equipped with an array of inter-war-period museum pieces. The bomber force had a single squadron of the latest Mark IV Blenheims. The rest was made up of Mark Is, supplemented by Vickers Wellesleys and Bristol Bombays. The fighters were all Hawker and Gloster biplanes. In time, aircraft numbers would expand vastly. In October 1941, the Western Desert Air Force (WDAF) which supported the Eighth Army in its back and forth battles across Egypt, Libya and Tunisia had sixteen squadrons (nine fighter, six medium bomber and one tactical reconnaissance) and fielded about 1,000 combat machines. A year later, there were twenty-nine squadrons and more than 1,500 aircraft, almost all new or newish types, more than twice the number the Axis could put in the air.

To stay in the war, Britain needed the resources of its overseas territories. The manpower of the Commonwealth would be a vital source of strength. The RAF was a particular beneficiary and, of the 340,000 men who served as aircrew in the course of the war, 134,000 came from abroad. The WDAF included squadrons from the South African Air Force, the Royal Australian Air Force, the Royal Canadian Air Force as well as exile units made up of Poles, Free

French and many other nationalities. Sons of the empire were well represented at the top. Arthur Longmore was born in New South Wales. Raymond Collishaw, the Desert Air Force's aggressive chief in 1940, and according to Arthur Tedder 'the very epitome of the offensive spirit', was born on Vancouver Island to Welsh parents who came to the RAF from the RNAS where he had ended the previous war as the service's highest scoring pilot. His successor, Arthur Coningham, left a rackety family background in New Zealand to join the RFC where he became known as 'Mary'. His father was a Test cricketer and also a con man who was forced to shift the family from Australia after he was exposed trying to blackmail a Catholic priest. The nickname, according to his biographer Vincent Orange, was 'worn down from the original Maori (then thought suitable for any New Zealander)'.[5] It stayed with him, with his blessing, for the rest of his life. He is a rather intangible figure now, dying soon after the war aged fifty-three when the airliner he was in disappeared in the Bermuda Triangle. 'Mary' would be as upright as his father was louche, a near-teetotaller who disapproved of swearing, in what was a boozy, expletive-rich milieu.

Australians in particular seemed at home in the desert. Philip Guedalla, a popular historian who travelled the region at the behest of the Air Ministry, put his finger on it after a visit to No. 3 Squadron. Meeting the pilots, equipped only with out-of-date Gladiators, he was struck by their air of 'reckless willingness and capacity to do something very soon'.[6]

The war in the Middle East got off to a good start. The Italians held most of the advantages. In Libya, a 210,000-strong army, operating within easy reach of home, stood ready under Marshal Graziani for the order to cross the border. Facing them were only 36,000 British and Commonwealth troops under the Middle East Commander-in-Chief, Archibald Wavell. At sea, the Mediterranean Fleet under Andrew Cunningham now had to contend with the Italian navy without the French, whose ships were either impounded or sunk following the British attack at Mers-el-Kébir in July 1940. The Italian air force had 329 aircraft in the immediate area against the RAF's 205. In the south, British land and air assets facing the Italians in Abyssinia and Somaliland were even thinner.

Despite the imbalance in forces, it was the British and the RAF who struck first. On the morning of 11 June, eight Blenheims of 45 Squadron came in low over the Italians' main airbase in eastern Libya at El Adem, south of Tobruk, and caught them utterly unprepared. The raiders were able to drop their bombs and incendiaries with little interference. The raid was followed by another in the afternoon. Eighteen aircraft were destroyed or damaged on the ground, and a pattern had been set of British aggression in defiance of the odds that kept the Italians on the defensive.

On 9 September Graziani's army finally attacked, crossing the border and covering fifty miles in two days to halt at Sidi Barrani on the coast. The British screening force withdrew in good order to Mersa Matruh, sixty miles to the east. From their base at Ma'aten Bagush, a few miles away, the RAF for the next few months kept the Italians off balance, bombing and strafing and never attacking the same target twice in succession.

Then, in early December, the British went on the attack in an operation that, for the first time since the war began, showed the Army and Air Force acting harmoniously and effectively in unison. Operation Compass was a complete success. On 9 December 30,000 British and Commonwealth troops under the vigorous leadership of Lieutenant General Richard O'Connor swept west in two columns, cutting through the Italian defences. Two months later Graziani's army was routed and the whole of Cyrenaica was in British hands. The ground forces were supported all the way by a steadily strengthening RAF (between September and the end of the year forty-one Wellingtons, eighty-seven Hurricanes and eighty-five Blenheim IVs arrived in theatre) which kept up a constant rhythm of operations.

All elements of air power were on display, strategic and tactical. In keeping with the precepts of the Air Ministry sages, the bombers undermined the Italian ability to wage war, bombing dumps and harbours. But they also attacked shipping, airfields and anything else that seemed likely to cause the enemy pain. The fighters provided reconnaissance and air cover as well as mounting a British version of *blitzkrieg*, shooting up the enemy in the path of the advancing troops. On the ground, soldiers and airmen worked together to plan joint operations that would apply violence as purposefully as possible. The result was a triumphant display of aggression when one was badly needed, and victory came cheap with fewer than 2,000 men dead and wounded. By the end, Egypt was out of danger and the acquisition of hundreds of miles of the south-east Mediterranean shoreline greatly extended the reach of the Air Force.

Things turned out equally well in the south. Once again, on paper the situation looked bleak. The Italians had 350,000 ground troops and an all-up total of 325 aircraft. The British forces amounted to about 19,000 men and 163 old-fashioned aeroplanes, widely dispersed around Kenya, Somaliland and Sudan. But most of the enemy soldiers were Africans whose loyalty was doubtful, their air force was plagued by maintenance problems and Ultra penetration of the Italian ciphers meant every hostile move was known. The Italian advances into British territory were pushed back by a pincer movement launched from Sudan and Kenya. On 6 April, Addis Ababa fell. Five weeks later the Italians surrendered.

Once again, the key to success was close co-operation between air and ground. At the spearhead of the Kenya force was the C-in-C of the RAF in East Africa, Air Commodore Bill Sowrey, and a flight of South African Air Force biplane fighters and light bombers which provided air support as needed 'on tap'. The aircraft belonged to the past but the service they provided was a vision of the future: a joined-up application of air and terrestrial power that would eventually sweep through North Africa, Italy and north-west Europe to deliver Allied victory.

The burden of operating at such long range and with sparse resources weighed on all the service chiefs. To get anywhere they would have to show a spirit of tolerance that had often been absent from the history of their dealings to date. Longmore and Wavell worked efficiently together from the outset, prompting the Foreign Secretary, Anthony Eden, to report back approvingly from a Middle East trip in October 1940 that 'liaison between the Army and the Air Force is excellent and the RAF are giving support for which no praise can be too high, given their limited resources'.[7]

The early success, compounded by the Fleet's victories against the Italians at sea, brought great strategic advantages and laid the basis for future success. The foundation was never to be built on. Early in 1941 aircraft and armour were switched away from Cyrenaica to Greece to protect against a German attack. In February, Rommel landed in Tripoli with the first elements of the Afrika Korps. The thin holding force was no match for his rapid and unexpected advance.

All that had been won would soon be lost and the ground would have to be clawed back slowly and painfully, this time from Germans not Italians. If different decisions had been made at the top the Italians might have been cleared from all of Libya, making a German intervention much more difficult. There would have been no need for a Battle of Alamein and victory in North Africa could have been wrapped up in months rather than years.

By no rational calculation did the Greek campaign seem winnable. Yet a decision that now looks senseless at the time seemed unavoidable. There were factors in play that outweighed strictly military calculations. Britain had pledged to go to the aid of Greece, following Italy's invasion of Albania in 1939, and the war leadership felt honour-bound to keep the promise. Churchill's entire strategy depended on luring America into the war, and he feared the negative response in Washington were Britain to break its word. Until that day came, America's material support was vital to build up the Middle East air fleet.

From January 1941 onwards, Longmore was forced to send one squadron after another to mostly inadequate and inaccessible Greek airfields. At the same time, he had to scrape together aircraft to defend Malta which, from the beginning of the new year, was under attack from Luftwaffe bombers based in Sicily.

By something like a miracle, Malta survived. Nothing that the Air Force could do was likely to tip the balance in Greece. The Nazi invasion was launched on 6 April. Twenty-one days later the Germans were in Athens. There was another disaster to come. In May, after ten days of desperate fighting, British forces evacuated Crete.

The token holding force left in Cyrenaica soon crumbled when Rommel immediately went on the attack confounding British expectations that there would be no offensive before May. By the middle of June, the British line was back where it started. For the next two years, the opposing forces pursued each other back and forth across a front that stretched from El Alamein in the east to Tunis in the west. For the Germans, the campaign was a distraction, a diversion from the titanic struggle on the Eastern Front. For the Allies, it was a precursor battle that had to be won before the reconquest of Europe could proceed. A great chance had been missed, but there was something to be salvaged from the wreckage of lost opportunities. North Africa was to provide the laboratory conditions in which the formula for eventual success was worked out.

As so often in the British war, it took the shock of failure to stimulate real action. Longmore's period of command was coming to an end. He had made enemies in London as a result of a steady flow of messages lamenting his lack of resources. In the early days, there was never enough of anything – machines, men or equipment. The climate seemed benign after the uncertain British summer and fog, mist, rain, sleet and snow of the long winter but the blue skies and sunshine brought their own problems. Perspex canopies buckled in the heat and the air that the engines sucked in was often laden with sand and dust, making maintenance schedules a Sisyphean nightmare. The air filters on Blenheims had to be serviced after five hours' flying time, an operation that took three hours. The grit penetrated everywhere, creeping into instruments and jamming the hinges of variable pitch propellers so they could not move from 'fine' to 'coarse' after take-off.

Longmore appeared to be a good man to handle a daunting situation. He understood the naval perspective from his days flying with the RNAS in the previous war, and was intelligent and cunning, shifting his aircraft around to create a false impression of strength; what Philip Guedalla called his 'happy gift for "bluffing a full house with a couple of pairs"'.[8] His grasp of the political side of command, though, was weak. He assumed that London would welcome his frank appreciations of his difficulties and be anxious to do what they could to help. This was naïve. The most important recipient of his reports soon became irritated with their importuning tone. Churchill seemed unable, or unwilling, to grasp the difficulties the

Air Force faced in maintaining aircraft and claimed not to understand the gap between Middle East Command's paper strength and its operational capabilities.

Even though aircraft began to arrive in numbers in the autumn of 1940, getting them battleworthy took time and there were always a large number of machines that were unserviceable due to the difficulty of local conditions. 'I was astonished to find that you have nearly 1,000 aircraft and 1,000 pilots and 16,000 air personnel in the Middle East,' Churchill wrote to Longmore on 12 November. 'I am most anxious to re-equip you with modern machines at the earliest moment; but surely out of all this establishment you ought to be able … to produce a substantially larger number of modern aircraft operationally fit?'[9] Churchill's testiness seems particularly ungracious given that the Middle East was the only place where there was a patch of light in an otherwise gloomy sky.

Nonetheless, he had a point. When, in the spring of 1941, Air Commodore Cyril Cooke arrived to take over as Chief Maintenance Officer he found the whole repair organization 'in a deplorable state. Accumulations of damaged aircraft were dotted about the vast Command, and there were practically no reserve machines complete in all respects.'[10] He pushed for the creation of a Maintenance Command like the one in the UK, which was eventually set up that summer under Air Vice Marshal Graham Dawson, a boyish dynamo with a domineering personality and a hatred of red tape. The existing repair and salvage unit in the desert was expanded and two more created, all fully mobile, a necessity in a constantly shifting war. At the main bases, Egyptians were hired to expand repair capacity, including recruits from the engineering faculty of Cairo University. Dawson found uses for everything. The limestone hills of al-Mokattam, on the south-eastern edge of Cairo, were honeycombed with caves excavated to supply stones for the Pyramids. Dawson had them cleaned up, floors cemented, walls whitewashed and power laid on to provide workshops for the overhaul of aero-engines as well as secure storage for 'everything from bombs to photo-paper'.[11]

Longmore's lamentations finally got him the sack. In May 1941, he was called back to London for discussions and never returned to

Egypt. If he had got the backing of the CAS he might have survived longer, but Portal, too, had turned against him. His place was taken by his deputy, Tedder, a far more subtle political operator who had warned his chief against testing patience in London.[12] Unlike Longmore, Tedder nurtured his relationship with Portal, sending him (at the request of the CAS) regular telegrams for his eyes only, giving unvarnished assessments of events, not only concerning the Air Force but all three services.

Longmore had got on well enough with the Army and Navy – indeed, his repeated assertions that they shared his dire view of the supply situation was one reason for his recall, encouraging the suspicion in the Air Ministry that he had gone native. Tedder was brilliant at managing the egos and sensitivities of his fellow chiefs, while at the same time quietly imposing the Air Force perspective on the conduct of the war.

The success of Operation Compass seemed to augur well for inter-service relations in the Middle East. The debacles in Greece and Crete and the setback in Cyrenaica ensured a resumption of the familiar crossfire of blame and recrimination. With the aircraft and aerodromes available to them and the Luftwaffe's overwhelming strength in numbers and bases it was unreasonable to expect the RAF to give anything like comprehensive protection to ships or ground troops. Nonetheless, according to Tedder, Cunningham, who enjoyed living up to his irascible sea-dog reputation, was 'prone to sending explosive messages to London about the alleged lack of air support to the Royal Navy'.[13] He also anticipated a repetition from the Army of the charges that had been levelled at the RAF following Dunkirk. While the fighting in Crete was still raging he confided to his diary: 'I am quite sure the Army will say we lost Crete because the RAF let them down. Actually, we have been put out of commission because the Army have lost all our bases for us and without bases one cannot do much ... Our fellows have been doing some incredible things over Crete these last few days, but they will never get the credit for doing the impossible.'[14]

Lord Louis Mountbatten, fresh from having his destroyer HMS *Kelly* sunk under him by Junkers 87 Stukas during the evacuation of Crete, confirmed this prediction. Tedder recounted how after being buttonholed by Mountbatten in Cairo, he 'heckled me extensively on the ability of the Hun to move forward quickly and establish, and operate from, forward bases'. Tedder explained patiently that German resources in the area dwarfed those of the RAF but Mountbatten's high connections and voluble opinions threatened potential trouble.

Later, when a good working relationship was eventually established, the Middle East would be cited as a paradigm of inter-service co-operation. At the beginning, though, Tedder was often exasperated by his colleagues, particularly the soldiers. 'The Army direction here makes me shudder,' he wrote on 11 April as the Afrika Korps pressed forward in Cyrenaica. 'We have got all our reorganisation to meet a new situation practically complete and working but they are still dithering as to … whether General So-and-so is not too junior to take command because George So-and-so is in the offing. 'Orrible!'[15] The Army's (to Tedder's mind) dismal hesitancy was on display when yet another crisis erupted in May after pro-German rebels launched a coup in Iraq. Wavell was reluctant to send a small emergency force, fearing it would be insufficient to crush the revolt, and preferred to wait until things had quietened on another front, freeing up troops for a proper expedition. Tedder recorded in his diary that 'two men and a boy could do *today* what it would require a division to do in a month's time'.[16]

These frustrations, he confided to his diary, meant that 'there are times when I nearly lose my temper with the Army'.[17] But he did not. A positive outlook, reinforced by a wryly humorous view of the world, steely self-control and a willingness to rehearse his arguments ad nauseam served him better. There was a lot to contend with. The recriminations over Crete inevitably raised the old question of whether it be better for the Air Force to be split up so that the Army and Navy could control their own air support. Eventually, sailors and soldiers would accept his argument that it was a choice between 'the feeble single stick and the bundle of faggots'.[18] Crete had proved beyond doubt 'the central fact of the war', that 'air superiority was the pre-requisite to all winning operations, whether at sea, on land or in the air'.[19] Victory required machines and men and a command and control operation that was closely meshed with the needs of the soldiers and sailors. Above all, it needed bases from which to operate at maximum effectiveness. 'This campaign,' Tedder had concluded in the early summer of 1941, 'is primarily a battle for aerodromes'.[20]

Tedder's prescriptions were given substance by a heartening improvement in RAF resources. Portal secured approval for a major Middle East reinforcement that would boost strength to fifty squadrons. In mid-May the 'Tiger' convoy docked, virtually intact, at Alexandria carrying 238 tanks and forty-three Hurricanes. At the same time, aircraft were being flown in from West Africa via the 'Takoradi Route'.

The 4,000-mile supply line across the waist of Africa was a heartening example of official foresight. Envisaging a day when Mussolini might act on his assertion that the Mediterranean was 'Mare Nostrum', an alternative route to Egypt had been mapped out before the war began. It was based on the infrastructure put in place by Imperial Airways to open a weekly civil passenger and mail air service between Lagos and Khartoum which began to operate in 1936. The RAF extended the chain to the port of Takoradi on the British Gold Coast, where ships delivered crated aircraft which were reassembled and flown in convoy, staging at Lagos, Kano, Maiduguri, Fort Lamy (in the hands of the Free French), Geneina and Khartoum, finishing at Abu Sueir, seventy miles north-east of Cairo. The first flight of reinforcements, one Blenheim and six Hurricanes, took off on 20 September 1940.

Operating the Takoradi Route soaked up nearly 7,000 men but the investment was worth it.[21] During the war it would feed more than 5,000 aeroplanes into theatre. With America's greater involvement and eventual entry as a belligerent the crates swinging off the cargo ships increasingly contained US machines – Curtiss Tomahawk, then Kittyhawk fighters, not as good as a Spitfire perhaps but the performance equivalent of a Hurricane. After reassembly, they had to be test-flown, often by pilots who had no previous experience of the type. James Pickering, a ferry pilot with No. 1 Aircraft Delivery Unit, remembered how his first briefing before climbing into a 'Tommy' was 'more of a warning than a source of useful information'. Their reputation 'had not been enhanced when the chief test pilot at Takoradi had been killed testing the first one re-erected from its crate'.[22]

All aircraft had their foibles. The Tomahawk's was a unit in the airscrew that leaked oil: 'Sand stuck to this. It covered the windscreen and quarter panels and blanked forward visibility when landing.' It also had a tendency to swing on touching down, which novices tried to correct by stabbing at the brakes, tipping the aircraft on its nose or collapsing the undercarriage.

Single-engine, single-seat aircraft made the journey in groups of six, led by a light bomber carrying a navigator and wireless operator who obtained bearings from the next staging post. The pilots were an eclectic bunch including Poles deemed too old for operational flying (among them a former commander of the Polish Air Force, Ludomil Rayski), Rhodesians and greenhorns arriving from England with only twenty hours on Hurricanes behind them. In a break with pre-war service practice the convoy leader, whose authority was absolute, was chosen on experience not seniority so a sergeant pilot could find himself commanding a flight of officers.

The five-day journey was testing, flying over hundreds of miles of thick forest or great patches of emptiness with only the faint trace of a wadi or an outcrop of rock for landmarks, where engine trouble or a navigational mistake could end in a lonely death. Sandstorms blew in from the Sahara blotting out landing grounds and electric tempests arrived suddenly out of cloudless skies, creating what Sam Pritchard, who flew the route often in a Bombay, described as 'a noisy pyrotechnic display with blood-orange haloes in front and blue flames sparking along the wings'.[23] The journey was also exciting and exotic. At Fort Lamy, giraffe-necked native women stooped over crops in the fields around the airfield. For the regular ferry pilots, there were also opportunities for illegal private enterprise. Early on it was discovered that gold purchased in West Africa fetched a much higher price in Khartoum and Cairo. All you had to do was dodge the customs and resist the temptation to be too greedy. A story did the rounds of a fighter pilot who was rumbled when his machine failed to get airborne due to the weight of gold hidden under his seat.

As Sam Pritchard discovered, snake and lizard skins involved no such difficulty. 'We found that python skins could be bought in

Kano for an average of £1 each and sold in Khartoum for an average of £2,' he wrote. This 'marvellous loot presented no weight problem when carried by air ... a bag of 100 python skins weighed so little it could be carried easily in one hand'. He and his crewmates took the precaution of arranging for a friendly wireless operator on the ground at Khartoum to deliver a coded tip-off as they approached if there was a customs van present, giving them time to jettison the loot. They never had to. He was soon accumulating £100 a trip as his share of the enterprise, but the profits evaporated rapidly in the bars and nightclubs of the city which provided 'a refuge for wealthy Arabs, Jews, Greeks [and] some fleet-footed Anglo-Saxons, as well as the most alluring prostitutes from many Middle Eastern territories'.

The Takoradi Route was only one trans-African pipeline for aircraft and supplies. The Americans set up a base at Accra which received long-range Liberators, Flying Fortresses and Marauders arriving from across the South Atlantic and fighters flown in from carriers for onward transmission as far as the Pacific theatre. From the autumn of 1941, the RAF base alongside the deep-water dock at Port Sudan in the Red Sea began assembling sea-delivered British and American fighters and American Boston and Baltimore medium bombers. They were then flown from the steamy seaside to the relative cool of the depot at Summit, in the hills sixty miles to the west, for modification to desert conditions before delivery to the squadrons.

At RAF Shaibah, near Basra at the head of the Persian Gulf, crated Bostons and Baltimores were put together for the benefit of the Russian air force. The British and Americans received no thanks for this largesse. The Russian aircrews James Pickering encountered were 'taciturn and suspicious. On arrival in Shaibah on a transport aircraft they checked the aircraft inventories and would not take the aircraft unless everything was accounted for. They wore uniform with buttoned up collar, regardless of the heat and humidity ...'[24] The RAF's encounters with their Soviet allies seldom left fond memories. Aircraft delivering supplies to Teheran after Iran was jointly occupied by British and the Soviet forces were routinely shot at by Russian flak batteries. After surviving this experience one crew were then ordered to help unload the cargo by a Russian officer.

For almost everyone, aircrew and ground crew alike, the journey into theatre was a formative part of their Middle East experience and left a strong impression. The transition from monochrome Britain to the dazzle of the Orient could be abrupt. Despite the risk from the Luftwaffe and Italians, the urgent need for aircraft meant that bombers with the endurance for the journey continued to fly in via the Mediterranean. For the ground crews the change was leisurely, a six-week voyage south through the Atlantic round the Cape of Good Hope, then through the Red Sea and Suez Canal into Egypt.

Neither route was easy. Flying meant an initial, dicey 1,200-mile hop from a southern England airfield to Gibraltar. Sam Pritchard was serving as a navigator with 105 bomber squadron when, in July 1942, the crew were summoned and told they were to deliver a new Blenheim Mark IV to Egypt. They took off from Portreath in Cornwall, the most westerly base in Britain, for the first leg. The flying time was estimated at seven hours, and the maximum fuel load they carried was for seven and a half. It was the longest trip Pritchard had ever done but he nonetheless ignored the briefing officer's advice to follow a course well out to sea, preferring to stay within sight of the coast even if it increased the risk of interception by Luftwaffe patrols. His boldness probably saved them. They struggled with a strong headwind and his pilot, Ben, 'went in straight over the harbour onto the runway with all fuel gauges registering zero'.[25] A Blenheim following immediately behind ran out of fuel just short of the runway and crash-landed in neutral Spain. The day before another went down into the sea off Cadiz with the same problem.

The sea voyage brought its own anxieties. In May 1943 Brian Kingcome was posted to Malta to lead 244 Wing. It was decided he would travel by boat rather than aeroplane, which would allow him to recuperate after a long period on ops. He travelled to Durban aboard the SS *Orion*, a luxurious P&O passenger liner in peacetime, now stripped of its refinements and serving as a troop carrier. The first part of the cruise was delightful: 'The weather was superb, the seas were calm [he wrote]. The flying fish flew and the tropical heat was tempered by the breeze created by our cruising speed of between fifteen and twenty knots. We were in a dream world and the grey clouds, rationed food and general shortages of war torn Britain hardly seemed to be real any longer.'[26] Then suddenly 'the dream was shattered'. Somewhere off the Canaries the on-board atmosphere changed abruptly. It took Kingcome some time to realize that the engines had stopped. 'The silence was paralysing, almost palpable ... we stood and waited wherever we happened to be on the ship, nerves on edge and sensing danger but blind to what it could be or from the direction it might come at us. Then, over the klaxon, sounded the duty officer's abrasive orders: "Boat stations!"' As they scrambled to their mustering points they heard the explanation: U-boats had been reported in the area.

These alarms were frequent in the first half of the voyage, but the threat reduced with the journey south. At Durban there was a run ashore where the local whites opened their homes to the troops. Then the fun was over as the sea miles passed and the mood of seriousness deepened as all on board prepared for whatever it was that lay ahead.

Their destination was exotic, a place that most of the passengers knew only from the *Children's Encyclopedia*, never imagining that they might see it themselves. Many were grateful for the opportunity for adventure that the war had handed to them, no matter that it came with risks attached. To young men who had never known anything but the muted backdrop of Britain's towns and countryside, and the essential order of everyday life, Egypt came as a shock. Ernest Bishop, a twenty-one-year-old fitter on his way to the main RAF base at Aboukir, was eager to get ashore when his troopship docked at Port Tewfik at the head of the Suez Canal. During the five-week voyage from Durban he and his comrades had 'seen only the sea' and their 'eyes were greedy for something new'.[27] After disembarking and being processed at a nearby transit camp, he and some friends headed off to explore the port. 'A native village lay between us and the town,' he wrote later. 'As we passed through it we were appalled by the squalor. There seemed to be no sanitation at all and the smell of the place was overpowering.' However, the men they saw lounging about 'in long white gowns were not at all perturbed by their unpleasant surroundings'. The black-gowned, heavily veiled women they passed took no notice of them. One was carrying an enormous bundle of melons and Bishop marvelled at her strength. Later, 'learning that women do most of the heavy work, I was more able to understand the Egyptian male's contentment'.

Sam Pritchard was repelled by the contemptuous attitude of the pre-war RAF towards the 'wogs' and 'sought to give them every benefit of the doubt'.[28] However, he found 'they were difficult to like and seemed to lack those qualities that I had been brought up to admire – if not always to practice – such as steadfastness, trustworthiness, loyalty, industry and courage'. The wealthier and better-educated seemed closer to the British ideal, 'but even they seemed unattractive because of their indifference to the vast majority who had nothing ...'

There was 'no great bond of affection between us and the Egyptians', and Pritchard was honest enough to understand why. Once, when walking through central Cairo he saw a teenage boy carrying a tray packed with trinkets approach a large, drunken soldier who had just emerged from the New Zealand Services Club. The Kiwi 'brought his great boot up under the tray producing a nuclear-like mushroom of combs, brushes, and other paraphernalia ...' The British passers-by, even some Egyptians, 'thought it was screamingly funny'. He concluded that 'in retrospect it was small wonder that the local populace disliked the foreigners in their midst'.

Ernest Bishop (far right) and pals

The British presence in Egypt had always been uneasy and its long history of military, political and financial interference had done much in the late nineteenth century to nurture the growth of Arab nationalism. The country had been declared a British protectorate in 1914 after the Ottoman Empire, of which Egypt was nominally a part, sided with the Germans. The British deposed the Khedive and replaced him with Fuad, a member of the same family. He was succeeded in 1936 by his son, Farouk, 'a rather fat youth in blue suiting and a gaudy tie', as Tedder described him after their first encounter, who felt bitterly the frequent humiliations he suffered at the hands of his protectors.[29] To the British he was sly and ungrateful, the epitome of wog delinquency. According to Pritchard, when at the end of June 1942 Rommel's advance had taken him to within striking distance of Cairo, his transport squadron's Bombays were fitted with bomb racks and given provisional orders to attack Farouk's palace if he decided to abandon Egypt's neutrality and declare for the Axis. Somewhat to his disappointment, the order never came.

Farouk's resentment of the British seemed to be reserved for the governing class. My father was canoeing with some friends off a beach near Alexandria one afternoon when Farouk's yacht appeared. A boat was despatched and the airmen, none above the rank of corporal, brought aboard for drinks. 'He was gracious, funny and not at all how we expected him to be,' he remembered years later.[30]

There was another culture shock in store for some of the new arrivals. The Treasury's notorious stinginess in the inter-war years seems not to have affected the living standards of the overseas Air Force. Sam Pritchard was delighted by luxurious conditions at Abu Sueir in the Canal Zone east of Cairo which opened in 1917 and had been successively a flying training school and a maintenance base. It had a cinema, a church and the accommodation for all ranks was spacious and cool. The sergeants' mess was 'what we imagined the Savoy would be like' with 'a club like atmosphere … a spacious bar, sumptuous ante-rooms and veranda and a billiard room with two full-sized tables'.[31] The members were another matter. Pritchard and his crewmates found the peacetime NCOs 'boorish and unfriendly', apparently resenting the fact that 'it had taken them many years of service to earn the privileges of rank whereas it took the new breed of aircrew only a matter of months'. With a tour on bombers under their belts, not to mention a hazardous journey out east, they decided that 'no pot-bellied old sweat from the Trenchard era was going to deprive us of our rightful inheritance'.

The interlude was brief. For those at the sharp end of the Middle East air war, the campaign was mainly lived in the wastes of sand and rock they called 'the blue'. Control of the airspace above it was the essential pre-condition of victory. Whoever won it would be able to interdict the enemy's supply lines by sea and land, destroy his stores, attack his airfields, harass his movements and kill his troops. To carry out these operations a flexible force was needed of light bombers, fighters and tactical battlefield machines capable of destroying armour. From its establishment in October 1941 the WDAF gradually accumulated the aircraft it needed to fulfil all these roles, while engaging in daily battles with the Luftwaffe and Regia Aeronautica for air supremacy.

By the autumn, the Eighth Army was ready to try and push the Germans out of Cyrenaica and relieve Tobruk, which had been under siege since May. Everyone engaged in Operation Crusader understood the central importance of air power, not least the New Zealand Prime Minister Peter Fraser who demanded assurances from Churchill that Kiwi troops would not have to undergo the ordeal they had endured in Greece and Crete of going into battle without adequate protection from the air. Tedder's cautious assessment of the numbers of available aircraft ignited Churchill's ire. Impatient as always for action and results, he interpreted this as an indication of defeatism and was all set to give Tedder the sack.[32]

His alliance with Portal saved him. He went forward to control the whole air operation which began well before the battle proper commenced. In the five weeks before the offensive opened on 18 November, the Air Force flew about three thousand sorties. The prelude gave Tedder 'the opportunity to show what air power could do when directed from one centre in accordance with a coherent plan'. Aircraft flying out of Malta bombed Naples, Palermo, Tripoli and

Benghazi, the enemy ports of departure and arrival, and attacked convoys on the high seas. The dumps where the goods that made it ashore were stored were subjected to a continuous hammering and the supply columns to the front areas regularly harassed. These attacks on the Axis logistics kept its fighters preoccupied, reducing their capacity to interfere with the Allied build-up. Tedder was confident that, overall, the Air Force would continue to give a very good account of itself. But as he wrote to his wife, success, and his continuation in post, depended on 'whether the soldiers do their stuff'. If they 'made a mess of it again there is no question at all but that I shall be made the scapegoat'.

By the middle of January 1942 Operation Crusader had succeeded in pushing the Germans out of Cyrenaica and relieving Tobruk, but it was clear that steam was running out and there would be no onward drive to the Axis headquarters at Tripoli. It was an all too predictable performance. Despite the Army's superior strength (680 tanks with 500 in reserve against Axis figures of less than 400) and the Allies' domination of the air, success had been laborious. Tedder found that the ground-force commander General Alan Cunningham, brother of the admiral, was easily dispirited and 'fluctuated between wishful optimism and the depths of pessimism'.[33] He also seemed obsessed with his opponent, telling Tedder during a visit to the front: 'I wish I knew what Rommel was going to do.' This struck him as 'a strange outlook for the commander of a superior force'. Auchinleck, who had succeeded Wavell as C-in-C, agreed and Cunningham was soon removed.

The air battle continued reasonably well. The WDAF had the advantage of numbers, with 1,000 aircraft facing a combined German and Italian force of 320. Bad weather and the reluctance of the Axis air to gamble with limited resources meant that opportunities for attrition were reduced. When combats did occur, the newly arrived Me 109Fs and Italian Macchi C202s proved superior to the Warhawks, Tomahawks, Kittyhawks and Hurricane IIs facing them. As Tedder ruefully remarked, a 'squadron of Spitfire Vs would have been worth a lot'. Policy in London was still to reserve the latest machines for the home front and it would not be until well into 1942 that the first Spits appeared.

One of Tedder's biggest frustrations was difficulty of providing effective close support to the advancing forces. There were plenty of medium bombers available to bomb the Germans on the ground, but poor communications and the problems of identifying friend from foe meant they were never put to full use. The battle 'showed only too clearly that we had not yet learned the secrets of bombing in the battle area'.

The initial success of Crusader was short-lived. Before January 1942 was out, Rommel was attacking once again and on the 29th he recaptured Benghazi. Huge air attacks on Malta made reinforcement easier and the reinvigorated Afrika Korps swept east once again. By the end of June, Tobruk had fallen and the Germans had reached El Alamein. The battle would ebb and flow throughout the summer until the new partnership of Alexander and Montgomery finally turned the tide in October.

For the airmen, life in the blue was exhausting, uncomfortable and dangerous. The ground troops were able to benefit from occasional lulls in the fighting. For the Air Force, the action was continuous. Neville Duke arrived in the desert just in time for the start of Crusader. He was not yet twenty, tall, lean, a natural pilot and not at all happy to be there. In the autumn of 1941 he had been ensconced with 92 Squadron at Biggin Hill, flying sweeps over France by day and hitting the London bars and clubs by night, when he was told he was being posted to Egypt. The bad news came with an assurance that the stint would only be for about six weeks. He arrived at Fayoum airport, south of Cairo, on 9 November with thirteen other fighter pilots, three of whom were killed within a few weeks of arriving.

His first glimpses of the blue were not encouraging. 'Arrived at Air Headquarters Western Desert at Sidi Hannish at 4 o'clock this afternoon,' he wrote in his laconic but revealing diary two days later. 'Not very impressed with the desert at all.'[34] The following day the newcomers were briefed by 'Mary' Coningham who informed them that their job was to 'knock down the thirty-odd Me109s the Huns possess and cover the army from bombing'. Duke was joining 112 Squadron as a flight commander, together with his 92 Squadron pal Peter 'Hunk' Humphreys. The CO came to pick him up in a car but

Duke noticed he was as 'tight as an owl and I was most put off and quite unhappy'. The following day he was introduced to the Tomahawk. He found it a poor substitute for his Spitfire. After being shown 'all the knobs and buttons' he took it up for a first flight 'and promptly crashed when I landed but only got a few bruises'. By now he was feeling sorry for himself. 'If only I could get home again,' he wrote. However, when he informed his fellow 112 Squadrons that he and 'Hunk' would be returning to the UK in six weeks 'everybody laughs and it rather hurts'.

It would be three days short of three years before Duke made it back. By then he was the top-scoring fighter pilot in the Mediterranean theatre, shooting down at least twenty-four enemy aircraft in Libya, Tunisia and Italy. His first German victim was flying one of the new Me 109Fs that were generally held to be superior to the Tomahawks. 'Squadron went ground strafing along the El Adem–Acroma road,' he recorded on 22 November. 'Whizzing along at telephone wire height – some fun. Wing sweep in the afternoon. Engaged by 15–20 Me109Fs. I got on the tail of one and followed him up. Got in a burst from stern quarter and its hood and pieces of fuselage disintegrated. Machine went into a vertical dive and he baled out. Flew round and round the pilot until he landed, then went down to look at him. I waved to him and he waved back. Poor devil thought I was going to strafe him as he initially dived behind a bush and lay flat.'

Duke was a Fighter Boy paradigm: cool, efficient, outwardly light-hearted and always game for fun. But a seam of sardonic melancholy runs through his observations. The war often seems a fatal game in which you kill and expect to be killed and none of it has a higher purpose or meaning. He felt no particular animus towards the enemy. The day before he downed the 109 he was on patrol near Tobruk when two Fiat CR42 biplanes appeared. 'Attacked same with P/O "Butch" Jeffries and Sgt Carson,' he recorded. 'Did three attacks on one which was flying at about 500 ft. He did a few turns and then went in to land. Turned over, after running a few yards, onto its back and the pilot was out like a shot. Butch and Carson started to shoot the poor devil but I couldn't do it, so I set his machine on fire. Went down to look at the pilot who was running with his hands up. His face was full of fear and the next time I saw him he was lying on the ground. There was no need to murder the poor devil as our troops were coming up …' This sort of air fighting produced contradictory emotions. Duke candidly admitted that 'it is a terrific thrill to come pelting out of the sun to let rip at the Huns with the .5s. To see your bullets making little spurts in the sand in front of a truck and then pull the nose up a bit until the spurts no longer rise and your bullets are hitting home.' But he could not 'help feeling sorry for the Jerry soldier … they run, poor little pitiful figures, trying to dodge the spurts of dust racing towards them'.

The pace of operations never slackened. On Monday 24 November, the squadron escorted Maryland light bombers on a raid near El Adem returning to their base, Landing Ground 110, to find it swamped with troops and aircraft falling back from an enemy breakout. The following day he shot up tanks and transport near Sidi Omar and took part in a wing sweep in the afternoon which ended in a fight with seventy enemy machines. There were further sweeps on three successive days. Then, on Sunday 30 November, the squadron ran into a 'circus of 30–40 enemy aircraft'. Duke managed to shoot down a Fiat G50 monoplane fighter, before he was jumped by an Me 109. He 'dodged 4–5 attacks and got in a few shots at him but he was too fast'.

'Finally he hit me in the port wing, and I think, the petrol tank. Machine turned on its back at about 500ft, out of control. Saw the ground rushing up and then I kicked the rudder and pushed the stick and prayed. Got control just in time and the machine hit the ground on its belly. Hopped out jolly quick and then darted behind some scrub and lay on my belly about 20 yards from the crash. The Hun came down and shot up my machine, which was already smoking and set it on fire. Horrible crack and whistle of bullets near me and I thought I was going to be strafed but the Hun cleared off. Started to walk across home but saw a lorry coming my way. Lay down behind another bush thinking they were Huns but as they went past I recognised the uniforms and popped up and gave 'em a yell.'

Five days later he was shot down again, and once more it was a 109 that had got the better of him and his Tomahawk. Though wounded in the leg by shell splinters he managed to crash-land at Tobruk, where he was patched up and sent back to Cairo in a Blenheim for a few days' rest.

Duke never learned to love the desert. The occasional trip to a beach, where the emerald inshore water shaded into an infinite expanse of electric blue, or the diamond-studded brilliance of the night skies, failed to compensate for the general misery of the climate. It rained in winter and baked in summer. The heat of the day was matched by the cold of the nights. And then there was the sand which 'gets in your eyes, ears, nose, mouth, hair, food, clothes, in fact sand everywhere ...'

In the blue, things never stayed still long enough for any degree of comfort to be established. Sam Pritchard arrived at Fuka, a satellite near the main 202 Group Ma'aten Bagush airbase in the autumn of 1941 to join 45 Squadron. It was equipped with Blenheims and had been given the joint task of tactical support for the Army combined with bombing attacks on ports like Bardia along the coast to the west where supplies for the Axis forward units came in. 'We settled down ... to "life in the blue" – sleeping in tents, eating in tents and relaxing in a sergeants' mess consisting of a wooden hut with a few wooden or cane armchairs, collapsible card tables and its essential bar,' he wrote.[35]

There were no camp beds. Instead he kipped down each night in 'a flattened bit of sand which we tried to shape so as to accommodate the hip and shoulder with a small amount of sand at the top for a pillow. This sculptured shape was then covered with a waterproof ground sheet and a doubled blanket – grey service issue of the coarsest quality – upon which one lay with one, two or three blankets on top' depending on the coldness of the night. Pritchard would have found the discomfort more bearable if everyone had been in the same boat. The knowledge that officers received a 'hard lying allowance' was 'an unnecessary and stupid source of disgruntlement'.

They ate the same field rations they would have been given anywhere where British forces found themselves in the world and which made no concession to climate or geography. When Norman Poole arrived at a forward base in Sétif in Algeria early in 1943 he found the 'food fairly dismal … we saw a good deal of Maconochie's meat and vegetable stew and other delights of wartime cuisine'.[36] Everything came in tins, even the bacon, and the drinking water tasted of chlorine. They supplemented the fare with eggs, bartered from locals in exchange for cigarettes. Player's – the airmen's favourite – and other well-known brands were not always available in the NAAFI. There was never any problem getting the officially issued 'V for Victory' which tasted, it was said, of camel dung and were smoked only as a last resort. The Arabs soon came to learn the difference, though they were sometimes conned into accepting them when they came disguised in a regular NAAFI pack.

On top of the other privations the sanitary arrangements were primitive. Water was always scarce. Baths, showers and hot water to shave with were a luxury. A trip to the latrines was not for the fainthearted. The set-up in Sétif was typical. 'The screens were some distance down wind, in accordance with the field training manual,' wrote Poole. The pits 'consisted of a long but stout tree-trunk suspended in a tree fork at an appropriate height'. The spoil from the excavated hole lay at the side to be kicked in when the job was done. The airmen thought it better not to face the ordeal alone and 'rather than make a solitary trip it was customary to make up a small party or at least a pair …'

On top of all this there was little off-duty amusement to be had. To alleviate boredom they sunbathed, played cards and bet on fights between captured scorpions. The mess – usually a stifling bell or ridge tent – lost much of its appeal when the supply of drink was unreliable. Beer – the Cairo-brewed Stella or hangover-inducing Canadian Black Label – and spirits would arrive on resupply convoys, or was sometimes flown in by enterprising crews. The South Africans benefited from a flow of Cape brandy, provided by their government. As the war moved west towards the vineyards of Algeria, rough red wine and sweet muscatel became available. The uncertainty of the flow meant that when alcohol arrived it was sometimes rationed, a few bottles of beer or tots of spirits a night. In times of abundance it did not sit around for long. Those in authority tried sometimes to dispel the reputation for booziness that hung about the Air Force but the truth was that airmen in general were a thirsty lot. Getting 'hoggers', getting 'amongst the beer' at 'pissys' and 'binges' feature with cheerful regularity in Neville Duke's diaries.

Drinking was therapy, a way of escaping the tensions, frustrations and privations. Jimmy Corbin, a Battle of Britain veteran, arrived at the Maison Blanche aerodrome in Algiers in November 1942 shortly after the US–Allied invasion. His nickname was 'Binder' due to a perceived disposition to grumble. In Algeria that winter there was much to bind about. His fighter squadron, 72, slept first on concrete floors, then under canvas at dispersal. The Luftwaffe bombed regularly and the weather was dreadful. Red wine was a rare solace. 'Got drunk on vin rouge with Chas Pryth Forde in the evening,' he recorded in his diary on 9 December.[37] Overnight it 'rained like hell again' and in the morning German bombers hit the town. 'Brassed off with moving about,' he wrote. 'Bags of mud that sticks like glue. Pushing kites for one and a half hours to make way for Beaus. Bloody tired. Covered in mud. A little wine relieves no end.'

The only real escape was a spot of leave, though a few days in Cairo was rarely restful. Off-duty airmen would dutifully visit the Pyramids and Sphinx and have their photographs taken aboard a camel. Then it was on to the city's multiple cinemas, restaurants, ice-cream parlours and, of course, bars and nightclubs. The egalitarian conditions of the blue, where officers and NCOs, aircrew and ground crew more or less endured the same conditions, did not apply in Cairo. The best hotels like the Continental and Shepheard's as well as the top restaurants and nightclubs were 'officers-only', as were most of the facilities of the sumptuous Gezira Sporting Club on the island of Zamalek. Sergeant Sam Pritchard felt the injustice keenly. As at least 50 per cent of those who flew were NCOs it 'meant that more than half of all aircrew were denied entry into decent hotels and restaurants'.[38] Such distinctions, he came to believe, could 'partly explain why Mr Churchill lost the post war election'.

He and his friend Jock got around the ban by sewing flight lieutenants' shoulder insignia on their bush jackets before they arrived in town. One evening in the Bardia, famous for its belly dancers, they 'got plastered in company with a very smart Wing Commander who was exceedingly friendly. At the maudlin stage we became buddies for life, planning to run an airline together after the war.' At this point Jock thought it safe to reveal that they were in fact sergeants in disguise. 'The Wing Commander roared with laughter and said "don't worry about that chaps – I'm only a f—— corporal!"'

There was no discrimination at Groppi's, the famous café-restaurant opened by a Swiss chocolatier in the Sharia Soliman Pasha in 1909. According to Pritchard, the founder's son Achille 'successfully resisted any attempts by the authorities to designate his establishment "for officers only" so it became a favourite haunt for RAF aircrew on leave'. He and his friends would start their day with an iced coffee in the café before moving on to the bar. They passed the evening in a 'largish room containing cocktail bars and a dancehall with a small stage for the band which could be opened out on dry balmy evenings'. For Pritchard, who had left a much-loved wife in England, the fun ended there and he stood at the bar 'watching the HQ wallahs and the Egyptians dancing with their bints'.

The city's 'Berka' district was stuffed with brothels for those who wanted them. Respectable female company was harder to find. At home the women of the WAAF were everywhere, in sizeable numbers on every RAF station, depot and facility. For the airmen they were the natural and obvious first source of friendship, sex and love. There were no WAAFs in the desert and very few in Egypt. By the end of 1942, about 200 were in theatre, all officers.[39] Local Palestinians, Greeks and other Allied nationals were hired for clerical and other trades, later reinforced by 2,000 airwomen sent out from Britain to serve all over Middle East Command.

For almost every Air Force member, as for almost every serviceman, life in the Middle East was intensely masculine. There is a sense in the diaries and memoirs that it was better that way. In Jimmy Corbin's surviving diaries covering the winter of 1942–3 there are occasional references to 'dames', 'females' and 'frippet' but his attempts to connect with them seem more dutiful than urgent. Arriving for a few days' leave with the rest of the pilots in Constantine, Algeria, at the beginning of February they soon identified the American Bar of the Casino as their watering hole of choice and noted the presence of 'loads of lush dames', but when they 'tried to get the form in the way of frippet' there was 'no joy'.[40] The following morning he 'went on a frippet hunt with Judd but no joy'. They consoled themselves with 'a hell of a session in [the] American Bar on egg flips'.

That night, at the Casino once more, Jimmy 'gazed with open mouth and a peculiar feeling in certain parts of the body at the beautiful dames'. However, looking was all he could do as 'the army seem to have the form wrapped', and the evening ended with another 'hell of a session' back in the requisitioned school where they were billeted.

The impression is of much talk but little action. One of the few recorded encounters turned out a rather melancholy business. A Beaufighter pilot described an evening spent in Naples in late 1943 in a flat in the city which the squadron officers had rented as a rest and recreation facility. 'Naples had always been well-provided with "hostesses" who were able to do a quick conversion course from German to English and the tenancy agreement seemed to include their hospitality,' he wrote. On his first visit with half a dozen others, including the CO, 'a couple of the girls joined us. This was quite a novel event and we were happy to share our wine with them and help them to improve their English.' When it 'got late enough to think of bed … the general view was that as I was the youngest – still only nineteen – I ought to entertain the youngest girl and the oldest girl was allocated to the oldest of our navigators'.

When they repaired to the bedroom the girl 'unbuttoned her dress and stepped out of it to reveal she was wearing a complicated arrangement of underwear … a foundation garment with suspenders holding up silk stockings'. His 'limited experience' to date 'was confined to passion killer WAAF knickers and lisle stockings'. The night was not a success. In the morning before the girl left 'she showed me her family photographs. I suppose they were calculated to increase her reward – and they did – but I was not proud of myself even though my reputation on the squadron advanced considerably.'

The airmen reinforced each other's spirits through an ethos of ragging, black humour and good-natured moaning. It needed a fair amount of maintenance, and sometimes the jolly façade crumbled.

Returning from a week's leave in Cairo on 15 December 1941, Neville Duke found 'the squadron is in a very poor state of morale. Everybody has had enough of the war.'[41] The following day the CO called him in to tell him that he was sending two of the pilots who had arrived with him home 'as he thinks they have "had" it'. Duke wrote that night that he 'could have cried on the spot when I heard that, as I know I have "had" this war good and proper. Got good and drunk …'

This frank admission from an outstandingly brave man surely reflected a wider mood. It remained hidden to the men at the top, who were perhaps not looking very hard for signs of war-weariness. At about the same time as Duke was recording his despair, Tedder visited some fighter squadrons in the blue and found 'the atmosphere among them was quite splendid … the whole tone amongst pilots and men was grand. I felt they were a much finer body of men than those of the First World War.'[42]

Retrospective contemplation of the place of the North Africa campaigns in the overall history of the war has bathed them in a kindly light, the 'end of the beginning' where the tide was turned and victory began to feel as if it was inevitable. That was not how it seemed at the time. For those who fought in the air, as for those in the sand and rock below, the desert war was an ordeal in which progress was almost always followed by a check or setback.

The airmen spent little time discussing the wider picture or questioning the competence of the personalities directing the war. In Sam Pritchard's account, what anger they might have felt was directed at civilians. 'We were satisfied from the information available to us that the British Army and its commanders were at a disadvantage simply because their equipment was inferior to that of the Germans and to a certain extent we felt the same about our equipment,' he wrote.[43] They were convinced that 'this inferiority was due to the stupidities of politicians and pacifists between the wars'.

Whether it was immediately discernible or not, victory at El Alamein in October 1942 was a pivotal point and from then on, no matter how difficult Rommel made it for the Allies, their eventual success was assured. A few weeks afterwards, US troops landed in Morocco and Algeria. Henceforth the RAF would always be working in alliance with the American air forces. The arrangement was cemented at the top by the partnership forged between Eisenhower and Tedder. Thanks to the hard-won knowledge acquired in the desert, they took forward a methodology of combined air–ground warfare that carried them unstoppably onwards through the landings in Sicily, Italy and Normandy to victory in the West.

11

'Eat, Drink and Be Merry ...'

Arthur Harris – 'Bomber' Harris as he became known to the world, but 'Butch' to the men who carried out his orders – liked shocking people. He presented himself as a leader for times of crisis, willing to confront hard decisions that weaker men would flinch from and to face uncomfortable truths with brutal frankness.

Even those accustomed to his ways were shaken by his reaction to a drama which blew up early in 1943. A comment scrawled on the bumf that flew back and forth between the departments involved in trying to sort the matter out, summed it up: 'This seems an incredible story!' wrote Reginald Maudling, the young private secretary to the Air Minister, Archibald Sinclair.[1]

The flap over an outbreak of venereal disease (VD) among Harris's men does not merit even a footnote in the official histories, whose authors, if they knew about it, perhaps regarded it as a small and rather sordid episode in the great saga of the strategic bombing campaign. But the tale has a larger significance. The small flashbulb lights up a big picture. At the centre is the bulky figure of Harris, who loomed over the wartime RAF, blustering and intimidating. Behind him stand the men he led, engaged in the most dangerous job of the British war. The after-image that lingers is stark, a chiaroscuro revealing the grim outlines of the bomber battle. One impression endures: far from sparing a new generation from the horrors of trench warfare as its advocates claimed, strategic bombing invented an aerial version of it, and flying bombers to Germany was to the Second World War what fighting on the Western Front was to the First.

The story began late in 1942 when the Air Ministry noted a sharp rise in the incidence of VD among RAF personnel. This was a serious matter. Treatment was with Sulfonamide antibiotics (penicillin had not yet come into widespread use) and infection could put a man on the sick list for several weeks.[2] The increase was highest in Bomber Command and particularly affected aircrew members. The situation prompted Sir Bertine Sutton, the officer in charge of personnel at the Air Ministry, to alert the chiefs of the various commands and ask for comments and possible remedies. As C-in-C of the command most effected, Harris's response had particular significance. He generally took an indulgent view when attempts were made from time to time to restrain the off-duty high-jinks of the Bomber Boys. This time, his reaction was savage.

On 9 January 1943, without consulting the Air Ministry, he wrote to his group commanders pointing out that the incidence of VD among aircrews was 35 per thousand per annum, 'four times that of all other RAF personnel in the Command'.[3] He went on:

> The consequences of this are far too serious for it to be regarded with tolerance as the natural result of war. At best, it shows criminal carelessness, but I am strongly inclined to believe that this is not the whole truth and that a substantial amount of deliberate malingering is involved … Every member of a crew who contracts Venereal Disease incapacitates not merely himself but breaks up his entire crew and I will not have the efficiency of the Command to carry on the war impaired by individual irresponsibility in this way. Still less do I propose to allow anyone who may hope to do so to gain advantage from deliberately exposing himself to infection.

He concluded with a terrible warning to anyone henceforth unlucky enough to fall victim to the 'clap'. 'In future … it will be the rule that anyone contracting Venereal Disease, irrespective of the stage he has reached in his operational tour, will be required to start afresh and complete his 30 sorties, as soon as he is in a fit state of health so to do.'

Without any evidence, Harris was accusing airmen of deliberately setting out to get infected in order to shirk their duty. More shockingly, in order to enforce sexual discipline, he was prepared to threaten his men with what might well be a sentence of death. In 1943 the chances of surviving a standard tour of thirty operations was about one in five.[4] To condemn a man who was nearing the end of his tour to start all over again for the crime of 'copping a dose' would be seen by many as amounting to a writ of execution.

Harris sent Sutton a copy of the letter claiming that his tough policy had the approval of the Chief of the Air Staff, Portal, himself. Perhaps for this reason, Sutton's criticisms of Harris's approach were mild. As an Air Marshal, Sutton was outranked by Harris and the tone of his correspondence with him is deferential, prompted no doubt by a wish to avoid provoking the Air Chief Marshal's fury.

It took him three weeks to make contact, offering the rather lame-sounding excuse that he 'wanted to wait until I could tell you that an [American-made] film' on VD was available for showing to RAF personnel. When he finally got down to business the approach was placatory. 'I was very glad to see that you were telling all your groups to tackle the subject of prevention of the disease with vigour,' he wrote.

However, he was 'surprised to note the particular action you suggested they should take'. With a reserve bordering on timidity, he listed his reasons: 'That one ought not to make the extension of operational tours a punishment in any way ... secondly that if people unfit [sic] are sent on them they will not be able to do their best in action against the enemy, and thirdly it may lead to concealment and that in turn leads to the spreading of the disease.'

There is no mention of the probable fatal consequences of the policy, nor of the charge of malingering. The soft approach did not work. Two days later, on 5 February, Harris wrote back that he was 'absolutely satisfied that no other form of deterrent will have the desired effect which is essential and urgent, and moreover, that this warning, which will not be made retrospective in action, will have the effect which is intended'.

It was left to the RAF's Director General of Medical Services, Sir Harold Whittingham, to fire a shot across Harris's bow. Harris had decided that the best method of delivering the threat of a repeat tour was via station or squadron medical officers. When

Whittingham heard of the order he was concerned by what he saw as a breach of medical ethics and condemned the idea of imposing 'a punishment for contracting disease'. On 25 February, a letter was sent from the Air Ministry stating that the 'present procedure lays us open to attack both in the House [of Commons] and in the Press'. It finished with a firm order: 'If any such instructions have been given they must be cancelled at once.'

Sutton assumed that Harris had backed off and the official focus now was on tackling VD through a programme of lectures by medical officers, more explicit than hitherto, on 'the physiology of sex … including the use of condoms' and screenings on stations of a US Army film on sexual hygiene.

The flap subsided. Then, in June 1943, news of the Harris order reached the ears of Archibald Sinclair. He learned about it only after a respected Labour MP, George Strauss, began making inquiries. Sinclair was annoyed at having been kept in the dark. He seems to have shared the view of his private secretary that the story was barely credible. 'Clearly, the methods of the Commander in Chief are objectionable,' he wrote to Sutton in July 1943. Harris, it seemed, had not rescinded his letter to the group commanders. Sinclair thundered that 'it should be made clear to him that it must be withdrawn at once'.

The intervention of the political brass generated action on all fronts. Philip Joubert, now an RAF Inspector General, was ordered to come up with a plan for combating what had become officially a 'scourge'. If Harris's draconian solution was ever applied – and there is no evidence I can find, documentary or anecdotal, either way – then it made no difference. The VD rate among bomber crews continued to climb in 1943, reaching a peak in August.

Joubert's inquiry took him to fifty-three stations across the operational commands in the company of Lord Amulree, a medical doctor. The report appeared on 17 September 1943 and its central conclusion was that 'indiscipline and idleness breed infection'. Joubert's tour seems to have left him with a poor impression of the conduct of airmen in general and bomber crews in particular. His solution was to make them more like soldiers, recommending that 'all RAF personnel including aircrew, must be trained to fight under their own officers and NCOs' – advice, which like most of that prof-fered in the report, was ignored by the Air Council.

What is most striking about the report is the absence of serious interest in the – surely relevant and certainly fascinating – questions of *why* the rate had risen and *why* it was so marked among the bomber crews?

The obvious explanation had been hinted at by Harris in a long letter to Sutton in which he set out justifications for his harsh approach – an important document that we will return to later. Repeating a tenaciously held but totally unsupported assertion, he wrote that 'there is not the least doubt that even after giving the fullest possible rein to the spirit of "Eat, Drink and be Merry" there is the very strongest possibility of deliberate malingering'.

The phrase, which would crop up regularly thereafter, of course continues: 'for tomorrow we die.' In the summer of 1943, there was every possibility that as a member of a Bomber Command aircrew you would die, if not tomorrow then at some point before the end of your operational tour. By the early months of 1943, only about seventeen out of a hundred men were likely to be alive after thirty operations. The survival rate for a second tour was a minuscule 2.5 per cent.[5] Senior commanders did their best to keep the informa-tion secret. 'I am extremely anxious that statistical information relating to the chances of survival of aircrews in certain types of operational employment should be confined to the smallest number of people,' Portal wrote to the Air Member for Training, at the end of 1942. 'The information can be so easily distorted and is then so dangerous to morale that all possible steps must be taken to safeguard it.'[6]

Though it might take a little time to sink in, the Bomber Boys knew soon enough what they had got themselves into. For a young man, fit and adventurous, the prospect of imminent extinction provided a plausible enough motive for wanting to live whatever remained of life to the full.

In the brief space he devoted to the subject, Joubert rejected the notion that the VD surge was a reflection of the fatalism felt by young warriors who assumed they were heading to their doom. As with Harris and his charge of malingering, he trusted to instinct and does not seem to have spoken to any airmen actually involved in operations, on the ground or in the air. He concluded that 'a large number' of infections were contracted in the last phase of training, at the end of courses at Operational Training Units (OTUs) and Heavy Conversion Units (HCUs) before crews joined their squadrons.

'The natural feeling of elation' that resulted, he wrote, 'leads to excess during the period of relaxation before the serious business of war has to be undertaken.' He went on: 'I do not believe that there is much of the "Let us eat, drink and be merry ..." feeling but rather a perfectly natural desire to show off. I should have expected to find a very high rate in the operational units if the former had been the case but the facts are against it.'

It was true that Lindholme, the station with the highest incidence of VD, housed two HCUs. Medical records put the infection rate at 85 per thousand per annum. According to Joubert, 'in many cases ... there is a record of a visit to Doncaster [the nearest town], a condition of drunkenness and a return to camp without taking any

precautions. In practically no case is the name of the woman known to the infected aircrew.'

The statistics confirmed that conversion units were the worst affected with a rate of 72.2 per thousand. But the rate in operational squadrons was still considerable, at 44.6. And a salient fact was, as Whittingham pointed out, that 'the incidence of venereal disease in air crews is about four times greater than in ground personnel in the command'. Ground crews worked hard but they had fixed hours, got time off, and were just as keen on beer and skittles as the aircrews. The big difference between the two groups was that one was facing imminent extinction and the other was not.

Joubert seemed reluctant to entertain this obvious explanation for the reckless encounters which his report described. At the Air Ministry, Sutton, too, tried to treat the issue as a problem that could be resolved in a tidy, bureaucratic manner. Like Joubert, he believed that more discipline, combined with greater pastoral care and 'welfare activities and discussion groups' were the way to keep the crews on the straight and narrow.

The men around Harris at Bomber Command headquarters in High Wycombe took a worldlier view. Responding to Sutton's proposals for a programme of 'useful diversions', Harris's chief administration officer, Arthur Sanders, gently pointed out some hard realities. After consulting with the command's medical authorities, his findings were that there was 'no evidence that one station is better than another because of a higher standard of welfare or of ethical counteraction'. The fact was that 'all station commanders are trying to do everything within their powers to provide compensatory attractions in the way of welfare activities, recreation and healthy diversions so that the personnel may be induced voluntarily to stay "in camp"'. Even so, despite 'all counter attractions [being] promoted *ad nauseam*, one is forced to the conclusion that these efforts at dissuasion … give no positive results'.

Nor was a ban on excursions to local towns a practical proposition. 'No doubt if we were to put places known to be sources of infection out of bounds, or at least put a ban on the pubs, cheap dance halls and night clubs etc., and if we controlled personal freedom and increased surveillance of promiscuity in public parks, back alleys etc., we could reduce the disease to almost pre-war level. But with what reactions!'

Young men were 'not normally very receptive of the teachings of self-control, restraint and abstinence in any form'. With aircrews, there were other powerful factors. They basked in the 'enhanced "hero-worship"' they encountered in pub, shop and cinema. But there was also the 'uncertainty of the span of life' and the 'strain arising out of the nature of [their] war occupation'. Sanders concluded that examination of the figures and taking the human factors into account '[forced] one to regard the hazard of operations as being a supreme factor in the incidence'. As far as Bomber Command HQ were concerned, then, 'eat, drink and be merry ...' explained almost everything.

One small detail from the story seems particularly poignant. The VD rate at Leeming, in Yorkshire was one of the highest but Joubert's inquiries led him to believe that the figure could well be an under-estimate. He warned that '[the] figures may not be by any means the total of actual infections since it is reported that a large number of M and B tabloids [tablets] ... have been found in missing aircrews' kit,' he reported. May and Baker tablets were antibiotics used for everything from urinary-tract infections to pneumonia. The impli-cation is that VD sufferers were not reporting sick but somehow getting hold of the necessary medication. Why they were unwilling to follow correct procedures and how they got hold of the tablets is open to conjecture. One possibility is that, having learned of Harris's directive, they sought the help of sympathetic medical officers who were willing to provide treatment off the books. In any case those few words paint a sad picture: a young airman treating himself in secret, going to his death with the vague memory of a shop-door grapple as his last, and perhaps only, experience of sex.

The founders of the RAF claimed to have invented a new form of warfare. Technology would speed things up and cut down casual-ties, both for the victorious and the defeated. Death was supposed to be a by-product of military action, not the primary purpose. The fatalism implicit in the VD episode, however, seems to belong to an earlier, but not that far-distant, era: it feels like the spirit of the trenches.

By the summer of 1943, the aircrews of Bomber Command were enmeshed in a terrible slogging match that, despite being fought in the air, had some of the characteristics of the struggle their fathers and uncles had endured in the front lines of Flanders a generation earlier. Their work was repetitive. Their losses, proportionately, were huge and seemingly without purpose. There was no progress that they could measure and they were forced to return to the same targets over and over again. The men who sent them there, they seldom saw.

This was not how the bomber war had been conceived but this is where it had ended up. It had arrived there largely because of the triumph of the Air Ministry doctrines that dominated the military thinking of the previous decade and the long-term planning decisions that had resulted. The fantasy of the 'knock-out blow' had been exposed almost immediately. The realization that Bomber Command was incapable of delivering the results it had promised took a little longer. As the war progressed there were constant calls for a reordering of priorities and a reallocation of air assets – to Coastal Command, as we have seen, and to meet the ever-growing needs of the Middle and Far Eastern theatres. But the bombing lobby prevailed and the investment that had been made in strategic bombing; in huge four-engine machines that could deliver the payloads to cripple German industry and fulfil the prophecies of Trenchard and his followers; and the physical and human resources to operate them, could not be unspent.

Everything about bombing was expensive; in money for the machines and bases and in time for the training of the aircrews. The Ford Motor Company in Manchester, which began producing the Rolls-Royce Merlin aero-engine, the power plant for the Lancaster bomber, in May 1941 cost £7 million to build and equip.[7] By the end of the war it employed 17,316 workers. The purchase price of a Lancaster in 1943 was £42,000, about £2 million in today's money.[8] During the war more than 7,000 were built in Britain alone as well as 6,000 Halifaxes and nearly 2,000 Stirlings.

Building a bomber station cost about £1 million (£59 million today). Bomber Command had started the war with twenty-seven, all with grass runways. In 1944, it had 128, all but two with concrete runways.[9] According to Harris, 'the education of a member of a bomber crew was the most expensive in the world', costing £10,000 (£589,000), 'enough to send ten men to Oxford or Cambridge for three years'.[10] Many of the RAF's eggs had been put in one basket. For better or worse, the air campaign against Germany was a central pillar of British strategy, and the logic was that to weaken it would undermine the whole construct.

This was the thinking that underpinned Churchill's statement of policy delivered to the War Cabinet on the first anniversary of the outbreak of the war, placing the hope of victory on the shoulders of the RAF, and in particular Bomber Command. Despite the abysmal results to date, Churchill was adamant that the way ahead was to 'develop the power to carry an increasing volume of explosives to Germany, so as to pulverize the entire industry and scientific structure on which the war effort and economic life of the enemy depend, while holding him at arm's length from our Island. In no other way at present visible can we hope to overcome the immense military power of Germany ...'[11]

It would be another eighteen months before bombing showed any signs of effectiveness. Despite this delay, the appalling losses in late 1941 that forced Churchill to call a suspension of operations until the following spring, and the huge change for the better in the strategic situation by the entry of first Russia, then America into the war, Britain's leaders stuck to the spirit of the plan. The arrival of the thirty-ton, four-engine bombers, better navigation aids, properly trained crews and a ruthless and energetic leader in the shape of Harris provided the 'power' that Churchill's speech looked forward to. From the summer of 1942 onwards the story can be told in terms of tonnages. In 1940 Bomber Command dropped 13,033 tons of bombs; in 1941, 31,704; in 1942, 45,561; in 1943, 157,457, in 1944, 525,718, and in 1945, up to 1 a.m. on 9 May, 181,740.[12] By the end of the war Bomber Command could deliver in twenty-four hours the same weight of bombs as the Luftwaffe had managed in the whole eight months of the 1940–41 Blitz.[13]

Support for the primacy of bombing was wide and deep. There was plenty of resentment from the other services and inside the RAF itself at Bomber Command's privileged status, but in the civilian world there was near-universal agreement that bombing Germany was the right and obvious thing to do. The consensus spanned the political spectrum and there were as many enthusiastic bombers on the left as on the right. The high-minded Marxist sympathizer Stafford Cripps, Minister of Aircraft Production in 1942, was a fervent supporter of bombing Germany. Another leading Labour intellectual, John Strachey, Eton-educated, a sometime Communist, joined the RAF and served as a public relations officer, broadcasting propaganda about the men of Bomber Command on the BBC.

In early 1942, there was at last something substantial to boast about. It was the raid on Cologne on the night of 30/31 May that demonstrated to the British people, the Germans and the world at large that an important shift had taken place in the direction of the air war. Every serviceable bomber, including aircraft from training units, was dragged in for the first Thousand Bomber Raid. This was the biggest air operation in history and set new records of violence, destroying 13,000 homes, nine hospitals, seventeen churches and numerous other public buildings and killing 469 people, all but fifty-eight of whom were civilians. Forty-three aircraft failed to return – just under 4 per cent of the force. These were the heaviest losses yet suffered by Bomber Command but deemed acceptable, given that the clear conditions favoured not only the bombers but also the German defences.[14]

Cologne was as much a propaganda as a military exercise. Newsreel crews were given access to briefings and filmed aircraft being bombed up. The commentaries that accompanied the reports are remarkably similar in tone and content. There are passing references to Cologne being 'of first importance to German war industry'. The overwhelming message, though, is that this is an act of retribution. The Pathé Gazette report, written and voiced by a veteran American journalist, Quentin Reynolds, started with a comparison based on his own experience of the Blitz. 'A year and a half ago I saw the Nazis concentrating their might on London,' he declaimed. 'From the clouds, hell was let loose ... as the flames roared, Londoners set their teeth and took it on the chin. But it wasn't a knock out. It gave birth to a grim determination that the Germans should pay dearly for such destruction. Then at last came the Spring morning when the people of London and other blitzed cities of Britain heard that the Royal Air Force had sent more than a thousand planes over Cologne and the Ruhr, the crews having instructions to "let 'em have it! Right on the chin!" And so it was ... RAF bombers dropped big beautiful bombs, right on the centre of the Nazis' war effort. An uppercut, right on the chin, creating havoc and fear in the hearts of the foolish people who put Hitler in power ...'[15]

The punch line was Harris's. All the newsreels carried footage of him dictating a message to his crews in which he exhorted them to 'press on your attack. If you succeed you will have delivered the most devastating blow against the very vitals of the enemy. Let him have it, right on the chin!' This was followed by a warning to Germany and a statement to the world of Bomber Command's intentions, which would soon be reinforced by the arrival of the air power of the United States Army. 'Cologne, Lübeck, Rostock. Those are only just the beginning. Let the Nazis take good note of the Western horizon. There they will see a cloud, as yet no bigger than a man's hand. But behind that hand lies the whole massive power of the United States of America. When the storm bursts over Germany, they will look back to the days of Lübeck and Rostock and Cologne as a man caught in the blasts of a hurricane will look back to the gentle zephyrs of last summer ...'

It was in this appearance that he delivered his most famous prophecy, all the more effective for being delivered in tones of cold certainty, devoid of histrionics: 'The Nazis entered this war under the rather childish delusion that they were going to bomb everybody else and nobody was going to bomb them ... they sowed the wind, and now they are going to reap the whirlwind.' The biblical theme of great sins inviting greater punishment was a favourite of Harris's. The Allied air attack on Hamburg launched in the last week of July 1943 that killed 30,000 was code-named Operation Gomorrah.

These sentiments were warmly endorsed by figures accepted on the left as moral arbiters, notably George Orwell who, in a BBC broadcast after Cologne, told listeners: 'In 1940, when the Germans were bombing Britain they did not expect retaliation on a very heavy scale ... the people of this country are not revengeful, but they remember what happened to themselves two years ago, and they remember how the Germans talked when they thought themselves safe from retaliation.'[16]

It was quite clear from the coverage what 'retaliation' meant to the Germans on the ground. The British Movietone News report explained that the smoke still covering the city days after the raid had made it impossible to include reconnaissance footage of the damage. Over images of roofless buildings, the voice track continued: 'but from these pictures of previous raid results, it's easy to imagine what Cologne looks like today'.[17] A cheerful airman then reports: 'We certainly gave Cologne a good pasting today. I looked down on the target and it was nothing but a sea of fire.'

The obvious message that mass air raids produced civilian casualties produced no outcry. There were a few brave dissenters who spoke out against area bombing, such as George Bell, the Anglican Bishop of Chichester, and the Labour MP Richard Stokes. But the vast majority agreed with Orwell that the Germans had had it coming, a view that persisted even when the scale of the destruction was revealed. In 1946, the pioneering documentary maker Humphrey Jennings made A Defeated People, which showed the consequences of the Allied victory. It opened with footage of a moonscape of pulverized streets and voiceovers in a variety of accents reflecting what Britons were saying about Germany. The first says: 'They asked for it. They got it!'[18]

The name of Arthur Harris would stick to the bombing war the way that Bernard Montgomery's stuck to El Alamein. It was his good luck to arrive at Bomber Command just as it reached effectiveness. It was his misfortune to be associated forever in everyone's mind as the prime mover behind area bombing, rather than the man who carried it out. If any one senior airman bears responsibility for the policy it is Portal, who was advocating 'a definite attempt with our offensive to affect the morale of the German people' by attacks 'with the prime aim of causing heavy material destruction' as early as October 1940.[19]

Harris complained about the misattribution but accepted there was little hope of correction. Given the gusto with which he entered into his role as the scourge of Germany, it was hardly surprising that he should get the blame rather than the cool, fastidious Portal, who was as surefooted as a chamois on the slippery slopes of power and whose distaste for publicity equalled Harris's enjoyment of it.

Seventy-five years on, Harris seems an unsympathetic figure, brutal of speech and manner and apparently indifferent to the human cost of the bombing campaign, whether of German women and children or his own men. The experience of the bomber crews may have some marked similarities with the lot of infantrymen in the trenches, but Harris was no Douglas Haig. The judgement that matters most to a commander is that of his own troops. 'Butch' won the respect, even the admiration, of many. In the company of men whose emotions were strictly rationed, he could also kindle a strange sort of liking.

Bomber Boys were by and large a bolshie lot. Many of them came from social backgrounds and areas of Britain which gave them no reason to respect the established order or take for granted the good faith or competence of the ruling class. Eric Banks, a Bradford boy who completed a tour as a rear gunner with 166 Squadron, had what was in some ways a typical attitude towards his duties. Brave, resourceful and punctilious when in the air, he resented attempts to impose petty rules and restrictions on the ground and did his best to thwart them. Yet his judgement on Harris was fulsome. 'He was a figure of the highest esteem, almost affection, from his "boys", he wrote.[20] 'I never saw the legendary leader, neither did I come across anyone else who had caught a glimpse of him. He did not tour around the bomber bases holding impromptu talks with his air and ground crews, sloganizing and entertaining his troops with light-hearted patter. Perhaps he surmised that his minions, young as most were, deserved better. From my small experience, I gained the impression that, to a man, they regarded their commander as one of their own – the highest praise of all.'

This verdict does not sit easily with some of Harris's attitudes and actions. He was opposed, for example, to setting a limit on operational tours, a practice he inherited on taking over. 'I am most unwilling to do anything to foster the idea that our crews are under some description of Trade Union contract to carry out a certain number of carefully-defined operational missions, after which they are free, at any rate for a fixed period, to take no more part in the war,' he wrote to the Air Ministry in February 1942.[21] As was sometimes the case, his habitual sarcasm disguised more nuanced thinking and a willingness to let things lie. In this case, he did nothing to alter the existing arrangement and his real point was that he thought it better to leave the length of a crew's tour for the squadron commander to decide, on the basis that he would know whether or not they had 'done their best'.

So it was with his attitude towards VD. In his letter replying to Sutton's querying of his policy of punishing sufferers with a second tour, he amplified the point made in the original signal to group commanders, and his justifications made a certain harsh sense. 'The personnel concerned must be regarded not as unfortunate individuals [he wrote] but as people who through their own action and their own carelessness ... have broken up a highly skilled and highly trained flying crew. It is not the individual but the crew that matters. These crews are first disrupted and then thrown out of gear perhaps for the rest of their tour. As a consequence, not only is the operational effort of the whole Command seriously reduced, but "patched up" crews are undoubtedly liable to suffer heavier casualties than crews who have been trained and learnt by long experience to work together as a team.'[22]

Cruel though the measure seemed, the Bomber Boys would not have denied the truth of Harris's words. The chemistry of a crew was a mysterious thing. In a brilliant display of imagination, the system allowed each team to select itself, pilot, navigator, bomb aimer and air gunners, milling round in a hangar until they coagulated into a unit in a process often described as resembling a mass blind date. Time and trial were needed to weave the web of trust needed to fly a huge aeroplane efficiently in conditions of extreme danger. The loss of one of the team for whatever reason was bad news, and, as Harris said, possibly fatal.

Norman Lee, a rear gunner with 428 Squadron, had finished three trips with his regular all-NCO crew when they were tasked with a raid on Milan. They were apprehensive about the operation, not just because it meant a ten-hour flight and crossing the Alps twice, but because their regular navigator had gone sick and they

Sardonic, humane and a star of the Mediterranean air war. Neville Duke snapped by Cecil Beaton.

Land-air co-operation in action: a Martin Baltimore of 55 Squadron silhouetted above a salvo of exploding bombs, dropped in a joint attack with the USAAF on Rommel's armour during the Battle of Alamein.

Unsung heroes. Short Sunderland and crew. Coastal Command's role in the existential struggle of the Battle of the Atlantic was often overlooked.

Depth charges from a sub-hunting Sunderland of 422 Squadron RCAF rock a U-boat in March 1944.

British industry was harnessed to the needs of the RAF. Here the de Havilland factory is churning out one of its most brilliant and versatile products – the Mosquito.

Ground crew working on a Bristol Beaufighter of 89 Squadron at a remote airstrip. The Burma campaign relied utterly on air power to succeed.

Percy Pickard like Guy Gibson was a favourite of RAF propaganda. Like Gibson, he insisted on returning to ops, and died in action.

Pilots of 132 Squadron with their CO Geoffrey Page (holding map) prepare to attack targets in France in the run-up to D-Day.

The RAF was a multinational, multi-ethnic force. Above, Polish pilots of 303 Squadron. And below, some of the 400 West Indian aircrew volunteers.

Though relations with the Army improved steadily throughout the war, the Air Force would get a large share of the blame for the debacle at Arnhem.

Arming a Typhoon during the Normandy campaign.

Slaughter in a country lane. The devastating result of a 'Tiffy' rocket attack on a German column in the Falaise Pocket.

Job done. Hitler's Berchtesgaden retreat after a last-minute visit by Bomber Command.

Airmen in Austria studying literature for the 1945 General Election. The democratic spirit of the wartime RAF would be echoed in the outcome.

It's a lovely day tomorrow …

were getting a young pilot officer as a replacement. 'This didn't please us much,' he wrote, 'not because he was an officer or because we doubted his technical competence … but because it was unsettling to have a stranger flying with us.'[23]

The outward journey was uneventful and the target was lightly defended. Soon after they turned for home the trouble started. The pilot lost his way and they found themselves over Paris, where 'they gave us a dreadful pasting. The searchlights had us coned for about ten minutes while the flak gunners threw everything they had at us.' The pilot, Johnny Harkins, ended the ordeal by finding sanctuary in a cloud, and eventually they reached the Channel coast. When they eventually landed, 'two of our engines actually died of thirst as we finished our landing run'.

Lee admitted that 'it was probably a bit brutal of us, but I don't think anyone spoke a single word to the poor old navigator after we left the aircraft. There was none of that sense of comradeship that is supposed to be generated by sharing and surmounting common dangers. Or rather that was just the trouble. The comradeship existed, but it was between the regular crew and it didn't include stand-in navigators who lost the way home.'

Almost every account of the experience makes it clear that in the later stages of training and for the duration of the tour, your crew were the most important people in the universe, crowding out thoughts of friends and family; even girlfriend or wife. Often the individual members had little in common and, in other circumstances, had their paths crossed no lasting relationship would have ensued. But as Lee said, shared danger and the responsibility each man shouldered for keeping the others alive created a deep attachment, the quality of which can perhaps only truly be understood by those who experienced it.

Eric Banks considered that joining the crew of Squadron Leader Stowell was 'without doubt the most important decision I ever made'. It was a typical Bomber Command jumble of backgrounds and nationalities. All but the pilot were sergeants. Banks, the wireless operator, had been a clerk before joining up. 'Tubby', the Canadian navigator, interrupted his science studies at university to volunteer. He was 'large, with a rather vacant fixed grin'. The mid-upper gunner was 'Whitey', from Shropshire, who had lied about his age to join the RAF. Jimmy, another Canadian, was a Methodist minister's son whose 'chief interest appeared to be "chicks" with whom he went dancing on just about every free evening'. 'Red', the bomb aimer, was the third Canadian in the crew and Banks's best friend. The last to join was Ernie, the flight engineer, from the East End of London who was 'the most accomplished booze artist I ever met'. He spent every evening 'propping up the bar of some Lincolnshire pub, quietly talking to anyone around drinking one pint every twelve minutes or so, and when the evening came to an end, collecting those of his companions who had fallen by the wayside and ensuring that they reached camp safely'.

Years later he still cherished memories of 'great hilarity, much revelry and above all, the unthinking loyalty and friendship of a small group of youngsters towards each other'. The odd man out was the pilot, who Banks gives the pseudonym 'Squadron Leader Stowell'. He was thirty-six years old, ancient by aircrew standards, a pre-war regular who had volunteered for flying duties with Bomber Command. He was the son of a senior official at the Colonial Office, and 'it soon became evident that he had no idea as to how the vast majority of British citizens lived'. The other crew members regarded Stowell as snobbish and offhand, though Banks charitably excused his manners on the grounds that he could not be blamed for his upbringing. On one of their first outings, however, his attitude provoked a mutiny. While still at the OTU at Peplow, Shropshire, they were returning from a cross-country daytime trip. As they approached the base, 'Tubby' the navigator warned the skipper to gain height as they were in danger of flying into the 1,335-ft-high Wrekin, which lay to the south of the station. Stowell 'replied that this was nonsense and [it] would be another twenty minutes or so before reaching the area of the airfield. He refused to gain altitude but the matter was resolved when the Wrekin appeared.'

After landing, 'Tubby' announced that this was 'the last time I fly with that bastard'. The rest agreed. They decided to report their decision to the Wing Commander in charge of flying training. He listened sympathetically and agreed that Stowell had acted improperly. 'He was naturally loath to break up a crew,' wrote Banks, 'and asked if we would consider continuing with Stowell for the moment until he had a tactful talk with him … we rather doubtfully agreed to this [but he] must have been as good as his word as we never had further nonsense of this sort again.'

Later, while they were doing their conversion course to Lancasters at Lindholme HCU, Stowell made an attempt to be sociable, asking Banks if he might join them on their nightly excursion to the village pub. Banks agreed, though the others received the news without enthusiasm. That evening in the bar 'the customers were as usual thick on the ground. He pushed his way through to us and insisted on buying a round, although we had just been served with our second whiskies.' Banks judged that 'by and large the evening was a success. He chatted amicably with us but we learned nothing about him that we did not already know.' The experiment was not repeated, and he would never be one of the boys.

Nonetheless, when they began their tour of operations flying out of Kirmington in north Lincolnshire with 166 Squadron, the rest of the crew came to respect his courage and skill. In late July the squadron took part in a raid on Le Havre. It was an evening operation but it was still broad daylight when they arrived. 'All went well until we were nearing our target and had commenced the bombing run,' Banks remembered. He was standing in the astrodome to get a view of the heavy flak barrage when he 'happened to glance upwards. To my horror, a Lancaster with bomb doors open was positioned exactly above us and … appeared almost within reach.' The rear gunner, Whitey, had seen it too and screamed a warning over the intercom. Stowell 'could not have known just what had occurred, but he certainly knew panic when he heard it. Our aircraft was thrown wildly to starboard as the bombs hurtled past our port wing. It was a magnificent reaction and Whitey and I breathed again.'

Their relief was premature. Banks assumed the skipper would abort the operation. All the other aircraft had completed their bombing runs and were heading for home. He was astonished to hear Stowell's voice in his earphones. '"We'll have to go around again," he said conversationally. It was as if he was suggesting another round of … golf.'

His first thought was that 'there was no way that a sole aircraft could, in daylight, fly through that flak barrage and come out the other side without phenomenal luck. I honestly doubt that I had any great feeling of terror ... Possibly I had passed the terror stage.'

With 'Red' the bomb aimer, calling directions, Stowell 'carefully handled the aircraft towards the target. He was quite oblivious to the lethal barrage and seemed no more concerned than any pilot on routine bombing range practice. "Bombs gone!" shouted Red. The aircraft banked steeply to port and in no time we were out of range of the German gunners.' Despite this extraordinary sang-froid, Banks believed there 'was nothing foolhardy about Stowell. He was just doing his job as instructed.'

Halfway through their tour the crew were told out of the blue that Stowell was being promoted and posted away to command 12 Squadron at Wickenby in Lincolnshire and they were to get a new skipper. At first this seemed like good news. Then they reconsidered. He was after all 'a competent pilot and had shown he did not panic in desperate situations ... we had completed fifteen ops with Stowell and shared the dangers and worries with him and survived'. Another thought struck them. What if his replacement was 'a gung-ho type who would really be "one of the boys"'? It was a relief when a few days after his departure they received a message that 'Wing Commander Stowell wanted "his boys" at Wickenby', where they would finish their tour, with the CO occasionally flying with them.

Harris believed there were similarities between what his men were doing and the experience of serving as an infantryman on the Western Front. They showed 'the courage of men with long-drawn apprehensions of "going over the top",' he wrote in a memoir, two years after the end of the war.[24] But he pointed out an important distinction. It was 'furthermore, the courage of the small hours, of men virtually alone, for at his battle station, the airman is virtually alone'.

Bomber crews operated in a capsule. On boarding their aircraft, men merged with machines. Flying towards enemy territory in the gathering dusk it was reassuring to see what Les Bartlett of 50 Squadron observed on his maiden op, a trip to Berlin on 22

November 1943. 'At 9,000 feet, still climbing, we break cloud,' he wrote in his diary.[25] 'It is almost dusk yet all around we can see shapes, vague yet resolute, all moving in the same direction. It is rather comforting to know you are not alone in your efforts ...' On their return, as they crossed the English coast, he realized that 'we are in the centre of a great armada, hundreds of little red, green and white navigation lights – actually they've been there all the time, without lights, but of course we couldn't see them.' Once night fell, the darkness swallowed your companions who might reveal themselves only as they loomed out of nowhere on a collision course over the target area or went up in a fireball, struck by flak or a night fighter's cannon shells.

Inside the skin of your Stirling or Halifax or Lancaster speech was strictly rationed. Once an operation began, the banter and easy familiarity ended and all was grave and serious. Outsiders they met in the towns and villages near the stations where they served 'would no doubt regard us as a bunch of happy clowns without a care in the world,' wrote Eric Banks. 'They would not have recognised us if they could have seen us at work. We regarded ourselves and each other as experts, each in his own particular field. And the fooling stopped when we donned our flying kit ...'

It annoyed Norman Lee how 'in films about the war, the crews seem to chatter away over the intercom all the time about popsies, wizard prangs and all the rest of it, always using Christian names and generally giving a rather happy-go-lucky impression'. His crew 'never did this ... we always followed the procedure when we spoke to one another: "rear gunner to pilot"; "pilot to navigator" and so on. No-one was ever addressed by his first name while we were in flight, which is as it should be.'

Personality was replaced by function. It was a lonely business, especially for a rear gunner like Lee, an arse-end Charlie marooned at the extremity of the Halifax connected to his mates only by intercom. The pilot, engineer and navigator were kept constantly busy but for the others there were long periods with nothing to do. Lee boasted that he was entirely without imagination, which he regarded as an attribute rather than a deficiency in his chosen line of work for it meant he hardly ever felt fear. It also meant he suffered more than most from boredom. The business of flying did nothing for him, and it was true that the glamour of aviation soon wore after a few hours in a bomber. 'The alleged poetry and beauty of it all left me cold,' he confessed. 'Going on an op in an aeroplane was just riding to work as far as I was concerned.'

His duties were 'to report flak positions or searchlights but otherwise it was dead quiet apart from the aircraft noise. I used to sing to myself the whole way there and back.' Lee recalled that during his tour in the summer of 1943, the gunners were instructed not to open fire at night fighters unless in dire necessity. 'Shooting enemy fighters down was not what the rear gunner existed for, but bringing the aircraft back,' he wrote. 'The vital part of the job was to spot the night fighters in time for the pilot to take evasive action. Firing your guns at the enemy was only a last resort if you failed to evade him, the point being that when you opened up with your guns you were giving a firework display, so if there was another fighter in the vicinity, he would spot it and join in the party.' After seventeen ops he had 'never fired my guns in anger'.

In his determinedly unheroic memoir, Lee several times makes the point that operations could often go off without the participants feeling any real sense of danger. His first trip with 428 was to Hamburg on 2 August 1943. The weather was atrocious, their Halifax was repeatedly struck by lightning, and of the thirty-two aircraft that set off from their station, Middleton St George in Yorkshire, only a handful reached the target. Lee's crew was not one of them and instead they dropped their bombs on Heligoland. The weather kept the night fighters on the ground and the flak gunners 'couldn't do much that night except poop off a few rounds, more as a gesture than in real hope'. He concluded that 'all in all, I can't say that this first taste of war impressed me very much'. The second and third trips were not much more eventful.

Even when things livened up, Lee felt insulated from events outside the aircraft and a sense of disconnection between the bomber and the bombed. Later, when, after being shot down he fell in with the French resistance, he was able to compare fighting in the air with fighting on the ground. 'Seeing the people you are shooting at makes you dry in the mouth, especially when you hit them,' he wrote. 'Hearing the bullets whistling around your unprotected body is quite another thing from seeing flak from the inside of an aeroplane.'

Little noise penetrated the aircraft because the roar of the engines drowned out everything. 'To us the whole affair was just a silent firework display, like Cinerama with the sound turned off. The searchlights poked about the sky. The flak explosions made puff-balls all round. The town below quietly burned and exploded. We were no more than spectators of it all. The only sense of reality came from the smell of cordite produced by the flak bursts, [which] came through despite the oxygen masks.'

This sense of isolation is echoed in the testimony of many Bomber Boys. They were delivering an abstract violence, turning the ground below into a boiling palette of reds and yellows, and it needed an effort of imagination to translate what they saw into dead bodies and shattered buildings. It took personal disaster to puncture the bubble. For Lee and his crew, it came on the night of 4 October 1943. They took off from Middleton St George at 17.25 to bomb Frankfurt. It was a clear evening, which favoured the night fighters who were further helped by marker flares dropped by Path Finder Force aircraft to direct the bomber stream to the target.

They were thirty minutes' flying time from Frankfurt when Lee saw a Junkers 88 about three hundred yards astern. 'I immediately told Johnny using the standard reporting procedure: "Rear gunner to pilot – prepare to corkscrew to starboard. Corkscrew starboard down – go!"' Johnny Harkins threw the aircraft into the approved manoeuvre, which involved falling away in the direction of the attacking fighter, then rolling and climbing. It seemed to be success-ful. As far as Lee could see, the attacker never opened fire. But 'there must have been another fighter working with him' for the bomber was raked from underneath, and both engines on the starboard fire burst into flames. Lee saw 'the starboard aileron sail past the tail and disappear. As it went, the flames from the engines were shooting past my rear turret on the starboard side. I remember Scotty the flight engineer yelling over the intercom, "the whole bloody aircraft's on fire." Indeed it was. The flames had reached back down the petrol feedlines and were setting the inside fuselage ablaze.'

Nobody panicked. Things were happening too fast for that. Harkins gave the order to bale out and it was every man for himself. Hunched in his position at the back of the aircraft Lee 'centralised the turret, opened the turret doors, grabbed my parachute which was hanging inside the fuselage' and clipped it on. He swung the turret away from the flames roaring down the starboard side and climbed onto the seat. The correct drill was to tumble out backwards but he 'didn't fancy this'. He went out feet first and a few seconds later 'there was a thump and an upward jerk on my chest and shoulders, and there I was dangling by my armpits on a cold night eighteen thousand feet somewhere over Europe ...' All the crew survived. Four were taken prisoner, but Lee and two others avoided capture. He landed near the Germany–Luxembourg border, and was sheltered by the head of the local resistance, who passed him on to the French underground. He would end up fighting with the Maquis in the South of France.

Lee was leaving the bombing war just as it was entering its most intense and costly phase. In November 1943 Harris was given a free hand to launch a series of massive raids on the German capital and other cities that became known as the Battle of Berlin. It lasted until March and aimed to prove once and for all the contention that it was possible to bring about the collapse of the enemy from the air. It was the aerial equivalent of the 'Big Push', beloved of First World War generals, and developed in much the same way. Initial success, raising hopes of a breakthrough, soon subsided. Gains dwindled as deaths rose. For those who took part in it there were none of the longueurs that Lee describes and every night there were dramas and catastrophes.

Les Bartlett arrived at Skellingthorpe in Lincolnshire to join 50 Squadron just as the battle got started. He was the bomb aimer with a crew skippered by Michael Beetham, who would gain a reputation as one of the most able and tenacious pilots in Bomber Command and end up Marshal of the RAF and Chief of the Air Staff. The life he described in his diary is one of almost constant hazard. Almost every operation, even those regarded as a 'piece of cake', resulted in significant losses. Perched in the nose of their Lancaster he had a stark view of the mayhem on the way to the target as night fighters slunk into the bomber stream, dealing death to their unsuspecting victims from below. During fourteen large raids on 'the Big City' between the middle of November 1943 and the end of January 1944, 384 aircraft were lost.[26] The campaign was a failure. As time passed, the raids became less effective and more costly. Most of the victims fell to the reorganized Luftwaffe night-fighter force which by the end could muster nearly 400 aircraft and Berlin, though battered, was still nowhere near surrendering when a halt was called.

The night of 30/31 March 1944 saw the biggest slaughter. The objective was Nuremburg, far away in Bavaria, which so far had been left off the target list. Bartlett recorded that when the crews learned their destination at the briefing, someone remarked: 'Oh this should be nice quiet stooge.' They took off at 10 p.m. and climbed to their operational height over the Channel. The first stage was uneventful. Then, wrote Bartlett, 'as we drew level with the south of the Ruhr Valley, things began to happen.

> Enemy night fighter flares were all around us and in no time at all, combats were taking place and aircraft were going down in flames on all sides. This aggravated the situation because each time a kite hit the deck a great glow lit up the area and night was turned into day making it easier still for the enemy fighters … I can remember looking out at the poor blighters going down and thinking to myself it must be our turn next, just a question of time … a Lancaster appeared on our port beam converging on a collision course, so we dropped a hundred feet or so to let him cross. He was only about two hundred yards on our starboard beam when 'crash' – a string of cannon shells hit him and down he went. The night fighter which got him must have been on our tail at the same time but with so much happening we didn't spot him.

As they altered course to approach Nuremburg, he 'looked down on the starboard beam at the area we had just passed … there were kites burning on the deck all over the place, bombs going off where they had been jettisoned by bombers damaged in combat and fires from their incendiaries across the whole area'. By the end of the night ninety-six aircraft had been lost, the largest number in a single operation in the history of Bomber Command. The catastrophe marked the close of the Battle of Berlin, but failed to shake Harris's conviction that crushing cities was a war-winning strategy.

Sharing such experiences forged a camaraderie which rendered the larger institutional identity of the Air Force remote and insignificant. The squadron, an important focus of loyalty for fighter pilots, does not seem to have featured greatly as an emotional point of reference for most bomber crews. A bomber station was a big, impersonal place, swarming with the two or three thousand ground staff needed to keep the fliers in the air. Each squadron had around a hundred and forty aircrew, whereas a fighter unit was a seventh of the size and there were usually two squadrons at each base. In 1943 and early 1944, when the losses were most intense, there was not enough time during the course of a tour to connect with your fellow airmen, who might be chatting in the canteen one day and vanished the next. In the six months from November 1943, during the Battle of Berlin, 50 Squadron lost nineteen crews, and only five completed a tour of operations.

Both earlier and later in Bomber Command's war, when the pace of operations was less hectic, some sort of squadron spirit had a chance to evolve and aircrew might get to know something of the character and quality of their superiors. During the darkest passage of the story, the relationship between directors and actors seems to have become more tenuous, and the crews' sense of identity tighter and more exclusive. You saw the base commander and the squadron commander at operational briefings, and perhaps when there was some administrative or disciplinary business to be dealt with, but the human scale of the enterprise was too big to allow much intimacy. Norman Lee and his crew 'scarcely saw an officer except at briefings or debriefings'. The commanders who flew disappeared with the same rapidity as everyone else. Five squadrons lost their COs in the first week of the Battle of Berlin.

Norman Lee claimed that talk of 'squadron spirit, morale and so on' was already redundant during his tour of duty with 428 Squadron, which ended halfway through when he was shot down just before the assault on the Big City got properly underway. 'To be frank, there just wasn't any,' he wrote. 'I never cared tuppence about the squadron as such, nor did the rest of our crew. But we did care for each other and this extended to our ground crew as well.' Officially the squadron belonged to the RCAF, but all but two of those flying with Lee were British. The ground crew, however, were Canadians. 'They looked after our aircraft [only] and our confidence in them was total. Nothing, absolutely nothing, was too much trouble, and they nursed our aircraft as if their lives depended on it as much as our own.'

Aircrew and ground crew took turns inviting each other out 'on the beer', a treat the better paid Canadians could afford more easily than the Brits. Lee 'particularly wanted to point this out, not because it rankled with us but because it didn't. We were a happy group together, and if there was indeed on the squadron as a whole anything that could be described as high morale, it was within the individual crews that it was generated.'

The death rate made any wider emotional association almost impossible. In the nine weeks that Lee was in action, 428 Squadron lost twenty-one crews on operations – that is almost the entire strength of an average bomber squadron. The turnover created an atmosphere of anonymity that numbed the emotions. Lee wrote that although 'the empty chairs appeared night after night … the truth is that in our squadron at least, it didn't much bother anyone – certainly not the crews … my crew was scarcely on the squadron long enough to get to know anyone properly, and as a matter of fact I don't think many other people were either. Nobody lasted long enough. The disappearance of people whose names you could barely fit to their faces produced little impact. Our feelings were that the other crews were either already there when we arrived so they didn't count, or else they joined us afterwards so they didn't count either.'

Conversely, the death of a member of the group, a rear gunner killed by flak, say, was felt intensely. The only time Lee 'saw a man go to pieces' was on returning from a mid-tour leave. 'There was an air-gunner on the squadron who joined our train at York. He ought to have returned the day before but had some compassionate reason for not having done so. When we got back to Middleton St George he learned that his crew had returned on time, gone on ops that night and gone missing. He had a complete nervous collapse and had to be taken off flying immediately.'

Operational flying created a confidence in your abilities and a faith in the competence of those around you that fostered a disinclination to show unquestioning respect for superiors and deference to orders that seemed pointless or stupid. Eric Banks noted early on in his training that it was those without combat experience who most revered the rules and that the closer you came to operations 'the less the bull'. The training staff seemed to understand that 'the types volunteering for flying duties were not those who would respond with any enthusiasm to the ... theory that only those who would jump to attention when shouted at were fit to fight the Hun'.

The instructors were 'gen men' who knew the reality of what they were preparing their charges for, yet spoke little about their exploits even in the pub. 'Gen men' were the only superiors Bomber Boys were likely to look up to, officers like Flight Lieutenant Les Gray, the signals leader at Wickenby, responsible for the wireless operators and who Banks was told by his colleagues on arrival was 'the best bloke you'll ever come across'. Having completed two tours and won the DFC he need never have flown again. However, against regulations, he had taken 'every opportunity of standing in for any wireless operator, or even gunner, who happened to be unfit for flying', often managing to get the trip credited to the absentee's total. His standing was further cemented by his institution of 'periodic piss-ups' at a hotel on the Lincoln Road, where all wireless operators were welcome provided they could hold their beer.

In this self-confident ambience, where respect was hard-won, Joubert's proposal that an attempt should be made to impose something like pre-war discipline on the crews seems absurd. A less rigid mind might have concluded that such efforts were not only futile but counter-productive. Instead, as his report made clear, during his tour of the bomber stations, where others might have recognized constructive informality, he saw slackness.

On his visit to Wyton, Cambridgeshire, he was unimpressed by the conduct of Wing Commander Tommy Rivett-Carnac who had just finished leading 156 Squadron of the Path Finder Force. 'It would appear that [he] needs training in his duties as commanding officer,' he wrote. 'I was particularly struck by the number of charges preferred by the APM [Assistant Provost Marshal] against the aircrew of his squadron which were dismissed by this officer.'[27] 'I also observed that some aircrew who had bad conduct sheets were nevertheless put up for promotion as a matter of course. In other words, bad behaviour was having no effect whatsoever on their careers.'

Rivett-Carnac was twenty-eight years old, South African-born, had a DFC and bar and was about to be awarded the DSO. As a Cranwell graduate and pre-war professional he might be expected to share Joubert's opinion about the need for firm discipline. Instead he seems to have taken the view that men facing death were entitled to a bit of fun.

The resistance that the aircrews showed to old-fashioned military discipline did not reflect any lack of commitment to their task. Norman Lee, a proud member of the awkward squad, recorded how 'when we were told at briefing ... "you're going to the Big City tonight," a great cheer went around the room'. Les Bartlett and his crew could not wait to start their tour of operations. 'Our luck is out,' he wrote in his diary on 10 November 1943, on learning that his crew was not on the list for 50 Squadron's trip to Modane on the French–Italian border. 'What a bind ... Good shooting you lucky people!'

It was another week before they were selected. 'Tonight's the night' runs the entry for 17 November. 'You can imagine how excited we felt as we put on our flying kit and drove out to the kite to do our Night Flying Test.' Then at 2 p.m. they were told that ops had been scrubbed due to poor visibility. 'What a disappointment,' he wrote.

Then at last, on 22 November, they made their debut. 'Briefing started at 1.30 pm and what do you think? It's the Big City ... Needless to say we were all very excited, because to an experienced crew Berlin is quite an assignment, so you can imagine what we felt like to be doing it as a first trip.'

Sitting in his bombing compartment after take-off his enthusiasm began to falter. 'I plug in my electric suit, make myself comfortable (if that is possible) and let my thoughts wander ... I realise what we are out to do and how frightened I really am ... In spite of the unsuitable surroundings I say a prayer to ask forgiveness for the murder of so many human beings by the dropping of my bombs, and also a prayer to ask for courage which I seem to lack at the moment, and for a safe flight to enable me to return to the land which I realise I love so much – to relatives and friends and to my wife who means more to me than anything in the world.'

This entry makes it clear that Bartlett was fully aware of what attacking the Big City meant for the population. Lee says that before his first trip to Berlin (on 23 August 1943), 'a ring was drawn around a sector of the city on the briefing map. The briefing officer pointed to it and said: "This is where you bomb and the next time you hit Berlin you'll bomb the area adjacent to it, and so on until the city is completely flattened."'

Lee knew 'perfectly well' that in the attacks on Berlin 'we were being sent to bomb civilians. I can't answer for all the other aircrews but as far as ours was concerned it didn't bother us. We felt the Germans had only themselves to blame. They had started it and now we were finishing it.' Once again the impersonal nature of the bombing war made that understanding easier to live with: 'It wasn't like a couple of infantrymen slugging it out with bayonets. It was just a technical job ... We didn't think about the people we were killing because we didn't see them.'

After his moment of reflection on his first trip, Les Bartlett's diary records no further qualms about civilian casualties. His accounts of raids become technical and dispassionate. Describing a trip to Stettin on 5 January 1944 he wrote: 'We settled down to bomb and I did a "bang on" run up on the centre of the city. The raid was highly concentrated and kites were bombing above and below and on all sides of us. Visibility was excellent and I could clearly see whole areas of houses and shops blasted and blazing like an inferno. The place "burned like a bastard" ...'[28]

He soon noticed that not everyone shared his eagerness for action. 'Ops tonight but just as we were going out to the kite it was scrubbed,' he wrote on 30 November, a week after. 'Loud cheers. The blokes just ran around in circles, dumped their kit and dashed off to town.' A few days later, after surviving a hair-raising fourth trip to Berlin (he would do ten in all), he and the crew felt the same way. 'Ops were on again but just as we were going out to the kites it was scrubbed and were we glad. We are going on leave in two days' time and feel much safer on the deck until we have had it.'

Operations brought little or no sense of progress. Eric Banks's first trip to Germany was to bomb Stuttgart, and when he left the city was swamped with smoke and fire. When he entered the briefing room the following day 'and saw that Stuttgart was again the target, I naively thought that this was rather overdoing things. From my view on the previous night I expected that the chaos below would be total and that not much would have escaped the attentions of the several hundred bombers.' This was in August of 1944. Stuttgart had first been attacked four years before, and in the first seven months of 1944 had already been subjected to six heavy raids.

In the end, the importance of each operation was that it brought you one step closer to the end of your tour and re-entry to a world where the prospect of a future could reasonably be entertained. That, perhaps, provided the main impetus to keep going. There was, of course, another force at work. The crews had no real choice in the matter. In the First World War dereliction of duty could mean a death sentence.

By 1940 the authorities had devised other deterrents for those who refused to fly on operations. There was an official reluctance to stigmatize men as exhibiting a 'Lack of Moral Fibre' (see page 139), which meant, before more humane procedures were introduced, they were stripped of their rank and placed on menial ground duties at another base. Guidelines emphasized that it was 'highly important … to eliminate any possibility of medical disability before a member of an aircrew is placed in [the LMF] category'.[29] Between February 1942 and the end of the war, the vast majority of those who dropped out were stated to be suffering from 'neurosis' (8,402) rather than LMF (1,029).

Sometimes, circumstances forced the issue, leading to a court martial. The offence came under the heading of 'failure to carry out a warlike operation'. It seems to have been an unwelcome last resort, and only a handful of cases appear in the records. One trial, on

31 August 1943, gives a grim taste of the pressures brave men were under, and a glimpse of the harsh face authority was prepared to show when it felt an example needed to be set.[30] The case related to four sergeants of 214 Squadron based at Chedburgh in Suffolk, members of the same all-NCO crew. In the last week of July, they had undergone a succession of sticky trips. During a mass raid on Hamburg on 24/25th, an exhaust burst into flames, attracting a night fighter which they managed to drive off. On the return leg, an engine caught fire and they staggered back to base, making an emergency landing which collapsed the undercarriage. Two nights later they were sent to Hamburg again but were forced to turn back when the rear turret jammed. The following night the squadron joined the third great operation in the Battle of Hamburg. After bombing, the crew found themselves apparently alone over the city and were 'coned' in searchlights for eight minutes while flak burst all around, hitting their Stirling in the port wing and tail.

They were coned again over Heligoland, and, almost out of fuel, were redirected to land at Stradishall, the main base. It was 7.15 a.m. before they got to bed. Few were able to sleep. At 2 p.m. they learned they were on ops again that night. Four of the team told their Australian captain they were too 'shaken up' to fly that night. He referred them to their flight commander who was unsympathetic and reported them to the Wing Commander who was Squadron CO.

They explained to him they felt unfit to operate and feared they would endanger each other if ordered to fly. According to one defendant, the CO 'appeared ... to have already made up his mind that we were to fly, and that was that, no matter what happened'. By his own admission, the Wing Commander hinted that they faced a firing squad if they refused, warning them: 'Do you realise the maximum penalty for this offence?' It made no difference. Although ordered to operate, they turned up at dispersal without their equipment and were arrested, charged and imprisoned in the guard house for the next thirty days.

The court martial revealed the system at its worst. There were ways to deal with such incidents which, if infrequent, were not uncommon. Flight commanders had the discretion to leave a crew off the battle order if they judged they were reaching the limit of their physical and mental endurance. One easy get-out was to treat the matter as a medical problem and refer the men to the MO. Instead, the CO was recorded in the transcript of the proceedings as having told the bomb aimer when he announced he felt unfit to fly: 'Ridiculous, man! You look all right to me.' The bullying tone of the prosecuting officer, who held the rank of squadron leader but flew a desk in the department of the Advocate General, sounds contemptible to modern ears. He put it to the crew's flight engineer, just nineteen years old: 'When you join the service, you are taught to do what you are told, whatever it may be. It is not for you to set up your own opinion against what you are told to do. Do you agree with that?'

'Yes, sir,' came the humble reply.

None of the accused was refusing to carry on with their tour, just seeking the shortest of respites before taking their place again in the line. 'All I actually needed was a night's sleep,' said the bomb aimer, a London policeman in peacetime. 'I thought I would be all right for the next night.' Instead, he and his comrades were sentenced to 112 days' detention, reduction to the ranks, and utterly undeserved ignominy. The upside was that they lived.

12

'Britain's Best Advertisement'

The shape of the war was always shifting. The flux touched everything: alliances, strategies, technologies, the ebb and flow of battle. The fixed points were the four warlords, Hitler and Stalin, Roosevelt and Churchill, seemingly immoveable above the great floods swirling around their feet.

War accelerates change. Since the start of hostilities, the RAF had raced in weeks and months through evolutionary processes that in peacetime would have taken years, expanding hugely in size and complexity so that in early 1944 it bore little outward resemblance to the Air Force of 1939. Its DNA might remain the same, but the external transformation had been as extraordinary as that of a mayfly, with the drab nymph shucking off its larval case to flutter free, fully formed and something marvellous to behold. The process had been painful and laborious but the suffering was worth it. In the spring of 1944, a year which brought real hope that this might be the last of the war, the RAF was a success that Britain could boast about.

By now it had won the good opinion of those who mattered most: the Americans. In March 1944, it was decided that the RAF would have its own public relations outlet in Washington and the Air Information Office opened two months later. The Wing Commander in charge set out its aims in a long memo. He started by saying how easy he found his current task. 'The raw material provided by the magnificent achievements of the Service and their high and constant news value has hardly needed any processing at all …'[1]

He went on: 'We cannot hope to *enhance* the prestige of the RAF. Throughout the world, it is a household word and in the United

States its reputation is so high that in some quarters it is almost regarded as something apart from, and superior to, Britain. Many people who dislike the British would not say a word against the RAF.' It was 'the service with the highest reputation in the outside world and ... therefore Britain's best advertisement'.

The Wing Commander's problem was that, with a second front about to open, the RAF's great standing might soon be eclipsed as American forces moved to centre stage. He urged his superiors 'to do everything possible to keep the RAF's share in the war from being forgotten by a fickle public'. There was much more at stake here than simply the good name of the Air Force. Underlining his words to reinforce his conviction, he urged that its fame should be broadcast as loudly as possible in order to 'enhance British prestige generally and to strengthen Britain's post war authority and influence'.

By now the early days of material shortage and tactical confusion, of blunders, humiliations and debacles were all but forgotten. The bad memories had been wiped away by a record of rising efficiency and steady success, wherever the Air Force operated across the globe. The failure of the Battle of Berlin to bomb Germany into submission did not darken the picture. Harris's grandiose hopes for the campaign had never been officially endorsed and it was relatively easy to present the episode as another phase in the ongoing programme of retribution and attrition, paving the way to victory. Bomber Command was as dear to British civilian hearts as Fighter Command had been in 1940, and the size, brute force and determination of the squadrons impressed American soldiers, politicians and civilians.

The British and American air forces had been working together since the Torch landings in North Africa in December 1942. Relations from the bottom to the top were on the whole reasonably smooth. With the invasion of Sicily, then Italy, the Americans had taken charge of events, but the shift in the balance of power and status had produced remarkably little resentment or obstructionism. The Allies worked together to devise tactics to deal with a fiendishly dogged and inventive enemy. The strategy they developed would be put to good use at the next great test they faced together – the invasion of north-western Europe.

The RAF understood that the best way to present its achievements was with a human face attached. The Air Ministry public relations team were often pre-war professionals, with an artistic and technical understanding of what was required. It included a creative writers' unit where the likes of Hilary St George Saunders, a novelist, and John Pudney, a journalist and poet, set talent to work, illuminating and celebrating the work of the Air Force. They were imaginative and willing to take risks, investing time and trust on the basis of instinctive judgements. H. E. Bates, then relatively unknown, was given a rank, a uniform and the run of RAF bases. The result was a series of short stories, published under the pseudonym 'Flying Officer X', which presented heroism in a nuanced and thoughtful way that drew the home front and the battlefield of the air close together.

At a more mundane level, airmen toured war factories, in an effort to link the workers' labours to the progress of the war. It was summed up in a 1944 cartoon by David Langdon, showing a manager briefing a visiting pilot on how to present his spiel: 'Start off with say, a saturation raid on Kiel and then lead up to the float chamber sprocket of our Bigley Carburettor.'

The Air Force was lucky to have in its ranks personalities who were as big and powerful as the aircraft it sent over Germany. At the pinnacle was Guy Gibson, famous for leading the May 1943 Dams Raid. The PR machine moved swiftly to spin propaganda gold from an exploit which displayed Bomber Command as a precise instrument that could strike with devastating effect at the German war machine. He was sent on an initial tour of Britain before heading off in the late summer for a progress through North America.

Gibson was scarcely representative of Bomber Command pilots. He was often touchy, rude and vain, in an environment where teamwork was essential. He was as far from being a typical Bomber Boy as Douglas Bader was from being a typical Fighter Boy. Gibson's reputation has become dented with the passing years and his record as a warrior qualified by his deficiencies as a human being. Richard Morris's 1994 biography made clear the misgivings of his peers. He was a 'bumptious bastard', always straining to prove himself and poor company in a world where conviviality was a religion.[2] Those further down the ladder could take a more forgiving view. Ted Mace, an aircraft electrician, served with Gibson on 106 Squadron. In the summer of 1944 he was climbing into a Lancaster at Coningsby when 'a staff car pulled up alongside and who should be the driver but my old CO Guy Gibson. He recognized me and remarked, "Hallo! One of my old boys." We had quite a conversation ...'[3] The grieving parents of boys taken from them before they were scarcely out of school would never forget the simple, heartfelt handwritten messages he added to the pro-forma letters expressing official regret at their loss.[4]

It was this face that Gibson showed to his American audiences. He sailed for Canada with the Prime Minister and Charles Portal on board the *Queen Mary* in August and began a series of press engagements, VIP encounters and talks. Gibson could be funny and self-deprecating in public, which made the passages of earnestness all the more effective. During one interview, he was asked why he wore two watches. One was in fact a wristband, a relic of his days as a Boy Scout, but Gibson replied disarmingly that 'this one looks good and the other one tells the time accurately'.[5] The little flash of innocence is a reminder that at the time he had just turned twenty-five.

In October, he began a coast-to-coast tour of the United States. In Hollywood, he stayed with Howard Hawks, the film director and powerful industry figure who was keen on making a movie of the Dams Raid. He commissioned a script from Roald Dahl, who, after a hectic career as a fighter pilot in North Africa, Greece and Palestine, had been declared medically unfit for flying duties. He was now a press attaché at the Washington embassy and had already attracted the attention of Walt Disney with his book *The Gremlins*, malign, troll-like creatures that in RAF mythology were blamed for mechanical mishaps.[6] The Dam Busters project died when the script was rejected by Barnes Wallis who thought it absurd, to be successfully resurrected a decade later.[7]

In December, Gibson returned to Britain. He immediately tried to get back on operations but was told instead to take leave and continue his propaganda work, this time writing a book which would be published as *Enemy Coast Ahead*, a frank, powerful account of his war, that is clearly mostly his own work. The attention he had received across the Atlantic had not improved him. Displays of arrogance and petulance were noted. Arthur Harris believed that the Americans 'had spoiled young Gibson', and the decision was taken not to repeat the performance with another Bomber Command hero and former 617 Squadron commander, Leonard Cheshire.[8] There was a brief flirtation with politics when, in February 1944, Gibson accepted an invitation to stand as Conservative candidate in a by-election at Macclesfield – and then backed out. His real desire was to return to the fight. His craving only deepened when the Normandy landings came and went without him playing a part.

His superiors were unwilling to indulge him, for his own good and for the image of the Air Force. A live hero was worth much more than a dead one. By string-pulling and persistence, however, he managed to manoeuvre his way back to the front line. On 19 September 1944, 5 Group were tasked with bombing three objectives in Rheydt and Mönchengladbach. Gibson was named as master bomber, monitoring the target marking and co-ordinating the main force bombing. The news was met with 'incredulity' by the crews taking part. He would be flying a Mosquito, a type he was relatively unfamiliar with, and orchestrating a complex raid with no previous experience of such operations.

The squadrons took off from Lincolnshire at dusk. One mishap followed another. The target marking went awry. Gibson's own attempt to drop indicators failed when they hung up on release. Main force aircraft were forced to loiter over the objective, increasing the risk from flak and night fighters. By the time the muddle was sorted it was too late. The attack was scattered and one of the aiming points went unbombed. The raiders left at 21.58. Gibson may have orbited for a minute or two assessing results. What happened next will probably never be known. Like Richthofen, Mannock, Ball and other legendary airmen before him, the precise details of Gibson's end are unclear. He and his navigator, Squadron Leader Jim Warwick, hit the ground at Steenbergen in Holland at about 22.30. The Germans cordoned off the area and sifted through the remains. Gibson was identified by a laundry tag on a sock.[9]

Gibson's death was the final tragedy in what, for all the attention and glory it attracted, seems now like a sad life. Growing up, he hardly ever saw his father, whose relationship with his children was chilly even by the standards of the day, and he shrank from his embarrassing mother who sought solace from her failed marriage in drink. At his public school, St Edward's in Oxford, he failed to read the codes correctly, tried too hard to be liked and was cold-shouldered by the elite he yearned to join. He had few friends and his relationship with his actress wife, Eve, was bumpy and argumentative. The judgement of the historian Malcolm Smith, that Gibson was 'a hollow man, starved of affection ... constantly trying to prove himself, truly unexceptional except for a dogged determination and a photogenic smile' seems harsh but probably not inaccurate.[10]

But, then, he never had the chance to develop a core. Gibson was just twenty-one when the war broke out, only twenty-six when he died. He had passed almost all his life in institutions, mixing almost exclusively with men. He could measure his worth only in terms of success in his trade, marked by ever more medals – a VC, DSO and bar, DFC and bar when he died – and the mounting entries in his log book. It was no wonder he was so desperate to get back on operations. The world of death was the only life he knew.

Fame was, by and large, a misfortune. It loaded another burden on men who already had enough to weigh them down. The stories of RAF celebrities rarely had happy endings. Leading Fighter Command poster boys ended up dead, like 'Paddy' Finucane and James Nicholson, the sole Battle of Britain VC, or prisoners of war like Douglas Bader and Bob Stanford Tuck.

Before Gibson, the most famous member of Bomber Command was Percy Charles Pickard. The film maker Harry Watt came across 'Pick' at a London party and asked the RAF to borrow him to play 'Squadron Leader Dickson', captain of F for Freddie in the 1941 hit drama-documentary *Target for Tonight*. Pickard stood out. Hugh Verity, who served with him, saw 'a big man, rather heavily built, with a pointed nose and very fair hair. He smoked a pipe. Whenever possible, on or off duty, he was accompanied by an Old English Sheepdog, Ming.'[11] He was the son of a Sheffield businessman who had moved the family to London. Pick was sent off to Framlingham College in Suffolk, where he was usually bottom of the class – possibly a result of dyslexia rather than inability.[12] He left school to work on the ranch of a school friend in Kenya where he revelled in riding, polo and the outdoor life. He returned to Britain in 1935 and he applied to join the Army. When they rejected him, he tried the RAF and was awarded a short service commission. By the time of the film he was already a veteran, having survived a tour of thirty-one operations flying Wellingtons with 99 Squadron, alongside his navigator, friend and comrade to the end, Alan Broadley.

Pickard was amiable and gregarious. His elder sister Helena was an actress, married to Cedric Hardwicke, a big name of British stage and screen. He and his wife, Dorothy, were happy and well matched. The attention that followed *Target for Tonight* had no apparent effect on him. In all these respects, he was very different from Gibson but they shared one thing in common: a seeming desperation to continue operational flying long after anyone expected them to.

While commanding a Czech squadron, 311, supposedly a 'rest' post, he insisted on going with them on their first raids over Germany. There followed three and a half months with 9 Squadron, in the thick of a grim period of the bomber offensive with heavy losses and few results. By the end of August, he and Broadley had chalked up sixty-four ops together, more than fulfilling their duty and entitling them to move to safer duties.

Neither grabbed the lifeline. In November, he joined 51 Squadron, tasked with high-level photographic reconnaissance. After a few trips, he was detached for a special mission. British scientists were anxious to learn the secrets of the German Würzburg radar system which they blamed for Bomber Command's heavy losses. An airborne raid was planned on the installation at Bruneval, on the heights overlooking the Channel, north of Le Havre. On the night of 27 February 1942, Pickard led the force that dropped a team of commandos on the site. The raid was a complete success. The team returned with vital pieces of the set, as well as a captured German technician, having sustained relatively few casualties.

His next posting was perhaps his most hazardous yet, commanding 161 Squadron which operated out of a clandestine aerodrome at Tempsford in Bedfordshire, ferrying Special Operations Executive agents in and out of occupied France. When Hugh Verity, who had volunteered to fly Lysanders, first met his new CO he noticed that 'though still in his twenties ... he seemed ten years older. One got the impression that he was driving himself hard and burning himself up.'[13]

When that job was finished, he was offered a safe post commanding a non-operational airfield. It was the autumn of 1943 and the RAF was restructuring to prepare for the invasion of northern Europe. The formation of 2nd Tactical Air Force combined squadrons from Fighter Command and light bombers from Bomber Command's 2 Group to create an instrument of integrated air power to support the Allied armies.

Pickard was determined to be part of it. He enlisted the help of an admirer, the 2 Group commander Basil Embry, who put him in charge of 140 Wing made up of three Mosquito squadrons based in Sculthorpe, Norfolk. Embry recognized that there was a problem with the appointment. Pickard's previous experience involved flying heavy bombers at high altitudes, or landing light Lysanders and Hudsons in French fields. The group was engaged in very different operations, screaming in at very low altitudes to hit small, usually well-defended targets. He and Broadley were a team again and Embry sent them off on familiarization trips to start with. On two occasions, they returned with significant damage to their Mosquito.

It seemed to Charles Patterson, by then a pilot with the RAF Film Unit that recorded the group's exploits, that Embry's well-meaning intervention was seriously misjudged. 'It was a wrong decision,' he said years after the war.[14] 'Embry ought to have recognised that after a hundred trips on night bombers there was no basis on which to start off a completely new career on low level daylight bombing ... not only was he operationally tired out – it's asking a lot of a man to adapt to something so completely new.' The signs of exhaustion were obvious. 'He was a nervous wreck. And he was obsessed with getting on operations but his brain was too tired to really sit down and tackle the detail ... his temper was very uncertain ... it was quite obvious that he should have been rested no matter how much he wanted to go on ...'

In February 1944, the group was tasked with a spectacular but extremely delicate mission. In the approach to D-Day, the French resistance grew in importance. They could provide vital intelligence and mount sabotage operations. German efforts to smash local networks intensified as expectation of the landings mounted. The organization in the Pas-de-Calais was hit hard with the arrest of senior figures who faced torture and death. Many were held by the Gestapo in a block in Amiens prison. Early in 1944 a local resistance chief begged the SOE in London to mount a rescue mission. The task was passed to 140 Wing.

The plan for Operation Jericho was bold and spectacular. The attack was timed for midday when the guards would be eating and the prisoners back in their cells. Six Mosquitoes from each of the three squadrons would attack in sequence. The first wave would blow holes in the prison outer walls. The second would take out the two guardrooms at either end of the main block. The explosions were expected to shake the cell doors off their hinges. The third wave was to be ordered in only as a last, dreadful resort. If the first attacks failed to breach the walls, the last one would bomb the prison out of existence, killing Germans, but also the French prisoners who would no longer be able to divulge under torture any details they might know about the landings.[15]

Basil Embry elected to lead the raid himself. He was overruled by his superiors, concerned at the potential loss of one of the key planners for the forthcoming invasion. He handed the job to Pickard. He would be flying with the Australians of 464 Squadron in the second wave, with the New Zealanders of 487 Squadron at the spearhead and 21 Squadron of the RAF in the rear.

The date was set for 17 February but the weather forced a postponement. It was no better the following day, but further delay was impossible. Pickard briefed his men at 8 a.m. at their new base at Hunsdon, Herts. They took off at 11 a.m. in a blizzard and were joined by a large force of Typhoon fighter escorts. Snow lay thick around the prison as the first wave of Mosquitoes arrived in two sections of three at a few minutes after midday, seeming to skim the ground as they raced in, dropped their bombs, then pulled up sharply to avoid smashing into the tall prison block beyond. They left behind two large breaches in the northern and eastern walls. The second wave was equally efficient, flattening the guardhouses. Pickard circled above, waiting for the smoke to clear to assess whether the job had been done. It had. There was no need for the third wave and he broadcast the signal, 'Red Daddy, Red Daddy', ordering them to head for home.

As the force turned away, the Mosquito piloted by Ian Ritchie of 464 Squadron was hit by ground fire and crashed at high speed. Ritchie survived but his navigator, Richard Sampson, was killed. Pickard was apparently checking out the wreckage when he was attacked by two Focke-Wulf 190s which had been scrambled from Grévillers airfield, thirty miles to the north-east. He managed to avoid their first attacks. Then a stream of fire blew off the Mosquito's tail and it rolled over and plunged down, crashing in flames near the village of Saint-Gratien.

It had been unwise to linger, but Pickard had not done anything wrong. His death cannot be attributed to the relative unfamiliarity of the aircraft or his inexperience of such operations. He had simply gone on too long and the odds had caught up with him. Charles Patterson later expressed regret that 'a man who'd made a stagger-ingly splendid contribution to the war was denied his future'.[16] Perhaps his fame, an unwillingness to let his public down, might have played a part in driving him back into danger. As he left no record of his thought processes it is impossible to know. One senses, though, that Pick was willingly doing what he felt he had to.

With so many of his friends and colleagues gone before, his own death must have seemed an inevitability. His mother, who was better placed than most to judge, surely got it right in the memorial notice she placed in *The Times* on the first anniversary of his death. As well as commemorating 'our darling "Boy"' and Alan Broadley, it also took the trouble to remember 'his many friends whom he was not afraid to join'.[17]

News of Pickard's death was delayed for a while and did not overshadow the success of the mission. About 400 prisoners escaped and 288 remained at large, including a key resistance leader, and the underground was able to regroup to play a part in the invasion. Inevitably, many were killed in the raid, some shot dead as they ran.

But in the ledger of war it counted as a success and a cheering one. An RAF Film and Photographic Unit Mosquito had been present and the footage was eventually played in cinemas across Britain and the free world. The commentary's praise of the 'perfect discrimination in this, one of the most difficult operations of the war' was no more than the truth.[18] It was a sword thrust in the dark heart of the enemy. The images of the smashed-up prison, swathed in smoke, and the reported sighting of men running through the breached walls were a marvellous symbol of retribution and salvation. Pickard's death was presented as a fitting end. He had 'died leading probably the most successful operation of his gallant and brilliant career' and had 'made sure the RAF paid another debt'. Further superbly executed raids against Gestapo headquarters in Denmark would follow.

The glory reflected from such feats added to the self-esteem of airmen and airwomen at every level, whether they served on the ground or in the air. The men at the top of the RAF were justified in feeling some satisfaction. Most were old enough to remember the struggles of the early years and the hostility they had faced from the soldiers and sailors. The spirit of resentment had not entirely disappeared. In the middle years of the war, in the constant battle for resources, it was usually the RAF which came out on top. The aerial war 'was given priority in materials, facilities for aircraft production and men for aircrew and technical needs'.[19] To the politicians, the Air Force represented value, delivering military results and boosting domestic morale, but also maintaining Britain's standing with the all-important Americans.

It had gone into the war armed with inadequate aircraft and no real understanding of how air power worked. The shock of combat had tested its organization, training methods and fighting techniques, sometimes close to the point of destruction, but it had emerged from each crisis tougher and wiser. Now it had the best machines in the air, a magnificent cadre of well-trained men to operate them, and drills to deal with most eventualities of battle. Luck, inevitably, played a part in the success story. But so, too, did judgement and the quality of the high command. Hectic expansion was possible because of the organizational framework put in place by Trenchard. The great improvement in aircraft was due to shrewd decisions by unsung planners whose names would never be known to the public and in technology to backroom players willing to try anything that offered a chance of success. Human resources were equally well managed, particularly the supply of aircrew, thanks to the foresight shown in schemes like the British Commonwealth Air Training Plan which trained nearly half the pilots, navigators, flight engineers, wireless operators, bomb aimers and air gunners who flew under the RAF standard in the war, in overseas flying schools, most of them in southern Africa and Canada.

After some initial hesitation on the part of Canada, the Dominions had made an extraordinarily generous response to Britain's predicament, and the Air Force had reason to be particularly thankful for their solidarity. The term 'RAF' is used routinely in this book but it is shorthand for what was in many ways an umbrella organization, providing an operational and administrative system covering elements of the Royal Australian, Royal Canadian, Royal New Zealand and South African Air Forces. Of the 487 squadrons in the RAF order of battle in June 1944, 100 were provided by the Dominions (forty-two by Canada, twenty-seven by South Africa, sixteen by Australia, nine by India and six by New Zealand).[20] In addition, there were many Dominion citizens serving in strictly RAF units. Of the 340,000 who served as aircrew in the Second World War, 134,000 men came from British overseas territories. Then there were the airmen from the conquered territories of Europe, the Poles, Czechs, French, Norwegians, Belgians, Dutch, Greeks and Yugoslavs. Their contribution was more than a token. The Poles had fourteen squadrons and 15,000 men in the RAF, which included their own ground staff.

Such a diverse force needed a strong identity to glue it together. The essential element was a sense of belonging to a worthwhile enterprise. In the participants' diaries, letters and memoirs there is a marked pride in their service. RAF life brought a degree of satisfaction that was perhaps harder to find elsewhere. In Bomber Command, despite the paucity of measurable progress, it was a feeling, expressed over and over again, that you were 'taking the fight to the enemy'. That meant striking back, exacting revenge, and perhaps bringing the end of the war a tiny bit closer. Bomber Command and Fighter Command had an intimate relationship with the enemy (Coastal less so). The violence they inflicted was direct and produced instant, if not necessarily lasting, results. In the spring of 1944, the RAF felt it was on the path to victory. As the snot froze in his nostrils, an able seaman looking out at the ice floes of the Arctic from the deck of HMS *Belfast* had been told often enough that if his convoy got through to Arkhangelsk or Murmansk he was making a real contribution to the war effort, but it probably did not seem much like it. A private in the Durham Light Infantry staring up at the peaks of the Gustav Line understood his courage was a factor in the drive to Rome, but what effort would be required for such minuscule observable gain!

Looking down from his Perspex perch in the nose of a Lancaster at the carpet of reds and yellows bubbling below, the bomb aimer knew that he was hurting Germany. Strangely, for all the repetition there was in the work described in Bomber Boys' accounts, a sense of futility is only rarely encountered. In the air war, effort and effect were almost instantaneous, as the cine-camera footage from operations makes dramatically clear. One can feel, at close second hand, the joy of a Coastal Command Wellington crew as their depth charges split the sea around a surfaced U-boat, or the savage thrill of pressing the firing button on the control column of a Typhoon and sending rockets snaking into a line of German trucks.

Many participants often claimed there was nothing personal about the violence. A typical voice was that of Andrew Hendrie, who flew with Coastal Command from 1942 to 1945 and later wrote its history.

'Coastal Command aircrew were concerned not with killing men but with sinking U-boats,' he wrote.[21] Others showed less detachment. Revenge was in the mix of motives. Writing to the parents of Flight Lieutenant Gray Healey, who was shot down by a night fighter during a raid on Essen in January 1943 and killed with the rest of the crew, Guy Gibson told them they could 'rest assured that the boys and I will hit those Huns even harder for doing this to you'.[22] Norman Lee volunteered for Bomber Command largely because his twin brother had done so. While he was still training, he heard that his Lancaster had failed to return from a raid on Wilhelmshaven. 'Although I felt deeply about my brother's death,' he wrote, 'it never occurred to me not to go on flying – rather the reverse. I wanted to get my own back.'[23]

After the Blitz, finer feelings evaporated. One day in the summer of 1941, Charles Patterson caught sight of the human face of the enemy. He had been sent with 114 Squadron on a daylight raid on the Knapsack power station near Cologne. It was a particularly risky operation and he set off with little hope of returning. He was in good spirits as they scudded home unscathed over the flat land near the German–Dutch border. He remembered flying 'on and on over these fields, past little villages and hamlets, the occasional individual diving into a ditch beneath us. Then just before we got to the German border, we flew over a typical German industrialist's Victorian semi-baronial mansion with turrets and things, and a garden ... I just got a glimpse beside a cedar tree of a table, large white tablecloth, all laid out for lunch ... and a group of people standing round it.

'As we whizzed over the top of this my gunner let fly and broke up the party. He felt that any rich Germans who were living like that ... deserved to be shot ... that sounds appalling, but at the time it seemed right and proper.'[24]

There were uplifting encounters, too, with people on the ground that reminded Patterson what the war was about. Flying back and forth over Holland as a Film Unit Mosquito pilot accompanying raids, 'a very interesting thing used to happen ... when they heard these low-flying aircraft coming towards them they knew they were probably British ... the Dutch country people used to run to the doors of their little houses and cottages and open and shut the door so they signalled a flashing light towards us of welcome. It was a very wonderful thing to see them doing this when one realised the terrible risks they were running in doing something that was purely a human gesture. It wasn't of any military value. They weren't damaging the enemy in any way. They were just risking their lives to do no more than wave us a greeting.'

It was the fliers who derived the most fulfilment from their work and who reaped the benefits that flowed from an admiring and thankful nation. A slate-blue uniform with an aircrew brevet meant free drinks in pubs and a privileged claim on female attention in bar, cinema queue and dance hall. Even the Yanks could not compete. Early in 1943, Norman Poole, a Beaufighter navigator, and his pilot friend Archie Mackinnon were on their way to Bristol to pick up a brand-new aircraft when they stopped at Swindon to change trains. A long wait was expected so they headed off in search of a pub. 'At one of the tables were four girls and about half a dozen US servicemen entertaining them,' he remembered.[25] The Americans had already 'established a commanding lead over British service-men in terms of pay, smoothness of uniform and delicious, ration-free goods'. They were also a source of nylon stockings, 'the key to a girl's heart and often a few other closely guarded treasures as well'.

Although Poole and Mackinnon 'didn't have nylons, we had an advantage that others didn't possess. We had "Wings"! We were still the glamour boys of the services and you couldn't blame us for trading on it.' They managed to get a message to the girls that they would 'love to see them outside if they could make their escape. I don't know how they managed it, perhaps a combined expedition to the toilet, but they got away and we joined up not only for another pub but one of them lived nearby … we got the Bristol train early next morning.'

For the four-fifths of the Air Force who never took to the skies, there was a share of the glory that reflected from the deeds of the aircrews. A squadron fitter or rigger had a relationship with an aeroplane, a pilot or a crew, that connected him with the struggle and gave him a stake in it. The pride that this generated – and the anger if it was felt that their effort was not being valued as it should – were revealed in a report to Mass Observation by the writer Roderic Papineau who, in the summer of 1941, was serving as a leading aircraftman with 256 Squadron, a night-fighter unit based at Squires Gate near Blackpool. He gave a verbatim account of a conversation with Corporal Crump, an 'expert maintenance fitter' who serviced the unit's Defiants. Crump explained that job satisfaction depended on a feeling that his labours had been worth it. When working on the Hurricanes of 111 Squadron at Croydon during the Battle of Britain his experience had been that 'you work on a kite carefully, sweat your guts out and then see it go up, dive on a formation of Jerries and actually watch three or four of them crashing all over the place as a result of your work ... you really feel keen. Next time that kite comes to your hangar for repair or a sixty-hour inspection, you turn her out shit-hot, every nut and bolt an absolute cert.'[26] Nowadays, he found, 'you don't get that incentive. Take "M" for instance. I'd just finished a thirty hour on that machine, taken the whole engine down and worked nearly a hundred hours to get the kite running sweet. Then some half-pissed idiot lands her 30 mph too fast and busts up the whole issue, probably joking about it in some mock-heroic way. I tell you, you don't feel keen on maintenance work unless the pilots are doing something worthwhile.'

Crump could afford to take a stern line as he was about to start aircrew training. The relationship between aircrew and ground crew was complicated. There was an obvious discrepancy in the risks each group faced. Douglas Bader made it clear that he regarded non-fliers as a lesser breed and the relationship between pilot and erk was that of master to servant. Len Hayden described how, while a fitter with 222 Squadron at Duxford in 1940, his flight sergeant told him he would be servicing the aircraft of a new pilot, warning him, 'he has no legs so you will have to assist him into the cockpit'.[27]

The two met on the grass in front of No. 1 Hangar where Bader's new Spitfire was parked. They shook hands. 'Bader then turned to his aircraft, and placing his left foot on the trailing edge and grasping the cockpit ... with his right hand started to heave himself heavenwards, assisted by a hefty shove up the arse by yours truly. This apparently was not what was required because red-faced and in a violent rage he dressed me down with some of the most colourful language I had ever heard. "All I want from you," he raged, "is to stand to attention with your arse to the trailing edge there" – indicating the position with the toe of his shoe.'

Hayden was not the deferential type, a confident craftsman who went on to be a crack motor racing mechanic. Yet he accepted this treatment and 'from then on we became friends'. Bader's arrogance was tempered by his own version of noblesse oblige. In return for

Hayden making sure not only his Spitfire but his MG sports car was in peak condition he would 'always see that the tea and rations brought to us on the airfield were to the best standard', ordering the duty cooks to make fresh tea for his ground crew rather than the 'sewage' they usually served up.

Some testimony reflects unease at the danger deficit. Overall, ground personnel were ten times less likely to die than aircrew. About 93,000 RAF, Dominion and Allied (i.e. Poles, Czechs, French etc.) aircrew were killed in the war on operations or in accidents. About 9,500 officers, NCOs and airmen were killed on the ground.[28] The discrepancy was particularly marked in Bomber Command. Over 55,000 aircrew were killed on operations or in accidents. The total of ground crew deaths in action was 530, a ratio of a hundred to one.[29]

A vague feeling of guilt ripples beneath the surface of the writings of John Sommerfield. In 'Hang Him Up to Dry', a story he wrote in May 1941, the narrator describes one of his ground crew companions laughing about a visit to the funfair in Blackpool and enthusing about a 'wizard bint' he was trailing. 'I lay back on the bunk with a cap over my eyes, half listening, thinking about the pilot and the gunner we had lost the night before, who still lay smouldering in little bits and pieces half a mile down the perimeter road.'[30] Sommerfield presented one pilot he served with as something more than a man of courage but as a paladin who was the embodiment of kindness and decency. In a story based on his ground crew experiences in Burma, he introduces Phil, a Spitfire pilot, 'who made you think of ... tennis-playing young men, strolling through peacetime summer evenings down rows of little redbrick houses with gardens in front of them and names like "The Acacias" on the garden gate, of ... young men in banks and offices who haven't yet started to take their jobs seriously, who go to musical comedies and come away humming the choruses, whose ambition is a sports car and a girl, or maybe a succession of girls to go with it.'[31] That, he wrote, was 'the sort of young man that so many of the pilots had been', but 'they weren't like that now. The war and their jobs had changed them, really changed what was inside them, as well as the way they talked and behaved.' Phil, however, had retained his innocence and cheerfulness, 'not the protective, wisecracking cheerfulness that most of the others wore like uniform, but simply from an abundance of good humour'.

Phil treats the erks as equals, but the difference between them becomes apparent when he climbs into the cockpit to take his aircraft, whose identity letter is 'L', for a test flight. 'I could see Phil's face bent over the instrument panel, and then he put on his mask and flying helmet. He didn't belong with us any more. Once in the seat, with the airscrew turning and a great torrent of sound pouring away from it, he became someone else, someone remote and inhuman, the brains of the machine.'

Later the same day the squadron is scrambled. The narrator and his companions, who observe the war and the Air Force with smart-aleck wit, are jolted out of their cynical pose.

'We watched them dwindle in the distance until they were out of sight and there was only a faint and distant aerial humming ... no-one spoke for a while, our ears strained for sounds from the sky. Tommy said suddenly, "L's got no overload tank you know."

'"He'll be all right," said Slush. "Phil's too sensible to try any hero stuff if he runs into a load of Japs."'

They wait anxiously until at last they see the aircraft returning. Phil's is not among them. At first, they refuse to believe that he has been shot down and cling to the hope he has baled out. But then one of the pilots confirms that he circled the wreckage and saw him 'all burnt up, lying half out of the cockpit'.

The hard-boiled façades melt away. 'Perce shook his large head slowly and disconsolately. "There's no doubt," he said. "That's the way it always is. It's always the best chaps that get knocked off."'

Whether you were flying or not, there seems to have been a degree of connectivity between all parts of the Air Force that reinforced an already vibrant *esprit de corps*. Gladys Partlett joined the WAAF in Brighton in 1942. She wanted to be a driver but the category was full up so she opted to be a cook, 'a decision I never regretted'.[32] The morning shift started at 4.30 a.m. and finished at 2 p.m. She spent her days labouring over cast-iron pots and coal-fired stoves. Food shortages and the demands of mass catering meant the culinary bar was set low and the official RAF cookbook makes grim reading today. Typical is the recipe for faggots which called for '3–5 lbs gristles and rinds. 8 lbs cooked meat. 9 lbs bread. 2 lbs onions. 8 oz faggot seasoning. Method: cook the rinds all day, cool off in cold water and mince finely …'[33]

Gladys and her colleagues, some of them 'the finest chefs from hotels like the Ritz and the Dorchester', took their duties as seriously as any rigger fitter, pilot or navigator, determined to improve standards and produce the best they could with the means available. The results were impressive. At RAF Stoney Cross in the New Forest they managed to vary breakfast; bacon and (powdered) egg one day, sausage and tinned tomatoes the other, and plentiful bread, margarine and marmalade. For lunch there was fish and chips or steak and kidney with a steamed pudding or semolina to follow.

When she moved to RAF Tarrant Rushton in Dorset in 1944, dinner in the officers' mess 'always began with soup, egg mayonnaise or hors d'oeuvres made from salad, diced beetroot, sardines, grated carrot and cheese. This would be followed by chops … mixed grills or roasts, served with sauté, creamed or chipped potatoes.' It was a time she would look back on as a great adventure, full of drama, enjoyment and fulfilment. She remembered Stoney Cross as having 'a very happy atmosphere. Often we would sing and everyone in the mess would join in.'

It felt like a community enterprise. The station commander had a Tiger Moth and would fly the cooks over the camp and around the Isle of Wight. At Scampton, crews routinely if unofficially took WAAFs on training flights. Aircraftwoman Morfydd Rose was a waitress in the sergeants' mess. Her boyfriend, Flying Officer Phil Burgess, was a navigator with 617 Squadron and would take part with his crew in the Dams Raid. Morfydd was friendly with Norm Barlow, the Australian captain, and the rest of the team, 'especially Harvey Glinz [the mid-upper gunner] and young Jacky Liddell', the rear gunner. They had two flights together and on one 'I remember Harvey saying, "if you do not have sex with us, we will drop you out of the plane in a parachute". Morfydd replied, '"OK Harvey, you can have first go" …'[34] Such repartee was par for the course. After flying, the doors of the mess 'would burst open and the aircrews would swarm in, shouting boisterously as we served the meal. We young WAAFs would have to endure a barrage of good-natured banter: "How is your sex life?" "I dreamed about you all night" … "Please serve us in the nude." We took it all in good part, because we knew the great strains they were under …'

Almost all the testimony suggests that fun was as important and vividly remembered a part of the RAF experience as the business of war. It took many shapes and forms, from a beer-fuelled sing-song around a piano in an East Anglia pub to cocktails in the American bar of the Savoy. The diaries of Betty Bullard, a thoughtful WAAF officer who came from a wealthy brewing family in Norwich and served with Transport Command, brim with jolly outings. On 10 April 1942, while serving at Honington, in Suffolk, she and a bunch of friends 'piled into cars' and headed to Norwich where they 'had dinner at The Castle. M got very whistled and I hoped I shouldn't meet anyone I knew. Saw Gledhills [her superior] but fortunately only when the party was behaving quite well and not throwing things about.'[35] On 19 April after a convivial night in the mess a party repaired to a married quarter where they 'drank beer and listened to [the] gramophone and everyone discovered I was ticklish. Oh dear, had a grand evening, a memorable one, but what will I feel like in the morning …' The following day there was 'an excellent lunch' in the mess to welcome a colleague's squadron leader brother with 'asparagus and masses to drink' and amusing anecdotes from Bob Boothby, the roguish Tory politician who was serving on the ground with 9 Squadron at the base. It did appear, as she observed, that 'life seems to be full of parties', and not just for a well-connected young women such as herself but for almost everybody.

The difference was that Betty was well able to handle the relaxation of social restraints that war brought in its wake. For some, the sudden freedom of life away from home was intoxicating but strewn with traps. The impositions and controls of service life were often matched by a lack of restraint off-duty. Every week there were base parties where drink was available. Stern parents and disapproving brothers were out of sight and out of mind and girls found themselves doing things they would never have countenanced before

Betty Bullard

they put on uniform. Sylvia Drake-Brockman, a by no means narrow-minded spinster, who as a senior WAAF officer was in charge of discipline and welfare of hundreds of girls, was shocked by a sight she witnessed after an American base sprang up not far from RAF Moreton-in-Marsh. 'It was positively embarrassing to return to the camp after 10 at night, the road was so full of couples locked in each other's arms,' she wrote.[36]

The result was inevitable at a time when sex education – including that offered to WAAFs – was minimal and contraception was not available to women. Drake-Brockman was much concerned with pregnancies, the rate of which increased as the war went on. Girls often tried to conceal their condition for as long as possible and she instituted a system where NCOs tipped her off if they suspected a case. Once summoned, the WAAF 'generally denied it to begin with but when I asked her to go to the Medical Officer for an examination so that the rumour could be quashed she admitted that the report was correct'.

Under the rules, pregnant women were discharged the service. There was an RAF maternity home for the many who could not bear the shame of going home to have their babies, 'but it was difficult to make use of this as it was so much in demand'. Most of the children seem to have been put up for adoption.

The free-and-easy nature of the wartime RAF was a source of deep concern to some senior officers steeped in the ways of the pre-war service. They watched with alarm as the strict hierarchies of the old RAF blurred, and smartness gave way to 'scruffiness'. Discipline was the responsibility of Edgar Ludlow-Hewitt who in 1940 was appointed the RAF's Inspector General after being removed from Bomber Command. In December 1942, the issue was considered serious enough to merit the appointment of a second IG, Philip Joubert.

Ludlow-Hewitt issued a series of reports bemoaning the decline of standards. He was particularly alarmed at what might be called the increasing civilianization of the Air Force. The tide of newcomers had brought the democratic spirit of an emerging Britain with them, threatening established customs and practices. In the summer of 1942 he complained that 'in many, I might almost say most units of the Air Force today, the NCOs have little disciplinary influence. They are regarded by the men rather as foremen of works in a factory.'[37]

Rank was no longer given automatic deference. 'It is not unusual for a station commander to go into a barrack room, reading room … bar or dining room where the men sitting about do not make a move to acknowledge his presence.' Smartness seemed optional and 'the tendency to scruffiness at home gets worse overseas and men [are] frequently seen on working parades unshaved. Officers, too, often appear unshaved, sometimes with half-grown beards without any reasonable excuse ...'

These worries seem to have been shared by many of those at the top. Commenting on the report, 'Jack' Slessor agreed that NCOs were no longer held in proper esteem. 'When I joined the RFC twenty-seven years ago as a Second Lieutenant, I looked upon a Sergeant or Flight Sergeant as being a hell of a chap and so did the men. Today every RAF station ... is lousy with Sergeants and Flight Sergeants – or rather men with three stripes on their sleeves ... a great many of them are completely undisciplined and they let the side down both in the sergeants' mess and out of it.'

Various remedies were proposed. Men should be 'paraded, inspected and marched to work'. At a high-level meeting in January 1944, it was even suggested that the cartoon character Pilot Officer Percy Prune, the shambolic novice who provided cautionary light relief in the training publication *Tee Emm*, was 'perhaps doing more harm than good'. The time had come 'to introduce a counterpart who should be a smart type with operational experience'.

If any of these measures were tried they seem to have done little good. Two years later, Ludlow-Hewitt was still warning that 'the greatest danger to ... morale is the importation into the service of the factory spirit with its suspicions, selfishness and distrust of authority'.

The truth was, as the Inspector General acknowledged honestly in a letter of June 1944 to a complaining colleague, that there was no link between appearance and efficiency. 'That you see untidy and scruffy airmen in the London streets, and officers as well often enough, does not really indicate low morale but simply ignorance,' he wrote. He went on: 'Indeed the Press seems to take particular pleasure in glorifying the unshaven, so much so that one [has] found again and again, that officers just as much as airmen think that being unshaven and scruffy is the hall mark of the genuine warrior.'

The casual approach to rules and dress, the partying and the urgent, impulsive sexual encounters were as structural an element in the war as bombs and rationing. It was a way of protecting yourself and carrying on against a background of constant tragedies. Those most intimately involved in the fighting added a further layer of insulation. The laconic response to loss has become a cliché of depictions of the RAF's war. It is exemplified by what Brian Kingcome portrayed as 'a typical conversation in a bar or … RAF mess'.[38]

> 'Heard about old Bill?'
> 'No. What's he up to, then?'
> 'Bought it yesterday.'
> 'Really? What happened?'
> 'Bounced by some 109s over Calais. Came down in flames.'
> 'Parachute?'
> 'No. Leastways, no one saw one.'
> 'Tough luck. Nice chap. Time for another?'

The accuracy of this reaction is confirmed by contemporaneous testimony. Sometime early in 1942, Australian navigator Walter 'Roo' Langworthy wrote from his bomber base to his WAAF girl-friend Sylvia Pickering bemoaning his 'miserable misfortune' at having been ordered to attend another funeral parade for a dead colleague.[39] He went on: 'Bad show really – still, that's how it goes. Now for pleasanter topics. Ain't the weather wonderful …'

Stiff upper lips could not be on permanent display. Morfydd Rose remembered standing by in the sergeants' mess to serve the crews their meal after returning from the Dams Raid, when they were told that eight of the aircraft would not be coming back. 'We all burst into tears,' she wrote. 'We looked around the … mess, the tables we had so hopefully laid out for the safe return of our young boys looked empty and pathetic.'[40]

The Second World War was a war of liberation, and liberation came in many forms and on many fronts. The triumph over Nazism brought other victories for freedom in its wake. For lower-class members of the RAF it created a sense of possibility. For those of the ruling class, an acceptance that merit spoke with many accents. Notions of masculine superiority were challenged and demolished by the overwhelming evidence to the contrary provided by a multitude of intelligent, efficient, dutiful and brave women.

The primacy of the white man was among the fallen bastions of pre-war thought. A few Indian pilots had served in the First World

War. The foundation of the Indian Air Force, an auxiliary formation, in 1932 opened the door to more Indian pilots and nine squadrons would fight in the Second World War.

In the RAF itself, pre-war policy had made membership of the white European races a requirement for joining. In October 1939, the need for manpower resulted in the dropping of the colour bar and in November 1940 recruiting began in the West Indies and Africa.[41]

In the Caribbean, the colonial education system stressed a familial link with Britain and many saw it as the mother country. The response was enthusiastic. Many thousands volunteered, of whom more than 400 were accepted as aircrew. Eighty women joined the WAAF. Their motives were the same mixture of idealism and adventurousness that impelled their British counterparts. Ulric Cross was working for the government in the railways department in Port of Spain, Trinidad, when the call came. 'The world was drowning in fascism,' he remembered. 'So I decided to do something about it and volunteer to fight in the RAF.'[42] Cross trained as a navigator, was commissioned and flew with 139 Squadron, Path Finder Force. He had an extraordinary war, flying three tours and eighty trips, including an astonishing twenty-two to Berlin. He finished the war as a squadron leader with a DFC and DSO and went on to a distinguished post-war legal career.

Africa produced only eighty volunteers, a result, it was said, of obstruction by reactionary colonial administrators. About 5,000 volunteers were put to work on the ground, in the West African Air Corps which supported the RAF in bases in Nigeria, the Gold Coast, Sierra Leone and Gambia. One who did make it past the prejudices of the local authorities was Flying Officer Akin Shenbanjo, a wireless operator with 76 Squadron, where his crew named their Halifax after him: 'Achtung! The Black Prince.'[43]

The aircrew came largely from the islands' best schools and the official assessment of their quality was glowing. 'The West Indian personnel selected for training have proved themselves capable of reaching the high technological standard required from operational aircrew and ... their discipline, spirit and general conduct is such as to enable them to carry out the ground duties of an officer or NCO with complete satisfaction,' concluded a report in 1944.[44]

This did not mean to say they could be treated entirely as equals. It went on to say that 'colour has not proved a drawback, either to them or their relations with their fellow officers or airmen – except in one respect – they have not proved suitable as captains of aircraft'. The perceived problem was not with them but with the rest of the crew. In a multi-crew aircraft, the pilot was the captain to whom the rest answered. The report considered that 'however good the individual may be, the mere fact that he is coloured may induce a feeling of lack of confidence in the members of the crew. It is a matter entirely beyond the Captain's control and while the feeling may be only subconscious, it will tend to lower the efficiency of the crew as a whole.'

This verdict does not seem to have been translated into strict policy, given the example of Flight Lieutenant Billy Strachan who started off as a wireless operator with 99 and 101 Squadrons and ended as a pilot flying Lancasters with 156 Squadron PFF.

The RAF's reputation as a meritocratic service where ability trumped background was validated by its openness to non-white airmen. Dropping the colour bar was not just a temporary expedient. It marked the advent of a new attitude in which discrimination was officially forbidden. An Air Ministry Confidential Order of June 1944 stated: 'All ranks should clearly understand that there is no colour bar in the Royal Air Force …' Any instance of 'discrimination on the grounds of colour by white officers or airmen or any attitude of hostility towards personnel of non-European descent should be immediately and severely checked'.[45]

The aircrew volunteers seem to have been accepted easily enough as exotic additions to the rich human mix that peopled the squadrons. Billy Strachan reflected that 'by any reasonable calculation one might have expected me to have suffered, if not discrimination, at least a constant barrage of racist jokes. I can confirm that this did not happen.'[46]

The aircrews' unique shared experience created a mutual understanding that dissolved the barriers of class, education and nationality that might have kept individuals apart in peacetime. It might be hoped that the same would be true of colour. On the ground, the picture is not quite so rosy. There is evidence of white staff bullying and verbally and physically abusing black airmen and unfairly blocking promotions. The victims did not take such treatments meekly and punch-ups ensued.

But the RAF lived up to the credo implicit in the decision to open its ranks. Caribbean aircrew mostly flew bombers, but they served in all the commands except Transport, where they could expect to visit countries where prejudice was entrenched. The islands produced fighter pilots like Flying Officer Jellicoe Scoon who flew Spitfires with 41 Squadron, then Typhoons with 198 Squadron, and Flight Lieutenant David Errol Chance who flew Beaufighters with Coastal Command's 603 Squadron against enemy shipping in the Aegean.

Many of those who survived went on to fame and success after the war. Michael Manley, who served in the RCAF, became Prime Minister of Jamaica. Cy Grant from Guyana was commissioned and served as a navigator with 103 Squadron before being shot down on his third trip during the Battle of the Ruhr. He spent the rest of the war in Stalag Luft III. He decided to stay on in Britain and become a barrister but found the Inns of Court less enlightened than the RAF and gave up the law. Instead, he took to stage and screen and in the 1950s was the first black face to be seen regularly on British TV.

The relative welcome that black volunteers found in the RAF was a pleasant contrast to the violent hostility that African-Americans encountered from their comrades in the armed forces of the United States where segregation was strictly enforced. Air Force policy was far in advance of the attitudes and hiring practices of most British firms of the time. Though it was not mentioned in the report of the Air Information Office in Washington, here was another area in which the RAF could claim to be 'Britain's best advertisement'.

13

Out of Sight

'Today the real adventure starts' reads the entry in Lucian Ercolani's diary for Saturday 12 December 1942. 'Arrived at 99 Squadron – right out in the jungle!'[1] The base was 'just bamboo huts and tents'. The mess bar was a 'tent open one end ... a hurricane lamp hanging down ... with a semi-circle of chairs'. He found the ramshackle set-up rather stimulating. 'In the evening after dinner, seeing [every-one] standing around under the light with glass in hand, the howls of the jackals outside, discussing the 'morrow's operation was a most impressive scene' as if they were all involved in an '"outpost of Empire" sort of racket'.

Ercolani was twenty-four, and a veteran bomber pilot who had already completed a tour of operations over Germany. Returning from a trip to Berlin in November 1941, his Wellington was hit by flak and most of the mid-section of the fuselage burned away. Despite the damage, he decided to try and make it back to base but was forced to ditch in the Channel. When the aircraft hit the water he was injured and went down with the wreck. Then the cockpit section broke free and bobbed to the surface. Ercolani scrambled out to join the rest of the crew in a dinghy, which floated for three days in the wintry seas undetected by searchers until it washed ashore on the southernmost tip of the Isle of Wight. The exploit earned him an immediate DSO for 'outstanding courage, initiative and devotion to duty'.[2]

Ercolani was the son of a prosperous Italian-born furniture designer and manufacturer who settled in High Wycombe, after moving from Italy in 1910. After Oundle public school, Lucian joined the family business and was all set for a conventional, prosperous life when the war took him off on an entirely different path. Ercolani had no literary pretension but his diaries are a gem. Heartfelt, artless, utterly genuine, they give a rare feel of the actuality of an overlooked campaign, as well as a glimpse into the mind of a decent man, dedicated to a duty that wrenched him from a much-loved wife and cherished family.

He arrived in India at the start of the great Allied push back against the Japanese eruption which had brought the enemy to northern Burma and the gates of the Raj. The fall of Singapore in

Lucian Ercolani with Cynthia at the Palace

February 1942 had been a strategic catastrophe for Britain and a huge psychological blow. The loss of this citadel of the Eastern empire had a chastening effect. There was an initial, abortive offensive to gain a foothold in the Arakan Peninsula in 1943. After that, the campaign of reconquest proceeded patiently. Lessons were learned, preparations were thorough and enough human and material resources dedicated to the enterprise to maximize the chances of success.

In contrast to the handful of squadrons allocated to the defence of Singapore, there would be abundant aircraft and aircrews available to support the armies on the ground and air power in all its forms would play a decisive part in the victory. Like the ground war, the air war in the Burma theatre had its own special character. In the accounts of those who fought it, there are few dogfights; indeed, the Japanese air force plays a minor role and the Allied air force would come to outnumber its opponents by three to one.[3] The most consistent enemies were the weather, the landscape and the logistical problems of mounting complicated missions over great distances, or operating from advanced bases like the one Ercolani arrived in, hacked out of the jungle by coolie labour. The courage of the airmen was measured less in feats of arms than of endurance and fortitude.

Jungle fighting called for a greatly expanded understanding of how air power could be most effectively used. Much of Burma was covered in forests and mountains and was short of roads and railways. There were no formal front lines and the fighting was done in pockets. The fighting would come to coalesce on three fronts in the west, centre and north of upper Burma. Increasingly, as well as providing firepower, the British and American air forces would be involved in moving troops and maintaining air bridges to forces cut off from conventional means of replenishing food, ammunition and medical supplies, as well as flying out casualties. The man who heaved the pallet out of the back of the Dakota to the 12th Army outpost beleaguered in the sea of tropical vegetation below became as essential a player in the enterprise as the fighter pilot or navigator, and the capacity to lift men and things at least as important as the ability to drop bombs.

Ercolani was arriving at 99 Squadron just as the offensive was starting. It was equipped with Wellingtons and tasked with hitting Japanese supply lines and destroying infrastructure. He had recently been promoted squadron leader and would be commanding a flight. He spent a few days getting re-accustomed to the 'good old Wimpey' and flew his first operation on 16 December. The trip was 'a special one ... a sort of army co-op affair'. Low cloud meant they failed to locate the target but Ercolani was pleased with his 'damned good' crew. 'The ice is broken, am not as [nervous] as was to begin with – roll on the war,' he wrote on his return.

In his diary entries, faithfully jotted down each night in the early days, Ercolani was honest about his doubts concerning his abilities and acknowledged his fears. The next op was four days later and the familiar butterflies stirred as the hour approached. 'In the morning [I] am dead keen and happy about the trip but by night always [seem] to get a bit apprehensive,' he confessed.

He had been assured on arrival that there was little to fear from the Japanese air force but the previous day a crew had reported having to dive away before finishing their bombing run after five fighters came up to them. On 20 December he was off again to an unspecified target, first flying to an advanced landing ground to refuel. The attacking force failed to form up on the way to their destination and arrived in dribs and drabs. Three of the first were set upon by fighters and he was 'scared as we did our run that fighters would then come after us', but 'nothing happened, took an extra photo and pushed off home, just crawling over the mountains'. Over the target they 'only saw some rather pathetic tracer miles away and three smoke puffs from AA'.

The rocky ridges, rising to nearly 20,000 feet in the north, seemed a much greater hazard than flak or Japanese Zeros. A fortnight later, after returning from an op near Mandalay, he recorded how he 'hated passing over those mountains – a nasty black night and the A/C [aircraft] seeming as though it's never going to make it as the hills get nearer and nearer. Even if you are above them, they still seem to tower above one.' He took to climbing to 14,500 feet to clear features that were reckoned to be 10,000 feet. In the airspace of the uplands he always felt 'a bit of a nag at the back of one's head wondering what we would do if an engine packed up …'

On the way back from an operation on 12 February he 'heard an A/C send an SOS, then "so long" – we wondered who it was – it made seem crossing the hills all the worse'. It turned out to be P-Peter, captained by a pilot named Watson who had celebrated his twenty-first birthday two days before. Watson managed to land without injury to himself or the crew. They were soon spotted by searching fighters and seem to have made it back to the nearby British lines.

This was remarkable good luck. Anyone surviving a crash was immediately confronted with a new array of deadly dangers: death from starvation, thirst, disease, or the bite of a host of venomous creatures. They could expect no mercy from the Japanese. The torture and execution of Allied airmen was officially sanctioned. One notorious incident exemplified the enemy attitude. On 31 January 1945, a Liberator with a nine-man crew carrying out an intelligence mission monitoring Japanese radar near Rangoon developed engine trouble and the captain ordered the crew to bale out. Six landed in the same area and were reunited. The others were believed to have died in the crash. The survivors headed west in the hope of reaching the coast. They sought help from a village head-man who tipped off the Japanese. The airmen were taken by boat down the Irrawaddy River to the Bassein district. The two officers in the group were taken off to Rangoon for further questioning. The NCOs were kept behind and relentlessly beaten. The worst treatment was reserved for the wireless operator, Flight Sergeant Stanley Woodbridge. He knew the codes and wavelengths used for links with ground operators who provided the co-ordinates of Japanese targets. Woodbridge revealed nothing. Eventually all four were beheaded.[4]

Ercolani arrived too early to benefit from a specialist training school set up in Poona to teach jungle survival skills. Before being sent to his squadron, Spitfire pilot Fred Dane completed the gruelling course. The school was 'in a large solid building situated in … hills overlooking dense jungle in all directions. How it got there and who built it in such isolation I never found out.'[5]

The classroom teaching was done by 'primitive natives from the Chin Hills in Northern Burma. They couldn't speak a word of English and all instruction had to be through an interpreter.' They learned how to make cooking utensils out of bamboo, trap and kill small animals including rats and snakes, and build fires to cook them on that gave off no tell-tale smoke. Then it was time to put their skills into practice. Groups of three were 'dropped off in the jungle with water bottles, a compass and a small amount of basic rations. Our base was a four-day trek in an easterly direction and we had to find our way back without maps.' Dane and his companions returned in time, all of them considerably thinner and 'suffering from ticks, bites, bleeding caused by leeches, dozens of insect bites and ... numerous abrasions and sores as the result of forcing a passage through the denser parts of the jungle.' The consensus was that, even with an elaborate survival kit, a pilot 'would have to be very lucky indeed to make it back from any distance in the jungle unless he was fortunate enough to stumble across friendly natives'.

The attitude of the local tribes was uncertain, as Alan Sammons, a Hurricane pilot with 20 Squadron operating out of a tiny forward airstrip on the Bay of Bengal, discovered. On 24 February he and his Canadian partner Eddy Fockler were taking a last stooge round at the end of an offensive recce over the southern tip of Arakan when 'bang – I copped it'.[6] A lucky shot from rifle or machine gun hit the engine coolant pipe line, 'steam flooded the cockpit and I became very warm indeed'. He was too far from friendly territory to reach it before the engine seized up so he headed for the coast and crash-landed in a mangrove swamp on the Mayu River. Amazingly, he was unhurt 'but the poor old kite was quite a wreck. The engine was broken away and was steaming in the swampy water, the wings were torn off and the fuselage was smashed in except for the cockpit.' He 'splashed through the water so that I could wave to Eddy who was circling overhead'. But Eddy failed to spot him. As the Hurricane eventually turned away and dwindled into the distance, Sammons was separated from the British forward position by more than fifty miles of hostile territory with only a rubber dinghy and a handful of Horlicks tablets and glucose sweets to sustain him.

He decided to seek help from the local inhabitants. He set off across the river in the dinghy but tides and currents defeated him and it was the afternoon of the following day before he got ashore and found a village. He waited for dusk, then 'seeing no sign of Japs I … approached the nearest hut around which a crowd soon gathered and with many salaams began to get down to the job of obtaining food and drink which I had been without for twenty-eight hours'. He was eventually given some watery rice, then, by means of sign language, tried to request that they take him by canoe, down the river and up the coast to the British front-line position at Maungdaw, where they would be given 'plenty of money as a reward'. Sammons understood they had agreed to set off with him in the morning. He was still cautious and determined to stay awake but exhaustion overtook him and he dozed off. He was woken up 'by the unpleasantness of a noose being tightened round my neck and several village stalwarts hanging on to me'. They robbed him of his revolver, sheath knife and escape kit, comprising compass, fishing line, matches, water purification tablets, silk scarf with printed map and £6 in silver rupees. He was then tied up 'securely and most uncomfortably' and they set off on a night march to a Japanese outpost where the tribesmen handed him over, receiving four blankets for their efforts.

After a desultory interrogation he was taken on a two-day trek north to what seemed to be a divisional headquarters where other Allied captives were being held. After several months they were moved down to the POW camp at the Central Prison in Rangoon where Sammons spent the next year. The prisoners subsisted on a near-starvation diet and were forbidden to communicate with each other. There were occasional beatings, but most of the suffering was caused by neglect, and the numbers were constantly thinned by deaths from beri-beri and dysentery. Their bony bodies were clothed in rags and maggots seethed in their open sores. In their misery, they showed astounding cheerfulness and ingenuity, using whatever tiny resource came their way to lighten the load of their appalling existences. 'To pass things from one cell to another we would throw a piece of string along … and attach our mess tins to the other end,' wrote Sammons. Smoking was forbidden but the prisoners 'used to make cigarettes from dog ends picked up while cleaning and any little scraps of newspaper'. Not all the guards were brutes. Sometimes, one would give a prisoner a light which he would then pass down the line of cells by means of the string and mess tin.

The dreadful prospect of a crash-landing meant the reliability of aero-engines took on an even greater importance. The ground crews had to be where the aircraft were based, or in the large number of advanced landing grounds that were planted in the middle of nowhere to extend operational reach. This often meant slaving twelve hours a day in sauna-bath humidity under constant attack from voracious insects, eating tinned and dehydrated food and sleeping in airless tents, with no diversions and few opportunities for escape. Ercolani's diary has many words of praise for their efforts and sympathy for their lot. One evening he went to check on a Wellington that needed attention and found 'the three senior NCOs at work on it together. They are an absolutely grand lot, never seen anything like it.'

The constant toing and froing of aircraft meant that even the most remote spots were kept supplied with booze flown in from Calcutta, and the familiar rituals of Air Force revelry were heard amid the steamy heat of the jungle. On 17 February 1943, Ercolani went for a few drinks in the mess, intending to take the 1 a.m. train to Calcutta for a few days' leave but a party developed which was 'such an utter shambles' that he missed it. There were 'chairs, tables, strewn all over the floor – Dicky Richardson with nothing on bar his identity discs. I put up a black – emptied a flower pot over W/C [Wing Commander] of 159. He was a bit cheesed. I don't mind but I do hope it has no repercussions on poor old Barry [his brother who flew with 159 Squadron].'

Leaves, as Ercolani admitted, were not particularly restful and down time could take as much out of you as operations. The routine followed the same lines that the RAF had established in Cairo, Algiers, Naples and any other city or town where there was the remotest possibility of a well-lubricated good time. 'Must say enjoyed the leave – am not really much better for it though,' he recorded early in March 1944. 'We stayed at the Grand Hotel, swam in the Calcutta Swimming Club in the mornings, had lunch time "sessions" which generally ended about four in the afternoon, then rested, or rather recovered – on then, to beat up the town in the evening. Spent a hell of a lot of cash …'

These excursions to Calcutta seemed only to emphasize the distance from home. The advanced landing grounds were carved out of an exotic landscape that pale-skinned young Britons had only encountered in comic books and films, full of wild beasts and primitive tribesmen. Calcutta, the nearest leave centre, seemed scarcely more civilized. Fred Dane felt 'the whole city seemed to pant in the heat'.[7] Misery was everywhere, worse than anything seen in the African ports of call on the voyage from Britain. He was appalled by the treatment by European and Indian alike of the rickshaw men, 'disease ridden skeletons' suffering from 'tuberculosis, hookworm and many other diseases … it was not unusual to see the passenger sitting back in the chair … kick out at the rickshaw wallah because he wasn't moving fast enough'.

One day in September 1943, while driving near Midnapur, Lucian Ercolani 'passed a station where a grain train was in. There were hundreds of Indians; men, women and children roaming around, all armed with staves and knives, some very long and thin, to poke through the doors and pierce the grain sacks so that it runs out. They catch some, then as the train pulls out, they scramble between the lines for the grains … it is a terrible sight to see some of them, just skin and bones.'

British rule did not seem to have done much for India. Resentment was palpable, and, to most who gave the matter thought, justifiable. The Allied servicemen were occupiers not liberators. Indian soldiers taken prisoner after the loss of Singapore and Malaya, together with thousands of volunteers, were now fighting alongside the Japanese in the Indian National Army, for liberation from British rule. Everyday transactions could be fractious and fraternization was rare. 'The troops treat the Indians, no matter what standing, as dirt,' Ercolani wrote following a riot in a canteen over the price of bananas.

The sour atmosphere intensified the yearning for home. On Easter Sunday 1944, while recovering from a bout of jaundice in the Himalayan hill station of Nainital, where the British went to escape the heat of Delhi, Ercolani was woken by the very English sound of bells tolling in the tower of St John in the Wilderness church. 'It reminded me of home when I used to get up early and go to … the Communion service with Mummy,' he wrote. 'What peaceful days those now seem. That Sunday morning always used to belong to Mummy and I.'

But more than home Ercolani yearned for his wife. He married Cynthia Douglas in June 1941 and she moved with him from aerodrome to aerodrome during his service in Britain. His diary throbs with the pain of separation. He recorded in bittersweet detail their parting in October 1942, at the door of the cottage they shared in Barton Bendish, Norfolk, when 'just before going we sat in the car … our last moment together. God, it was terrible. We kissed each other goodbye. She got out of the car with tears just beginning to well out of her eyes and looked in the window of the car and waved. I drove on and waved back through the sunshine roof and had a last glimpse of her standing in the road outside the cottage with her camel coat over her pyjamas.'

It was not quite the final farewell. Flying up to Blackpool, prior to setting sail for the East, he took the aircraft down low over the cottage, just as he used to 'beat up' their lodgings near the base at Stradishall before setting off on an op. She came out, 'jumping up and down and waving goodbye'.

He was oppressed by the same thought that clouded every farewell. 'Will I ever see her again?' It would be nearly three years before they were reunited. Time and distance only seem to have intensified his feelings. Her picture went with him everywhere, the focus of a nightly ritual. 'Said goodnight to Cyn and the photo I took on our anniversary smiled back goodnight.' There are almost daily references to how much he missed her and every good time he recounts is qualified by the thought that it would have been even better if she was there to share it. Cynthia wanted to join the WAAF. He had misgivings, fearing she was too sensitive for service life. She went ahead anyway, trying to wangle a posting to India to be near him. It didn't work out but the story had a happy ending. Despite his fears that they would reunite as strangers, their marriage seems to have successfully picked up where it left off.

Duty offered a shape and purpose to a dislocated existence. In the Far East theatre the ideological element to the conflict was less obvious than it was in Europe and the Mediterranean. The Japanese were ciphers, their culture and beliefs opaque and unknowable, and their cruelty and fanaticism made it hard to regard them as entirely human, 'no better than a horrible animal,' concluded Ercolani. He wanted to 'hit them good and hard'. Over Germany he had experienced a 'slightly different feeling … felt it was a job to be done more than anything else'.

Well-executed operations brought a sense of progress, each one a step nearer home. Ercolani was present from the beginning of the major air effort in Burma until well after the end. When long-range Liberators arrived to beef up the bomber force in September 1943 he moved to the newly formed 355 Squadron, flying missions involving round trips of 2,000 miles against enemy supply routes including the Burma–Siam railway, partly built by the slave labour of Allied prisoners. A year later he returned to 99 Squadron as CO. Although not required to, he led many of the most difficult raids himself, attacking supply dumps, railway targets and enemy headquarters. When, in the spring of 1945, the battle for Burma was won he moved on to command 159 Squadron, part of a target-marking force, engaged in operations that could take more than twenty hours.

His achievements are barely mentioned in the diaries. He took satisfaction in a job well done, though no pleasure in destruction. Early on he was one of three aircraft taking part in a diversionary raid on 'some obscure town' in enemy hands. He wrote later that they 'certainly laced that place up. Felt a bit guilty about it. It was undefended and just sheer butchery. Bombed in two sticks from 3,500 and [machine-gunned]. I didn't like that but the gunners would never have forgiven me if I hadn't [let them].'

Occasionally, though, a glow of professional satisfaction shows through. A raid with 159 Squadron on 13 May 1945 was 'a really successful op. Our job was to destroy a bridge over 1200 miles away – a bomb aimer's dream. It was laid flat and was a wonderful sight. The first few bombs didn't get it, then down it went. We felt like singing …'

The Burma campaign was just part of the wider, American-led struggle against the Japanese in the Far East. From August 1943, all Allied land, sea and air forces in the operational area covering India, Burma, Malaya, Ceylon, Siam and parts of Sumatra were fused into South East Asia Command, under a British chief, Louis Mountbatten. The air forces were placed under an RAF officer, Richard Peirse, who had made a good recovery after being sacked as C-in-C Bomber Command by Portal in January 1942.[8] His number two was an American, Major General George Stratemeyer, who issued a memorable order of the day establishing the spirit of the joint enterprise. 'We must merge into one unified force,' he declared, 'in thought and in deed, neither English nor American, with the faults of neither and the virtues of both. We must establish in Asia a record of Allied Air Victory of which we can all be proud in the years to come. Let us write it now in the skies over Burma.'[9]

The official history judged that the campaign 'showed how well and gallantly this exhortation was fulfilled'.[10] Nonetheless, command arrangements were notoriously complicated and however well the elements co-operated operationally there were differences of style on the ground that could grate. During a leave in Calcutta Lucian Ercolani bumped into a senior American airman at the 300 Club. 'We were all a bit whissholed and he started to tell us about how damned marvellous the United States Army Air Forces are,' he wrote.[11] 'They seem to get a medal for practically damn-all. There's no doubt they are a good lot of fellows but their standards are so different to ours. He talks of the number of ships he has sunk. When we get down to actual facts he is not so certain. Also they have very little interest … in the RAF, whereas a lot of the RAF boys try to find out all they can from the Yanks. We can't be all that bad … we've been doing the job a lot longer and have far greater experience.'

The landscape of Burma made conventional campaigning impossible. Aircraft became an essential means of moving troops around the battle fronts and keeping them supplied in place. The transportation and logistical capacity provided by aircraft were fundamental to the Allied victory. The first long-range penetration operation mounted by the Chindits in February 1943 was unsustainable without regular air drops by the RAF. The second, which began in

February 1944, relied on American aeroplanes and gliders of the 1st Air Commando Group to insert troops behind enemy lines.

All activity on the ground, offensive or defensive, had to be sustained from the air. In late 1943 the British 14th Army under General Bill Slim launched its great effort to seize back Burma. It started with another attempt to take the Arakan Peninsula led by XV Corps. The Japanese responded with the tactics of infiltrating British lines and threatening encirclement, forcing a withdrawal which had worked well the previous year. They appeared to be about to succeed again, and the headquarters of the 7th Indian Division was overrun. Instead of falling back, though, the threatened units were told to stand and fight. The calculation was that the Allies' great advantage in air power would mean the defenders could be kept supplied with enough rations, ammunition and medical supplies to hold out indefinitely. The Japanese would have to rely on overland transport, which could be disrupted by air attacks, and eventually forced to retire.

So it turned out. The 7th Indian Division withdrew into a jungle compound, 1,200 yards in diameter, which became known as the 'Admin Box', where they staved off the besiegers from 5 to 23 February. In that time, Dakotas flew 714 sorties dropping 2,300 tons of supplies to them and other troops. They faced some initial opposition from Japanese fighters, who were soon driven from the skies by three squadrons of Spitfires operating from airfields around Chittagong. The Japanese losses of about 5,000 men were fewer than those of the Allies. But their methods had been successfully countered and the pattern was set for the remainder of the Burma campaign.

Shortly afterwards, the Japanese launched their own major offensive. Central to the plan was the destruction of the British forces around Imphal, the capital of the state of Manipur, which commanded the approach to Assam and the Raj. Imphal was surrounded in early March, and the strategic town of Kohima to the north on 4 April. The siege of Imphal lasted four months, that of Kohima, eleven weeks. Both were decisive defeats for the Japanese, the largest they had suffered to date, and marked a turning point in the Burma campaign.

Once again, it was resupply by air that determined the outcome. The seventy-six transport aircraft of SEAC, reinforced by twenty C-46 twin-engine Curtiss Commandos diverted from their duties flying over the 'Hump' of the Eastern Himalayas to convoy supplies to the Nationalist Chinese forces of Chiang Kai-shek, kept up a continuous shuttle to the enclaves. They lifted 19,000 tons of materiel, flew in 12,000 fresh men and took out 13,000 casualties and 43,000 non-combatants. The supplies included a million gallons of fuel, a thousand bags of mail and forty million cigarettes.[12]

In these battles and at every stage of the campaign, the 14th Army could rely on the support from the RAF's 3rd Tactical Air Force as well as units of the USAAF Tenth Air Force to provide close air support and act as aerial artillery. Fred Dane arrived in theatre to join 155 Squadron at Meiktila in central Burma just after it fell to the Allies in March 1945. The fourteen pilots were a typical mix of nationalities: two Australians, a New Zealander, a South African and a Canadian, the rest British. They were kept busy, flying up to seventeen sorties a day as the army pushed south down the Sittang River towards Rangoon.

The Spitfires operated in groups of two or four, sometimes eight, depending on the size of the objective, bombing and strafing with cannon fire as the enemy floundered back through the paddy fields. All attacks were at low level. 'Sometimes the target would be a few mud huts, that the Japs had taken and the army wanted destroyed,' Dane wrote.[13] 'Often the only target indicator would be two thin strips of white cloth, some distance apart, pointing towards the enemy strong point. The attacking aircraft would have to judge the interception point and [hit] an unseen target obscured by jungle, perhaps within a few hundred yards of our own troops.'

They had to contend with anti-aircraft fire, often very accurate. The main danger, though, was from the weather, which during the monsoon was more vicious and destructive than anything the Japanese air force could now contrive. The pilots lived in dread of cumulonimbus clouds, huge thunderheads which reared upwards from below rocky ridge lines for 35,000 feet. They 'had the reputation of disintegrating an aircraft unlucky enough to accidentally fly into them', torn apart by drastically varying wind currents. The tropical clouds harboured their own malevolent micro climate, blotting out light, whipping up hailstorms and coating wings with ice. Great banks of 'cumulonims' could stretch for a hundred miles or more, and the only way through was underneath, if the cloud base allowed it. Even then, 'the turbulence, wind shear and buffeting were extreme'. Flying beneath the clouds Dane was once struck by lightning and 'temporarily lost control … the plane was engulfed in a blue haze, mini flashes of lightning [flickered] between the prop blades and the radio was wrecked'.

The push south to the Japanese main base in the port of Rangoon was given added urgency by the fact that American transport aircraft were due to be withdrawn at the end of May for use elsewhere and the prospect of the approaching monsoon. If the city had not fallen by the time the rains came, victory in Burma would be delayed by months. As 14th Army closed from the north, it was decided to mount an amphibious assault from the south. On 1 May, a battalion of Gurkhas parachuted onto flat land near Elephant Point, south-west of Rangoon. At the same time the Royal Navy was tasked with leading a flotilla of seaborne troops up the Rangoon River.

The end was a merciful anti-climax. On the evening of 29 April, after lights out was called in Rangoon jail, one of the prisoners of war, Dick Corbett, had been unable to sleep. He heard the revving of lorries and the smell of burning paper. The guards had gone. Alan Sammons remembered him 'immediately arousing us all and in no time several men were scrambling over the compound and rousing the members of the other blocks'.[14] The senior officer among the prisoners, Wing Commander Lionel Hudson of the Royal Australian Air Force, took charge and a Union Jack used for numerous burial services was hoisted over the prison. A little later a large painted sign appeared on the roof for the benefit of Allied aircraft: JAPS GONE. BRITISH HERE. EXTRACT DIGIT.

14

Black and White

Merston aerodrome used to lie just south of the main Bognor Regis to Chichester road, between the English Channel and the West Sussex Downs. There is no trace of it today. A ghostly airman returning would see only cereal fields flanked by row after row of polytunnels filled with ripening soft fruit; nothing at all that hints at the stupendous enterprise these few acres were once part of. In the early summer of 1944 Merston was a temporary airfield, with two steel mesh runways laid over the dirt, and tents instead of huts for the air and ground staff. It was home to 145 Wing of the RAF, made up of two fighter squadrons manned by the Free French, another, mainly British, Spitfire squadron plus a transport unit flying Douglas DC-3 Dakotas.

On the evening of 5 June, officers were called to a briefing from the CO. Group Captain Adolph 'Sailor' Malan was a celebrated Battle of Britain pilot, a South African of Afrikaner stock. He looked pugnacious with his close-cut blond hair and square jaw and was famous for his aggression in the air. On the ground, he was surprisingly mild and introspective. The audience had a good idea of what he was about to say. 'He came into the tent and informed us, quite quietly, that the show was on,' wrote one of those present, an RAF Regiment officer called John Rolfe to a female friend a year later.[1] 'I can capture the atmosphere easily now. The smell of the tent in the hot sun, and one of the tent flaps banging in the wind. As he spoke we heard the first wave of gliders going over, and suddenly it dawned on me that it was our supreme effort ...'

The sound and sight of aeroplanes overhead, of all shapes and sizes and in vast, amazing numbers, would be indelibly imprinted on the memories of everyone in southern England that summer. Thirty-eight years afterwards John Keegan recalled how as a boy he watched the Somerset countryside fill up with the troops and war machines and then, one night, suddenly empty.

> One evening the sky over our house began to fill with the sound of aircraft, which swelled until it overflowed the darkness from edge to edge. Its first tremors had taken my parents into the garden, and as the roar grew I followed and stood between them to gaze awestruck at the constellation of red, green and yellow lights which rode across the heavens and streamed southwards towards the sea. It seemed as if every aircraft in the world was in flight, as wave followed wave without intermission ...[2]

In this first, great southward-heading flock were 1,000 heavy bombers with night-fighter escorts, tasked with pounding the reinforced concrete strong points and gun emplacements of the Atlantic Wall, transports laden with paratroopers and tugs towing gliders crammed with infantrymen. Further north, a decoy operation was underway as 617 squadron, the Dam Busters, scattered bundles of tinfoil Window, which lit up German radar screens, creating the impression of an invasion fleet approaching the Pas de Calais at seven knots and for a few crucial hours sowing confusion about where the real blow was falling.

Just before dawn, it was the turn of the fighters and fighter bombers. At Merston, the pilots were told they would be providing dawn-to-dusk cover of the invasion. They were to operate over Omaha Beach, on the Calvados coast where the Americans met the fiercest resistance of the day. For the airmen looking down, the carpet of ships butting across the Channel was an awesome sight that matched the spectacle the air fleet presented in the skies. Flight Lieutenant Stanley de Vere, a twenty-five-year-old New Zealander fighter pilot who was temporarily on ground control duties, wangled himself onto a patrol in the middle of the afternoon. 'It was amazing,' he wrote in his diary. 'From Portsmouth Harbour and Southampton to the beachhead was [a] lane of every type of craft, from battleships to small infantry landing craft. Warships, from battleships to small corvettes were hurrying around each convoy and fussing like a hen over her chicks. Then just off the beachhead still greater numbers of ships ... were lying, the battleships shelling enemy positions on the shore. Saw one destroyer which had been sunk, its funnels and some of the superstructure were showing above the water ...'[3]

Ken 'Paddy' French, a Spitfire pilot with 66 Squadron, was thrilled by the panoramic view of the warships belching shells and the landing craft running up the beaches but felt 'strangely detached from it all'.[4] The tongues of flame shooting from gun barrels, the flash of exploding shells, were oddly soundless and it was hard to grasp that the scene was accompanied by 'terrible noise and the fact that thousands of men were dying on the beaches below'.

While marvelling at the armada, French's main thought had been relief that, should he be shot down, there were plenty of boats to pick him up. As it turned out, it was two days before he saw enemy aircraft. Flying back to base with another squadron member after both developed engine trouble, they spotted a pair of Me 109s. They were 'pretty sure they had seen us as they emitted a little puff of smoke indicating that they were accelerating'. But they were speeding away, not towards them. The Luftwaffe, for the moment at least, were in no mood or condition for a fight.

The Allies would enjoy the priceless asset of the freedom of the skies for most of the campaign. Air superiority was a *sine qua non* of the Overlord plan. Lavish air power was essential to cover the landing beaches as the armies struggled ashore, to shield them from the inevitable counter-attacks as they carved out a bridgehead, to prepare the ground for the push forward, and to create the conditions for the breakout that led to victory. Clearly, this called for the closest possible co-operation between land and air, as Bernard Montgomery, commanding the Allied ground forces in Normandy, spelled out in a letter to Miles Dempsey, commander of the British Second Army, a month before the landing. 'I feel very strongly ... that we can achieve no real success unless each Army and its accompanying Air Force can weld itself into one entity,' he declared.[5] He looked forward to the continuation of the happy situation that had developed in the Middle East and Italy where 'the spirit of unity went right down to the individual soldier and airman'.

The Normandy enterprise would reassemble some of the key players in those campaigns. Arthur Tedder, who had worked side by side with Monty since 1942, was Deputy Supreme Allied Commander and co-ordinator of air activities. The great desert air warrior Arthur Coningham was chief of the RAF's 2nd Tactical Air Force, a huge assembly of light bombers and the new generation of fighter-bombers that would roam the battlefield that summer. Familiarity did not breed affection or respect. As head of the Desert Air Force, Coningham had fallen out badly with Montgomery over his failure to fall on Rommel's retreating army after Alamein. Tedder derided his claims to great generalship and deplored his boastfulness and publicity seeking. In early 1943 he shared his opinion with US General George Patton. Monty, he wrote, was 'a little fellow of average ability who has had such a build-up that he thinks of himself as Napoleon – he is not'.[6] Nothing that happened in Normandy would cause him, or Coningham, to revise their opinions.

The air operations that preceded Overlord were intelligently conceived and executed on a massive scale. Never before had air power been used with such care and in such quantity. The sharp efficiency demonstrated by the Allied air forces before and during the campaign stood out against the duller performance of the forces on the ground. The landings themselves were a brilliant success but thereafter progress disappointed. For all his bold talk, Montgomery showed his habitual caution. His commanders bungled opportunities and misunderstandings and balls-ups abounded. Monty's tricky personality guaranteed trouble with his chief, Eisenhower, and the leading American generals Bradley and Patton. His insistence that everything was going according to his master plan sounded increasingly hollow as weeks passed and the crucial Caen sector, which he had led everyone to believe could be taken on D-Day, remained firmly in German hands.

The Allied armies were up against the most formidable soldiers in the world, courageous and fanatically determined, who made maximum use of the difficult terrain and their still considerable resources, directed by field commanders of the calibre of Erwin Rommel. On the other hand, the invaders had the priceless asset of a huge air force which did everything that was asked of it swiftly and effectively. For months before the first soldiers hit the beaches, the Allied squadrons had been working to a plan that would undermine the Luftwaffe's powers and shape the battlefield to the Allies' liking. Before the air campaign started, the USAAF and Bomber Command launched a week-long assault on German aircraft factories, designed to structurally undermine the Luftwaffe by attacking its industrial base, as well as luring it into an attritional battle to whittle away aircraft and aircrew. The continual losses the German air force suffered on the three fronts it was fighting on in the spring of 1944 meant that, when the time came, it was unable to contribute much to the defence of Normandy, let alone seriously challenge the Allies in the air.

The preparations and the post-invasion air campaign were the responsibility of the Allied Expeditionary Air Force (AEAF) under Trafford Leigh-Mallory, who was moved from Fighter Command to become Commander-in-Chief in November 1943. It grouped together the new formations created for the invasion; the RAF's 2nd Tactical Air Force (2nd TAF) and the United States Ninth Air Force (9th USAF) as well as units of Fighter Command. Leigh-Mallory did not, however, control either Bomber Command or the United States Strategic Air Forces in Europe, which for the time being remained at the disposal of the Combined Chiefs of Staff. He was far from being the ideal man for the job. Many of his British and American peers regarded Leigh-Mallory as uncongenial and incompetent, and friction over control was guaranteed.

AEAF was nonetheless a hive of original thinking. In January 1944, a bombing committee was set up whose members included Professor Solly Zuckerman, a South African-born zoologist who had worked with Tedder in Italy studying the effects of bombardment. He and other experts evolved the 'transportation plan' aimed at paralysing German rail communications by first attacking marshalling yards and maintenance and repair facilities in the wider network, before moving on to tactical targets like bridges, locomotives and rolling stock inside the invasion zone. The certainty of

Fifth wheel. Leigh-Mallory

civilian casualties alarmed politicians, senior airmen and Eisenhower himself. Predictably, the plan was opposed by Arthur Harris and his US counterpart Carl Spaatz on the grounds that it would divert their bombers from their proper function of destroying Germany's industry and undermining civilian morale.

The success of experimental operations in March against rail centres in France and Belgium, significant civilian deaths notwithstanding, persuaded military and political leaders to back it. By

D-Day, eighty railway targets had been attacked and, in the words of the official history, 'the movement of German troops and material by rail had thus become a matter of very great difficulty and hazard ... such trains as still ran moved very slowly, were forced to make long detours and travelled only at night. The enemy had no freedom of movement in a large part of France and Belgium and would therefore find it difficult, if not impossible, to marshal troops quickly for a decisive counter attack ...'[7]

In the weeks before the landing, airfields, coastal batteries and radar sites were blasted up and down the coast of northern France, and, in the last days, bridges over the Seine. At least as many raids were mounted outside the landing zone as in it. Thus was maintained the deception that the real invasion was aimed at the Pas-de-Calais, a bluff that succeeded beyond the wildest hopes of the Allies, planting a misconception in the Germans' minds that would endure for many weeks after D-Day.

In the spring and early summer of 1944, temporary airfields like Merston sprang up like mushrooms in bucolic corners of southern England. The familiar fighters of the RAF had undergone an evolution. The Spitfires of 66 Squadron could now carry 500lb bombs, to add another dimension to their capabilities. Dive-bombing had come late to the Air Force and it took some time to work out the best method of delivery. 'Paddy' French recalled how initially they would 'fly over the target at 10,000 feet and when we saw it appear behind our wing we would turn over on our backs, going into a steep dive aiming at the target'.[8] At 2,000 feet, the pilot was supposed to 'pull out of the dive and count three seconds' before releasing his bomb, yanking the stick back as the ground approached at 300mph, then swooping upwards again to avoid anti-aircraft fire. At this point, French 'always blacked out because of the G-force but the plane would keep climbing and you would come round again'. He found the technique 'rather haphazard and accuracy could not be guaranteed'. The pilots soon came up with a better method, which was both safer and much more effective: 'We would come right down low and fly the plane directly at the target, and at the last second release the bomb so that it would go straight into the target and at the same time you would lift the plane over the top. You couldn't really miss.'

More formal training was on offer to the men leading the fighter-bomber units. Six months before D-Day, Geoffrey Page, commanding 132 Squadron, was sent on a course at the Fighter Training School at Milfield in Northumberland, which had just opened to teach leaders the special skills needed for close support operations flown from front-line airfields. There was snow on the ground when he arrived which contrasted with 'the cosy warmth of the officers mess'.[9] There he met 'a milling throng of cheerful young men [who] despite their ... youth sported the ranks of squadron leaders and wing commanders combined with decorations for gallantry. Together they represented the spearhead of leadership in the air for the coming invasion ...'

After breakfast on the first day, they listened to a welcoming speech from a young air commodore who quickly got down to essentials, telling them 'for the next three weeks you will fire your guns and practise dive bombing until it is second nature. On the beaches near here are convoys of ... lorries of different shapes and sizes. There are also tanks. These you will attack with cannons and rockets followed by an inspection on foot of the damage caused ... you will learn through trial and error the best angle of attack for thin and thick-skinned vehicles. On the bombing ranges you will obtain a proficiency previously thought impossible. You will set a standard for the pilots in your squadron, a standard that you must demand that they in turn attain. You will keep up the highest traditions of the Royal Air Force.'

With the spring, the new techniques were put into practice. On D-Day minus sixty, 66 Squadron bombed a site in a wood near Abbeville. The pilots learned later that it was a launch ramp for the V-1 flying bombs which would later begin cascading on London and the South East. They went off on low-level sweeps, ranging beyond Paris, with orders to engage targets of opportunity, and escorted bombers attacking railway junctions. At the end of May, they struck at radar stations in the Pas-de-Calais, part of an ongoing effort that would end with the destruction of all six long-range scanners south of Boulogne and the reduction of four-fifths of the enemy early warning and gun laying capacity.[10]

The squadron was part of the 2nd TAF which, together with the

9th USAF Force, could muster 2,434 fighters and fighter-bombers and about 700 light and medium bombers. They were reinforced by the might of Bomber Command. For the crews, the diversion away from pulverizing German cities onto tactical targets in France was welcome, bringing relief from their grim nightly routines and generating the feeling that they were making a palpable contribution towards victory. After some initial blustering, Harris accepted the new situation with reasonable grace and would turn out to be a reliable partner to the Overlord armies.

The invasion preparations marked a new and more positive phase of Bomber Command's war. On the night of 5/6 April 144 Lancasters of 5 Group attacked and badly damaged an aircraft factory in Toulouse. The precision of the raid was in part due to the low-level marking carried out by a Mosquito flown by Leonard Cheshire, the innovative and apparently nerveless CO of 617 Squadron. For the next two months, British and American bombers hit railway targets, military bases, arms and ordnance factories, ammunition dumps, and as the date grew closer, coastal batteries and strongpoints. Despite improved accuracy, German reinforced concrete proved highly resistant to destruction and on D-Day damage to the seaward defences was less than the Army commanders had hoped. Despite the steady plastering, enough infrastructure survived to make the American landing at Omaha Beach a bloody affair.

On 5 June, the airmen learned that the prelude was over. The ground crews broke off their normal duties to paint broad black and white stripes around their Spitfires' wings. The livery would let troops on the ground – and trigger-happy gunners on ship or shore who even at this stage in the war would reflexively fire at anything that appeared overhead – know that the machine above was friend, not foe.

The stripes were an unintentional symbol of dramatically changed circumstances, the difference between night and day. The last time British troops had been in action in France was in June 1940, falling back on the beaches of Dunkirk before an unstoppable enemy under a sky that, to their eyes, the RAF appeared to have vacated. Now they were returning, and no soldier would be able to claim that the Air Force had let them down. The victory that followed was a feat of co-ordination and co-operation involving all arms, but it was only possible because of the Allies' command of the air, a fact that was now apparent to all. At last air power had been accepted, not as an adjunct to the efforts of troops on the ground or ships at sea. It was the ingredient that determined success or failure.

Next to Dwight Eisenhower in the Allied command structure stood the RAF officer who had done more than anyone else to embed this reality in British military thinking. Arthur Tedder first met Ike in North Africa late in 1942 and soon took a professional liking to him. The feeling was mutual, and in time the shared regard developed a human dimension. Tedder's outward amiability masked a temperament that was chilly, sharp and reserved. His feelings for his chief were unusually warm and he chose him as his best man when, after his first wife Rosalinde was killed in a plane crash, he married the vivacious and independent-minded Marie 'Toppy' Black. She shared his affection for the American, writing to her mother: 'I like Ike so much. He is a dear, honest-to-God straight, good man and a very great friend of ours.'[11]

They were excellent partners for a fraught task. The Allies' outward similarities masked acute differences in outlook, approach and the ultimate objectives that lay beyond immediate war aims. They were managing a team that included some monstrous egotists – led by Montgomery for the British and Patton for the Americans. Handling national and personal sensitivities required Olympian tact and iron self-control. Both men possessed them and although the ride was often rocky, their mastery of Alliance diplomacy made a crucial contribution to victory.

In January 1944 Tedder and Coningham were recalled to Britain to join Eisenhower for the countdown to D-Day. They brought with them enormous experience, the glow of victory and a shared outlook. The nature of the air war fought through North Africa, Sicily and Italy had to some extent been formed by Coningham's ideas and leadership. In February 1943, he was given command of the British and American tactical forces in Tunisia. The team carried the Allies through the expulsion of the Axis forces from Tunisia, the Sicily landings and the invasion of Italy. At every stage lessons were learned and technologies and tactics were refined that would be applied triumphantly in the next stage of the air war.

On D-Day, 171 squadrons roamed over the troops toiling ashore. The almost total lack of opposition meant they were barely needed and hopes faded for a decisive first-day battle that would wipe the Luftwaffe from the skies. When dusk fell, the bag was a paltry twelve Junkers 88s.[12] On 10 June, tactical support and air-cover units began to move across the Channel. Waiting for them at Sainte Croix-sur-Mer was an airfield, thrown together from portable components by the RAF Servicing Commandos and Airfield Construction Branch wings. By the time the Normandy campaign was finished there would be thirty-one in the British zone and fifty in the American area of operations, most of them constructed under fire.

For Britain-based ground crews who manned the invasion force bases, Normandy would bring a dramatic change to their routines. Harry Clift, an armourer with 175 Squadron, arrived by Dakota on the morning of 17 June. They touched down at airstrip B5 at Le Fresne-Camilly, north-west of Caen. Before landing they were told to unload as quickly as possible and then carry aboard a party of wounded who would be lying on stretchers by the runway. The aircraft threw up clouds of dust, alerting the German 88mm gunners who opened fire on the runway. He and his comrades scrambled out and flung themselves to the ground 'much to the amusement of the wounded'.[13] The shells landed a hundred yards away and they were assured by the veterans that they would soon get used to it. 'After that we only dropped to the ground for the close ones and ignored the others.'

In sunny weather – by no means constant in a summer of freakish cloud and rain – the thick dust, a compound of limestone and powdered dirt, was a menace. Each take-off and landing would send it swirling around the airfield forcing the armourers to swathe their heads in scarves and shield their eyes with anti-gas goggles to protect them from the blast from the propellers. It worked its way into the 20mm cannon, causing many stoppages and clogging the air intake system of the Merlin engines, so that desert filters from North Africa had to be fitted. The problem would eventually be reduced by laying bitumen-coated strips on the runways and spraying them with water at night.

Life was tough for the crews, working all the hours of daylight, subject to frequent shelling and strafing, sleeping in tents, or at least trying to against a constant background roar of aircraft and artillery. There were many compensating satisfactions. They were right on the front line and the 175 Squadron armourers 'could watch our Typhoons take off … form up over the sea, fly inland to the target, dive on to their target, release their rockets, pull out of the dive and circle the strip ready to land. It gave us the feeling that we were personally involved in the attack.'

The pilots provided a running commentary on the progress of the battle. Sometimes the ground crews made their own direct contribution. At Le Fresne-Camilly, exasperated at the attentions of the Luftwaffe who would shoot them up on their way back to their bases after attacking the beachhead, they made a gun-pit out of sand bags and installed twin Browning .303s. One day they brought down a marauding Focke-Wulf 190.

For once there was a feeling that, further up the chain, the effort was appreciated. One day they received the ultimate accolade. 'We were told to smarten up and gather at the side of the runway,' Clift recalled. 'When we arrived there we found a large crowd of all ranks who like us were wondering what it was all about.' After a while a light aircraft landed and rolled to a stop nearby. 'In the rear cockpit was Winston Churchill who stood up … and gave us a pep talk, telling us how he and everyone back home were thinking of us and how proud they all were at the way we were fighting the enemy.'

Harry Clift would go all the way to Germany but it was the first weeks that stuck most vividly in his mind. 'It was hard work, we were in danger most of the time, but we had an important job to do and we were allowed to get on with it without interference or red tape. In those early days we found a feeling of camaraderie between all ranks which was to stay with us throughout the campaign.'

Among the British pilots were many who had been fighting since the beginning of the war. They could remember the daunting odds, the scant resources, the desperation and the exhaustion of the Battle of Britain. Now there was a lavish supply of aeroplanes and pilots and the only shortage was the paucity of enemies to come up and fight. For some, Normandy was an opportunity to pay off old scores.

Geoffrey Page had baled out over the Channel in August 1940. He was badly burned when they picked him up and spent the next two years at Queen Victoria Hospital, East Grinstead, where he was one of the pioneering plastic surgeon Archibald McIndoe's 'guinea pigs', undergoing multiple operations. Sometimes the orderlies would push the patients out onto the hospital lawn, where they watched Spitfires on their way to sweeps over northern France. 'How my heart yearned to be one of them, and not just a burnt cripple,' he wrote.[14] 'I made a bitter vow to myself that, for each operation I underwent, I would destroy one enemy aircraft when I returned to flying.' He overcame many bureaucratic obstacles to get a chance to fulfil this promise and in June arrived in France at the head of 132 Squadron. Initially, he was disappointed by the Luftwaffe's absence and had to content himself shooting up targets of opportunity on the ground. Although he 'exulted in the sight of my cannon shells ripping into the lurching vehicles as they careened about the narrow Normandy lanes like stricken animals, my lust lay in the desire to destroy enemy aircraft'.

Then, one day, while on a test flight with another pilot thirty miles behind the enemy lines, he got his chance, running into a formation of thirty Me 109s near Lisieux. Despite the odds, he plunged to attack. In the dogfight that followed Page was hit by a cannon shell and wounded in the leg. The red mist cleared. He dived to tree-top level, and pulling out, looked round to see only a lone Messerschmitt was now dogging him. 'Hatred brought with it a new strength,' he wrote. His opponent pulled up the nose of his aircraft to get enough deflection on his target. The move was fatal. Already on the point of stalling when the pilot opened fire 'the recoil slowed the [aircraft] sufficiently to flick over and strike the trees twenty feet below. Circling the funeral pyre I watched the column of black smoke rising with morbid fascination.'

For Pierre Clostermann, Normandy represented a further opportunity to restore the honour of France. He was a diplomat's son with family roots in Alsace and Lorraine who was studying aeronautical engineering at California Institute of Technology at the start of the war. Before he could return home, France had fallen. He made a circuitous journey to England, and after training joined first 341

(Alsace) Squadron, before transferring to 602 Squadron, where he flew Spitfires over France. Five days after D-Day, he set foot again in his homeland. The squadron was told to overnight at the landing ground at Bazenville, just south of the British landing beaches. He and his friend Jacques Remlinger were given the honour of putting down first and dressed for the occasion in their best dark blue uniforms. The great moment was a let-down. They landed in a cloud of dust which 'penetrated everywhere, darkened the sky, suffocated us … for 500 yards round the landing strip all green had disappeared – every growing thing was covered by a thick layer, stirred by the slightest breeze'.[15] Their first night was interrupted by the drone of a twin-engine aircraft and the swish of a falling bomb. 'I dived under a lorry … the earth quivered, a burning gust of air slapped our faces and glowing splinters bespattered the tent, the trees and the lorry and bounced back sizzling on the dew-covered grass.'

Like the German army, the Luftwaffe used what resources they had to great effect. The narrow bridgehead behind the landing beaches was so choked with troops, ammunition dumps, concentrations of armour and aircraft that, as Clostermann said, 'they could scarcely fail to score a bull practically every time'. The greatest hazards faced by Allied pilots in Normandy were the expertly operated 20mm light flak guns that protected airfields and the 88mm anti-tank guns of the infantry. After the initial avoidance of air-to-air combat, the Germans did come up to fight, sometimes with devastating effect.[16]

The Luftwaffe, though, had no hope of turning the battle. Their enemy overwhelmed them in every department. The first units ashore arrived with radar systems and mobile air–ground control posts, allowing commanders to request air strikes which, most of the time, materialized.

Coningham pressed on with the methods he had developed in North Africa and Italy. The essential challenge of close air support was how to concentrate firepower on tactical targets in the shortest possible time. Coningham's solution was the 'cab rank' system. It involved placing an air controller with the advancing troops, who could call on permanent air patrols loitering on the edge of the battle zone. The aircraft would carry a list of pre-arranged objectives but could be switched immediately if required to targets of opportunity or to relieve an immediate threat.

In Normandy, the system reached its apotheosis, finally fulfilling the devastating potential of air–armour fusion glimpsed on the battlefields of the Western Front a generation earlier. On the road to Berlin, the 'brown jobs' and the Brylcreem Boys marched side by side. On the British side the new methods were incarnated in the muscular form of the Hawker Typhoon (for the Americans it would be the P-47 Thunderbolt), loved by every Allied footslogger, dreaded and hated by his German foe. The 'Tiffy' was a speedier, deadlier descendant of the Fighter Command stalwart of the Battle of Britain. Its development had been marred by technical setbacks and, initially, it earned a reputation among pilots as a killer when put into a dive. By the summer of 1944 it was the perfect machine for the campaign, capable of 400mph and packing firepower that made the eight Browning .303-calibre machine guns of the 1940 Hurricane seem like peashooters.

According to Harry Clift, a typical armament load consisted of 'four boxes of 20 mm ammunition. Each box contained a belt of 140 rounds, made up alternatively of two High Explosive and two Armour Piercing/Incendiary shells throughout the belt.' Next came 'eight rocket motors weighing 20lbs each and already fitted with fins and saddles by the armourers' assistants working at the bomb dump'. Screwed into each was a 60lb High Explosive Warhead. The rockets were mounted on rails under the wings and fired electrically. A newsreel commentary claimed one Tiffy could deliver the equivalent of a destroyer's broadside and just one missile could transform a tank into a hunk of glowing metal.[17]

The Germans received their first taste of what fighter bombers could deliver at dawn on D-Day plus one. The Panzer Lehr division was caught as it moved forward in five columns from Alençon, eighty-five miles south of the beachhead. The attacks went on all morning. Before they had even sighted the invasion forces they had lost ninety supply lorries, forty fuel trucks, eighty-four half-track fighting vehicles and several 88mm guns.

Only five days after the landings, Rommel reported to Field Marshal Keitel that 'the enemy has complete control of the air over the battle area up to a distance of about 100 kilometres behind the front [which] immobilizes almost all traffic by day on roads or in open country … in the country behind, all roads are exposed to continual air attack and it is therefore very difficult to bring up the necessary supplies of fuel and munitions …'[18] Generals were as vulnerable as everyone else. On 17 July, Rommel's staff car was caught in the open by a Spitfire of 412 Squadron, a Canadian unit. Rommel was badly wounded and invalided back to Germany, never to return to the battlefield.

The defenders were under attack on sea as well as land. The attempt by U-boats to stem the flow of men and logistics across the Channel exposed them to the attentions of Coastal Command which, in four days following D-Day, attacked twenty-five submarines, sinking six of them.

The picture on the ground was rather different. The continuing inability of the British to take Caen prompted Leigh-Mallory, eight days after the invasion, to suggest a raid by light and heavy bombers to 'unfreeze' the situation.[19] The tactical use of heavies had been tried before in February during the battle of Monte Cassino in southern Italy when American bombers dropped 1,400 tons of bombs on a hilltop monastery overlooking the Allies' route to Rome. The attack achieved little. There were no troops on hand to follow up and German paratroopers moved into the rubble to establish strong defensive positions. The proposal was rejected by Tedder, apparently on the grounds that Leigh-Mallory was trespassing on Coningham's area of responsibility. Bomber Command and the US Strategic Air Force were anyway opposed to the operation, fearing the front lines were too close and accuracy too questionable to prevent friendly casualties.

Three weeks later, with the capture of Caen no nearer, Montgomery grabbed at Leigh-Mallory's plan. On 7 July, AEAF HQ at Stanmore in Middlesex discussed a request for Bomber Command to blast a path for a renewed assault by carpet-bombing the northern approaches to Caen. Tedder, who had been leading the criticism of Monty, disliked the development, believing it could encourage continual Army requests for heavy bomber support, diverting them from more pressing duties, but did not object.

In one hour on the late evening of 7 July, 457 Bomber Command aircraft dropped 2,363 tons of bombs on northern Caen. The effect was spectacular but the results relatively insignificant. Two days of bitter fighting followed, resulting in the capture of half the city but the bombardment seems to have brought few advantages. apart from boosting morale. There was no proper co-ordination between air and ground and though the defenders were shaken up, few were killed. Showing the same fanatical determination that would mark every stage of the German retreat, they fell back to positions on the south of the city to block any further advance and the strategic position remained the same.

Despite the disappointing results, Montgomery gave a wildly optimistic account of the episode and British and American heavy bombers launched six further massive air raids before German resistance in Normandy cracked. The risk to civilians was obvious. About 3,000 French men, women and children were killed in Caen alone between 6 June and 19 July. The French historian Henri Amouroux put the civilian death toll for the campaign at more than 50,000.[20] The bombs had the same effect on French towns as they did on German ones. About 75 per cent of the fabric of Caen, ancient churches, university and all were demolished by the attacks. Nor were the liberating troops spared from the inevitable inaccuracies. The preparatory bombardment for Operation Cobra, the American attack on Saint-Lô at the end of July, killed about a hundred GIs and wounded another 500.

The effort was an attempt to break out of the cramped hedge and lane 'bocage' of the Cherbourg Pensinsula and into the easier country to the south where the US divisions could sweep west to secure the ports of Brittany and east towards Paris. The massive air assault of 25 July involving 1,500 heavy bombers dropping 3,400 tons of bombs, opened the first big cracks in the German defences.

In early August the US Third Army under Patton had secured Brittany and was ready to swing back to join the First Army, which was now moving eastwards. The end was hastened by a typical intervention from Hitler. Viewing events from his retreat at Berchtesgaden he perceived the desperate situation as 'a unique, never recurring opportunity for a complete reversal of the situation'.[21] He ordered

Panzer units in Normandy into a counter-attack to recapture the neck of the Cherbourg Peninsula and cut off American forces in Brittany. The German Seventh Army moved forward to be enveloped by the advancing Americans as British and Canadian forces moved in behind them. The trap they were caught in would become known as the Falaise Pocket.

On 13 August, Hitler finally accepted reality and gave permission for a fallback to the Seine. The Germans attempted an orderly retreat, delaying their departure. When, on the 17th, they took to the roads leading east and north-east from Falaise, they made a terrible rendezvous with the predators of the 2nd TAF. The retreat was spotted by Wing Commander Charles Green, who reported back to Harry Broadhurst, commanding 83 Group, that he was 'so low I could see not only the black crosses on the vehicles but the square heads of the drivers'. The weather prevented operations that morning but the fleeing Germans came under continuous attack. The official history recorded that 'as evening fell, pilots … were greeted with a display of white handkerchiefs and cloths waved by despairing drivers. No notice was taken of this attempt to surrender. None of our land forces was anywhere in the neighbourhood to round up the would-be prisoners, and to cease fire would merely have allowed the enemy to move unmolested to the Seine.'

The debris became a war tourist attraction in the days ahead. Airmen had the unusual experience of witnessing the effects of their efforts. Stanley de Vere set off from Falaise hoping to find an abandoned vehicle for the squadron's use. He was out of luck. The road east to Trun, he recorded in his diary, was 'littered with wrecks, nearly all burnt out and some not recognisable as vehicles at all'.[22] Beyond Trun, he saw mounds of dead horses, pressed into service as artillery transport when petrol ran out, and 'the bodies of Germans began to make an appearance … the sight and smell of these dead Germans didn't worry me much more than if they were horses really'. In a village he came across a 'jerry tank' with 'a body lying over the top of the track, its head and arms hanging down and altogether looking a horrible sight with eyes and mouth gaping and skin quite black …'

Many vehicles had taken to side roads and farm tracks in a futile attempt to avoid their fate. A witness who was forced to detour because the main road was impassable found 'cars of every description, many of them Citroens, Renaults and other French makes, strewed the fields, mingled with horses dead in the shafts of stolen carts and even old-fashioned traps of two generations ago'.[23] He noticed 'one up to date limousine, painted with the stippled green and brown camouflage affected by the Germans. It contained on the back seat a colonel and his smartly-dressed mistress. Each had been shot through the chest with cannon shells …' Further on in a leafy lane was a mile-long traffic jam from which all life was extinct. At its head and tail were a smashed-up armoured car. Every vehicle had been hit by rockets. 'Grey-clad, dust-powdered bodies were sprawled everywhere, propped against trees, flopped over driving seats or running boards …' Pilots flying over the scene the following day reported that even at 15,000 feet the stench of death reached their nostrils.

The carnage in the lane bore the hallmarks of a classic Typhoon attack in which the lead and rear vehicles were rocketed first to immobilize the column which could then be annihilated systematically. There was no escape. Harry Clift recorded that at this phase of the fighting the Typhoon's payload was arranged so that half the rockets were an antipersonnel type 'to explode at ground level and deal with the crew'.[24] If any survivors 'tried to escape by running through the cornfields, they left a trail which could easily be seen from the air. Then they were strafed with cannon fire.'

The fugitives were harried every yard of the way. Sweeping over the small bands of escapees, Geoffrey Page found his anger turning to pity. At first he revelled in the pursuit. When he came across a group of 'arrogant German soldiers, sitting outside on [a] farmhouse steps playing cards' he 'stopped their game with a few hundred rounds of bullets and their arrogance disappeared rapidly'.[25] Then he 'met a man who will haunt me to my dying day'. He calculated that by now he had 'probably killed several hundred people but from the air it was completely impersonal, and made no mental impact'.

When out on a hunt for German aircraft, he saw a small cloud of dust rising, revealing a motorbike and rider. He went down to investigate and saw the bike was camouflaged and the rider wore uniform;

a legitimate military target. 'As I placed the orange reflected dot of my gunsight on the centre of his body, he looked straight up at me, and I knew that the moment of truth had arrived,' he wrote.[26] 'As I stabbed the gun button he threw up his left arm as if to shield his face from the impact. I cursed him … for making such a simple, pathetic human gesture, and loathed myself as I saw man and bike disappear in a torrent of bullets. I returned to base, and found it difficult to talk to anyone for several days. I can still see his face and the raised arm.'

The 2nd TAF averaged 1,200 sorties a day for ten days, turning defeat into headlong retreat. On 25 August, the German garrison in Paris surrendered. The pent-up force of the Allied advance broke free, falling on the backs of the retreating Germans. The pursuers could barely keep up with them. On 3 September, the fifth anniversary of the outbreak of war, Stanley de Vere had gone down with food poisoning. The rest of the squadron were sent off that morning and he wandered down to the flight office to find how they were faring, to hear that they were 'coming back again without having operated'. The reason for their return, he wrote in his diary, 'was that the bomb line had suddenly been moved forward and our boys would have possibly been strafing our forward troops, thinking them to be Huns!'[27]

15

The Hyacinths of Spring

For the Tactical Air Force squadrons keeping step with the advance across Europe, there was plenty of work, bombing and strafing, but ample time off to enjoy the pleasures and privileges accorded to the liberators. Everywhere, they were swamped with gratitude. Paddy French was in a small party sent on a recce to Lille to see if the airfield was fit for occupation by 66 Squadron. It was. Having sent a message to HQ, they 'decided we would smarten up and go into the town'.[1] As they got ready they 'heard sounds outside and found it was the local people starting to gather. There was much hand shaking and shouts of "Vive la France" and "Vive l'Angleterre." We eventually got away and drove into town where we were mobbed. We were eventually rescued by the police ...'

John Rolfe of the RAF Regiment wrote to his friend Joan Durnford in Cheshire, describing the reception given to his armoured car unit when it arrived in Ghent early in November with 'people standing at their doors and cheering, waving and blowing kisses – all very embarrassing'. Later he found the 'poor devils ... are pathetically anxious to make friends and practically fight each other to give you things they are so grateful ...'[2]

The gratitude could become oppressive. Stanley de Vere's Kiwi amiability was tested by a young Frenchman from Lille who took to dropping in on the squadron. 'He has been coming to our quarters to speak to us [bringing] cakes, fruit and tomatoes etc.,' he confided to his diary on 4 October. 'Really very kind of him ... but the trouble is he seems to come almost every day and stays a long time talking incessantly ... we haven't had the heart to tell him to scram.'[3]

These gifts involved sacrifice. Rolfe reported that the Belgians were 'very short of food – pitifully so … coal is terribly short'. It was 'literally true that a tablet of soap, a bar of chocolate or even twenty cigarettes will get you *anything*'. Yet for all the privations, 'the people will never ask you for anything for services rendered, they just want to be friends'.

De Vere and his comrades were probably too modest to see what heroic figures they cut in the eyes of their Belgian admirer. They were young men like himself, who instead of having to endure the suffering and humiliation of defeat and occupation, were saviours, whose skill, courage and sacrifice had lifted the terrible yoke. The ravages of life under the Germans were all too apparent. Paddy French noticed what looked like a graveyard next to the Lille airfield and a few days later saw people digging there. A man spotted him and came over and told him that the plots contained the bodies of

Brussels breathes again

about eighty men, women and children, hostages murdered by the Germans a few months before. He took him over to one pit and 'apart from the smell it was a horrible sight. The bodies of four men with their hands tied behind their backs.'

The German appetite for destruction seemed insatiable. In Ghent, Rolfe reported, 'the sanitary arrangements leave much to be desired … from what I have learned Jerry connected up the town's main water supply with the sewerage system and then blew the lot sky high. A typical piece of German beastliness.'

The pilots took the opportunity to explore their new surroundings during their frequent downtime before wining and dining at night. A sense that things were settling down was reinforced by the arrival of an inexorable visitor. When 66 Squadron moved to Grimbergen, near Brussels, base personnel were told to stand by to welcome Lord Trenchard. It can only be wondered what, if anything, his presence meant to the young men, many of them Norwegian aircrew. He seemed an 'old man' in the eyes of Paddy French, who Trenchard buttonholed for a few minutes, apparently relieved at finding a native English speaker among the throng of foreigners in Air Force Blue.

The semi-domesticity of life could foster a false sense of security. The Germans were still capable of biting back. On 3 November, with the squadron now based near Brussels, de Vere was tasked with a bombing and strafing attack on Klundert in southern Holland where a German rearguard was holding up the advance. 'We saw lots of planes over the town having their whack and then we started on ours,' he wrote in his diary that night in an entry that reveals the extraordinary proximity that 'close air support' could involve.[4]

'The flak was pretty intense and rather accurate – more than we had expected. I saw streams of it following close behind me several times. Noticed a large vehicle parked in the centre of town, so went down on it using guns and let my bomb go close by, hoping to damage some buildings where the Hun might be. Decided to give the vehicle another dose so came round again and squirted more stuff into it and the street and buildings round about. By the time I was at the bottom of the "pull-out" I was a bit lower than a church steeple and passed close to it. Was thinking what a good thing it was

I didn't fly into it when there was a hell of a thumping bang and my eyes were full of glass splinters. A 20 or 30 mm shell had struck the windscreen and shattered it leaving a hole about 6 inches in diameter ... after a few seconds of furious blinking I found I could see OK out of my right eye and fairly well out of the left, but both felt crammed full of this fine glass ...' He had a painful journey back to base reflecting 'on how lucky I had just been. A 100th of a second later and the shell would simply have wiped my head off.'

The scale of the task still lying ahead became clear at the end of September at Arnhem. The Allied advance slowed drastically as supply lines lengthened and logistical difficulties multiplied. Resupply was made more difficult by the German strategy of leaving garrisons behind in the French Channel ports with orders to fight to the death. On 4 September, the British Second Army (with assistance from the local resistance) took Antwerp intact, but the Scheldt Estuary on which it lay remained in German hands so that the port facilities could not be exploited.

Eisenhower was determined to maintain the Allied advance on a broad front and urged Montgomery to break through to Antwerp. Monty had his own ideas. He proposed instead 'one really powerful and full-blooded thrust towards Berlin ...' commanded, naturally, by himself.[5] It aimed to propel a large force across the waterways guarding the northern frontiers of Germany, thereby circumventing the man-made defences of the Siegfried Line and catching the German army in a pincer movement. The crucial element was surprise, which was to be achieved by the landing of a huge airborne force to seize bridges over the rivers Maas, two branches of the Rhine and several canals and tributaries. This was Operation Market. In Operation Garden, armoured forces would then drive north from Belgium to link up and pour across the captured bridges into Germany to take the Ruhr region whose industries kept the German war effort alive. Largely in the interests of maintaining Allied harmony, Eisenhower agreed.

Operation Market was the greatest air assault attempted to date. Taking part would be 34,600 men of the American 101st and 82nd Airborne Divisions, the British 1st Airborne Division and the Polish Brigade.[6] About 20,000 would jump into their landing zones. The rest would be towed there in gliders. A force of 1,438 Dakotas and 321 converted bombers, plus more than 3,000 gliders, was available. The swift adoption of Montgomery's plan meant preparations were rushed. It was originally sanctioned on 10 September for execution on the 14th but on the 12th it was postponed until the 17th.[7] Thus, the detailed planning took a week compared to the months dedicated to preparing the airborne operations in Sicily and Normandy. The element of shock was diminished by the fact that there were still not enough resources to get all the troops on the ground on the first day, forcing a phased delivery.

The opening moves of Market went well. The great majority of the troops reached their drop zones without meeting significant flak or fighters, and arrived where they were supposed to. The 1st Airborne Division's objective was the road bridge over the Nederrijn (Nether Rhine) in the Dutch city of Arnhem, but the landing zone chosen required a significant march to secure it. The progress of the troops alerted the defenders and by the time they reached the bridge they did not have the numbers to capture it. The heroic debacle that ensued dispelled hope that the war might be over by Christmas.

The operation was described in enthralling detail by Sergeant Arthur Rigby, a member of the Glider Pilot Regiment. Its members were trained by the RAF but controlled by the Army and fought alongside the men they transported. Rigby was disappointed to miss out on the D-Day glider operation and had spent a frustrating summer in England. His account, written while fresh in his mind a few weeks after his capture, records that a number of airborne ops were scheduled and then abruptly cancelled during the period, for 'each time … there was no time to mount it before the ground troops had overrun the ground, so rapid was the advance'.[8] His testimony reveals a high degree of training and competence on the part of the aircrews that absolves them from any blame for the catastrophe.

Rigby remembered a stir at the end of August at his base at Brize Norton, 'suggesting something was afoot'. It was confirmed around 10 September when the group was ordered to move to Manston on the North Foreland in Kent, in order to put their upcoming objective within range of their Albemarle tug aircraft. There they stayed

for a week before the target was revealed. They would be transport-
ing the men of the 1st Airborne Division to a Landing Zone (LZ)
near Arnhem then joining the operation to capture and hold the
bridge until relieved. On the morning of Sunday 17 September, as
the sun burned off the mist and with 'everyone in high spirits', they
got ready for take-off. Rigby and his co-pilot, Sergeant Ted Healey,
were at the controls of their usual glider, an Airspeed Horsa, sixty-
seven feet long with an eighty-eight-foot wingspan, which they
nicknamed 'Droopy'. They were carrying a six-pounder anti-tank
gun and three-man crew plus a jeep to tow it, as well as their own
Bren gun, rifle and ammunition.

Marshals orchestrated the complex take-off schedule and at 10.40
a.m. it was their turn. The tug took up the slack on the tow rope and
'the glider started to roll gently forward and to rapidly gain momen-
tum. 20 … 40 … 60 … 80 … 85 … 90! Ease back on the column
and the old Droop came off the deck as smoothly as she always did
and we rose to about fifty feet and settled down at that height until
the tug got airborne, and as she did just that, so we started gently to
climb ahead of her rise, all very smoothly and gracefully.' From the
cockpit, the sky seemed 'literally full of aircraft … Dakotas, Stirlings,
Albemarles, Horsa and Hamilcar gliders, and here and there
Typhoon and Thunderbolt fighters sliding around like black and
white minnows in a pool of pike'. He was a little nervous crossing
the coast but it was only when they passed Nijmegen on their right
that they saw the first puffs of flak, far away and ineffectual.

Rigby handed the controls to Ted Healey to take charge of the
landing while he cast off the tow rope. Then 'we were in free flight
and heading towards the Landing Zone. Everything was quiet …
other than the rushing sound of the wind as we swept on, no
gunfire, nothing.'

They landed at 1.20 p.m. in what looked like a potato field in a
cloud of dust that left them coughing and spluttering. The back of
the Horsa unbolted. The jeep rolled off, they hitched up the gun
and took their place in the column in the road next to the LZ. A
Hamilcar came in too fast and flipped over, killing everyone on
board. It was a routine tragedy and did little to spoil the feeling that
everything was going well. A little way away, 'parachute troops were

floating down … the sky was full of them'. Apart from the aircraft engines 'there was not a sound, no gunfire … it was as if we had landed in Holland completely unnoticed'.

It was three hours before the force was assembled and ready to move off. Half of the troops were to stay behind together with the Divisional HQ to secure the landing zones and drop zones [DZs] for the second lift due the following day. That meant there were only about 700 men to tackle the objective. The LZs and DZs were seven and in some cases eight miles from Arnhem, well beyond the range of the HQ radios, which, it turned out, were tuned to the wrong frequencies.

Eventually, the column set off, taking a road close to the Rhine which led through the district of Oosterbeek. The weather seemed propitious. It was a 'perfect Sunday afternoon, sunny and warm and very suburbanly quiet. We passed some houses on the way and there were men digging their gardens and mowing their lawns just as though it was quite usual to have an entire airborne division drop in …'

Then people emerged from their houses and 'it was like a royal progress; men, women and children were standing along the pavements and in their front gardens, throwing posies of marigolds to us, giving us apples and bottles of wine, shouting "Welcome! Welcome! Four years we have waited," shaking our hands. Little boys ran along with us, their faces shining.'

Oosterbeek was a few kilometres west of Arnhem. It stood on high ground at the edge of fields that sloped away to the Rhine a mile or two away. A steel cantilevered railway bridge ran across it. They paused while a party of Royal Engineers set off to deal with any demolition charges. They had only gone a very short time when the crackle of rifle and machine guns drifted across the fields. Then there was 'a tremendous roar of explosives and the railway bridge began to collapse in a pall of dust and smoke'.

There followed what seemed to Arthur 'quite a dangerous delay. Quite obviously, the officers in the column were taken by surprise by the sudden appearance of enemy resistance after the quiet start of the operation and it was some time before there was any forward movement.'

After a skirmish on route they arrived at dusk to find Arnhem 'a ghost town'. As they approached the north end of the bridge, the shooting started, with 'terrific crashes and bangs and enormous explosions'. Arthur and Ted helped the gun party manhandle the six-pounder into position. Arthur acted as loader and they opened fire. Their target was 'a concrete pillbox about half-way up the approach ramp to the bridge, from which quite a lot of opposition was emanating and we had to either knock it out or quieten the occupants down while a flame thrower party could get in close enough to deal with it. We pumped three shells into it and the firing died down ... we were told to hold our fire and quite suddenly there was an enormous burst of flame and black smoke around the strong point, followed by the most terrifying screaming ...'

The clean streets, tidy houses and neatly trimmed gardens of Arnhem became an intimate battleground. Arthur and his fellow glider pilots dodged from house to house, beating back infantry attacks, while each one was gradually demolished around them by tank and artillery fire. It is only on Tuesday 19 September – the third day of the operation – that that there is any mention of aircraft in his account, and the aeroplanes that appeared were German. He recorded that before noon 'the Luftwaffe had a go at us. A gaggle of Messerschmitts came over low over the houses with the cannon and machine guns blazing away, going like the clappers.' One clipped the cathedral spire and crashed, and 'they didn't try anymore straf-ing after that'. It was not necessary. On Wednesday, as ammunition and all forms of supplies dwindled, casualties mounted, and hopes of the long-promised relief faded, group by group, the gallant band surrendered. The old Army cry, heard at Dunkirk of 'where are the RAF?' does not appear in Arthur Rigby's story. No one could blame him for uttering it.

The Allied air forces' performance would attract much of the blame for the failure of Market Garden. The first, veiled, criticism was voiced three months after the debacle and it came from a very authoritative, if not disinterested, source. In his after-action report of 10 January 1945, the commanding officer of the 1st Airborne Division, Major General Roy Urquhart, chose his words cautiously but their meaning was clear. 'An Airborne Division is designed to fight as a whole,' he wrote.[9] 'If the Division is split and committed to a 2nd lift some 24 hrs later then, owing to the necessity of allotting part of the first lift to protect the DZs and LZs of the following troops, the effective strength for immediate offensive action of the Div is reduced to that of a B[rigade].'

So, the operation had been weakened from the beginning by the failure to deliver all the airborne attackers in one go. It was further undermined by the choice of landing sites, chosen, it appeared, because of appreciations of the strength of anti-aircraft artillery around the target which were 'very pessimistic' as it turned out. 'When the balance sheet of casualties at Arnhem is made,' he ventured, 'it would appear a reasonable risk to have landed the Div much closer to the objective chosen, even in the face of some enemy flak. It has always been the rule when planning that the maximum distance from the LZ or DZ to the objective should not exceed 5 miles. In the ARNHEM operation the distance was 7 miles and in some cases 8 miles. An extra two minutes flying time in the face of flak, if not too severe, would have put the Div – always supposing that the ground was suitable – much nearer its objective. Initial surprise … was obtained, but the effect … was lost owing to the time lag of 4hrs before the troops could arrive at the objective.'

Finally, there was the absence of the fighter-bombers which in the campaign so far had been the Army's constant companions. 'Close air support during the first afternoon … would have been invaluable,' Urquhart wrote. 'If there had been a "cab rank" available, the effect on the enemy would have been considerable. Close air support during the period when the troops were in movement might easily have turned the scale and allowed the whole of 1 Para B[rigade] to have concentrated near the main ARNHEM bridge.'

Successive historians, including loyal friends of the RAF, have largely agreed with the soldier's view. Recently, a strong defence of the Air Force planning and performance by Sebastian Ritchie of the RAF Air Historical Branch makes the case convincingly that culpability for the failure cannot be as neatly assigned as the Airborne version claims and that 'the Allied air forces were not primarily responsible for Market Garden's failure'.[10]

The multitude of what-ifs inherent in Market Garden seem likely to ensure that it will be endlessly and inconclusively debated. The fact was that the Allies did not cross the Rhine until March. In the interim the Germans gathered enough strength to mount a last fightback, on the ground and in the air. On 16 December 1944, the commander-in-chief in the West, Gerd von Rundstedt, launched the fiercest counter-attack since the landings. The thrust through the Ardennes was soon beaten back, with the Allied tactical air forces as well as British and American heavy bombers helping to stop the advance in its tracks by Boxing Day. The Luftwaffe, or what remained of it, played a minor part in the operation. On 1 January, they put in a dramatic appearance.

'Started 1945 in fine fashion,' wrote Stanley de Vere in his diary.[11] He woke up in Brussels having celebrated the New Year with appropriate enthusiasm and after breakfast 'heard the sound of aeroplanes … and a burst of cannon fire … rushed downstairs and out into the street. There, scarcely able to believe my eyes, I saw a number of FW 190s and Me 109s circling low over the city. From the direction of Evere aerodrome came dense clouds of black smoke … after waiting for a few minutes I expected to see swarms of Spitfires etc. nipping in to put a finish to the Huns but I think I saw only one … very little AA could be heard and the cheeky buggers continued milling [around] over the centre of Brussels for about twenty minutes.'

The feeble anti-aircraft fire was evidence of the Allies' low estimate of the threat the Luftwaffe now posed. Before the end of September, 2nd TAF's commander Arthur Coningham had ordered heavy guns to be withdrawn from the airfields and camouflage netting to be sent back to the base depots.[12] His force was now concentrated in a relatively small number of congested bases in Belgium and Holland, presenting an attractive and vulnerable target if the resources could be found to mount an effective assault.

The Luftwaffe took their chance. Planning for Operation Bodenplatte, as it was code-named, began at the start of December. An ill-assorted force of a wide array of types – about 800 aircraft in all – was scraped together, piloted by every man available, from experienced instructor to raw novice. The attacks and air combats that day destroyed about 300 Allied aircraft, as well as killing men on the ground, forty in the British area alone. The operation proved to be a minor setback for the Allies. For the Luftwaffe, it was all but fatal. More than 140 airmen were killed and seventy were captured. The Allied losses were soon made up. The German aircraft and personnel were by now irreplaceable. The Luftwaffe could no longer mount an effective defence of German airspace or interfere significantly when the Rhine was crossed at last. The roof of the Reich had fallen in.

The bombardment of German cities had resumed long before. In mid-September, Arthur Harris was formally released from the clutches of Supreme Headquarters Allied Expeditionary Force in Europe and the heavy bomber squadrons returned to Air Ministry control. Things would not be quite as before. All future operations were required to fit into Eisenhower's overall plans, and heavy bombers provided to support the troops when required. This still left enormous spare capacity. The number of front-line aircraft increased by half in 1944. A single group could now drop as much tonnage as the whole of Bomber Command managed two years earlier.

What to do with all these bombs? Harris was determined to persist with area attacks. But there were now powerful voices with a claim on his squadrons and his formula for success was under challenge. The intention at the top was that Bomber Command should continue focusing on specific targets, in particular synthetic oil production and the Reich's transportation system. Portal and the Air Ministry favoured an emphasis on the former, Tedder and the senior Allied commanders on the ground in Europe, the latter. At the end of September, a directive issued to Bomber Command and the American Eighth Air Force gave priority to oil, with rail and waterway networks and tank and vehicle factories joint second. Harris fell reluctantly into line and railway junctions, canals and synthetic oil plants like the Leuna and Braunkohle refineries joined the target lists alongside the old favourites. Nonetheless, his generous interpretation of the scope of the new orders meant that area attacks would continue until the end.

Almost half the tonnage of bombs dropped by Bomber Command in between 1939 and 1945 was delivered in the last nine months of the war. The opposition was lighter now with the German night-fighter force in decline, and increased accuracy and refined marking meant destruction was maximized.

The defenders could still draw blood. In January 1945, the command lost 179 aircraft in operations against Germany. But the swish of the reaper's scythe was heard less frequently now and the business no longer felt so much like dicing with death.

The vulnerability of German cities was horrifyingly demonstrated on the night of 13/14 February 1945. Dresden has become a symbol of the moral dubiety of the Strategic Air Campaign. In fact, the attack was not intended as an exercise in area bombing. It was an Army support operation, aimed at easing the Soviet advance, and Harris was simply following instructions. Much of the testimony of those who took part conveys a sense that this was just another op, memorable because of the spectacular results and the subsequent furore.

However, there were some who felt unease as Bomber Command turned its attention to places that had until now not been touched. Kelso Robinson, an Australian wireless operator with 550 Squadron, was part of a force tasked to attack railway yards in Hildesheim, in Lower Saxony, on 22 March. No trouble from fighters was expected and they set off in daylight. Robinson felt 'stronger than usual twinges of doubt about the morality of our actions as I saw the town spread out in clear view beneath, a small, clean looking city, apparently undamaged by any previous bombing. Surrounded by fields, it could have been England …'[13]

But then came a reminder that the war was not yet over. Somehow, their Lancaster got detached from the bomber stream and ended up near the flak defences of Cologne which 'soon had us in their sights … ominous black puffs of exploding shells began to appear around us as the Germans improved their aim and soon the sound of shrapnel … like a heavy hailstorm could be heard spattering against the fuselage. Ahead of us, getting slowly closer, was the Rhine, the other side of which lay safety. Our engines were at full power and we were weaving violently to present as difficult a target as possible, but of course there is little sense of speed when travelling at high altitude … and we seemed to be hanging still in the air, a sitting target.'

He recalled 'having a peculiar detached feeling, not really fear, more a sense of regret that my life was to finish now, with so much unexperienced and unaccomplished. I expected to die, but mercifully did not think of what that might mean, the pain and the terror, perhaps burning alive ... I even had a thought for the German gunners, no doubt young men not unlike ourselves, willingly or unwillingly doing their military duty. What a thrill they would get if they were able to send us crashing to the ground in flames.'

The ordeal went on for ten minutes before they crossed the Rhine. They counted more than a hundred holes in the fuselage and tailplane. Their luck had held. Otherwise they might have joined the other eight Lancasters from the squadron lost on operations that month.

Robinson's qualms about Hildesheim were justified. What was meant to be a precise operation turned out to be 'virtually an area attack'.[14] The bombing survey carried out by the RAF after the war reported 70 per cent of the town destroyed, and local records show 1,645 were killed. It was in keeping with the apocalyptic destruction that airmen were now beginning to see close up as the front line moved across Germany.

'During my travels I passed through a number of towns which have featured largely in the news,' wrote John Rolfe of the RAF Regiment to Joan Durnford at the end of April.[15] 'The devastation is terrible. I have seen *nothing* in England to compare with them, not even in the most badly blitzed towns. It really is a terrible sight, Joan, to see a town the size of Sheffield *completely* wiped out, not one house left standing or habitable. Nothing to be seen but piles of rubble and still smoking ruins. The dust and the smells were awful of course ...'

Armourer Harry Clift was sent with his squadron to Schleswig in May. On the journey, they breasted a hill 'and there in the valley below lay the city of Hamburg. We were used to seeing the destruction of towns caused by bombing raids but had never seen anything like this. As we drove through the city all the buildings for mile after mile had been reduced to rubble about one storey high. The smell of dead bodies still buried in the rubble was quite sickening.'[16]

When Rolfe saw civilians moving through the ruins, queuing up for food and water, he was 'inclined to feel pity ... but I realised that if Jerry had had his way the same scene would have been taking place in England'. Clift had recently encountered a Nazi breeding centre where Aryan women from occupied countries were put to mate with German servicemen, and witnessed the skeletal, pyjama-clad survivors of Belsen. Rolfe had seen photographs of German atrocities committed in France which provoked him to exclaim in one of his letters: 'You could not credit that such deeds could be perpetrated by anyone with the vestige of a soul.'

He was educated, thoughtful, a liberal in politics, yet, viewing the destruction, he had to 'confess to a feeling of savage pleasure at seeing the way the war has recoiled on the German heads'. The belief that this was just retribution is mixed with mystification at the psychological forces that led the Germans to this pass. 'I should like to get behind the German mind and find out what they really think of their Führer and their responsibility for the war,' he wrote to Joan on 24 April 1945. 'If ever we wanted to show the German people as a whole what warfare on their own territory is like then what is happening now will fulfil that want and amply repay them for years of aggression upon other countries. They are getting it back with bags of interest and I rejoice in it. I am glad that the war did not end before we entered Germany.'

There was little chance to ask the defeated directly. Crossing into the occupied zones servicemen were met with large signs warning them against fraternizing with the enemy, though inevitably this was ignored by the adventurous.

Rolfe's first impression was of a people habituated to fear from whichever source it emanated. 'In some places they were disposed to be friendly,' he wrote. More often they were 'scared stiff and hopped out of the way whenever possible … in one place where we stopped for two days I was told by the Bürgermeister that the people … were convinced that our purpose was to burn the place down and line [them] up and shoot them.' His initial feeling was that Germany could never recover. The dead towns 'can be completely written off. I can't see that they will ever rise again.' The quiet acceptance in defeat, and the way they were prepared to carry out the orders of their new masters with the same meek efficiency as they had the old seemed contemptible at first. But at the end of July, he wrote admiringly that 'the German capacity for work is phenomenal. They have repaired more damage in Bonn in one month than the French have tackled in a year. What a marvellous thing it would be if this could be turned to work for good instead of aggression …'

The amount of time devoted to thinking about the future had naturally increased as the end approached. In the course of the war, reflection waxed and waned according to circumstances. In the early days, there are few mentions in the diaries and letters of airmen and women of what it is they are fighting for, apart from survival, the defence of the values of decency and the defeat of an enemy with whom there could be no accommodation. It was this message that Chamberlain had first delivered in his 3 September speech, when he defined the 'evil things' they would be fighting against, and which Churchill had brilliantly developed.

The bigger question, of what they were fighting *for*, did not take long to appear on the public agenda. It was put there by *Picture Post* in its 'Plan for Britain' issue, published in January 1941 which called for a minimum wage, national health service, children's allowances and other reforms which would be formulated officially in the Beveridge Report of November 1942.

Mass Observation tried from time to time to gauge the political mood of the services, by gathering personal reports and commissioning surveys. The results are inevitably patchy and unscientific but nonetheless revealing. In August 1941 John Sommerfeld wrote from his RAF camp to Tom Harrisson of MO, regretting that only 'about one in fifty see a daily paper … talk about the political aspect of the war is rare and ill-informed'.[17] In July 1944 a campaign began to get servicemen to register as voters, and a brown buff form, No. 2040, was sent to all RAF stations near and far. MO attempted a survey on the registration process across the forces and the results showed a wildly varied picture. In one Army unit with a 'high standard of efficiency', the MO correspondent reported that of the sixty-eight men in his unit only six bothered to fill in the form.[18]

The RAF take-up rates recorded were much higher. In one unit 85 per cent registered, in another 92–95 per cent. This seems to have less to do with the political enthusiasm of the airmen than a policy of encouragement decided on at a reasonably high level. One MO reporter described an officer delivering 'a brief but convincing talk of the desirability of registering … everything was done to encourage personnel to realise the importance both to themselves and the nation in general'.

A leading aircraftman was quoted as claiming he had 'never previously encountered a body of men so "Left-Wing" as the RAF. I reckon they must be ninety-per cent Left, from officers downwards.' However, the attitude he goes on to describe sounds more cynical than ideological: 'One view I heard recently, "only hypocrites and humbugs stood for parliament so it doesn't matter who we vote for."' It was echoed emphatically by an anonymous WAAF who declared: 'They're all a bleeding lot of swindlers, out for themselves – one's no better than the rest, Conservative or Labour, it's me first every time.'

Behind this general disillusionment lay a vague but powerful feeling that after the war things would have to be different. It is evident in the evening chat of the Far Eastern ground crews counting the days until they can go home, recorded in John Sommerfield's short stories. In 'Worm's Eye View' the narrator and his friend Tommy are chatting on their bunks about post-Demob life. He warns that they may be going back to 'the same sort of job again that we'd had before the war, only for less pay maybe and provided that we're lucky enough to get jobs at all'.[19]

> 'There'll have to be a big change in the way things are done,' Tommy interrupted. 'Everybody feels there's *got* to be a big change.'
>
> How often had I heard that said lately, more and more frequently as time went on …
>
> 'Yes,' I replied. 'A change is needed and there'll be one all right. But whether it's for the better or worse depends on us, – on us alone.'

The narrator goes outside and stands 'watching the squadron taking off in the brilliant moonlight and drone away into the distance … though I was very tired I was unwilling to go back to the tent's narrow stuffiness'. Instead he lit a pipe and lay down on the warm sand. 'The past was dead, the future would be as we made it. I rolled over on my stomach and began to write:

> Winter is the time of war
> But a spring comes with hyacinths
> Whose blossoms are the banners of peace
> Foretelling rich harvests of freedom
> For the towns and seasons of our future ...

In Europe, the future finally dawned at 2.41 on the morning of 7 May when at Supreme Headquarters Allied Expeditionary Force headquarters in Reims, General Alfred Jodl signed the unconditional surrender documents for all the German armed forces. The joy that erupted took many forms. On VE Day WAAF cook Gladys Partlett left Tarrant Rushton to visit a friend in nearby Wimborne Minster. They pushed a piano into the street and a party began 'in which the whole town seemed to be joining in'.[20] She was on duty to prepare breakfast the following morning. It was impossible to get back to the base that night but she hitched a lift in the morning 'only to find that everyone was drunk. The mess was a mess ... aircrew were riding motorcycles through the dining room and the duckpond was full of furniture and drunken officers.'

At Hustedt-Schwerin airfield near Celle, Harry Clift and his comrades started the day with a game of football with the officers, and spent the afternoon drinking hock out of pint mugs. As darkness fell they 'had a huge bonfire and used signal cartridges as fireworks. Someone towed an Me 109 on the bonfire but in their merry state forgot to remove the ammunition.' As the tracer zipped harmlessly into the darkness he looked back to see 'a wonderful sight after so many years of blackout ... the lights from the buildings and the tents shining out over the aerodrome'.[21]

Epilogue

Brothers and Sisters

On the damp Saturday afternoon of 8 June 1946, the crowds packing the Mall in London for the first anniversary of Victory in Europe celebrations looked up as the air filled with the rumble of aero-engines sounding from the east. Out of the dishcloth-grey clouds a small shape appeared over Admiralty Arch and flashed past to disappear into the murk above Buckingham Palace. The blunt outlines of a Hurricane were instantly recognizable, an enduring symbol of the guts and skill that had won the Battle of Britain.

It was followed by a stream of 306 aeroplanes large and small, each type reflecting an aspect of the air war. There were Sunderlands from Coastal Command, twelve Lancasters from 35 Squadron of Bomber Command and Spitfires, then Mosquitoes and Beaufighters, the jacks-of-all-trades of the Air Force, Fireflies and Seafires of the Fleet Air Arm. After twenty minutes, the propeller throb was drowned out by the roar of jet engines. The crowds barely had time to register the sleek forms of the new Meteors and Vampires of Fighter Command before they had vanished.

Less than a year after the end of the war, the aircraft that had won it already belonged to a rapidly receding past. The commanding place of air power and the Royal Air Force in the story, though, was already assured. The squadrons had been in action every day of the conflict, often in conjunction with the Army and Navy but much of the time on their own. Victory was the work of many – soldier, sailor, airman and civilian – but, though they did not make the claim themselves, the Air Force can fairly be said to have made the most significant contribution. It was Fighter Command which, in the summer of 1940, kept Britain in the war, creating the essential

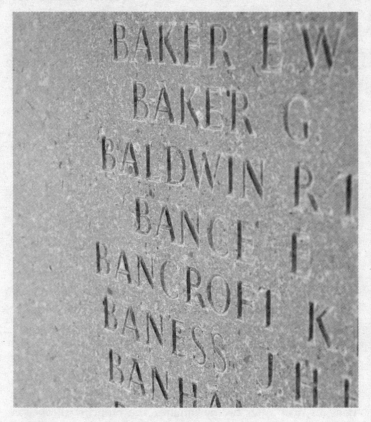

The Many – some of the more than 20,000 dead airmen with no known grave commemorated at Runnymede

conditions for a landing in north-west Europe and the ultimate defeat of Germany. It was Bomber Command that had led the fight back, taking the war to Germany by the only means available and slowly dismantling its ability to make war. If not for Coastal Command, the struggle to keep the sea lanes open would have been lost and Britain starved into submission. Without the efforts of all arms of the Air Force and the alliance with the USAAF, the invasion of Normandy might have been much bloodier and the march to Berlin a great deal longer. During the conflict, air power had become inextricably fused with action on land and sea and superiority over the enemy in the air accepted as the essential prerequisite for success.

In the course of the war the RAF had grown gigantically. In May 1945, it numbered 1,079,835 men and women, compared with the 173,958 it had started out with, and 9,200 aircraft compared with a front-line strength of 1,911 at the beginning.[1] A tight, white, socially restricted elite had burgeoned into a heterodox host of nationalities, races drawn from every milieu.

The force had expanded to fill the ravenous demands of the war and when it ended much of the organization became redundant. At the same time the factors that had shaped its evolution altered dramatically. The last act of the conflict seemed to spell the end of the era of total warfare and the opening of a new age that required a new air force. On 6 August, the first atomic bomb burst over Hiroshima followed three days later by one on Nagasaki, ending the war with Japan. With the coming of the Cold War, Britain and America would henceforth base their national security on a policy of deterrence with fleets of long-range nuclear bombers at its heart.

The process of dismantling a vast force took time. For most airmen, demobilization could not come fast enough. As Bomber Boy Eric Banks observed, 'whatever [their] RAF experiences, they remained civilians at heart'.[2] Respect for the force, pride in its achievements and gratitude for the friendships forged along the way notwithstanding, they still 'had no interest whatsoever in the peacetime pursuits of the service'.

The slow rate of demobilization was resented, particularly overseas where many had served for years without seeing home or loved ones. In January 1946, a wave of strikes rippled across bases in India, and the Far East. Hundreds of ground staff downed tools in protest at the slow rate of repatriation. The 'factory spirit' feared by Ludlow-Hewitt in his reports on discipline as Inspector General lay dormant in the wartime service. With the overwhelming Labour victory in the 1945 General Election – a result which the Forces vote had done much to bring about – the trade union ethos was everywhere in the ascendant.

The RAF's internal report into the disaffection tried to blame the trouble on a 'well organised minority' of troublemakers and claimed that the episodes had caused a 'serious loss of prestige to the Junior Service at a time when it was universally recognised that Air Power had been one of the deciding factors in World War II'.[3] From the accounts of those involved in the protests, it seems more like the justifiable frustration of patriotic men who had kept their side of the bargain and simply wanted to go home. On the morning of 22 January 1946 Flight Mechanic R. J. Adams and his crewmates reported for duty at the Mauripur base outside Karachi to find 'everything was dead quiet'.[4] On learning that a strike was underway they set off back to their tents but were overtaken by the engineering officer in a jeep who asked them where they were going.

'"Back to the camp sir," said we. "We are on strike." I'm sure had he insisted we would have gone back but he said "OK then" ... he did not make things unpleasant as he could have done. Indeed, there was no unpleasantness at any time during the strike. It was a strange situation for us all. We had been subject to military discipline for years and we knew what we were doing was really mutiny.'

The protest was led by NCOs, none of them pre-war regulars, but seems to have had the sympathy of the officers on the spot. According to Adams 'the organisation and management ... was nothing less than brilliant. Everything had been thought through and acted upon superbly.' The leaders knew very well that Mauripur was an essential link in the airline route operating eastwards from Cairo and on to Singapore and even a short closure could bring chaos. After three days and fervent assurances from visiting senior officers and leading figures in Air Command South East Asia that grievances would be addressed, the strike was called off, mostly with no consequences for the ringleaders. The other protests were similarly dealt with.[5]

The episode was perhaps to be expected. The men on strike were skilled, self-confident and proud. They had accepted service customs and discipline for the duration of hostilities but they had never lost their aversion to bullshit. The slow pace of the demobilization and repatriation programme seemed exactly that.

The RAF had no interest in preserving the more flexible character of the citizen Air Force and was anxious to return as soon as possible to its pre-war, professional identity. The attitude was apparent in ways that were small, but revealing. While the war was on, many bases held dances at which all ranks were welcome. Previously the practice had been for officers to attend NCOs' or airmen's parties by invitation only and then to stay for only a short time.[6] The trend towards more democratic socializing had been noted anxiously by the ever-vigilant Ludlow-Hewitt who warned that, though 'we have to remember ... that today we have a citizen Air Force', the matter still 'required careful consideration'. After discussion, it was decided to let the dances continue. After the war the Director General of Personnel, Dermot Boyle, summed up the new mood by stating that though they had served a 'very necessary and useful purpose in wartime' it was now 'common ground that "all ranks" dances are to be deprecated ... since they may lead to the inescapable barriers, however intangible they may be, between different ranks being broken down too far, with the result that discipline might suffer'.[7]

Ludlow-Hewitt's strictures seem tinged with nostalgia for the pre-war era. But it was in this, broadened phase of the RAF's life, when Tom, Dick and Harry, Joan, Kath and Betty flooded into its ranks that it lived its hour of greatest glory. Its deeds and triumphs, great and small, were largely the achievements of the birds of passage, and it was the image they created that fired the imagination of Britain and the world.

By 1945 everyone knew about the RAF. Fighter Command's victory in the summer of 1940 was famous not merely as a military success but as a triumph of the spirit and the brave, apparently carefree young pilots were the embodiment of the values they were willing to die for.

With Bomber Command, the picture was more complicated. Their achievements soon came to be questioned on the grounds of both utility and morality. The RAF's own post-war survey showed that, until the last period of the campaign, the spectacular destruction meted out had not had quite the devastating effect on industrial production that had been expected. The conclusion drawn by some critics, that the strategic bombing campaign was a massive waste of life and effort, was however inaccurate and unjust.

The bomber cult that shaped pre-war development, misguided though it seems in hindsight, made sense to many at the time, and once the commitment to strategic bombing was made there was no real choice but to stick to the plan. Trial, error and the acceleration of technology that always comes with war meant that by the end the prophecy was fulfilled. In the judgement of the official historians, whose four-volume account of the history treated Harris and the bomber zealots with admirably stern detachment, 'both cumulatively in largely indirect ways and eventually in a more immediate and direct manner, strategic bombing ... made a contribution to victory which was decisive'.[8]

The charge that the huge civilian casualties resulting from area bombing amounted to an Allied war crime came later, in time to trouble the old age of brave men who had not welcomed war and had no say in how it was conducted. Kelso Robinson was unusual in admitting to 'nagging doubts about the morality of what I was doing' during his tour of operations in 1944–5, which included the raid on Dresden.[9] However he 'fairly easily assuaged my conscience by reflecting that what we were doing was carrying out the policy of the highest in the land ... and supported almost completely by the public at large'. Looking back half a century later, he wrote: 'I do not think my viewpoint has changed. In spite of the horror, the indiscriminate killing and maiming ... I think the bombing policy was probably right. War is horrible ... once a nation has become involved in a war it is the responsibility of the political leaders and commanders to win ... as quickly as possible and with minimum casualties to their own side. It is not possible to fight and win a war under some kind of Marquis of Queensbury rules.'

If the man who directed the policy, and pressed on with it even when Churchill's enthusiasm cooled, had any qualms, he kept them to himself. What went on behind Peter Portal's hooded eyes would remain his secret. It was not necessary to penetrate his thought processes to appreciate his brilliance. The youngest of the wartime service chiefs, he was the coolest and shrewdest, the unflappable opposite of hot-tempered Alan Brooke, apparently inexhaustible when Dudley Pound was visibly flagging. These qualities would be much needed in his dealings with his peers. As late as the summer of 1942, he was still fending off Army and Navy efforts to bend the Air Force to their wills. The Royal Marine General Sir Leslie Hollis, who observed him in conference with the Chiefs of Staff, 'never saw him ruffled, even under vicious and uninformed attacks on the Air Force. He would sit surveying the critic coldly from beneath his heavy-lidded eyes, never raising his voice or losing his temper, but replying to rhetoric with facts.'[10]

Portal was the best chief the service could have hoped for, and among the men he presided over were several superbly suited to their place and time. Tedder, Dowding and Harris were very different men. They seem granite figures now, terrifying in their certainty. What they shared was a certain clairvoyance, and the enormous energy and self-belief needed to push their vision through the thickets of the decision-making process and make it a reality. Their service was well rewarded. They ended up heaped with honours bestowed by Britain and her grateful allies. Portal had already been made a Marshal of the Royal Air Force in January 1944. In August 1945 he became a baron and in January 1946 a viscount, as well as being awarded the Order of Merit, to join the row upon row of silverware that jangled on his chest.[11]

For the mass of those who served, their reward was their memories. The war diverted them from a course whose direction was largely set by their background and education, taking them down unexpected paths and into unusual company. 'I quite enjoy the idea of not knowing what will happen to me,' wrote Betty Bullard in her diary eleven days after the outbreak of war.[12] Her career in the WAAF would bring responsibilities, adventures and friendships that a woman of her background would never have experienced in peacetime. 'Sergeants party tonight which I rather enjoyed' ran a typical entry a few years later.

For women who had hitherto served only under men, serving with them could prove a liberation and a validation of their worth. Sylvia Drake-Brockman discovered a new self as a highly efficient WAAF officer, as competent at giving orders as acting on them. In the RAF she found men who treated her as something approaching an equal. Among her papers is a letter she clearly cherished, from Group Captain Peter Jones, the station commander at West Kirby, a despatch centre for personnel going overseas, received after she had been posted away in his absence. 'Dear D-B,' it read. 'It was a shock to come back and find no wise woman to greet me. I shall miss you and you must know that I have appreciated our talks together about all sorts of subjects …'[13]

For hundreds of thousands of ordinary people who in peacetime could expect only a small ration of excitement and fulfilment, war was the great opportunity. It swept away the restricted vistas of normal life, revealing possibilities that were unimaginable hitherto. Fred Dane, who fantasized about being an RAF pilot growing up in west London in the 1930s, remembered a moment when he was just completing his training at an OTU in Egypt. He wrote: 'I was stooging around at 30,000 feet in clear, blue empty sky, wallowing a little in the rarefied atmosphere and admiring the magnificent view across to Ismaelia, the Suez Canal, on to the Sinai Desert and then to the minute curve of the earth on the far horizon. In that grand isolation, it occurred to me that had it not been for the war, instead of flying a Spitfire high over the desert of Egypt I should probably be working at a bench in some dreary factory on the Perivale Trading Estate.'[14]

The Second World War is lodged in our collective memory as the Good War. For all its contradictions, confusions and bitter ironies, it was the closest thing to a clear-cut moral conflict that we are likely to see. The sense that the effort was being made in the name of decency permeates the testimony of the ordinary players in the struggle. Everyone who wrote anything about their war refers to a feeling of solidarity that incubated among people who in other circumstances would probably have never mixed, a sense that, even in such socially stratified times, what combined people was greater than what separated them. For those in the front line, the camaraderie had a special quality that only they could feel, and which endured long afterwards. 'I am a shy man,' wrote Kelso Robinson, 'but I can go to a meeting of former aircrew whom I do not know and immediately feel at home. It's not that we talk about the war, but the sense of a shared extraordinary experience gives us a feeling of common brotherhood.'[15]

It was made more intense by the ghostly presence of the absentees. In all 102,592 British, Dominion and Allied personnel were killed serving in the wartime RAF.[16] Another 31,011 were wounded.

The balance of casualties in favour of death reveals the thick layer of added hazard involved in fighting in aeroplanes. By choosing to serve in the air they had identified themselves as adventurous and high-spirited, ready for challenges and thirsty for life; just the people needed to build a new world from the rubble of the old.

Acknowledgements

In this book I have tried whenever possible to draw on contemporaneous sources – letters, diaries, as well as official documents, etc. – supplemented by post-facto recollections and memoirs. So my first thanks – sadly posthumous in most cases now – are to all those men and women at every level of the wartime RAF who felt moved to write down their experiences. Why one person chooses to record events and another not is a mystery. I am just grateful that the impulse exists. Tattered journals, pale blue notepaper with the RAF crest, flimsy airmail letter-cards and faded ink are for me the mother lode as I go about my historical prospecting. Every nugget has value. Much of the writing has a freshness and honesty that is sometimes lacking in professional accounts. All of it reinforces my continuing wonderment at the qualities and achievements of an extraordinary generation of men and women. I am consequently very grateful to those families who, understanding the importance of their loved ones' testimony, added its riches to the public trove of stories.

My thanks are therefore also due to the staffs of the libraries who curate and manage the material and who have been so helpful to me during my researches. I'm particularly indebted to Peter Devitt of the Royal Air Force Museum at Hendon, for his enthusiasm for the project and his many insights and observations, which illuminated what is a very large landscape. The Liddle Collection in the Brotherton Library at Leeds University was a rich source of new material and the team there made my life a lot easier with their professionalism and courtesy. The early period research owes a lot to Tim Pierce and the staff at the College Hall Library, Cranwell. Alina Nachescu and Cristina Neagu at the Portal Archive at Christ

Church College, Oxford, were unfailingly helpful. Thanks too once again, to the staffs of the Imperial War Museum, the National Archives, the British Library and the London Library.

A big thank you too to old friends for encouragement, help and advice, notably Maurice Byrne in Dublin and Richard Foreman, Sebastian Cox, Head of the Air Historical Branch of the RAF, and John Nichol in the UK. Dr Robert Owen, the official historian of 617 Squadron, did me the huge service of reading the manuscript, criticizing and correcting to greatly beneficial effect. For those errors that remain, the fault is mine.

As always the HarperCollins team was a joy to work with. To Arabella Pike, Richard Collins, Iain Hunt, Julian Humphries and Helen Ellis, my sincere gratitude for your talent, good-natured professionalism and generosity in smoothing the way.

Notes

PROLOGUE: FIRSTWAY

1. The National Archive [TNA] AIR 41/9.
2. Vincent Orange, *Tedder: Quietly in Command*, Frank Cass, 2004, p. 242.
3. Ibid., p. 152.
4. TNA AIR 41/9.
5. Susan Ottaway, *Dambuster: A Life of Guy Gibson VC*, Pen and Sword, 2003, p. 136.
6. Sir Charles Webster and Noble Frankland, *The Strategic Air Offensive Against Germany, 1939–1945*, HMSO, 1961, vol. IV, p. 456.
7. www.tophilo.com
8. Roger A. Freeman, *The Mighty Eighth: A History of the Units, Men and Machines of the US 8th Air Force*, Cassell, 2000, p. 2.
9. *Picture Post*, Saturday 8 October 1938.
10. *Men of the RAF*, Oxford University Press, 1942, p. 78.
11. John Keegan, *Six Armies in Normandy*, Book Club Associates, 1982, p. 9.
12. *Picture Post*, 7 October 1939.
13. Ibid., 28 October 1939.
14. Diary of John Thornley, Mass Observation Archive, University of Sussex, Diarist No. 5212.
15. Bernard Fergusson, preface to Sir John Kennedy, *The Business of War*, Hutchinson, 1957, p. xix.
16. *Picture Post*, 28 October 1939.

1: THE BIG ONE

1. Fred Whitfield, *We Sat Alone, Diary of Rear Gunner*, unpublished manuscript, Liddle Collection, Brotherton Library, University of Leeds.
2. TNA AIR 14/3135.
3. Whitfield, op. cit.
4. Ibid.
5. Imperial War Museum [IWM] Sound Archive 2207.
6. Patrick Otter, *Lincolnshire Airfields in the Second World War*, Countryside Books, 2002, p. 29.
7. IWM Sound Archive 2207.
8. Wikipedia: 'Consolidated B-24 Liberator'.
9. IWM Sound Archive 2207.
10. Alan Cooper, *Beyond the Dams to the Tirpitz*, Goodall Publications, 1991, p. 158.
11. Martin Filler, *Hanging Out With Hitler*, New York Review of Books, 17 December 2015–13 January 2016.
12. Despina Stratigakos, *Hitler At Home*, Yale University Press, 2015, p. 81.
13. Willi Frischauer, *Goering*, Odhams Press, 1951, p. 261.
14. IWM Sound Archive 2207.
15. 9 Squadron Operations Record Book [ORB], 9 Squadron Archive, RAF Marham.
16. IWM Sound Archive 2207.
17. 9 Squadron ORB.
18. Whitfield, op. cit.
19. Emmy Goering, *My Life with Goering*, David Bruce and Watson, 1972, p. 124.

20. Irmgard Hunt, *On Hitler's Mountain: Overcoming the Legacy of a Nazi Childhood*, William Morrow, 2005, pp. 220–3.
21. Whitfield, op. cit.

2: A COTTAGE OR A CASTLE?

1. Recollections of Group Captain Arnold Wall, RAF Museum, Hendon.
2. Sir John Slessor, *The Central Blue: Recollections and Reflections*, Cassell, 1956, p. 31.
3. Maurice Dean, *The Royal Air Force and Two World Wars*, Cassell, 1979, p. 20.
4. Malcolm Smith, *British Air Strategy Between the Wars*, Oxford, 1984, p. 18.
5. TNA AIR 1/29/15/1/141/3 (3625).
6. TNA T 161/282 (3657).
7. Slessor, op. cit., p. 45.
8. Viscount Portal Archive, Christ Church College, Oxford.
9. Henry Probert, *High Commanders of the Royal Air Force*, HMSO, 1991, p. 4.
10. Ibid., p. xxi.
11. Smith, op. cit., pp. 23, 43.
12. Ibid., p. 42.
13. Wall, op. cit.
14. By Leo Amery, Under Secretary for the Colonial Office [Wikipedia: Somaliland Campaign 1920].
15. H. Montgomery Hyde, *British Air Policy Between the Wars*, Heinemann, 1976, p. 230.
16. Sir Philip Joubert de la Ferté, *The Third Service, The Story behind the Royal Air Force*, Thames & Hudson, 1955, p. 70.
17. *Journal of the Royal Air Force College*, vol. XV, Spring 1935, no 1.
18. All the following statistics are based on an analysis of data contained in the *List of Graduates, The Royal Air Force College Cranwell, February 5 1920–December 18 1962*, published by the Old Cranwellian Association.
19. Brian Kingcome, *A Willingness to Die*, Tempus, 1999, p. 19.

20. Tony Mansell, *Flying Start: educational and social factors in the recruitment of pilots of the Royal Air Force in the interwar years*, History of Education, 1997, vol. 26, no. 1, pp. 71–90.
21. Analysis of List of Graduates.
22. Peter Townsend, *Time and Chance*, Book Club Associates, 1978, p. 57.
23. Kingcome, op. cit., pp. 34–5.
24. Tim Vigors, *Life's Too Short to Cry*, Grub Street, 2006, p. 61.
25. Kingcome, op. cit., p. 24.
26. *Journal of the RAF College*, vol. XV, Spring 1935, no 1.
27. Townsend, op. cit., p. 110.
28. Kingcome, op. cit., p. 36.
29. Townsend, op. cit., p. 74.
30. Analysis of List of Graduates.
31. John James, *The Paladins, a social history of the RAF up to the outbreak of World War II*, Macdonald, 1990, p. 106.
32. 'The RAF of the Future' by Major C. C. Turner, *Journal of the Royal Air Force College*, vol. XIV, Spring 1934.
33. John Terraine, *The Right of the Line, The Royal Air Force in the European War, 1939–1945*, Hodder & Stoughton, 1985, p. 4.
34. James, op. cit., p. 113.
35. Hubert Rawlinson, *Chronicles of a Trenchard's Brat by 565663*, unpublished manuscript, RAF Museum, Hendon, B683.
36. James, op. cit., p. 108.
37. Analysis of List of Graduates.
38. Ibid.
39. James, op. cit., p. 113.
40. TNA AIR 32/15. Air Historical Branch Monograph: History of Flying Training, Part II: Organisation.
41. Probert, op. cit., p. 24.
42. Townsend, op. cit., p. 120.

3: SMOKE AND MIRRORS

1. Sir John Slessor, *The Central Blue*, Cassell, 1956, p. 163.
2. Malcolm Smith, *British Air Strategy Between the Wars*, Oxford, 1984, p. 336.

3. For a full analysis see Smith, op. cit., pp. 44–75.

4. Ibid., p. 6.

5. The full transcript can be read on www.emersonkent.com

6. Slessor, op. cit., p. 167.

7. Ibid., p. 204.

8. Though information from the air raids on Barcelona in March 1938 was used by the Home Office to try and determine casualty rates in an all-out German air assault. David Edgerton, *Britain's War Machine*, Penguin, 2012, p. 36.

9. *Chief of Staff, the Diaries of Lieutenant-General Sir Henry Pownall*, edited by Brian Bond, Leo Cooper, vol. I, *1933–1940*, p. 38.

10. Ibid., p. 49.

11. Ibid., p. 135.

12. *The War Narrative of Major General Sir John Kennedy*, William Morrow, New York, 1958, p. 7.

13. Ibid.

14. Pownall, op. cit., p. 203.

15. Kennedy, op. cit., p. 36.

16. Ibid., p. 37.

17. Ironside claimed that Hore-Belisha's limited grasp had led to a crucial misunderstanding when discussing with General Gamelin the time it took to build a 'pillbox' strongpoint. The minister thought he said three days when the Frenchman had said three weeks. The resulting controversy ended in Hore-Belisha's departure from the War Office.

18. See 'Double Lives – a history of sex and secrecy at Westminster', Michael Bloch, *Guardian*, 16 May 2015.

19. TNA AIR 6/39.

20. H. Montgomery Hyde, *British Air Policy Between the Wars*, Heinemann, 1976, Appendices VII and VIII.

21. Philip Joubert de la Ferté, *The Third Service*, Thames & Hudson, 1955, p. 126.

22. Montgomery Hyde, op. cit., p. 462.

23. Slessor, op. cit., p. 159.

24. *The Times*, 19 October 1937.

25. David Irving, *The Rise and Fall of the Luftwaffe: The Life of Erhard Milch*, Weidenfeld & Nicolson, 1973, p. 58.

26. *The Times*, 20 October 1937.

27. Richard G. Smith, *Hornchurch Scramble*, Grub Street, 2000, p. 32.

28. *Flight*, 23 October 1937.

29. Montgomery Hyde, op. cit., p. 395.

30. Slessor, op. cit., p. 158.

31. Montgomery Hyde, op. cit., p. 407.

32. Ibid., p. 418.

33. John Terraine, *The Right of the Line*, Hodder & Stoughton, 1985, p. 76.

34. Denis Richards and Hilary St George Saunders, *The Royal Air Force 1939–1945*, vol. I, p. 63.

35. Montgomery Hyde, op. cit., p. 361.

36. TNA AIR 8/226.

37. Ibid.

38. Andrew Boyle, *Trenchard*, Collins, 1962, p. 710.

4: BRYLCREEM BOYS

1. Eric Partridge, *A Concise Dictionary of Slang and Unconventional English*, Routledge, 1989.

2. After the war he had a distinguished career as a psychologist.

3. Richard Passmore, *Blenheim Boy*, Thomas Harmsworth, 1981, p. 14.

4. TNA AIR 20/8992. The precise figure is 1,201,106.

5. TNA AIR 32/15.

6. Ibid.

7. I am indebted to Dr Tony Mansell for the insights in his paper 'Flying Start: educational and social factors in the recruitment of the Royal Air Force in the interwar years', in *History of Education*, 1997, vol. 26, no. 1, pp. 71–90.

8. TNA AIR 32/15.

9. Sir John Slessor, *The Central Blue*, Cassell, 1956, p. 160.

10. Vincent Orange, *Tedder: Quietly in Command*, Frank Cass, 2004, p. 36.

11. Ibid.

12. John Terraine, *The Right of the Line*, Hodder & Stoughton, 1985, p. 43.

13. Peter Townsend, *Time and Chance*, Book Club Associates, 1978, p. 95.

14. TNA AIR 32/15.
15. Mansell, op. cit., p. 87.
16. TNA AIR 32/15.
17. John Llewellyn Rhys, *England Is My Village*, Faber & Faber, 1942, pp. 76–7.
18. Ibid., pp. 23–4.
19. Analysis of data from Ken Wynn, *Men of the Battle of Britain*, Gliddon Books, 1989.
20. TNA AIR 41/9.
21. Colin Cruddas, *Those Fabulous Flying Years, Joy Riding and Flying Circuses Between the Wars*, Air Britain, 203, p. 52.
22. Ibid., p. 58.
23. Charles Fenwick, *Dear Mother*, unpublished memoir, p. 4.
24. IWM Images, PST 14624.
25. Len Hayden, unpublished memoirs, RAF Museum, Hendon.
26. IWM Documents 4207.
27. TNA AIR 6/56.
28. TNA AIR 6/41.
29. IWM Sound Archive 008901/16.
30. TNA AIR 6/27.
31. IWM Sound Archive 12217.
32. IWM Sound Archive 10961.
33. Christopher Foxley-Norris, *A Lighter Shade of Blue*, Ian Allen, 1978, p. 8.
34. Interview with the author.
35. AVM Smyth, *Abrupt Sierras*, Wilton, 2001, p. 49.
36. Interview with the author.
37. IWM Sound Archive 8901/16.
38. A. W. T. Tedder, *With Prejudice: The War Memoirs of Marshal of the Royal Air Force Lord Tedder*, Cassell, 1966, p. 5.
39. Bob Doe, *Fighter Pilot*, Spellmount, 1991, p. 7.
40. Edward Hearn, *The Chronicle of a Passer By*, unpublished memoir.
41. TNA AIR 6/27.
42. Ibid.

5: 'THERE'S SOMETHING IN THE AIR'

1. Roger Broad, *Conscription in Britain: The Militarisation of a Generation*, Routledge, 2006, p. 144. The RAF would remain the most popular choice until late 1942 when it was overtaken by the Navy (see Table VI in H. M. D. Parker, below, for figures).
2. H. M. D. Parker, *Manpower: A study of War Time Policy and Administration*, HMSO, 1957, Table VI.
3. TNA AIR 20/8992.
4. Ibid.
5. Ibid.
6. Broad, op. cit., p. 146.
7. House of Commons Library, Social and General Statistics SN/SG/4252.
8. F. S. Reed, 'One Scruffy Erk', unpublished memoir, RAF Museum, Hendon, X001–2307.
9. 'Lawson Memorandum', RAF Air Historical Branch, Northolt, Middlesex.
10. Denis Richards, *The Royal Air Force 1939–45*, vol. I, *The Fight at Odds*, HMSO, 1953, p. 229.
11. John Sommerfield, letter to Tom Harrisson, 27 November 1940, Mass Observation Archive [MOA], University of Sussex.
12. TNA AIR 20/8992.
13. IWM Sound Archive 32219.
14. TNA AIR 20/8992.
15. Diary of John Thornley, MOA, Diarist No. 5212.
16. Norman Lee [with Geoffrey French], *Lower Crust War*, unpublished memoir, Liddle Collection, Brotherton Library, University of Leeds.
17. Sam Pritchard, unpublished memoir, RAF Museum, Hendon.
18. Ibid.
19. Ibid.
20. Edward Mace, unpublished memoirs of RAF service, Liddle Collection, Brotherton Library, University of Leeds.
21. Lee, op. cit.
22. Letter from John Sommerfield to Tom Harrisson, MOA.
23. John Sommerfield, *The Survivors*, John Lehmann, 1947, p. 141.
24. MOA, Sussex.
25. Eric Partridge, *A Dictionary of RAF Slang*, Michael Joseph, 1945, p. 8.
26. 9 Squadron Line Book, RAF Marham.
27. *Picture Post*, 28 October 1939.

28. James Hampton, *Selected for Aircrew*, Air Research Publications, 1993, p. 116. He added that, had he done so, he would probably 'not be here today'.

29. Letters of Edwin Thomas, IWM 67/281/1.

30. *Sunday Express*, 31 December 1939.

31. S. P. Mackenzie, *British War Films, 1939–45, The Cinema and the Services*, Hambledon, 2001, pp. 33–4.

32. IWM 67/281/1.

33. TNA AIR 20/8992.

34. John Frayn Turner, *The WAAF at War*, Pen and Sword, 2011, p. 129.

35. Sylvia Drake-Brockman, *Memories of the Women's Auxiliary Air Force 1940–1946*, unpublished memoir, RAF Museum, Hendon.

36. Marjorie Hazell, *All The Same Buttons*, unpublished memoir, RAF Museum, Hendon.

37. Initial WAAF policy was that women would be posted to a base near their homes.

6: 'TRAGIC, CRIMINALLY TRAGIC'

1. Sir John Slessor, *The Central Blue*, Cassell, 1956, p. 234.

2. Guy Gibson, *Enemy Coast Ahead*, Crecy, 2003, p. 30.

3. Peter Johnson, *The Withered Garland, Reflections and Doubts of a Bomber*, New European Publications, 1995, pp. 132–3.

4. Peter Townsend, *Time and Chance*, Book Club Associates, 1978, p. 102.

5. Tim Vigors, *Life's Too Short to Cry*, Grub Street, 2006, p. 78.

6. John Terraine, *The Right of the Line*, Hodder & Stoughton, 1985, p. xi.

7. Slessor, op. cit., p. 234.

8. Stephen Bungay, *The Most Dangerous Enemy*, Aurum Press, 2001, p. 93.

9. TNA AIR 41/4 [RAF Air Historical Branch, Flying Training 1934–42].

10. Mark Barber, *RAF Fighter Command Pilot, The Western Front 1939–42*, Osprey, 2012, p. 14.

11. TNA AIR 41/4.

12. Ibid.

13. Ibid.

14. Ibid.

15. Sir Charles Webster and Noble Frankland, *The Strategic Air Offensive Against Germany*, HMSO, 1961, vol. I, p. 112.

16. Ibid., I, p. 205.

17. Ibid., I, pp. 179–80.

18. Jonathan Falconer, *Bomber Command Handbook*, Sutton Publishing, 1998, p. 41.

19. Hubert R. Allen, *British Bombing Policy During the Second World War*, Fonthill, 2016, p. 75.

20. TNA AIR 6/39.

21. Webster and Frankland, op. cit., I, p. 116.

22. Terraine, op. cit., p. 88.

23. TNA AIR 6/39.

24. Webster and Frankland, op. cit., IV, pp. 99–102.

25. Slessor, op. cit., pp. 205–6.

26. Denis Richards, *Royal Air Force, 1939–45*, HMSO, 1953, vol. I, p. 38.

27. Webster and Frankland, op. cit., I, pp. 116–17.

28. Richards, op. cit., p. 38.

29. Eric Banks, *The Laughing Boys*, unpublished memoir, Liddle Collection, Brotherton Library, University of Leeds.

30. Norman Lee, *Lower Crust War*, unpublished memoir, Liddle Collection, Brotherton Library, University of Leeds.

31. Falconer, op. cit., p. 77.

32. Allen, op. cit., p. 77.

33. Martin Middlebrook and Chris Everitt, *The Bomber Command War Diaries, An Operational Reference Book, 1939–1945*, Penguin, 1990, p. 12.

34. *Daily Telegraph*, 9 September 1939.

35. Webster and Frankland, op. cit., I, p. 203.

36. Lord Portal Archive, Christ Church College, Oxford.

37. Lord Portal Archive, Christ Church College, Oxford. AVM William Yool interview with Denis Richards 6/10/72. The anecdote recalls the opening scene in Powell and Pressburger's *The Life and Death of Colonel Blimp*.

38. Lord Portal Archive, Christ Church College, Oxford. AVM Hugh Walmsley interview with Denis Richards.
39. Lord Portal Archive, Christ Church College, Oxford.
40. *RAF College Cadet Magazine*, vol. 1, April 1921, No. 2.
41. AVM Smyth, *Abrupt Sierras*, Wilton, 1965, p. 84.
42. IWM Sound Archive 11772.
43. Richards, op. cit., p. 109.
44. Webster and Frankland, op. cit., I, pp. 118–19.
45. Richards, op. cit., p. 110.
46. Ibid., p. 116.
47. Papers of Len Clarke, RAF Museum, Hendon.
48. Richards, op. cit., p. 142.
49. Christopher Foxley-Norris, *A Lighter Shade of Blue*, Ian Allen, 1978, p. 16.
50. Recollections of Group Captain Arnold Wall, RAF Museum, Hendon.
51. TNA AIR 20/4325.
52. Slessor, op. cit., p. 367.
53. Foxley-Norris, op. cit., p. 16.

7: THE BATTLE

1. Diary of James Barclay, RAF Museum, Hendon.
2. The full despatch is available on www.spitfiresite.com
3. TNA AIR 6/41.
4. TNA AIR 6/70.
5. Barclay, op. cit.
6. Private Papers of Pilot Officer D. H. Wissler, IWM Documents 786.
7. Barclay, op. cit.
8. Ibid.
9. Letters of Denys Mileham, Mileham family archive.
10. War Diary of No. 73 Squadron RAF July 1940–January 1941. IWM Documents 9422.
11. IWM Sound Archive 12217.
12. Letter included in 73 Squadron War Diary, op. cit.
13. George Barclay [edited by Humphrey Wynn], *Angels 22: A Self-Portrait of a Fighter Pilot*, Arrow, 1977, p. 89.

14. Group Captain R. Deacon Elliot, Unofficial History of 72 Squadron, RAF Museum, Hendon.
15. AIR 16/1032.
16. Cecil Beaton, *Winged Squadron*, Hutchinson, 1942, p. 6.
17. Paul Richey, *Fighter Pilot*, Guild, 1990, p. 143.
18. Deacon Elliot, op. cit.
19. Kenneth G. Wynn, *Men of the Battle of Britain*, Gliddon, 1989.
20. Deacon Elliot, op. cit.
21. Barclay, *Angels 22*, p. 101.
22. Leng, op. cit.
23. Barclay, *Angels 22*, p. 103.
24. Beaton, op. cit., p. 6.
25. Mackenzie, op. cit., p. 45.
26. Ibid., p. 38.

8: FIGHTING THE NIGHT

1. Private Papers of Squadron Leader H. E. Bodien DFC, IWM Documents 17660.
2. Denis Richards, *Royal Air Force 1939–45*, HMSO, 1953, vol. I, p. 201.
3. Ibid., p. 206.
4. AVM Desmond Hughes, *Unfinished Memoirs: A personal history*, unpublished MS in possession of author.
5. Hughes, op. cit.
6. Richards, op. cit., p. 204.
7. Hughes, op. cit.
8. Bodien, op. cit.
9. John Golley, *John 'Cat's Eyes' Cunningham, The Aviation Legend*, Airlife, 1999, pp. 34–5.
10. IWM Sound Archive recording 12155.
11. Golley, op. cit., p. 38.
12. Richards, op. cit., p. 215.
13. Golley, op. cit., p. 53.
14. Home Intelligence weekly report 4 October, 1940. Mass Observation Archive, University of Sussex.
15. Home Intelligence Report, 11–18 December, 1940. MOA.
16. Civilian Attitudes to the Navy compared with the Army and RAF. MOA.
17. Home Intelligence Report, 11–18 December, 1940. MOA.

18. Brian Kingcome, *A Willingness to Die*, Tempus, 1999, pp. 14–15.
19. S. P. Mackenzie, *British War Films, 1939–45*, Hambledon, 2001, p. 39.
20. *Winged Words: Our Airmen Speak for Themselves*, PRO, 1941, pp. 99–100.
21. *Picture Post*, 14 September 1940.
22. Home Intelligence Report, 12–19 March, 1941. MOA.
23. Home Intelligence Report, 26 March–2 April, 1941. MOA.
24. Sir Charles Webster and Noble Frankland, *The Strategic Air Offensive Against Germany, 1939–1945*, HMSO, 1961, vol. I, p. 153.
25. Ibid., p. 154.
26. Ibid., p. 157.
27. *Dictionary of National Biography*, 'Newall, Cyril Lewis Norton' by Vincent Orange.
28. Private Papers of E. F. Fry DFM, IWM Documents 15155.
29. Michael Paris, 'The RAF on Screen', *History Today*, vol. 40, issue 8, August 1990.
30. Richards, op. cit., p. 383.
31. Sholto Douglas, *Years of Command*, Collins, 1966, p. 114.
32. Richards, op. cit., p. 384.
33. Ibid., pp. 384–5.
34. Ibid., p. 385.
35. Donald Caldwell, *The JG 26 War Diary*, vol. I, *1929–1942*, Grub Street, 1996, p. 199.
36. Cuthbert Orde, *Pilots of Fighter Command*, Harrap, 1942, p. 32.
37. Figures from Maurice Byrne in his review of Anthony Cooper, *Paddy Finucane and the Legend of the Kenley Wing*, Foothill, 2016, p. 175.
38. Anthony Cooper, *Paddy Finucane and the Legend of the Kenley Wing*, op. cit., pp. 175–7.

9: TEN MILLION MILES OF SEA

1. readings rafbf.org
2. John Terraine, *The Right of the Line, The Royal Air Force in the European War 1939–1945*, Hodder & Stoughton, 1985, p. 226.
3. Andrew Hendrie, *The Cinderella Service, RAF Coastal Command 1939–1945*, Pen and Sword, 2010, p. 27.
4. Sir Philip Joubert de la Ferté, *The Third Service*, Thames & Hudson, 1955, p. 132.
5. Tony Spooner, *In Full Flight*, Wingham Press, 1991, p. 116.
6. Group Captain Guy Bolland, unpublished memoir, RAF Museum, Hendon.
7. See Roy Conyers Nesbit, *An Expendable Squadron, The Story of 217 Squadron, Coastal Command, 1939–1945*, Pen and Sword, 2014, for a full account.
8. Bolland, op. cit.
9. *The Gazette*, 13 March 1942.
10. Air Ministry, *Coastal Command*, HMSO, 1942, pp. 28–9.
11. TNA AIR 2/5995.
12. Spooner, op. cit., p. 156.
13. *Coastal Command*, HMSO, pp. 28–9.
14. Spooner, op. cit., p. 158.
15. Hendrie, op. cit., p. 208.
16. Denis Richards, *Royal Air Force, 1939–45*, HMSO, 1953, I, p. 227.
17. Spooner, op. cit., p. 159.
18. *Coastal Command*, HMSO, p. 66.
19. Terraine, op. cit., p. 230.
20. *Coastal Command*, HMSO, p. 101.
21. Ibid., p. 101.
22. Joubert, op. cit., p. 155.
23. Webster and Frankland, op. cit., I, p. 327.
24. Ibid., p. 325.
25. Terraine, op. cit., p. 452.
26. Webster and Frankland, op. cit., 1, p. 340.
27. Ibid., pp. 341–3.
28. Stafford Cripps set out the arguments in a general form in a debate in the House of Commons.
29. Terraine, op. cit., p. 402.
30. Ibid., p. 403.
31. Tony Spooner, op. cit., p. 238.
32. Wikipedia, 'Leigh Light'.
33. Spooner, op. cit., p. 245.
34. Hendry, op. cit., p. 230.
35. Sir John Slessor, *The Central Blue*, Cassell, 1956, p. 468.

CHAPTER TEN: THE BLUE

1. Sam Pritchard, *By the Centre*, unpublished memoir, RAF Museum, Hendon.
2. 'Bobby Gibbes Writes on Fear' [From 'You Live But Once' by Wing Commander Robert H. Gibbes, www.3squadron.org.au].
3. Denis Richards, *Royal Air Force, 1939–45*, HMSO, 1953, p. 242.
4. John Terraine, *The Right of the Line*, Hodder & Stoughton, 1985, p. 304.
5. Vincent Orange, 'Sir Arthur Coningham,' *Dictionary of National Biography*.
6. Philip Guedalla, *Middle East 1940–1942, A Study in Air Power*, Hodder & Stoughton, 1944, p. 83.
7. Terraine, op. cit., p. 313.
8. Guedalla, op. cit., p. 157.
9. Terraine, op. cit., p. 309.
10. Denis Richards and Hilary St George Saunders, *Royal Air Force 1939–1945*, HMSO, 1954, vol. II, p. 163.
11. Ibid., II, p. 166.
12. A. W. T. Tedder, *With Prejudice, The War Memoirs of Marshal of the Royal Air Force Lord Tedder*, Cassell, 1966, p. 82.
13. Ibid., p. 95.
14. Ibid., p. 107.
15. Ibid., p. 70.
16. Ibid., p. 93.
17. Ibid., p. 101.
18. Ibid., p. 95.
19. Ibid., p. 105.
20. Ibid., p. 107.
21. Papers of J. Pickering, 1939–45 RAF, Liddle Collection, Brotherton Library, University of Leeds.
22. Ibid.
23. Pritchard, op. cit.
24. Pritchard, op. cit.
25. Pritchard, op. cit.
26. Brian Kingcome, *A Willingness to Die*, Tempus, 1999, p. 145.
27. Papers of Kathleen Bishop.
28. Pritchard, op. cit.
29. Tedder, op. cit., p. 165.
30. Family anecdote.
31. Pritchard, op. cit.
32. See Tedder, op. cit., pp. 176–90 for his account of this episode.
33. Ibid., p. 198.
34. *The War Diaries of Neville Duke, 1941–1944*, edited by Norman Franks, Grub Street, 1995, p. 32.
35. Pritchard, op. cit.
36. Wing Commander Norman Poole, unpublished memoirs, RAF Museum, Hendon.
37. Diary of W. J. Corbin, 1939–45 RAF, Liddle Collection, Brotherton Library, University of Leeds.
38. Pritchard, op. cit.
39. John Frayn Turner, *The WAAF at War*, Pen and Sword, 2011, pp. 169–70.
40. Corbin, op. cit.
41. Duke, op. cit., p. 45.
42. Tedder, op. cit., p. 200.
43. Pritchard, op. cit.

11: 'EAT, DRINK AND BE MERRY …'

1. TNA AIR 2/5995. Maudling would go on to become a Conservative politician, serving as Chancellor of the Exchequer, 1962–4. He volunteered for the RAF at the start of the war but was rejected for flying duties because of poor eyesight and served in intelligence before going to work for Sinclair.
2. TNA AIR 2/5995. Sir Harold Whittingham, Director General of Medical Services RAF to Sir Bertine Sutton, 27 December 1943 (3759).
3. All references to correspondence on the controversy are from AIR 2/5995 'Control of Venereal Diseases in the RAF – Proposed Defence Regulations' unless end note number indicates otherwise.
4. Mark K. Wells, *Courage in Air Warfare*, Cass, 1995, p. 127.
5. Ibid.
6. TNA AIR 20/2860.
7. David Edgerton, *Britain's War Machine*, Penguin, 2012, pp. 202–3.
8. Ibid., p. 364.
9. Ibid., p. 199.
10. Sir Arthur Harris, *Bomber Offensive*, Pen and Sword, 2005, p. 98.

11. Denis Richards, *Royal Air Force 1939–1945*, HMSO, 1953, p. 229.
12. Sir Charles Webster and Noble Frankland, *The Strategic Air Offensive Against Germany*, HMSO, 1961, vol. IV, Appendix 44.
13. Edgerton, op. cit., p. 285.
14. Martin Middlebrook and Chris Everitt, *The Bomber Command War Diaries, An Operational Reference Book, 1939–1945*, Penguin, 1985, p. 272.
15. YouTube, 'On The Chin', 1942.
16. Patrick Bishop, *Bomber Boys: Fighting Back 1940–45*, Harper Press, 2007, p. 100.
17. YouTube, British Movietone News, 'Gigantic 1,000 Bomber Raid', 1942.
18. Philip M. Taylor, *Munitions of the Mind, A History of Propaganda from the Ancient World to the Present Day*, Manchester University Press, 1990, p. 233.
19. Bishop, op. cit., p. 72.
20. Eric Banks, *The Laughing Boys*, unpublished memoir, Liddle Collection, Brotherton Library, University of Leeds.
21. Wells, op. cit., p. 126.
22. TNA AIR 2/5995.
23. Norman Lee and Geoffrey French, *The Lower Crust War*, unpublished memoir, Liddle Collection, Brotherton Library, University of Leeds.
24. Harris, op. cit., p. 267.
25. Diary of Flight Lieutenant Les Bartlett, Liddle Collection, Brotherton Library, University of Leeds.
26. Middlebrook and Everitt, op. cit., p. 448.
27. TNA AIR 8/730 5777.
28. Bartlett, op. cit.
29. See my *Bomber Boys*, pp. 247–55 for a full discussion of the subject.
30. TNA AIR 18/15 et al.

12: 'BRITAIN'S BEST ADVERTISEMENT'

1. TNA AIR 41/9 RAF Air Historical Branch, 'Propaganda and Publicity'.
2. See Malcolm Smith's verdict in *History*, vol. 82, no. 267 (July 1997), pp. 540–41.
3. Edward Mace, unpublished memoirs, Liddle Collection, Brotherton Library, University of Leeds.
4. Susan Ottaway, *Dambuster: A Life of Guy Gibson VC*, Pen and Sword, 2003, p. 95.
5. Ibid., p. 130.
6. Dahl's story *The Gremlins* based on the RAF name for mythical creatures blamed for mechanical glitches on aircraft was bought and developed by Disney though no film appeared.
7. Richard Morris, with Colin Dobinson, *Guy Gibson*, Viking, 1994, pp. 207–8.
8. Ibid., p. 210.
9. Ibid., pp. 284–5.
10. Smith, op. cit.
11. Hugh Verity, *We Landed by Moonlight*, Air Data Publications, 1995, p. 13.
12. Adrian Orchard, Group Captain Percy Charles 'Pick' Pickard www.oldframlinghamian.com
13. Verity, op. cit., p. 13.
14. IWM Sound Archive 8901.
15. Orchard, op. cit.
16. Patterson, op. cit.
17. *The Times*, 19 February 1945.
18. Pathé News, 'The Jailbreakers', www.youtube.com
19. Roger Broad, *Conscription in Britain 1939–1963: The Militarisation of a Generation*, Routledge, 2006, p. 50.
20. Hilary St George Saunders, *Royal Air Force, 1939–45*, HMSO, 1954, vol. III, p. 370.
21. Andrew Hendrie, *The Cinderella Service*, Pen and Sword, 2010, p. 129.
22. Ottaway, op. cit., p. 95.
23. Norman Lee and Geoffrey French, *The Lower Crust War*, unpublished memoir, Liddle Collection, Brotherton Library, University of Leeds.
24. Patterson, op. cit.
25. Wing Commander Norman Poole, unpublished memoir, RAF Museum, Hendon.

26. Roderic Papineau report to Tom Harrisson, 18 June 1941, Mass Observation Archive, University of Sussex.
27. Hayden, op. cit.
28. TNA AIR 20/6211.
29. Sir Charles Webster and Noble Frankland, *The Strategic Air Offensive Against Germany, 1939–1945*, HMSO, 1961, vol. IV, Appendix 41.
30. Roderic Papineau, MOA, University of Sussex.
31. John Sommerfield, *The Survivors*, John Lehmann, 1947, p. 76.
32. G. M. Partlett, *Memories of the WAAF 1942–1946*, unpublished memoir, Liddle Collection, Brotherton Library, University of Leeds.
33. RAF Manual of Cooking and Dietary, April 1942, in Partlett file, Liddle Collection, Brotherton Library, University of Leeds.
34. Morfydd Brooks, Letter to Dr Peter Liddle, 30.05.1997, Liddle Collection, Brotherton Library, University of Leeds.
35. Diaries of Betty Bullard, Liddle Collection, Brotherton Library, University of Leeds.
36. Sylvia Drake-Brockman, *Memories of the Women's Auxiliary Air Force, 1940–1946*, unpublished memoir, RAF Museum, Hendon.
37. TNA AIR 20/4583.
38. Brian Kingcome, *A Willingness to Die*, Tempus, 1999, p. 149.
39. Mrs Sylvia Watts, letters and memorabilia, Liddle Collection, Brotherton Library, University of Leeds.
40. Morfydd Rose, op. cit.
41. RAF Museum online exhibition, 'Pilots of the Caribbean', www.rafmuseum.org.uk
42. www.caribbeanaircrew-ww2.com
43. RAF Museum online exhibition.
44. Kurt Burling, 'Flyers of the Caribbean,' 13 November 2014, BBC London Online.
45. RAF Museum online exhibition.
46. Ibid.

13: OUT OF SIGHT

1. Diaries of Wing Commander L. B. Ercolani, IWM Documents 15352.
2. Obituary, 'Wing Commander Lucian Ercolani', *Daily Telegraph*, 7 April 2010.
3. Brian Bond and Kyoichi Tachikawa, *British and Japanese Leadership in the Far Eastern War*, Frank Cass, 2004, pp. 124–6.
4. www.aircrewremembered.com. Woodbridge was later honoured with the award of the George Cross. Two of his executioners were tried for war crimes and hanged in Rangoon in 1947.
5. F. Dane, unpublished memoir, IWM Documents 18824.
6. A. B. Sammons, 'Experiences as a Jap Prisoner of War', IWM Documents 2525.
7. Dane, op. cit.
8. His comeback would be hampered somewhat by his affair with Lady [Jessie] Auchinleck, wife of Field Marshal Sir Claude Auchinleck, the Army commander in India.
9. Hilary St George Saunders, *Royal Air Force, 1939–45*, HMSO, 1954, vol. III, p. 310.
10. Ibid.
11. Ercolani, op. cit.
12. Battle of Imphal, Wikipedia.
13. Dane, op. cit.
14. Sammons, op. cit.

14: BLACK AND WHITE

1. Letters of Flight Lieutenant John Rolfe, RAF Museum, Hendon.
2. John Keegan, *Six Armies in Normandy*, Book Club Associates, 1982, pp. 14–15.
3. Diary of Flight Lieutenant Stanley Bruce de Vere, IWM Documents 17213.
4. Ken 'Paddy' French, *My Early Life*, unpublished memoir, RAF Museum, Hendon.
5. Carlo D'Este, *Decision in Normandy*, Collins, 1983, Appendix A.

6. Vincent Orange, *Tedder: Quietly in Command*, Frank Cass, 2004, p. 218.
7. Hilary St George Saunders, *Royal Air Force, 1939–45*, HMSO, 1954, vol. III, p. 89.
8. French, op. cit.
9. Geoffrey Page, *Shot Down in Flames*, Grub Street, 1999, p. 134.
10. St George Saunders, op. cit., p. 95.
11. Vincent Orange, op. cit., p. 233.
12. St George Saunders, op. cit., p. 115.
13. Private Papers of H. E. Clift, IWM Documents 12270.
14. Page, op. cit., p. 116.
15. Pierre Clostermann, *The Big Show*, Weidenfeld & Nicolson, 2004, p. 171.
16. D'Este, op. cit., Appendix B.
17. YouTube, British Movietone News 'The RAF's Airborne Artillery'.
18. St George Saunders, op. cit., p. 123.
19. D'Este, op. cit., pp. 225–8.
20. The Bombing of Normandy, Wikipedia.
21. St George Saunders, op. cit., p. 136.
22. De Vere, op. cit.
23. St George Saunders, op. cit., p. 136.
24. Clift, op. cit.
25. Page, op. cit., p. 149.
26. Ibid., p. 150.
27. De Vere, op. cit.

15: THE HYACINTHS OF SPRING

1. Ken 'Paddy' French, *My Early Life*, unpublished memoir, RAF Museum, Hendon.
2. Letters of Flight Lieutenant John Rolfe, RAF Museum, Hendon.
3. Diary of Flight Lieutenant Stanley Bruce de Vere, Diaries, IWM Documents 17213.
4. Ibid.
5. Sebastian Ritchie, *Arnhem, Myth and Reality: Airborne Warfare, Air Power and the Failure of Operation Market Garden*, Robert Hale, 2011, p. 90.
6. Operation Market Garden, Wikipedia.
7. Ritchie, op. cit., p. 12.
8. Sergeant Arthur Rigby, War Time Log, Liddle Collection, Brotherton Library, University of Leeds.
9. Ritchie, op. cit., p. 16.
10. Ibid., p. 257.
11. De Vere, op. cit.
12. Hilary St George Saunders, *Royal Air Force 1939–45*, HMSO, 1954, vol. III, p. 208.
13. Kelso Robinson, unpublished memoir, Liddle Collection, Brotherton Library, University of Leeds.
14. Middlebrook and Everitt, op. cit., p. 685.
15. Rolfe, op. cit.
16. Private Papers of H. E. Clift, IWM Documents 12270.
17. Mass Observation Archive, University of Sussex.
18. The Forces Vote: A Mass Observation Report, 19 July, 1944. MOA, University of Sussex.
19. John Sommerfield, *The Survivors*, John Lehmann, 1947, pp. 27–30.
20. G. M. Partlett, *Memories of the WAAF 1942–1946*, unpublished memoir, Liddle Collection, Brotherton Library, University of Leeds.
21. Clift, op. cit.

EPILOGUE: BROTHERS AND SISTERS

1. Hilary St George Saunders, *Royal Air Force 1939–45*, HMSO, 1954, vol. III, p. 371.
2. Eric Banks, *The Laughing Boys*, unpublished memoir, Liddle Collection, Brotherton Library, University of Leeds.
3. TNA AIR 23/1986.
4. Eyewitness recollections of the airmen's strike at Mauripur, Karachi, in 1946 by ex LAC T. J. Adams, RAF Museum, Hendon.
5. An AC2, N. H. Cymbalist was imprisoned for ten years for promoting a strike at Base Headquarters, Singapore, but, after a few months, the sentence was quashed.
6. TNA AIR 57/2.
7. Ibid.

8. Sir Charles Webster and Noble Frankland, *The Strategic Air Offensive Against Germany, 1939–1945*, HMSO, 1961, vol. III, p. 310.

9. Kelso Robinson, unpublished memoir, Liddle Collection, Brotherton Library, University of Leeds.

10. Denis Richards, *Portal of Hungerford*, Heinemann, 1977, p. 204.

11. Harris was said to have been passed over for a peerage at the end of the war but maintained he had never wanted one. Churchill offered to ennoble him in 1951 but he declined, accepting instead a baronetcy.

12. Diaries of Betty Bullard, Liddle Collection, Brotherton Library, University of Leeds.

13. Sylvia Drake-Brockman, *Memories of the Women's Auxiliary Air Force, 1940–1946*, unpublished memoir, RAF Museum, Hendon.

14. F. Dane, unpublished memoir, IWM Documents, 18824.

15. Robinson, op. cit.

16. TNA AIR 20/6211. The figures are as of 31 May 1947. Another 117 from all categories are listed as missing.

Illustration Credits

Hugh Trenchard inspects men of the RAF Regiment (© *Imperial War Museums, CH 8705*)

RAF recruits signing up (*Photo by M. McNeill/Fox Photos/Getty Images*)

WAAF camera gun technicians (*Photo by © Hulton-Deutsch Collection/CORBIS/Corbis via Getty Images*)

Hugh Dowding with Fighter Boys (© *Imperial War Museums, CH 16283*)

Spitfires in formation (*Photo by Fg Off. B. J. Daventry/IWM via Getty Images*)

George Barclay with 249 Squadron comrades (*ww2images.com*)

Paddy Finucane at RAF Kenley, 20 September 1941 (*Pictorial Press Ltd/Alamy Stock Photo*)

Eric Lock drawn by Cuthbert Orde (© *Imperial War Museums, ART LD 2363*)

'Peter' Portal (*Photo by: Universal History Archive/UIG via Getty Images*)

Arthur Harris (© *Imperial War Museums, TR 1092*)

AVRO Lancaster (*Photo by Hulton Archive/Getty Images*)

Aircrew prepare to board a Short Stirling, 1942 (*Photo by Charles E. Brown/IWM via Getty Images*)

Vickers Wellingtons in formation (*Photo by Charles E. Brown/Royal Air Force Museum/Getty Images*)

Arthur Tedder (© *Imperial War Museums, TR 1487*)

Arthur 'Mary' Coningham (© *Imperial War Museums, TR 1497*)

Neville Duke (© *Imperial War Museums, HU 112294*)

Martin Baltimore of 55 Squadron (© *Imperial War Museums, CM 3844*)

Short Sunderland and crew (*Photo by Fox Photos/Hulton Archive/Getty Images*)

Sub-hunting Sunderland attacking U-boat, March 1944 (© *Imperial War Museums, C 4287*)

RAF Mosquitos at the de Havilland factory (© *Imperial War Museums, TR 1426*)

Bristol Beaufighter of 89 Squadron (© *Imperial War Museums, CF 511*)

Percy Pickard (© *Imperial War Museums, HU 98865*)

Pilots of 132 Squadron with CO Geoffrey Page (© *Imperial War Museums, CH 12889*)

Polish pilots of 303 Squadron (*Photo by Fox Photos/Hulton Archive/ Getty Images*)

Paratroopers, planes and gliders litter the skies during Operation Market Garden in September 1944 (*Photo by © CORBIS/Corbis via Getty Images*)

Arming a Typhoon during the Normandy campaign (*Photo by Fox Photos/Getty Images*)

Slaughter in a country lane, Falaise Pocket (© *Imperial War Museums, CL 910*)

Hitler's Berchtesgarden retreat after visit by Bomber Command (*Photo by © Hulton-Deutsch Collection/CORBIS/Corbis via Getty Images*)

Airmen in Austria studying literature for the 1945 General Election (© *Imperial War Museums, CL 2980*)

It's a lovely day tomorrow, celebrations in Whitehall (*Photo by Fox Photos/Getty Images*)

Index